Advancing Smarter and More Secure Industrial Applications Using AI, IoT, and Blockchain Technology

Kavita Saini
Galgotias University, India

Pethuru Raj
Reliance Jio Platforms Ltd., Bangalore, India

A volume in the Advances in Systems Analysis, Software Engineering, and High Performance Computing (ASASEHPC) Book Series

Published in the United States of America by
  IGI Global
  Engineering Science Reference (an imprint of IGI Global)
  701 E. Chocolate Avenue
  Hershey PA, USA 17033
  Tel: 717-533-8845
  Fax: 717-533-8661
  E-mail: cust@igi-global.com
  Web site: http://www.igi-global.com

Library of Congress Cataloging-in-Publication Data

Names: Saini, Kavita, 1976- editor. | Chelliah, Pethuru Raj, 1968- editor.
Title: Advancing smarter and more secure industrial applications using AI,
   IoT, and blockchain technology / Kavita Saini and Pethuru Raj Chelliah,
   editor.
Description: Hershey, PA : Engineering Science Reference, [2021] | Includes
   bibliographical references and index. | Summary: "This book articulates
   and accentuates various AI algorithms, fresh innovations in the IoT and
   blockchain spaces explaining how suggested AI algorithms come in handy
   in producing predictive and prescriptive insights out of big data"--
   Provided by publisher.
Identifiers: LCCN 2021013865 (print) | LCCN 2021013866 (ebook) | ISBN
   9781799883678 (h/c) | ISBN 9781668442838 (s/c) | ISBN 9781799883685
   (eISBN)
Subjects: LCSH: Blockchains (Databases)--Industrial applications. |
   Artificial intelligence--Industrial applications. | Internet of
   things--Industrial applications.
Classification: LCC QA76.9.B56 A38 2021 (print) | LCC QA76.9.B56 (ebook)
   | DDC 006.3--dc23
LC record available at https://lccn.loc.gov/2021013865
LC ebook record available at https://lccn.loc.gov/2021013866

This book is published in the IGI Global book series Advances in Systems Analysis, Software Engineering, and High Performance Computing (ASASEHPC) (ISSN: 2327-3453; eISSN: 2327-3461)

British Cataloguing in Publication Data
A Cataloguing in Publication record for this book is available from the British Library.

For electronic access to this publication, please contact: eresources@igi-global.com.

Advances in Systems Analysis, Software Engineering, and High Performance Computing (ASASEHPC) Book Series

Vijayan Sugumaran
Oakland University, USA

ISSN:2327-3453
EISSN:2327-3461

Mission

The theory and practice of computing applications and distributed systems has emerged as one of the key areas of research driving innovations in business, engineering, and science. The fields of software engineering, systems analysis, and high performance computing offer a wide range of applications and solutions in solving computational problems for any modern organization.

The **Advances in Systems Analysis, Software Engineering, and High Performance Computing (ASASEHPC) Book Series** brings together research in the areas of distributed computing, systems and software engineering, high performance computing, and service science. This collection of publications is useful for academics, researchers, and practitioners seeking the latest practices and knowledge in this field.

Coverage

- Engineering Environments
- Metadata and Semantic Web
- Computer Graphics
- Virtual Data Systems
- Computer System Analysis
- Network Management
- Performance Modelling
- Computer Networking
- Parallel Architectures
- Enterprise Information Systems

IGI Global is currently accepting manuscripts for publication within this series. To submit a proposal for a volume in this series, please contact our Acquisition Editors at Acquisitions@igi-global.com or visit: http://www.igi-global.com/publish/.

Titles in this Series

For a list of additional titles in this series, please visit: http://www.igi-global.com/book-series/advances-systems-analysis-software-engineering/73689.

Design, Applications, and Maintenance of Cyber-Physical Systems
Pierluigi Rea (University of Cagliari, Italy) Erika Ottaviano (University of Cassino and Southern Lazio, Italy)
José Machado (University of Minho, Portugal) and Katarzyna Antosz (Rzeszow University of Technology Poland)
Engineering Science Reference • © 2021 • 314pp • H/C (ISBN: 9781799867210) • US $225.00

Methodologies and Applications of Computational Statistics for Machine Intelligence
Debabrata Samanta (Christ University (Deemed), India) Raghavendra Rao Althar (QMS, First American India,
Bangalore, India) Sabyasachi Pramanik (Haldia Institute of Technology, India) and Soumi Dutta (Institute of Engineering and Management, Kolkata, India)
Engineering Science Reference • © 2021 • 277pp • H/C (ISBN: 9781799877011) • US $245.00

Handbook of Research on Software Quality Innovation in Interactive Systems
Francisco Vicente Cipolla-Ficarra (Latin Association of Human-Computer Interaction, Spain & International Association of Interactive Communication, Italy)
Engineering Science Reference • © 2021 • 501pp • H/C (ISBN: 9781799870104) • US $295.00

Handbook of Research on Methodologies and Applications of Supercomputing
Veljko Milutinović (Indiana University, Bloomington, USA) and Miloš Kotlar (University of Belgrade, Serbia)
Engineering Science Reference • © 2021 • 393pp • H/C (ISBN: 9781799871569) • US $345.00

MATLAB® With Applications in Mechanics and Tribology
Leonid Burstein (Independent Researcher, Israel)
Engineering Science Reference • © 2021 • 368pp • H/C (ISBN: 9781799870784) • US $195.00

Advancements in Fuzzy Reliability Theory
Akshay Kumar (Graphic Era Hill University, India) Mangey Ram (Department of Mathematics, Graphic Era
(Deemed to be University), India) and Om Prakash Yadav (North Dakota State University, USA)
Engineering Science Reference • © 2021 • 322pp • H/C (ISBN: 9781799875642) • US $245.00

Impacts and Challenges of Cloud Business Intelligence
Shadi Aljawarneh (Jordan University of Science and Technology, Jordan) and Manisha Malhotra (Chandigarh
University, India)
Business Science Reference • © 2021 • 263pp • H/C (ISBN: 9781799850403) • US $195.00

701 East Chocolate Avenue, Hershey, PA 17033, USA
Tel: 717-533-8845 x100 • Fax: 717-533-8661
E-Mail: cust@igi-global.com • www.igi-global.com

Table of Contents

Meghena Danasekar, School of Information Technology and Engineering, Vellore Institute of Technology, Vellore, India
Brindha K., School of Information Technology and Engineering, Vellore Institute of Technology, Vellore, India

Detailed Table of Contents

Chapter 1

Yuan Sun, Walvax Biotechnology Co., Ltd., China
Syed Imran Ali, University of Huddersfield, UK

A traceable, transparent, and authentic pharmaceutical supply chain (PSC) could provide a guarantee for drug safety, quality, and a better public health protection. A thorough review of the PSC and future research agenda are necessary to understand the IoT and blockchain applications in PSC provenance. A systematic review was conducted to study how IoT and blockchain could help to cope with the challenges faced by the current PSC. The descriptive and thematic analysis was conducted to reveal the research trends, chronological and geographical distribution of research, and themes. The main findings were focused on the challenges faced by the current PSC, opportunities for implementing IoT and blockchain in PSC, as well as the application of IoT and blockchain in pharmaceutical package and transportation processes. Additionally, the study summarizes the framework of IoT and blockchain integration in PSC.

Chapter 2

Dhaya R., King Khalid University, Saudi Arabia
Kanthavel R., King Khalid University, Saudi Arabia

Edge computing is an open information technology design that is empowering mobile computing and internet of things innovations. Edge computing is the arrangement of the process that is significant because it makes as good as ever ways for mechanical and undertaking level organizations to amplify operational proficiency, improve execution and security, computerize all center business measures, and guarantee consistently on accessibility. The effectiveness of edge computing depends on the assessment of the cleverness of IoT-supported gadgets and the way of clustering our IoT devices. Even though edge computing can give convincing advantages across a huge number of utilization cases, the innovation is a long way from foolproof. Past the conventional issues of organization constraints, a few key contemplations can influence the reception of edge computing. This chapter deals with the viewpoints on the challenges of multi-access edge computing that specially focuses on network bandwidth, distributed computing, latency, security, backup, data accumulation, control and management, and scale.

Chapter 3

Oshin Rawlley, Birla Institute of Technology and Science, Pilani, India
Shashank Gupta, Birla Institute of Technology and Science, Pilani, India

In this chapter, the authors present a comprehensive review on how the fog computing-based IoT can be utilized for the outbreak prevention and its existing control systems. The authors have also explained how numerous edge computing devices (e.g., sensors/actuators, RFID systems, webcams, drones, etc.) are playing a key role in controlling this disease using IoT protocols like 6LoWPAN. In addition, the authors also emphasize IoT security attacks and vulnerabilities which are prevalent in the existing infrastructure setup of smart cities. The key aspects of emerging uses of IoT (such as smart retail store automation, smart transportation, smart waste management, etc.) are described that played a key role in controlling this epidemic in the existing infrastructure of sustainable smart cities. Finally, some future research directions are also discussed that highlight the steps in mitigating the effect of this pandemic using fog-enabled IoT and AI techniques.

Chapter 4

Dhaya R., King Khalid University, Saudi Arabia
Kanthavel R., King Khalid University, Saudi Arabia

The fifth generation (5G) network advancement focus is to help mixed upright applications by associating heterogeneous gadgets and machines with extreme upgrades regarding high quality of administration, extended organization limit, and improved framework throughput regardless of significant difficulties like decentralization, straightforwardness, dangers of information interoperability, network protection, and security weaknesses. The challenges and limitations of other intelligent 5G internet of networks (5G IoTs) are also to be met by using blockchain technology with the integration of cloud computing and edge computing technologies. In this chapter, the authors render an elaborated analytics of the empowering of blockchain technology in intelligent networks that include 5G networks and 5G-based IoT. The solutions for the spectrum management, data sharing, security, and privacy in 5G networks will also be analyzed. It is believed that the proposed chapter would definitely be useful for the researchers in the field of blockchain in intelligent networks.

Chapter 5

Maissa Daoud, University of Sfax, Tunisia

Considering the conditions that we are living in since 2020 and the cases of death caused by covid, all the researchers of the world have participated in defending humanity from this epidemic. Like all these people, the author has thought about what she cannot reduce but to specify the number of cases in an environment thanks to this project called "SARS-COV-2 watch," and this measures the temperature of the owner and also informs him in the case of someone close to him at a distance less than one meter who is infected. The proposed SARS-COV-2 watch design consists of a case to place all components, a metal cap to conduct heat into the main temperature sensor, an LCD screen to display the temperature data, and a button to activate the temperature conversion and display it on the LCD screen. In order to inform the watch wearer that there is someone around him with high temperature, the author integrated a vibrating module. This small vibrating motor is ideal for projects with haptic feedback.

Chapter 6

    Saugata Dutta, Galgotias University, India
    Kavita Saini, Galgotias University, India

This chapter covers an introductory overview of blockchain using Python code. This chapter will give a basic understanding of using Python codes in development of blockchain. The chapter throws light on beginner-level blockchain creation which will help in understanding developing an advance blockchain project using Python codes. This chapter covers basic building blocks which will help in creating various functions and methods to enhance the blockchain in terms of security. This will also help students in creating advanced level of Python program in creating better mining algorithms, better queue management, enhanced and secured transactions, consensus algorithm, wallets, and accounts.

Chapter 7

    Kazim Rizvi, Vellore Institute of Technology, India
    Bhavisha J. Dholakia, Vellore Institute of Technology, India
    Aditya Kaushik, Vellore Institute of Technology, India
    Aswani Kumar Cherukuri, Vellore Institute of Technology, India
    Chandra Mouliswaran S., Vellore Institute of Technology, India

For an individual or a small organization, protecting and securing content could be a new and challenging task. The existing options do not completely fulfill the demands for today's content consumption and security while providing a good customer experience. The authors came across this problem of content security as a small group while building an application and tried to find a simple solution to secure content for playback on Android, so that the end users would be able to stream seamlessly and without any hindrance caused due to the enhanced security. They explore the way of securing video content through AES and using HLS to enable streaming of those video files over the internet. At the client's end, they have used Google's exoplayer to decrypt the data and play it directly after authentication and authorization. They performed a comparative analysis of the current models with the given model of securing content. Overall, with the aim to create an end-to-end module, they show how all the elements interact and work together as a system to provide protection against external threats.

Chapter 8

    N. S. Gowri Ganesh, Malla Reddy College of Engineering and Technology, India
    N. G. Mukunth Venkatesh, Panimalar Engineeting College, Chennai, India

Industry 4.0 and smart manufacturing are expected to transform current practices into new milestones of exponential growth with high intensity of velocity, scope, and system impact. Technological advancements in the fields such as artificial intelligence, internet of things (IoT), blockchain technology, and cyber physical systems have resulted in a breakthrough in capturing the potential to boost income levels and an improvement in the quality of life of various sectors of people worldwide. A continuous stream of input data generated by IoT devices can assist to closely monitor an industry's various production phases. Edge computing and AI process these data at the end node, while blockchain technology provides a distributed secure data environment for both financial and non-financial applications. Security measures must be built into all manufacturing systems, allowing for failsafe production and cyber threat protection. In this chapter, the authors look at how these technologies can be used in a variety of scenarios to boost productivity in the industry and its environmental elements.

IoT is a dispersed stage that bolsters the improvement of disseminated IoT applications. Subsequently, it gives an IoT computerization framework that encourages both the foundation definition and the framework arrangement. This framework incorporates programming arrangement devices to send administrations and applications everywhere on the IoT figuring framework. The previous work accepts that the model breaking time is longer than the model update time frame. The engineering approach comprises two sections: industrial IoT gadgets and their cloud worker. The cloud worker comprises two modules. The assault screen module records the most recent assault data for Industrial IoT gadgets as per their areas or types. The module deals with a library comprising of all the revealed assault plans. When the assault screen module recognizes some new assault for a gadget, it will require the instrument to download the relating assault plot with the end goal of ill-disposed retraining. The enhanced suggestion improves availability by 8.54% and security by 9.54%.

Blockchain is a peer-to-peer (P2P) distributed ledger technology that provides openness and confidence for a new age of transactional applications. The fundamental fabric for bitcoin is blockchain, which is a design pattern made up of three core elements: a distributed network, a public ledger, and digital transactions. Digital transactions are recorded in a public ledger by members of the distributed network. Members of the network run algorithms to test and validate the planned transaction before adding it to the network. The latest transaction is applied to the public ledger if a number of the network participants believe that the transaction is legitimate. In minutes or seconds, changes to the public ledger are mirrored in all copies of the blockchain. A transaction is immutable after it has been added and cannot be reversed or deleted. No one user of the network has the ability to tamper with or change data, and everybody in the network has a full copy of the blockchain. Blockchain is a peer-to-peer (P2P) network of nodes made up of network members.

This chapter investigates the security issues identified with the file cloud storage to ensure the security of client information in cloud information server. The authors have proposed a modified RSA algorithm with multiple keys and CRT to ensure confidentiality of data coupled with hashing through SHA-512 to maintain integrity. This work has made a secure data exchange app where files are encrypted using the RSA-CRT algorithm and hashed later. On successfully implementing the work, they observed that the proposed technique is more secure than the original RSA algorithm and RSA-CRT. Furthermore, it enhanced the algorithm performance for decryption because it employed the CRT for decryption; thus, the proposed technique proved to be faster than RSA with multi keys.

Chapter 12

In this chapter, an overview of two IoT applications, smart badge and smart mask, are used to protect employees working in a crowded environment. The smart mask protects the wearer from inhaling very small microbes that are transmitted through the airways (such as influenza virus or coronavirus), filters the air, controls the presence of $CO2$, and measures the body temperature. The smart badge measures the wearer temperature. It is equipped with an SOS panic alarm for indoor and outdoor workers. By pressing the SOS button, the device communicates with pre-recorded IDs so that the victim can talk and alert the emergency services. Thanks to the GPS functionality, it is possible to precisely locate the user via a Google Map link.

Chapter 13

The work utilizes an alliance blockchain, where a lot of foreordained hubs control the agreement convention. Different devices can produce information and send the information to the information pool. All agreement hubs cooperate to update the client repudiation list that improves the unwavering quality of the frame. Clients submit search demands through the blockchain. A client sends a fractional token to the blockchain, and agreement hubs produce the total with the client's trait keys. At that point, the cloud can play out a quest with the total token for the client. The cloud asks the related time-coordinated pre-unscrambling key of the client from the blockchain to pre-decode. The framework is proportionate to a release board where we record all client open personality keys, client unscrambling keys, key update messages, and pre-decoding keys. The cloud can utilize those keys to pre-decrypt for clients, and accord hubs are liable for refreshing keys for non-renounced clients. The proposal increases security by 3.82% and improves trust by 5.09%.

Chapter 14

The Indian retail sector is transforming rapidly propelled by rising household income, technology advancements, e-commerce, and increased expectations. Radical changes are evident in the retail landscape with the advent of the internet. New innovative technologies are being used by the retailers in order to provide seamless and unique shopping experience to the customer. Internet of things is one of the technologies creating competitive advantage in the world of retailing, and now smart retailing is in trend to cater to enhanced customer expectations. This study aims to understand concept and explain applications of internet of things in retailing and also discusses IoT as an opportunity for retailers, companies using IoT technology, and obstacles in adopting IoT especially in the retail sector.

Chapter 15

Sudha Senthilkumar, School of Computer Science and Engineering, Vellore Institute of Technology, Vellore, India

Meghena Danasekar, School of Information Technology and Engineering, Vellore Institute of Technology, Vellore, India

Brindha K., School of Information Technology and Engineering, Vellore Institute of Technology, Vellore, India

Gardening is a nice activity. It is not possible to monitor and tend to a garden 24 hours a day, so we need a smart gardening system that can monitor and tend to the garden as we want it. In today's busy world, we forget to nourish and water plants that make our home clean and soothing. It would be really helpful if we get a notification on our phones about our plant health and needs. Taking account of this, the authors came up with the idea of building a smart garden with an IoT plant monitoring system. After the data is processed and verified, a notification is sent about the plant's health. An automated gardening system is designed to enable us to manage gardening, including monitoring moisture, temperature, and humidity. This chapter is on an IoT-based smart garden monitoring system which senses the requirement of the plant and provides it with water as the soil loses its moisture. Thing-speak and Blynk application are used to view sensor data from remote locations.

Preface

Lately, across industry verticals, there is a widespread acceptance and adoption of a slew of trend-setting digital technologies and tools, which come handy in quickly and easily producing and running scores of service-oriented, event-driven, people-centric, process-aware, cloud-native, business-critical and technology-agnostic digital applications. There are a number of revolutions and evolutions in the form of process excellence, integrated platforms, enabling patterns and products, best practices and optimized procedures in the digital space these days. All these path-breaking innovations and disruptions have laid down a stimulating foundation for the ensuing digital era. The result is that worldwide enterprises are keen on strategizing and embracing the proven and potential digital technologies in order to be ahead of their competitors in delivering premium offerings (product, solution and service), in envisaging fresh avenues to increase their revenues, in sharply enhancing customer experience, in significantly raising the productivity through efficient resource utilization, and in expanding the market and brand value.

Precisely speaking, with the smart leverage of a bevy of digital technologies, we can delectably expect digitally transformed enterprises, governments, cities, universities, retailing, healthcare, etc. The implications are definitely many and varied. Not only businesses get hugely benefited but also individuals are to receive a flurry of advantages in taking decisions, plunging into deals and deeds. That is, the aspects of digitization and digitalization are to strengthen not only business houses but also people in their everyday assignments and obligations. In other words, we are steadily journeying from business IT towards people IT. In this transformation, there are a few futuristic and fabulous technologies such as artificial intelligence (AI), the Internet of Things (IoT), and Blockchain. There are other serious digital technologies such as microservices architecture (MSA), event-driven architecture (EDA), software-defined cloud infrastructures, big, fast and streaming data analytics methods, 5G connectivity, a stream of newer computing paradigms such as cloud-native, serverless and edge computing, digital twins, cybersecurity, etc.

In this book, we specifical target AI, the IoT and blockchain with the sole aim of articulating how this trinity of pioneering technologies fuses well to empower product and tool vendors, system integrators, service providers, researchers, solution organizations and others to envisage and implement a dazzling array of sophisticated and secure software applications.

The IoT domain is a collection of powerful technologies and methods to invoke and involve a larger number of multifaceted digitized objects (physical, mechanical and electrical systems in our everyday environments get turned into digitized objects by incorporating scores of digitization and edge technologies such as sensors, actuators, chips, controllers, codes, stickers, beacons, LED lights, etc.), electronics systems, and software applications (hosted in local and remote IT environments) to produce an astounding amount of digital data. Through the connectivity (wired as well as wireless) methods, the

IoT data gets gleaned and transmitted to appropriate analytics platforms running in hyperscale clouds or for proximate processing through edge clouds to emit out useful insights. In short, the IoT paradigm is to generate a lot of digital data.

We all would have heard and read that digital data is turning out to be an astute and strategic asset for any establishment and enterprise to march ahead in their aspirations and ambitions. Therefore, it is mandated to meticulously collect, cleanse and crunch data to extract actionable insights, which can be fed back to software systems, electronics devices, and digitized entities to exhibit intelligent behaviour. The process of translating data into information and into knowledge gets serious and sagacious attention from IT experts and exponents. Here comes the biggest role of AI processing. Transitioning data to useful knowledge is the prime role being played by AI algorithms, frameworks, platforms, accelerators, specialized engines, etc. For building and executing intelligent applications, AI is the way forward. Not only software applications but also all kinds of medical instruments, defence equipment, information appliances, handhelds, smartphones, kitchen utilities and wares, industrial machineries, robots, drones, consumer electronics, transport vehicles, etc. get the much-needed intelligence in time in order to be cognitive in their offerings, operations and outputs. With the surging popularity of AI methods, the dream of producing intelligent systems and environments (smarter homes, hotels, hospitals, etc.) is all set to become a grandiose reality.

Finally, in the extremely connected era, digital entities, devices and applications are liable to be attacked by evil doers and brilliant hackers remotely. The cyberattacks are consistently on the rise and their ingenuity is simply astounding. The security, safety and privacy of data, and properties are in danger with the advancement of cyber technologies and tools. Thus, it is indispensable that data, application, network, device and infrastructure security can't be compromised at any cost. Thus came a slew of security-enablement mechanisms. Especially with the pervasive and persuasive nature of IoT devices, sensors, and workloads, the data and device security aspects garner a sincere attention in the recent past. The traditional security approaches and applications are found insufficient in such a deeply connected world. Interestingly blockchain is being touted as the best-in-class method for ensuring unbreakable and impenetrable security for software systems and digitized assets. This book has many well-written chapters to insightfully articulate and accentuate these three breakthrough technologies in detail for enlightening our esteemed readers.

To summarize, we can very well take this analogy. Our physical body components such as hands, legs, eyes, nose, etc. create, collect and pass on a variety of data from internal as well as external sources to our brain and all the refined data gets stored in our memory. These information-gathering elements are typically called as the IoT modules. The brain is the AI tool and the memory is the tamper-proof and integrity-guaranteed blockchain database to be the single source of truth.

ORGANIZATION OF BOOK

Chapter 1: A traceable, transparent and authentic pharmaceutical supply chain (PSC) could provide a guarantee for drug safety, quality, and a better public health protection. A thorough review of the PSC and future research agenda are necessary to understand the IoT and Blockchain applications in PSC provenance. A systematic review was conducted to study how IoT and blockchain could help to cope with the challenges faced by the current PSC. The descriptive and thematic analysis was conducted to reveal the research trends, chronological and geographical distribution of research, and themes. The main findings were focused on the challenges faced by the current PSC, opportunities for implementing IoT and blockchain in PSC, as well as the application of IoT and blockchain in pharmaceutical package and transportation processes. Additionally, the study summarizes the framework of IoT and blockchain integration in PSC.

Chapter 2: Edge computing is an open Information Technology design that empowering mobile computing and Internet of Things innovations. Edge computing is the arrangement of the process that is significant because it makes as good as ever ways for mechanical and undertaking level organizations to amplify operational proficiency, improve execution and security, computerize all center business measures, and guarantee consistently on accessibility. The effectiveness of edge computing depends on the assessment of the cleverness of IoT-supported gadgets and the way of clustering our IoT devices. Even though edge computing can give convincing advantages across a huge number of utilization cases, the innovation is a long way from foolproof. Past the conventional issues of organization constraints, a few key contemplation can influence the reception of edge computing. This chapter deals with the viewpoints on the challenges of multi-access Edge Computing that specially focuses on network bandwidth, distributed computing, latency, security, backup, data accumulation, control and management, and scale.

Chapter 3: In this chapter, the authors present a comprehensive review on how the fog computing-based IoT can be utilized for the outbreak prevention and its existing control systems. The authors have also explained how numerous edge computing devices (for e.g., sensors/actuators, RFID systems, Webcams, Drones, etc.) are playing a key role in controlling this disease using IoT protocols like 6LoWPAN. In addition, the authors also emphasize on IoT security attacks and vulnerabilities which are prevalent in the existing infrastructure setup of smart cities. The key aspects of emerging uses of IoT (such as Smart Retail Store Automation, smart transportation, smart waste management, etc.) are described that played a key role in controlling this epidemic in the existing infrastructure of sustainable smart cities. Finally, some future research directions are also discussed that highlights the steps in mitigating the effect of this pandemic using Fog-enabled IoT and AI techniques.

Chapter 4: The fifth generation (5G) networks advancement focus to help mixed upright applications by associating heterogeneous gadgets and machines with extreme upgrades regarding high quality of administration, extended organization limit and improved framework throughput regardless of significant difficulties like decentralization, straightforwardness, dangers of information interoperability, network protection and security weaknesses. The challenges and limitations of other intelligent 5G intelligent Internet of Networks (5G IoTs) are also to be met out by using Blockchain technology with the integration of cloud computing and Edge computing technologies. In this Chapter, we render a elaborated analytics of the empowering of Blackchain technology in intelligent networks that includes 5G networks and 5G based IoT. The solutions for the spectrum management, data sharing, security and privacy in 5G networks will also be analyzed. It is believed that the proposed chapter would definitely be useful for the researchers in the field of Blackchain in intelligent networks.

Chapter 5: Considering the conditions that we are living in since 2020 and the cases of death caused by COVID, all the researchers of the world have participated in defending humanity from this epidemic in the same way as the doctors but in their own way. Like all these people, I have thought about what I cannot even reduce but to specify the number of cases in an environment thanks to this project called "SARS-COV-2 watch" and this onel measure the temperature each time of it owner also informs him in case of someone close to him at a distance less than one meter. The proposed SARS-COV-2 watch design consists of a case to place all components, a metal cap to conduct heat into the main temperature sensor, an LCD screen to display the temperature data and a button to activate the temperature conversion and display it on the LCD screen. In order to inform the watch wearer that there is someone around him with high temperature, I integrated a vibrating module. This small vibrating motor is ideal for projects with haptic feedback.

Chapter 6: This chapter covers an introductory overview of blockchain using python code. This chapter will give a basic understanding of using python codes in development of blockchain. The chapter throws light on beginner level blockchain creation which will help in understanding developing an advance blockchain project using python codes. This chapter covers basic building blocks where which will help in creating various functions and methods to enhance the blockchain in terms of security. This will also help students in creating advanced level of python program in creating better mining algorithms, better queue management, enhanced and secured transactions, consensus algorithm, wallets and accounts.

Chapter 7: For an individual or a small organization, protecting and securing its own content could be a new and challenging task. The existing options do not completely fulfill the demands for today's content consumption and security while providing a good customer experience. We came across this problem of content security as a small group while building an application and tried to find a simple solution to secure content for playback on Android, so that our end users would be able to stream seamlessly and without any hindrance caused due to the enhanced security. We explore the way of securing video content through AES and using HLS to enable streaming of those video files over the internet. At the client's end we have used Google's exoplayer to decrypt the data and play it directly after authentication and authorization. We performed a comparative analysis of the current models with the given model of securing content. Overall, with the aim to create an end to end module, we show how all the elements interact and work together as a system to provide protection against external threats.

Chapter 8: Industry4.0 and smart manufacturing is expected to transform current practices into new milestones of exponential growth with high intensity of velocity, scope, and system impact. Technological advancements in the fields such as artificial intelligence,Internet of Things(IoT), blockchain technology and cyber physical systems have resulted in a breakthrough in capturing the potential to boost income levels and an improvement in the quality of life of various sectors of people worldwide. A continuous stream of input data generated by IoT devices can assist to closely monitor an industry's various production phases. Edge computing and AI process these data at the end node, while blockchain technology provides a distributed secure data environment for both financial and non-financial applications. Security measures must be built into all manufacturing systems, allowing for failsafe production and cyber threat protection. In this chapter, we will look at how these technologies can be used in a variety of scenarios to boost productivity in the industry and its environmental elements.

Chapter 9: IoT is a dispersed stage that bolsters the improvement of disseminated IoT applications. Subsequently, it gives an IoT computerization framework that encourages both the foundation definition and the framework arrangement. This framework incorporates programming arrangement devices to send administrations and applications everywhere on the IoT figuring framework. The previous work accepts that the model breaking time is longer than the model update time frame. The engineering approach comprises two sections Industrial IoT gadgets and their cloud worker. The cloud worker comprises of two modules. The assault screen module records the most recent assault data for Industrial IoT gadgets as per their areas or types. The module deals with a library comprising of all the revealed assault plans. When the assault screen module recognizes some new assault for a gadget, it will require the instrument to download the relating assault plot with the end goal of ill-disposed retraining. The enhanced suggestion improves the earlier by increasing availability by 8.54% and security by 9.54%.

Chapter 10: Blockchain is a peer-to-peer (P2P) distributed ledger technology that provides openness and confidence for a new age of transactional applications. The fundamental fabric for Bitcoin is blockchain, which is a design pattern made up of three core elements: a distributed network, a public ledger, and digital transactions. Digital transactions are recorded in a public ledger by members of the distributed network. Members of the network run algorithms to test and validate the planned transaction before adding it to the network. The latest transaction is applied to the public ledger if a number of the network participants believe that the transaction is legitimate. In minutes or seconds, changes to the public ledger are mirrored in all copies of the blockchain. A transaction is immutable after it has been added and cannot be reversed or deleted. No one user of the network has the ability to tamper with or change data and everybody in the network has a full copy of the blockchain. Blockchain is a peer-to-peer (P2P) network of nodes made up of network members.

Chapter 11: Our work investigates the security issues identified with the file cloud storage To ensure the security of clients' information in cloud information server, we have proposed a modified RSA algorithm with multiple keys and CRT to ensure confidentiality of data coupled with hashing through SHA-512 to maintain integrity. This work has made a secure data exchange app where files are encrypted using the RSA-CRT algorithm and hashed later. On successfully implementing our work, we observed that the proposed technique is more secure than the original RSA algorithm and RSA-CRT. Furthermore, it enhanced the algorithm performance for decryption because it employed the CRT for decryption; thus the proposed technique proved to be faster than RSA with multi keys.

Chapter 12: In this chapter, an overview of two IOT applications: smart badge and smart mask, used to protect employees working in a crowded environment. The smart mask protects the wearer from inhaling very small microbes that are transmitted through the airways (such as influenza virus or corona virus), filters the air, controls the presence of CO_2 and measures the body temperature. The smart badge measures the wearer temperature. It is equipped with an SOS panic alarm for indoor and outdoor workers. By pressing the SOS button, the device communicates with pre-recorded IDs so that the victim can talk and alert the emergency services. Thanks to the GPS functionality, it is possible to precisely locate the user via a Google Map link.

Chapter 13: The work utilizes an alliance blockchain, where a lot of foreordained hubs control the agreement convention. Different devices can produce information and send the information to the information pool. All agreement hubs cooperate to update the client repudiation list that improves the unwavering quality of the frame. Clients submit search demands through the blockchain. A client sends a fractional token to the blockchain, and agreement hubs produce the total with the client's trait keys. At that point, the cloud can play out a quest with the total token for the client. The cloud asks the related time-coordinated pre-unscrambling key of the client from the blockchain to pre-decode. The framework is proportionate to a release board where we record all client open personality keys, client unscrambling keys, key update messages, and pre-decoding keys. The cloud can utilize those keys to pre-decrypt for clients, and accord hubs are liable for refreshing keys for non-renounced clients. The proposal increases security by 3.82% and improves trust by 5.09%.

Chapter 14: Indian retail sector is transforming rapidly propelling by rising household income, technology advancements, e-commerce, and increased expectations. Radical changes are evident in retail landscape with the advent of internet. New innovative technologies are being used by the retailers in order to provide seamless and unique shopping experience to the customer. Internet of things is one of technology creating competitive advantage in the world of retailing and now smart retailing is in trend to cater enhanced customer expectations. This study aims to understand concept and explain applications of Internet of Things in retailing and also discuss IoT as an opportunity for retailers, companies using IoT technology and obstacles in adopting IoT especially in retail sector.

Chapter 15: Gardening is a nice activity. It is not possible to monitor and tend to a garden 24 hours a day, so we need a smart gardening system that can monitor and tend to the garden as we want it. In today's busy world, we forget to nourish and water plants that make our home clean and soothing. It would be really helpful if we get a notification on our phones about our plant's health and needs. Taking account of this we came up with the idea of building a smart garden with IoT plant monitoring system. After the data is processed and verified, accordingly a notification is sent about the plant's health. An automated gardening system is designed to enable us to manage gardening, including monitoring moisture, temperature, and humidity. This paper on IOT based smart garden monitoring system which senses the requirement of the plant and provides it with water as the soil loses its moisture. Thing-speak and Blynk application is used to view those sensor data from remote location.

Kavita Saini

Pethuru Raj

Chapter 1
Internet of Things (IoT) and Blockchain Applications in Pharmaceutical Supply Chain Provenance to Achieve Traceability, Transparency, and Authenticity

Yuan Sun
Walvax Biotechnology Co., Ltd., China

Syed Imran Ali
ⓘ https://orcid.org/0000-0002-6553-8210
University of Huddersfield, UK

ABSTRACT

A traceable, transparent, and authentic pharmaceutical supply chain (PSC) could provide a guarantee for drug safety, quality, and a better public health protection. A thorough review of the PSC and future research agenda are necessary to understand the IoT and blockchain applications in PSC provenance. A systematic review was conducted to study how IoT and blockchain could help to cope with the challenges faced by the current PSC. The descriptive and thematic analysis was conducted to reveal the research trends, chronological and geographical distribution of research, and themes. The main findings were focused on the challenges faced by the current PSC, opportunities for implementing IoT and blockchain in PSC, as well as the application of IoT and blockchain in pharmaceutical package and transportation processes. Additionally, the study summarizes the framework of IoT and blockchain integration in PSC.

DOI: 10.4018/978-1-7998-8367-8.ch001

INTRODUCTION

Medicine supplies are one of the building blocks of healthcare systems (WHO, 2010). In the present health-conscious society, the satisfactory quality and regulatory compliance of drugs have gained enormous attention globally due to the significant risk of counterfeit and unqualified medicines that could pose to consumer health (Sylim et al., 2018). From manufacturing to consumption, there are multiple partners and intermediaries involved in the pharmaceutical supply chain (PSC). This brings about great traceability challenges in present centralized systems such as single point of failure, data manipulation, interoperability, security, stakeholder agreement, implementation cost, lack of standardization and regulations (Premkumar and C, 2020, Uddin et at., 2021). Operating with legacy information platforms could not assist the collaboration amongst multiple participants of PSC (Vecchione, 2017). It also could not support the tracking and tracing of sources required to ensure quality, regulatory compliance, and drug security.

Internet of things (IoT) and Blockchain technology have been brought to the forefront of global attention in different industries. The application of IoT in supply chain management could support real-time information update and monitoring (Premkumar and C, 2020). The blockchain technology could document everything related to the whole supply chain and allow information sharing across the distribution network in a secure manner (Bocek et al., 2017). Implementation of drug provenance across the whole PSC is essential to strengthen the governance and supervision of the pharma market (Sylim et al., 2018). Hence, the application of IoT and Blockchain in PSC would have a tremendous role in future pharmaceutical domain. The application of IoT and blockchain could help to achieve the target of track and trace capability, authenticity and transparency by improving the collaboration, as well as, information sharing amongst the PSC stakeholders.

BACKGROUND

Pharmaceutical Supply Chain

Supply chain is defined as a network of participants who cooperatively work together to convert basic materials into a specific finished product which is valued by end-customers (Settanni, Harrington and Srai, 2017). Supply chain also involves controlling, managing, and improving the flow of materials and information from suppliers to end-users (Harrison, et al., 2019, Uddin et at., 2021). Therefore, the PSC is a network between firms to produce, manage, distribute medicine and all the relevant information to the final buyer. The aim of PSC is aligning enterprises in enabling achievement of improving health status by pharmaceutical provision (Settanni, Harrington and Srai, 2017, Musamih et al., 2021). The PSC is complex, and its quality control process is strict (Vecchione, 2017, Ahmadi et al., 2020). From the aspect of involved participants, a typical PSC contains more than one participant. It not only includes the raw material suppliers, manufacturers, wholesalers, warehouse, distributors, retailers, and end-customers, but also the information agencies, government regulatory department such as Food and Drug Administration (FDA) (Sylim et al., 2018a, Uddin et at., 2021).

The distribution network and regulations of PSC are complex. There are two distribution levels in PSC. Firstly, pharmaceutical manufacturers supply medicine from the point of production to the wholesaler, and this is also called the first level of drug distribution. In the second level of drug distribution, the products are transported from wholesalers to retailers, hospitals, or pharmacies (Jangir et al., 2019, Sunny et al., 2020). In some cases, manufacturers also distribute medicine directly to the government purchasers (Olson et al., 2018). From the aspect of regulation, the manufacturing of pharmaceutical must be in full compliance with Good Manufacturing Practice (GMP) to ensure that medicinal products are consistently manufactured and controlled to the quality standards appropriate to their intended use and as required by the product specification (WHO, 2010). The distribution chain of medical products must follow Good Distribution Practices (GDP) to guarantee the original quality of medicine (WHO, 2010). The whole PSC is supervised and monitored by FDA (Uddin et at., 2021). The typical physical drug distribution and information flow of PSC is shown in Figure 1.

Figure 1. The pharmaceutical supply chain

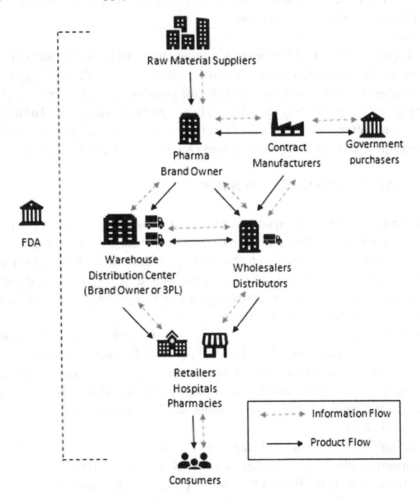

The Definition of the Internet of Things (IoT)

The Internet of things (IoT), is one of the latest IT evolvements, it's the concept of connecting devices and internet to facilitate data collection, sharing, and transmission over a network (Ben-Daya, Hassini and Bahroun, 2019, Jha et al., 2019, Kari et al., 2019). Xu et al. (2014) indicated that the IoT network is composed of four fundamental layers as follows. The detailed architecture of IoT is as follows:.

1. Sensing Layer

    Existing hardware is integrated in this layer. Wireless smart systems with sensors or special tags such as RFID could sense the physical thing, as well as it acquires and exchange data amongst different devices.

2. Networking Layer

    The function of the networking layer is to provide the essential network support and allow aggregation and sharing of information within the network.

3. Service Layer

    Services would be created and managed in this layer. It aims to provide services to satisfy users' needs based on middleware technology.

4. Interface Layer

    This layer enables users with different devices or applications to interact with the system, which allows IoT to acquire and process massive volume of value data. Giving the focus on the characteristics of IoT and the supply chain, IoT could be defined as a network that could connect physical things digitally (Ben-Daya, Hassini and Bahroun, 2019). The digital connection model could sense and interact with several partners in a supply chain to achieve information sharing, quickness, visibility, and tracking (Xu, He and Li, 2014; Clauson et al., 2018).

The Definition of Blockchain Technology

Blockchain technology was created to support bitcoin transactions at first but as it develops, it has evolved to be more than a platform for storage of financial transactions managed by cryptography. For instance, there are some cases related to blockchain technology application in the health, food and agriculture industry (Rejeb, Keogh and Treiblmaier, 2019). It is defined as "a decentralized database that could store and share data with trusted partners across a peer-to-peer computer network in a secure, tamper proof environment" (Radanović and Likić, 2018).

Blockchain follows a decentralized network model and the data is shared and continuously synchronized across all nodes in the network (Sylim et al., 2018b). Blockchain consists of several blocks, with each block containing verified transactions, timestamp, current hash code and the hash code of the previous block (Xie et al., 2019). The new block is always connected with the previous block forming a chain of blocks arranged chronologically, so any change would occur disharmony (Pandey and Litoriya, 2020; De Aguiar et al., 2020).

Generally, there are three types of blockchains, which are the public blockchain, the private blockchain and the consortium blockchain (De Aguiar et al., 2020; Molina, Delgado and Tarazona, 2019). The public blockchain, such as the Bitcoin network, is permission-less, and records are transparent to all nodes (Abbas et al., 2020). For the private blockchain, only the authorized participants could access the records, which provides a higher degree of privacy (De Aguiar et al., 2020). In the consortium blockchain, some records could be public while a part of records only could be shown to the specific private participants (Abbas et al., 2020).

Treiblmaier (2019) pointed out that the main characteristics of blockchain are data immutability, transparency, decentralization, time-stamped, tamper proof and security. Immutability does not allow modifying digital data within the network, which could create an immutable and actual environment for all transactions across the network (Radanović and Likić, 2018; Wu et al., 2017). The transparency of Blockchains is especially critical for tracking products along the supply chain as it enables users to read-only access to previous information and to inspect the content of smart contracts (Kshetri, 2018).

JUSTIFICATION OF RESEARCH

The rationale behind doing this research is the provenance to achieve traceability, transparency and authenticity in the PSC. The current PSC are being increasingly complicated and heterogeneous as more internal and external stakeholders are involved. In this case, Information Technology (IT) has become and will continue to be an indispensable driving force for effective management of stakeholders across the supply chain (Rejeb, et al. 2019,). IT is capable of integrating internal processes, external vendors, as well as customers, therefore, the capability of acquiring, transmitting and communicating information within the supply chain network could be improved (Ben-Daya, Hassini and Bahroun, 2019). Hence, IoT and blockchain are the latest technologies. IoT could obtain real-time data to provide digital footprints (Ben-Daya, Hassini and Bahroun, 2019, Musamih et al., 2021), and Blockchain could provide better provenance with full traceability within the supply chain (Clauson et al., 2018). The application of IoT and blockchains could bring a paradigm shift in various areas of a PSC. So far, there is a lot of research related to blockchain or IoT application in a supply chain. For instance, an agricultural supply chain has achieved traceability by implementing blockchain (Kamble, Gunasekaran and Sharma, 2020, Sunny et al., 2020), while Walmart used blockchain to track food for better safety (Hyperledger, 2019). These literature reviews and case studies shows that IoT and blockchain application has a promising opportunity in information management and provenance in supply chains. But there is not much research focus on the IoT and blockchain application in the PSC. Therefore, this chapter would explore the application IoT and blockchain in PSC provenance to implement authenticity, traceability and transparency.

AIMS AND OBJECTIVES

This chapter follows a Systematic Literature Review (SLR) to conduct the comprehensive search for academic and practitioner literature that is related to the topic of IoT and Blockchain applications in the PSC provenance to achieve traceability, transparency, and authenticity. The SLR methodology could enable the research process to be more structured, reliable, comprehensive and transparent.

The three main **objectives** of the chapter are:

1. Objective 1:
   To identify the challenges for achieving traceability, transparency and authenticity in PSC from the existing research.
   a. -What challenges are faced by current PSC and what actors caused those challenges?
2. Objective 2:
   To produce a descriptive analysis of the opportunities and issues that IoT and blockchain application have on the aspect of information management and provenance in PSC.
   b. -What are the opportunities for IoT and blockchain application in PSC?

3.   Objective 3:
      To provide valid insights into the main themes, methods, findings and models of IoT and blockchain
            applications in PSC.
   c.   -How to combine the IoT and blockchain in PSC provenance to implement traceability, trans-
         parency, and authenticity?

MOTIVATION OF WORK

This chapter researches the application of Blockchain and IoT technology towards the PSC to achieve traceability, transparency and authenticity. The scope of the study mainly covers two processes, which are the drug packaging and transportation processes (figure 2).

Figure 2. Scope mapping of the chapter

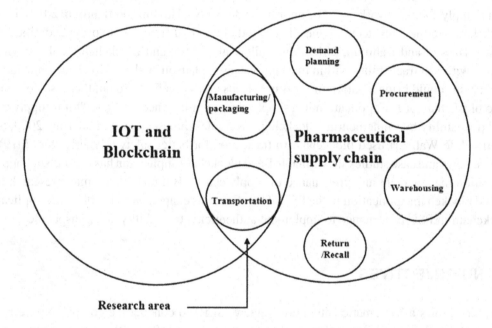

For the packaging process, it involves packaging requirements. In the transportation process, it includes three aspects (Premkumar and C, 2020). The first aspect involves real-time monitoring of the medicine movement and its transportation environment (humidity and temperature). Second, it involves the collaboration of trading participants by sharing and verifying records transactions in a tamper proof environment. Third, is to ensure compliance with FDA and other regulatory track and trace guidelines. What is more important is decreasing the risk of introducing counterfeit medicine during the process.

To answer the research question and objectives, the present review will systematically extract the literature from the multiple databases such as, ABI Inform, EBSCO and SCOPUS, which provides a great deal of academic and practitioner literature concerning the application of IoT and blockchain in the PSC.

METHODOLOGY

The systematic literature review (SLR) method is adopted in this chapter to achieve the aforementioned objectives. The SLR is a clear, and repeatable methodology for locating, reviewing, evaluating and synthesizing the existing relevant studies on a specific topic comprehensively (Saunders, Mark N.K., et al, 2009; Okoli, 2015).

SLR is derived from medical sciences, and its importance has been recognized in other fields over the time as the process of SLR is clear, scientific, transparent, and replicable (Tranfield, Denyer and Smart, 2003). Tranfield, Denyer and Smart (2003) indicated that the SLR method could help to guarantee collected literature falls within a specific research scope. At the same time, this method could help reviewers to mitigate the biases and imbalance when evaluating and synthesizing the contribution and findings of the studies. As such, the SLR can be considered as a useful methodology that could help the reviewer to collect and review studies around the topic from a wide range of databases. At the same time, it could provide reliable evidence for interpreting the findings in this chapter sufficiently (Armitage and Keeble-allen, 2008).

The Comparison of Systematic Literature Review and Traditional Review

Popay et al. (2006) recommended applying SLR when reviewing literature because when compared to traditional review methods, the benefits of SLR are prominent. The detailed differences between the traditional review and SLR are listed in table 1.

Table 1. The comparison of traditional and systematic literature review

Differences	Good quality SLR	Traditional reviews
Review question	Begin with clear question to be answered or hypothesis to be tested.	May also begin with clear question to be answered, but they more often include general discussion of subject with no stated hypothesis.
Searching for relevant studies	Attempt to collect all relevant published and unpublished studies to limit influence of publication and other biases.	Usually do not strive to collect all relevant papers.
Deciding studies to be reviewed	Involve detailed selection criteria of what type of papers could be selected to limit selection bias on behalf of reviewer	Usually do not describe the selected criteria.
Assessing study quality	Involve quality appraisal and description evaluation of each study which increases the standard of reviews.	Do not consider quality of evidence and lack of clear methodology.
Summarize study results	The study results are most methodologically sound, which are based on the conclusions of studies reviewed	Usually do not differentiate between methodologically sound and unsound studies

Source: (Armitage and Keeble-allen, 2008)

Stages of Systematic Literature Review

To achieve transparency, comprehensiveness and objectivity, the systematic literature review was conducted in four stages as seen in Figure 3.

Scoping

The first stage of SLR is scoping that is mapping relevant literature with specific research questions. The main focus of this research on provenance of PSC with traceability, transparency and authenticity. The technologies like Blockchain and IoT are used for enhancing the provenance. To achieve this following research questions are formulated:

RQ.1. What are traceability issues in present PSC?
RQ.2. In what ways blockchain and IoT aided in enhancing traceability of PSC?
RQ.3. What are the challenges faced by PSC in achieving provenance?
RQ.4. What are the opportunities in implementing IoT and blockchain in PSC?

Figure 3. Systematic literature review stages

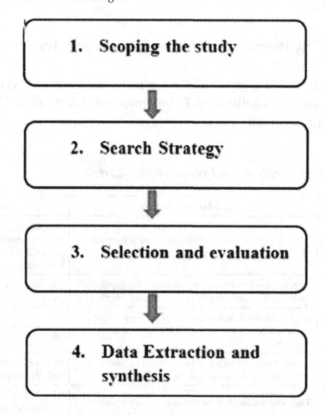

Search Strategy

Establishing a search strategy is a crucial stage for searching relevant literature. In this subsection, the purpose of developing a search strategy is to identify applicable information sources related to IoT and blockchain applications in PSC. Appropriate databases, search strings and keywords need to be defined in this stage. Notably, the search strings or keywords might need to be modified according to the evaluation of the search result.

Database Selection

Appropriate data sources can facilitate a comprehensive SLR. Three suitable databases were selected for conducting the research, and they are ABI Inform, SCOPUS, and Business Source Complete (EBSCO). The characteristics and brief introduction of selected databases is described in table 2.

Keywords and Search Strings

Four groups of keywords have been designed for the main search, which are IoT, Blockchain and Pharmaceutical supply chain. To generate the search strings with high usability, these keywords were modified after the initial searching and reading of references. Table 3 presents the search strings.

Using the logical operator 'AND' to combine these individual strings. The search strings is **(Pharmaceutical* OR drug* OR medicine OR vaccin*) AND ("supply chain*" OR "supply network*" OR "distribution network*" OR "demand chain*" OR "value chain*") AND (Blockchain OR "internet of things" OR "web of things" OR "artificial intelligence" OR "big data")**

Table 2. The characteristics of selected databases

Database	Characteristics
ABI/Inform (ProQuest)	ABI/INFORM has the gold standard in the field of business research databases. ABI/INFORM consists of over 40 million business-related documents and 90% of the documents contain full text. It includes content such as journals, key trade publications, business press, conference proceedings and market reports.
EBSCO (Business Source Complete)	EBSCO is the foremost provider of research databases, journals, magazine, e-books and discovery service to libraries of all kinds. It provides "over 550,000 e-books plus subscription management services for 360,000 e-journals, e-journal packages and print journals".
SCOPUS	Scopus offers more than 5,000 international publishers. It includes scientific journals, books and conference proceedings in different broad fields.

Table 3. Keywords identification

Keywords	String
pharmaceutical	Pharmaceutical* OR drug* OR medicine OR vaccin*
Supply chain	"supply chain*" OR "supply network*" OR "distribution network*" OR "demand chain*" OR "value chain*"
Blockchain and IoT	Blockchain OR "internet of things" OR "web of things" OR "artificial intelligence" OR "big data"

Selection and Evaluation

The main operations in this stage are setting robust selection criteria, conducting the title, abstract screening and full-text screening to select the articles from the preliminary search result. Aiming to ensure the relevance and quality of the literature and constrain the number of final references needed to be read.

Criteria for the First Screening

The first screening focus on the title and abstract. Setting the exclusion criteria to explain the reason of certain literature will be removed from the research. The detailed criteria of this step is outlined in Table 4.

Table 4. The exclusion criteria with reasons

Criteria	Exclusion	Rationale
Relevance	Articles out of the topic of interest	To avoid unproductive research and resource waste caused.
Language	Non-English articles	To avoid misunderstanding that might be occurred in translation.
Time coverage	Articles published before 2010 (expect for articles which are highly relevant and quality.)	Articles published long time ago might have restricted contribution to recent research due to the rapid development of technologies.
Type of publication	Any type of publication other than academic journals (expect for articles which are highly relevant)	To control the quality of selected articles as well as to ensure these articles are eligible and provide the best evidence to support current review.
Peer-review	Articles which are not peer reviewed	To guarantee the quality and validity of articles.
Availability	Articles which cannot be acquired as full text	Full-text availability would constrain effective evaluation of the literature.

Criteria for Full-Text Screening

The articles should be further evaluated for the usability, quality and relevance through full paper screening to select a fewer number of articles for review. The aim of this step is to look for points which are traceable, transparent, and authentic. This is to select articles that could support achieving the objectives, contribute to develop research as well as provide the necessary information.

Data Extraction and Synthesis

Data extraction is a process of extracting and recording useful data from the selected articles to prepare information for synthesis. In order to ensure the transparency, traceability of the review process, as well as to facilitate the exploration of articles, the authors have extracted all the details on data extraction form i.e. Table 5 (Tranfield, Denyer and Smart, 2003).

Table 5. The data extraction form

Ref No
Citation:
Title:
Author(s):
Journal / Source:
Year:
Country of origin
Key words:
Content of Article
Research Question(s)/Objectives:
Study Method:
Quality assessment
Relevant themes
Grounding Literature:
Contribution
Scope covered
Key Findings
Key prepositions and arguments:
Limitations and Scope for further research:
Synthesis/ Key contribution to review question

Reporting of the Findings

The data extraction forms were used for reporting the results in descriptive analysis. Meanwhile, the extraction forms also helped in the logical characteristics of the topic and organization of various literature to develop themes and framework.

DESCRIPTIVE FINDINGS

Detailed descriptive findings of the selected literature from three databases would be provided in this section. The data findings include the characteristics of the article source, the year of publication, research types and the number of papers per journal. The descriptive statistics would be presented both in figures and percentages in visible charts or tables for better explanation and review.

The SLR Execution Results

399 references were obtained from the three databases by adopting search strings mentioned in methodology section. The database named SCOPUS provided 174 articles. ABI/Inform provided 158 articles and EBSCO contributed 67 papers. Figure 4 shows the contribution of the initial research result from

each database. It is clear that SCOPUS captured the most papers, contributing about 44% of the whole search followed by ABI/Inform and EBSCO accounting for around 39% and 17% separately.

Figure 4. The initial results from database searching

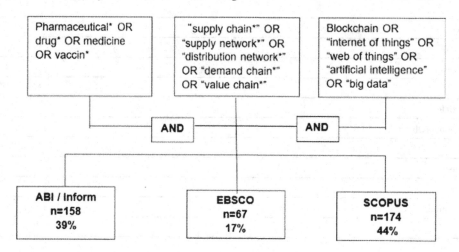

The process included screening all the relevant papers according to the selection criteria. It lays emphasis on quality control. The selected studies are highly correlated with the research topic. Articles were screened based on the publication year between 2010 to 2020 in the English language, and they are from full-text academically and scholarly (peer-reviewed) journals. At the same time, selected studies intend to include the papers that had been cited highly and the journals with high ranking in the academic field. After de-duplication and screening, the total number of articles for this review are 52. The records of the outcomes are shown in Figure 5.

The Distribution of Selected Articles Based on Source Types

52 articles collected from three databases could be considered as eligible sources for the research since the data retrieved from these electronic databases were dependable and effective. All of these databases offer advanced limitation and filtering function, as well as provide some key information of each individual article such as citation times to support the quality analysis. Figure 6 presents the statistics of the source types of the selected articles. It is clear from the pie chart that a majority of literature related to IoT or blockchain applications in PSC were from conference papers, with about 44%. For academic peer-reviewed journals, 37% contribute to the final selected articles. The academic journals were written by researchers or experts in a particular academic area. The detailed data of overall articles can be divided into four different source types:

- 19 Academic peer-reviewed journals
- 24 Conference papers
- 8 Trade journals
- 1 Book chapter

Figure 5. Flow diagram of literature search and selection criteria

```
┌─────────────────────────────────────────────────────────┐
│   399 records identified through database searching       │
│  ABI/Inform: n=158    EBSCO: n=67    SCOPUS: n=174        │
└─────────────────────────────────────────────────────────┘
                          │
                          ▼
┌─────────────────────────────────────────────────────────┐
│        Total number of de-duplication n=320               │
└─────────────────────────────────────────────────────────┘

     Screening
                                    ┌──────────────────────────────────┐
                                    │ Records excluded for not meeting │
                                    │ inclusion criteria               │
                                    │ •not in English: n=6             │
                                    │ •not published after 2010: n=17  │
                                    │ •Full text not available: n=20   │
                                    │ • not relevance: n=146           │
                                    └──────────────────────────────────┘
                          │
                          ▼
┌─────────────────────────────────────────────────────────┐
│   Records first screening (Title, abstract &keywords)    │
│                      n=131                                │
└─────────────────────────────────────────────────────────┘
                          │
                          ▼
┌─────────────────────────────────────────────────────────┐
│   Academic and scholarly (peer reviewed) journals         │
│                      n=40                                 │
└─────────────────────────────────────────────────────────┘
                                          │
                                          ▼
                              ┌──────────────────────────────┐
                              │ Second screening (Full text) │
┌────────────────────────────┐│           n=19               │
│ Additional  articles        │└──────────────────────────────┘
│ included:                   │            │
│ • trade journals: n=8       │            ▼
│ • conference papers: n=24   │ ┌──────────────────────────────┐
│ • book chapter: n=1         │ │       Total result           │
└────────────────────────────┘ │           n=52               │
                               └──────────────────────────────┘
```

Figure 6. The distribution of selected literature based on source types

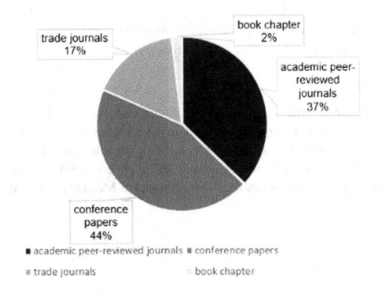

Chronological Distribution

Only articles published between 2010 and 2020 were included in the final review list that is based on the exclusion criteria. Figure 7 shows the distribution of selected articles' across publication years. As per the chosen search strings, the time span of articles came out to be 8 years, with the earliest article dating back to the year 2010 and the latest contribution was from the year 2020. The data presents that the highest rate of articles used in this research published in 2019, which is 33%, followed by 2020, 2018, and 2017 with 24%, 22%, and 9% respectively. From 2015 to 2019, the number of research papers increases with the advance of time significantly.

Journals Contributed to the Review

Figure 7. The distribution of articles published between 2010 and 2020

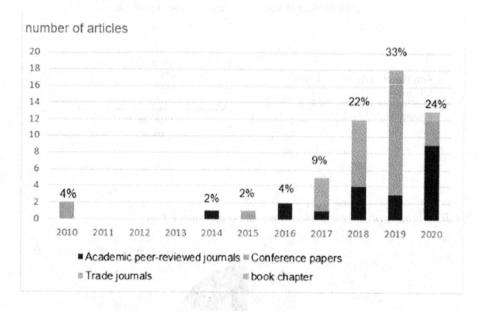

Table 6 depicts the reviewed articles that were from 18 different journals. The table includes information about the name, field and CABS ranking of academic journals, as well as the number of articles per journal. From figure 8, it is evident that 25% of articles were from the 2 and 4-star ranking journals on the basis of the CABS 2018 Journal Guide. However, 20% of papers were from 1-star ranking and 65% of articles were from non-ranked journals such as the Journal of Medical Internet Research.

Table 6. The list of academic journals contributed to the review

No.	Academic journals	Field	Journal Ranking	Number of articles
1	Production & Operations Management	Ops &Tech	4	1
2	Computers & Industrial Engineering	Ops &Tech	2	1
3	International Journal of Information Management.	Info man	2	1
4	Journal of the Association for Information Systems	Info man	2	1
5	International Journal of Physical Distribution & Logistics Management	Ops &Tech	2	1
6	Intelligent Systems in Accounting, Finance & Management	Finance	1	1
7	International Journal of Engineering Business Management	Ops &Tech	1	1
8	ACM Computing Surveys	n/a	n/a	1
9	Applied Health Economics and Health Policy	n/a	n/a	1
10	Electronics (Switzerland)	n/a	n/a	2
11	Information (Switzerland)	n/a	n/a	1
12	International Journal of Advanced Science and Technology	n/a	n/a	1
13	International Journal of Environmental Research and Public Health	n/a	n/a	1
14	International Journal of Scientific and Technology Research	n/a	n/a	2
15	Journal of Information Security and Applications	n/a	n/a	1
16	Journal of Medical Internet Research	n/a	n/a	1
17	Wireless Personal Communications	n/a	n/a	1
Total				19

Note:
Ops &Tech = Operations and Technology Management
Info man = Information Management
n/a = not applicable
Source: the author (2020)

Figure 8. Percentage distribution of number of articles by journal rank

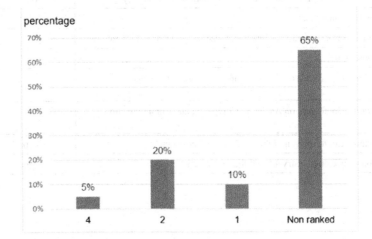

Apart from the academic journals, there were 24 conference papers, 9 trade journals and 1 book chapter that could provide highly relevant and up-to-date information about the research area. The retained information covered various aspects concerning IoT, blockchain and other new tech and combination strategies to address the concerns related to transparency, traceability and authenticity of PSC. The details of the conference papers are shown in Table 7.

Table 7. The list of conference papers contributed to the review

No.	Conference papers	Year	Number of articles
1	The 5th International Conference on Computer Sciences and Convergence Information Technology	2010	1
2	The 8th International Conference on Supply Chain Management and Information Systems: Logistics Systems and Engineering	2010	1
3	Communications in Computer and Information Science	2015&2019	2
4	IFIP/IEEE International Symposium on Integrated Network and Service Management	2017	1
5	Advances in Transdisciplinary Engineering	2018	1
6	IEEE 2018 International Congress on Cybermatics	2018	1
7	Lecture Notes of the Institute for Computer Sciences, Social-Informatics and Telecommunications Engineering	2018	1
8	The 10th International Conference on Computing, Communication and Networking Technologies	2019	2
9	The 11th International Conference on Communication Systems and Networks	2019	1
10	The 6th IEEE International Conference on Advances in Computing, Communication and Control	2019	1
11	The 6th International Conference on Information Technology, Computer and Electrical Engineering	2019	1
12	ACM International Conference Proceeding Series	2019	1
13	2019 IEEE Region 10 Conference	2019	1
14	IFIP Advances in Information and Communication Technology	2019	1
15	International Conference on "Information Technology and Nanotechnology"	2019	1
16	Lecture Notes in Computer Science	2019	1
17	2019 IEEE International Conference on Intelligent Systems and Green Technology	2019	1
18	Winter Simulation Conference	2019	1
19	The 9th International Conference on Cloud Computing, Data Science and Engineering	2019	1
20	The 6th International Conference on Advanced Computing and Communication Systems	2020	1
21	The 6th International Conference on Mobile and Secure Services	2020	1
22	International Conference on Industry 4.0 and Smart Manufacturing	2020	1

Figure 9. Geographical distributions of articles

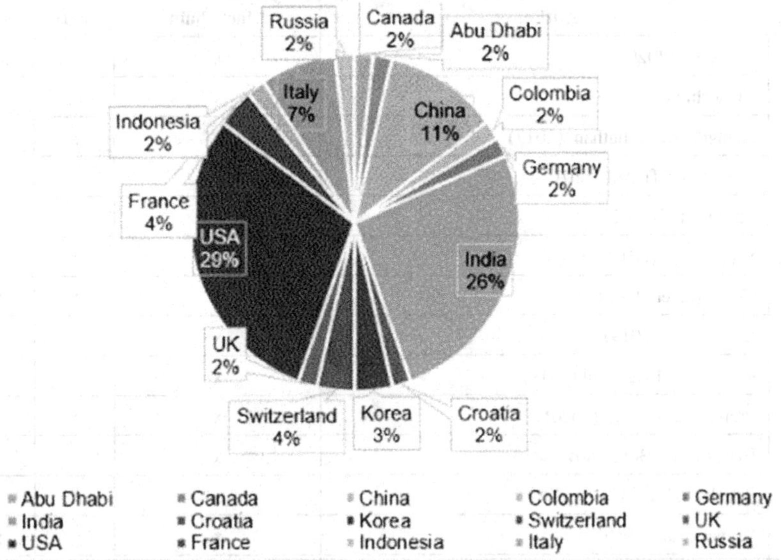

Table 8. The research themes

Document type	Author	Blockchain	IoT	PP	TP	IM
Academic Journal	Yong et al. (2019)	x				x
	De Aguiar et al. (2020)	x	x		x	x
	Abbas et al. (2020)	x		X		x
	Slym et al. (2018)	x			x	x
	Jamil et al. (2019)	x				x
	Wu et al. (2017)	x			x	x
	Kumari and Saini (2020)	x				x
	Papert, Rimpler and Pflaum (2016)		x	X	x	x
	Tseng et al. (2018)	x	x	X	x	x
	Radanovic and Likic (2018)	x				x
	Pandey and Litoriya (2020)	x			x	x
	Yadav, Selva and Tandon (2020)	x	x			x
	Srivastava et al. (2019)	x	x		x	x
	Rotunno et al. (2014)		x	X		x
	Dwivedi, Amin and Vollala (2020)	x	x			x
	Chanson et al. (2018)	x	x			x
	Hasan et al. (2019)	x	x		x	x
	Kim and Laskowski (2018)	x	x			x
	Kshetri (2018)	x				x

Continued on following page

Table 8. Continued

Document type	Author	Blockchain	IoT	PP	TP	IM
Conference paper	Fernando (2020)	x				x
	Chiacchio et al. (2019)	x	x	x		x
	Alangot and Achuthan. (2017)	x	x			x
	Kumar and Tripathi (2019)	x				x
	Molina et al. (2019)	x				x
	Sahoo et al. (2019)	x	x	x	x	x
	Chiacchio et al. (2020)	x	x	x		x
	Jangir et al. (2019)	x		x		x
	Raj, Rai and Agarwal (2019)	x				x
	Premkumar and C. (2020)	x	x	x	x	x
	Bryatov and Borodinov (2019)	x				x
	Bocek et al. (2017)	x	x		x	x
	Kumar et al. (2019)	x		x		x
	Ahmadi et al. (2020)	x	x	x		x
	Huang, Wu and Long (2018)	x		x		x
	Ting et al. (2020)		x			x
	Botcha, Chakravarthy and Anurag (2019)	x	x	x		x
	Barchetti et al. (2020)		x	x		x
	Zhou and Piramuthu (2014)		x			x
	Chitre et al. (2020)	x	x	x		x
	Shi, Yi and Kuang (2019)	x	x	x		x
	Benatia et al. (2018)		x	x		x
	Sinclair, Shahriar and Zhang (2019)	x				x
	Xie, Wang and Ye (2019)	x				x
Trade journal	Anon (2018)		x			x
	Vecchione (2017)	x				x
	Thaul (2015)	x				x
	Shanley (2018)		x	x		x
	Marbury (2019)	x				x
	Shanley (2017)		x		x	x
	Haughwout (2018)	x	x			x
	Redman (2019)	x				x
Book Chapter	Anand et al. (2020)	x				x
	Number of articles per theme	44	28	18	12	52

Note: IM =information management
PP = Package process
TP = Transport process

Geographical Distribution of Articles

The countries of origin could offer another way of looking into the situation of IoT and blockchain applications in PSC, as different locations might have different research levels of technology application. Figure 9 shows the geographic of the selected articles. It is found that authors from the USA published the most numbers of relevant articles, which are 29%. India takes up 26% of the total articles, followed by China (11%) and Italy (7%).

The Identification of Research Themes

The relevant papers collected from the SLR process revealed insightful knowledge and strategies for adoption of IoT and blockchain technologies in PSC. To obtain more findings in a specific area, the collected articles should be classified as different insight themes that match the scope of the study by analyzing. Table 8 demonstrates the themes of all reviewed studies covered within the framework for addressing the research questions of this chapter.

THEMATIC ANALYSIS

This section provides a detailed analysis of the findings from the reviewed articles. It is confirmed from the reviewed articles that the IoT and blockchain have enormous potential for resolving existing problems in the PSC and creating a traceable, transparent and authentic pharmaceutical supply environment. Before analyzing the thematic contribution, it would be helpful to understand the current challenges and problems in the current PSC. Therefore, this section would start with the findings related to traditional PSC followed by a discussion of findings categorized into two main themes, which are application and opportunities of IoT and blockchain technologies in PSC. Finally, the combination strategy of the IoT and blockchain is discussed in the context of PSC.

Traditional Pharmaceutical Supply Chain

Challenges in Traditional PSC

There are several participants involved in the PSC, as a result it becomes complex in today's business world. Recent studies indicated that pharmaceutical industries are facing challenges. There are many challenges but three universal challenges in the PSC are discussed below:

Poor Product Traceability

Insufficient drug traceability is one of the issues that has been in existence for a long time. There are several published studies which defined this problem as an immense challenge in PSC (Sahoo et al., 2019; Dwivedi, Amin and Vollala, 2020). Traceability is crucial in guaranteeing that the drugs have complied with the regulations and products are delivered to end customers safely (Dwivedi, Amin and Vollala, 2020). It is also the basis for customer confidence building in the pharmaceutical market (Chiacchio et al., 2019). However, Kim and Laskowski (2018) explained that pharmaceutical provenance evaluation in today's PSC is complex because of its inter-organizational nature. Furthermore, Srivastava et al. (2019) pointed out that the unsatisfactory information sharing, information transmission delay and inefficient drug traceability system made it hard to track drugs and ensure the provenance and authenticity.

As for the present track and trace system in PSC, Chitre et al. (2019) indicated that drug traceability could be achieved by integrating IT systems from manufacturers to retailers. Although this practice is in compliance with the regulations related to traceability, however, there are some concerns in the adoption of such a system. Firstly, as Pandey and Litoriya (2020) mentioned, this is a centralized system that might occur as a single point of failure. Yong et al. (2020), Kumari and Saini (2020) also suggested the same opinion that the centralized information system is risky. At the same time, they underlined that data is highly prone to be deleted or tampered when the central server is attacked. Secondly, all the transactions data is stored in a database managed by a third-party that would decrease the privacy and reliability of records as the middleman could obtain and modify drug information easily (Huang, Wu and Long, 2018; Chitre et al., 2019). Thirdly, end-users are out of the system. According to the studies by Chitre et al. (2019) and Pandey (2020), the record processing usually starts from the manufacturer and end before reaching the end-users. Furthermore, manual operations are involved in current data collection and sharing mechanisms, where human error might occur (Ting et al., 2010). Hence, the present systems have some shortcomings including data security, data transparency, data transmission delays, poor compatibility of the IT systems. They could not meet the demand for tracking and tracing of drugs.

Low Transparency

The lack of transparency is another major issue in the current complex PSC. Several publications indicated this problem, such as Tseng et al. (2018), Kumari and Saini (2020), as well as Dwivedi, Amin and Vollala (2020). Jamil et al. (2019) mentioned that low transparency related to information and transaction. The root cause of the low transparency is the absence of an appropriate information transmission system or mechanism. Currently, different enterprises might use different systems to record information, which would lead to a problem with compatibility (Dwivedi, Amin and Vollala, 2020). In this situation, it is hard to guarantee the integrity and timeliness of the information flow. The missing data, information asymmetry, or block would lead to a non-transparent supply chain (Tseng et al., 2018). In addition, although the development of information technology allows the integration of different kinds of IT system, but there is still a risk of poor product traceability.

The low transparency and visibility would have some bad effects on PSC management since there are gaps where fake drugs may be introduced into the market (Shi, Yi and Kuang, 2019; Abbas et al., 2020). At the same time, the low transparency in PSC would result in a low trust relationship between partners (Thaul, 2015; Jangir et al., 2019). Fernando, Meyliana and Surjandy (2019) emphasized on maintaining the trust relationship among different types of companies, which is consistent with the view of Dwivedi (2020), Chitre et al. (2019), and Ting et al. (2010). Lacking trust in PSC would greatly hinder cooperation and collaboration between partners.

In order to alleviate the transparency, visibility and traceability issues, there are some monitoring technologies that have been suggested to collect data in recent years. Barcode, QR code, RFID are relatively mature identification technologies adopted in the PSC, despite their capabilities being somewhat limited (Barchetti et al., 2010; Papert, Rimpler and Pflaum, 2016a; Hasan et al., 2019). From previous literature, it could be seen that such identification technologies could help to offer a degree of information visibility and transparency in PSC but at the risks of privacy, wireless attacks, modifying and reusing of data (Jamil et al., 2019; Kumar and Tripathi, 2019; Dwivedi, Amin and Vollala, 2020).

In the aspect of identification capability, barcode can only define one kind of product, which is disadvantageous for PSC (Ting et al., 2010). As for the read and write capability, data in the barcode and data matrix code is fixed. Both of these two techniques do not support adding further information at the drug level (Papert, Rimpler and Pflaum, 2016). Moreover, in the view of the read range, the barcode requires a laser beam to scan without any obstacles. The broken or polluted barcode could not be identified (Ting et al., 2010). On the other hand, RFID has more advantages, Ting et al. (2010) indicated that RFID allows the assignment of unique ID to each item, which is beneficial in tracking specific products. Furthermore, the read range of RFID technology is also longer than the barcode and is not limited by an obstacle. However, the popularity of the RFID system is not very high (Molina, Delgado and Tarazona, 2019). In addition, Raj, Rai and Agarwal (2019) and Kumar (2019) noted that RFID and QR code can be imitated and cloned easily with the growing skills and techniques, which also poses a threat to authenticity of data in PSC.

The Lack of Authenticity

The authenticity of drugs in current complex PSC is hard to ensure as there are several distribution channels for drugs, which involves multiple processes and enterprises. The most challenging issue about authenticity is drug counterfeiting. Several publications documented that counterfeit and fake drug is a major threat to the pharmaceutical industry (Tseng et al., 2018; Jamil et al., 2019; Kumari and Saini, 2020; Pandey and Litoriya, 2020). It is prevalent in the developing countries and in the areas that lack strict surveillance (Sylim et al., 2018; Pandey and Litoriya, 2020). The quality of fictitious drugs is poor and non-standard, which would have a negative effect on consumer's health (Abbas et al., 2020). At the same time, this kind of phenomenon would cause low public confidence in the effectiveness of the authentic drugs, influence the reputation of the companies in the PSC, as well as it leads to revenue losses of the medical company (Papert, Rimpler and Pflaum, 2016; Sahoo et al., 2019).

Some researchers have argued that the appearance of fake drugs was due to low transparency and visibility in the current PSC (Shi, Yi and Kuang, 2019; Kumar et al., 2019; Abbas et al., 2020). Although some technologies such as barcode and RFID have already been implemented in PSC, they could not prevent counterfeit drugs in the market and ensure the authenticity of the products effectively (Papert, Rimpler and Pflaum, 2016; Tseng et al., 2018; Anand et al., 2020).

Another problem related to PSC authenticity is information records. Molina, Delgado and Tarazona (2019) described that every participant in PSC has different tasks and each enterprise has its own information and IT system. Because of the IT system compatibility issue, participants of PSC exchange information through paper-based records. Another method is using a centralized database management by a third-party. Moreover, there is a possibility of fabrication and tampering of a centralized database maintained by an intermediary (Huang, Wu and Long, 2018). These potential risks pose a threat to authenticity and efficient government supervision, which might even cause serious security issues.

Limitations and Requirements

Based on the comprehensive analysis of the current PSC situation, present technologies and IT support systems, it could be seen that those current practices and adopted techniques are inadequate for achieving the target of traceability, transparency and authenticity in PSC. Thus, as highlighted by Abbas et al., (2020), Yong et al. (2020) and Kumar and Tripathi (2019), there is need to develop a trustworthy and tamper proof information network to help address the issues and challenges in current PSC. Such a network is required to record and share information related to drugs accurately and securely from its raw material suppliers through manufacturers and wholesalers to end-users (Huang, Wu and Long, 2018; Pandey and Litoriya, 2020). Meanwhile, it requires that the network offer higher visibility and transparency to the government regulator, as well as, gives assistance in drug traceability in a complex international PSC to prove the provenance of medicine (Kim and Laskowski, 2018a; Kim and Laskowski, 2018a).

Applying IoT and Blockchain in PSC

IoT Technology in PSC

IoT Application

IoT implementation is on the basis of the emergence of IoT sensors or tags like loggers, RFID, barcode and QR code, etc. (Xu et al.,2014). As mentioned earlier, barcode, QR code, and RFID are identification technologies adopted in the current PSC, which could help PSC to identify goods quickly and offer a degree of information visibility.

In addition, the serialization is an IoT technology. It was identified as the anti-counterfeit solution when the EU published a regulation that all Rx products (prescription drugs) must have a safety label supporting verification check in the whole PSC (Chiacchio et al., 2020). According to the description of Chiacchio (2020), it requires the allocation of a unique serial number linked to drug production data such as batch number, production data and item identification code in the form of data matrix code, and then label the number on the drug package. With the unique identifier and the hierarchy matrix from the serialization software, the drug could be tracked from the outer to the inner package level. Currently, advanced technology enables operation machines to generate a serial number, print labels, packing automatically, as well as connect with the Internet to realize the IoT paradigm (Chiacchio et al., 2019, Jha et al., 2019).

Opportunities for IoT

According to IoT application, different kinds of IoT sensors can capture detailed real-time data related to the environment, products and locations as well as timestamps (Shanley, 2017; Kim and Laskowski, 2018b; Chanson et al., 2019). Therefore, the emergence of IoT technology in supply chain management is in favor of providing digital footprints and building a real-time information communication and product monitoring network (DE AGUIAR et al., 2020; Premkumar and C, 2020, Khari et al., 2019). With real-time sharing, the network could support to integrate partners (Xie et al., 2019). A similar opinion was provided by Srivastava et al. (2019) that the combination of sensor and network enables data exchanges between objectives and mechanism. As mentioned before, the IoT sensors like RFID, QR Code were adopted frequently to collect and provide a large amount of data in PSC, which could help to provide the digital footprints of drugs through PSC. However, some new challenges related to security and privacy have been brought by the usage of IoT devices, as indicated by Chanson et al. (2019).

Blockchain Technology in PSC

Blockchain Application

A PSC management system based on Hyperledger fabrics was developed in the study of Abbas et al. (2020) to solve the problems of fraud vaccine record and expired vaccines. Companies involved in the PSC from raw material to final clients are included as participants in the system. The authors in their study indicated that the simulation results were satisfactory. In the same year, another blockchain-based system was designed. Smart contracts were developed in the vaccine Ethereum blockchain for supervision (Yong et al., 2020), which could provide a tamper proof environment for tracking vaccines. However, the research only chose three key institutions to join the network, which does not correspond with the actual situation. In addition, the system for tracking and checking the delivery process was provided by Molina, Delgado and Tarazona (2019). The system adopted Hyperledger blockchain technology. However, this approach was just based on the case study, and may not be practical. Jamil et al. (2019) recommended a novel and secure system for documenting medicine supply chain records by using Hyperledger Fabric blockchain.

It could be found that there are two kinds of blockchain platforms, which are Hyperledger fabrics and Ethereum platforms. There are some differences between these two platforms. The above studies showed that both of two platforms are feasible in improving PSC. Pharmaceutical companies could choose the appropriate platform according to the requirements to develop a system. Differences between the two platforms are summarized below:

1.   Ethereum platform

Ethereum is a public network with an available framework that anyone could develop and use as decentralized applications (Yong et al., 2020). De Aguiar et al. (2020) underlined the framework of Ethereum that could offer a platform to support smart contracts, which could create a more reliable and secure flexible environment for transactions. Moreover, it usually comes with data encryption as a default (Sylim et al., 2018a).

2.   Hyperleger fabric platform

Hyperleger fabric is a private network, which could provide better performance and privacy as the platform is modularized and only authorized participants could trust and access the system (Sylim et al., 2018a; Kumar and Tripathi, 2019). Yadav, Selva and Tandon (2020) indicated private blockchain could be the convincing use case of the PSC.

Opportunities of Blockchain

The advantages of blockchain have made it an attractive technology in recent years. The blockchain owns many great strengths such as decentralization, time-stamped, data immutability, transparency and privacy, etc. (Xie et al., 2019; Chanson et al., 2019; De Aguiar et al., 2020). Ever-increasing studies also discussed the potential benefits that blockchains could bring to PSC.

1.   Transparency and visibility

Studies conducted by Abbas et al. (2020), Jangir et al. (2019) and Yadav, Selva and Tandon (2020) mentioned that the features of distributed storage mode and decentralization could improve the visibility and transparency of PSC. The decentralized ledger enables data and transactions to be stored and shared by all network participants without the use of middleman (Radanović and Likić, 2018; Redman, 2019; Molina, Delgado and Tarazona, 2019). The end-to-end visibility enables consistent monitoring, thereby improving the supervision of end-to-end PSC (Dwivedi, Amin and Vollala, 2020).

2.   Traceability

The connection of each block with timestamp ensures that records in blockchain are in strict order. Therefore, it could provide the information provenance and keep track of drugs in PSC (Dwivedi, Amin and Vollala, 2020b). Moreover, this nature could provide convincing evidence for investigation if there are any deviations or problems during the drug distribution process (Fernando, Meyliana and Surjandy, 2019).

3.   Security and privacy

Yong et al. (2020) and Srivastava et al. (2019) added that the blockchain could be a solution to tackle the barriers of privacy and security in PSC as the blocks are tied through cryptographic hashing and the data could be accessed by having specific permission. Transactions are stored in a block with a unique hash value, each block in the framework is always connected with the previous one (Marbury, 2019; Ting et al., 2010). Any change is impossible in blockchain as it would cause a disharmony situation, and the resultant change would not be accepted by the network (Jangir et al., 2019; Pandey and Litoriya, 2020). So, data in the blockchain is immutable and tamper proof, which is beneficial to deal with the problems of authenticity and security to ensure the drug quality and reliability (Abbas et al., 2020) Moreover, the decentralization could improve the network safety and decrease the possibility of network failure effectively, since data is distributed in many nodes and is also updated in real-time (Molina, Delgado and Tarazona, 2019; Kumari and Saini, 2020).

4.   Smart contract application

Sylim et al. (2018) and Chiacchio et al. (2020) indicated the smart contract is the best application of blockchain that could bring several benefits to PSC. Firstly, Xie et al. (2019), Srivastava et al. (2019) and Fernando, Meyliana and Surjandy (2019) pointed out the smart contracts support in executing transaction verification without middleman automatically prevent various attacks in PSC, such as deviation, counterfeiting and theft. Secondly, the smart contracts could be written into the blockchain as a digital format, which enables partners in the same business to follow the defined rules (Chiacchio et al., 2020). Third, with an appropriate smart contract, the system could provide a more reliable, secure and flexible environment for transactions (Markarian, 2018; Sylim et al., 2018).

5.   Other benefits

In addition to the above-mentioned features, other characteristics could also bring benefits to PSC. For instance, the consensus algorithm in blockchain could avoid the problem of the duplicate transaction and it ensures that only the validated information could be uploaded into the network (Abbas et al., 2020).

Combination of IoT and Blockchain in PSC

In recent years, great effort has been devoted to the study of IoT and blockchain technology. Previous publications mentioned properties of blockchain which are useful to mitigate issues of data privacy and security in IoT (Shanley, 2018; Chanson et al., 2019). With blockchain, IoT could have many versatile and decentralized platforms, and therefore IoT could execute the works better (Dwivedi, Amin and Vollala, 2020a). De Aguiar et al. (2020) mentioned that blockchain could assist in managing and sharing the information from IoT in the healthcare area. Similarly, Sylim et al. (2018) and Haughwout (2018) underlined blockchain that could be a channel for integrating the anti-counterfeit mechanisms into the IoT and improve the interoperability of different unrelated systems. De Aguiar et al. (2020) and Ahmadi et al. (2020) also pointed out that integrating blockchain and IoT could offer capabilities of un-forgeability and trackability, which would help to decrease the possibility of drug diversion and theft.

Application in the Packaging Process

As opinion provided by Premkumar and C. (2020), the combination of IoT and blockchain could allow the manufacturers to realize and excel at digital twin initiatives that enable enterprises to monitor the whole lifecycle of products. Premkumar and C. (2020) described that IoT could support data monitoring and updating in real-time, while blockchain could record all information securely and immutably. There are some specific requirements for the packaging process when implementing IoT and blockchain. The studies conducted by Huang, Wu and Long (2018), Sylim et al.(2018), Chiacchio et al. (2019) and Pandey and Lotoriya (2020) presented the system design and special requirements, such as:.

- **RFID and Blockchain**

Barcode and RFID technology are adopted in a system called Drugledger designed by Huang, Wu and Long (2018). The author described that the RFID or barcode is encoded with raw data and it would be labelled on the packages of drugs. Only the certificated enterprise could join the Drugledger as a node, which could ensure the network security. The author highlighted the encoded hash of raw data would serve as metadata added into the system for querying the whole tracking and tracing information. Therefore, it requires participants in PSC to scan QR or RFID tags on the package to get the encoded hash when transactions happen. In particular, since the system considered different packaging levels and the situation of repackaging and unpacking. So, Drugledger blockchain could support recording transactions and movement of drugs with the different-level package.

- **RFID, GTIN with Blockchain**

In 2018, a drug surveillance system was developed by Sylim et al. (2018). To ensure the system could take effect, it requires a RFID and GTIN (global identifier number) following GS1 standard to be allocated to each physical drug unit and shipment package separately for creating the manufacturing and shipping pedigrees. Furthermore, the package contains the specific information such as hash code and the above two pedigrees. The authenticity of the drug could be verified by scanning the RFID, and then the verified transaction would be encrypted and entered into the network by participants of PSC. This process would continue from production to the final sale point. With entire data flow, end-users could scan the code to check the drug distribution history, confirming the drug provenance. Nevertheless, the main limitation of the presented system is invalid for tracking fake drug distribution outside the official PSC.

- **QR Code and Blockchain**

Pandey and Lotoriya (2020) proposed a system-based QR code and blockchain. The package of each sales unit, sub-package and sale, whole-carton are printed with a unique QR code that contains key production information such as batch number, production date and expiry date, etc. The information of the drug could be obtained and checked easily with the help of various information identifier. Partners in PSC could verify drug authenticity via scanning QR code and then record verified information on the ledger. As the QR code has already registered at the beginning, counterfeit drugs could be detected by the system automatically through checking whether the products with the same ID has been recorded before. The integral information flow enables tracking drugs throughout the PSC, which could provide provenance evaluation. Also, the end-consumers could verify drug authenticity. However, this study only works in a limited geographical area, and could not ensure the effectiveness in other areas. Also, the system could only be effective for medicines that are authorized in the system.

- **Serialisation and Blockchain**

The serialisation technology enables each level of the drug to have a unique serial number on its package, with the hierarchy matrix list generated by a serialisation software. This ensures that the product could be tracked (Chiacchio et al., 2019). The role and functions of the serial number is similar to the information identifiers such as QR code and RFID mentioned above. In order to combine the blockchain with the serialisation system, a BC server would have to be developed for realizing the information transmission that facilitates the storage of the hierarchy matrix in the blockchain. Moreover, the interaction of servers and smart contracts would generate a QR code as the unique electronic identity for each drug. Similarly, the QR code would be labelled on the package of the corresponding drug. The system enables the final client to verify the authenticity of the drug by scanning the QR code on the package. The effectiveness of the system would already be confirmed through testing. The authors found that the Ethereum has a little delay for generating QR code, which might decrease the production capacity in the packaging process. Therefore, there might be a need to investigate other blockchain platforms with lower latency and higher transaction (Chiacchio et al., 2020).

- **Serial Number, Fingerprint and Blockchain**

A new information identifier named fingerprint was adopted in a model proposed by Sahoo et al. (2019). In particular, the fingerprint is hard to copy, and could ensure authenticity. Sahoo et al. (2019) described that all participants in the PSC are included in the network. A serial number and unique fingerprint of the drug's manufacture would be attached to each package of sale unit. Meanwhile, the serial numbers of the inner products would be contained in the drug package at the transportation level. The verified transactions, information about serial number would be scanned and recorded on the blockchain in real-time by participants in the PSC, which made the footprints of the drug visible in the blockchain. Also, the model allowed end-users to review relative data by scanning the drug serial number through a cloud platform of blockchain.

Application in the Transportation Process

There are some temperature-sensitive drugs, whose quality would be affected by the unsuitable environment. According to the GDP regulation, it requires recording of temperature during the distribution process to ensure consistent quality and any deviation must be reported (Papert, Rimpler and Pflaum, 2016a; Bocek et al., 2017). Several studies indicated the advantages of applying IoT and blockchain in real-time drug environment monitoring. Hastig and Sodhi (2020) adverted the IoT technology including RFID tags and sensors would help to monitor the temperature change in the end-to-end PSC. Besides, Sahoo et al.(2019) also suggested that attaching IoT sensors like wireless sensors or GPS to the drug package helps in environment and location monitoring. However, the number of studies related to IoT and blockchain application in transportation are limited.

A company named Modum.io. designed a system using IoT devices and Ethereum blockchain technology to assist in drug temperature monitoring, and therefore, guarantee regulatory compliance and effective quality control over the transportation process (Bocek et al., 2017). The compositions of the system are shown in Table 9.

Table 9. Architectures of system designed by Modum.io. company

Architecture	Components	Function
IoT devices	Bluetooth sensors	provide temperature data
Database	n/a	Data and user credentials storage
Smart contracts	n/a	Defining transactions to guarantee that the temperature during the entire transportation complies with regulation.
Server	n/a	Serve as interfaces and support communication between blockchain and front-end-user.
Mobile devices	n/a	Enable end-users to do operations such as new shipment registration and keeping track of temperature record.
Ethereum blockchain network	n/a	Store intelligent smart contract code, Verify temperature data resisted in the front-end.

Source: (Bocek et al., 2017).

According to studies of Bocek et al. (2017), a tracking number would be attached to the drug package, and each sensor owns an address number. Sensor devices are placed at the appropriate point of the shipment. The temperature would be recorded by the sensor continuously and then stored in its database. The temperature data would be downloaded by scanning the tracking number on the drug package to connect the sensor, and then data could be sent to smart contracts. In this way, participants in the blockchain could verify the data. The approach could enhance regulatory compliance and guarantee quality control during transportation.

This study proved it is possible to adopt IoT and blockchain technology in the drug transportation process to record and monitor the environment change. With continuous monitoring, the drug quality could be better guaranteed. The architectures were designed by Modum.io. The company provided a rough idea and method of combining IoT and blockchain in the PSC. However, it only focused on temperature monitoring, which is limited. In future studies and practice, researchers or companies could choose the right IoT sensor and blockchain platform to develop other functions such as humidity, location and other information monitoring in the transportation process based on this architecture.

Framework for Combining IoT and Blockchain in PSC

In light of the problems in the current PSC. An architectural design for the PSC management system has been proposed by Shi, Yi and Kuang (2019). The model is based on the blockchain and IoT techniques. It is composed of six modules. (1) IoT module, (2) Application module, (3) Certificate authority, (4) Transaction private module, (5) Smart contract module, (6) Fabric blockchain. Shi, Yi and Kuang (2019) indicated that the model could ensure that data is transparent, authentic, not tampered with, and traceable. The functional test results were satisfactory.

By combining the studies related to IoT and blockchain in PSC, authors summarized a basic framework for integrating IoT and blockchain in the PSC, which could give a detailed idea about how to combine two technologies in PSC for obtaining several advantages. The detailed system modules are described in table 10.

Table 10. Modules of PSC system

Module	Composition	Function
IoT module	Data acquisition devices (GPS, Barcode, serial number, RFID, sensors and their networks)	Collect and upload data in real-time
Application module	• Data uploaded sub-module, • Data query sub-module.	• Receive data, • Query data • Transfer various data from IoT devices to privacy module. • As interface, to support conmmunication between IoT devices and blockchain network • enable end users to do operations via mobile application
Database	n/a	Data and user credentials storage
Certificate authority	n/a	• Generating public key and private key, • Provide version number for each member in the blockchain
Transaction private module	Key participants in the network (manufacturers, wholesalers, retailers, carriers etc.)	Data encryption and decryption, ensure privacy and security
Smart contract module	n/a	• Provide AIP (Application Programming Interface) deploy, call, execute and logout contract. • Defining transactions to guarantee the temperature in whole transportation is regulatory compliance.
Blockchain platform	Ethereum platform or Hyperleger fabric platform	• Connect nodes of participants, • Store intelligent smart contract code, • Store or return data in blockchain.

Source: Shi, Yi and Kuang (2019) and (Bocek et al., 2017)

The drug company could choose diffident kinds of IoT devices and blockchain platforms based on the demand and its requirement. Besides IoT devices and blockchain platforms, other models could also help to establish a connection and realize functions for participants and users. Therefore, the company could view the above multiple models as a basic framework to develop their own PSC management system to integrate IoT and blockchain.

Challenge of IoT and Blockchain Application in PSC

As the appearance of IoT and blockchain combination is not for a long time and it is clear that the pharmaceutical industry is highly regulated. Therefore, there are several challenges when applying the new integrated technology in the PSC.

1. Lacking regulations and policy

There are some risks to the privacy and surety of IoT. Although several studies confirmed that IoT and blockchain applications could bring great advantages to PSC. With the sustained growth of IoT-based data sharing, a lack of regulation to enhance the governance of data sharing based on IoT might lead to high risks in security and privacy (Srivastava et al., 2019). Secondly, there are no policies to incentivize technology implementation (Sylim et al., 2018a).

2. Acceptance

The superiority of IoT and blockchain application in PSC could only be achieved when all companies involved in the PSC are willing to participate in the network. So, making the blockchain accepted by the pharmaceutical industry and to promote the application is a challenging task (Huang, Wu and Long 2018; Srivastava et al., 2019).

3. Writing of smart contracts

Smart contracts are the most advantageous application that could bring huge benefits to the supply chain. However, writing smart contracts faces some challenges. Firstly, the programming language of smart contracts is new, and it is hard to maintain. Secondly, the efficiency of transaction execution is low, reason being all transactions are executed amongst all the nodes (Sylim et al., 2018; Abbas et al., 2020).

4. Efficiency of blockchain

With the increase in number of nodes and transactions in the network, more verification is required for the transaction to be executed. As a result the throughput of blockchain would negatively affect the efficiency of PSC (Zhou et al., 2019).

5. Other barriers

Radanović and Likić (2018) suggested that blockchain technology is still immature and public or expert knowledge is insufficient.

CONCLUSION

Review of Objectives

The authors consider that all the objectives set out in this chapter have been achieved.

Objective 1: The literature was summarized with relative information related to main challenges or issues in PSC. Three main challenges that are faced by PSC are poor traceability, low transparency, and lack of authenticity. Some of the problems as discussed in the review of complex PSC environment are different practices of enterprises, insufficient information management systems, unsatisfactory track and trace system, etc.

Objective 2: Descriptive analysis was conducted for the opportunities and issues that IoT and blockchain application have on the aspect of information management and provenance in PSC. There is a short description of the existing IoT devices applied in PSC and the proposed blockchain system in this chapter. The publications on IoT and blockchain applications in current PSC showed potential opportunities. Nevertheless, most of the blockchain systems proposed by researchers lacked system effectiveness. The challenges discussed in the review include the aspects of regulation, expertise, as well as the acceptance of the pharmaceutical industry. All of these challenges would influence the effectiveness of implementing IoT and blockchain in the PSC.

Objective 3: An effort was made to achieve this objective by dividing it into 2 parts which is the combination of IoT and Blockchain application in PSC and the suggested framework for integrating IoT and blockchain in PSC. Although developing blockchain for PSC management is still at the initial phase, multiple pieces of research have already demonstrated that the application of IoT and blockchain in PSC could provide a secure, authentic, reliable, trustworthy, immutable, traceable as well as tamper proof environment to support the PSC. That application could facilitate the collection of drug information, record and share information and transactions with involved participants in PSC. With the integral and reliable information flow, the transparency, traceability and authenticity of PSC could be improved effectively. Hence, problems such as counterfeit drugs and low trust relationships amongst partners of PSC could be resolved. For the IoT and blockchain integration, this chapter focused on the packaging process and transportation process. More importantly, this chapter provides a rough basic framework of IoT and blockchain combination structure in PSC based on the review of existing studies, which presents the essential models when combining IoT and blockchain.

The Limitations and Future Research

The findings of this study must be seen in the light of following limitations. Firstly, the sample size and the number of academic literatures used for the review. As blockchain and IoT integration technology are still in the initial phase, there is limited research done on this topic. Therefore, the number of selected academic peer-reviewed journals, journal papers and conference papers are unbalanced. Furthermore, the ranking of most selected scholarly papers is unspecific. Secondly, there were only few articles related to the implementation of IoT and blockchain in the drug transportation process, which might be because IoT and blockchain application is still in the initial phase. Finally, the framework provided in this chapter is by combining IoT and Blockchain in PSC. It is composed of six modules. (1) IoT module, (2) Application module, (3) Certificate authority, (4) Transaction private module, (5) Smart contract module, and (6) Fabric blockchain. Further research should be conducted to simulate the framework, enabling a stepped approach towards best practice.

REFERENCES

Abbas, K., Afaq, M., Khan, T. A., & Song, W.-C. (2020). A blockchain and machine learning-based drug supply chain management and recommendation system for smart pharmaceutical industry. *Electronics (Switzerland)*, *9*(5), 852.

Ahmadi, V., Benjelloun, S., El Kik, M., Sharma, T., Chi, H., & Zhou, W. (2020). Drug Governance: IoT-based Blockchain Implementation in the Pharmaceutical Supply Chain. *6th International Conference on Mobile and Secure Services, MOBISECSERV 2020*, 1–8. 10.1109/MobiSecServ48690.2020.9042950

Alangot, B., & Achuthan, K. (2017, August). Trace and track: Enhanced pharma supply chain infrastructure to prevent fraud. In *International Conference on Ubiquitous Communications and Network Computing* (pp. 189-195). Springer.

Anand, R., Niyas, K., Gupta, S., & Revathy, S. (2020). Anti-counterfeit on medicine detection using blockchain technology. *Lecture Notes in Networks and Systems*, *89*, 1223–1232. doi:10.1007/978-981-15-0146-3_119

Anon. (2018). 2018 Major Pharma Packaging Trends. In *Pharmaceutical Processing*. Advantage Business Media.

Arksey, H., & O'Malley, L. (2005). Scoping studies: Towards a methodological framework. *International Journal of Social Research Methodology: Theory and Practice*, *8*(1), 19–32. doi:10.1080/1364557032000119616

Armitage, A., & Keeble-allen, D. (2008). Undertaking a Structured Literature Review or Structuring a Literature Review: Tales from the... by Academic Conferences and publishing International – Issuu. *7th European Conference on ...*, *6(2)*, 103–114.

Barchetti, U., Bucciero, A., De Blasi, M., Guido, A. L., Mainetti, L., & Patrono, L. (2010). Impact of RFID, EPC and B2B on traceability management of the pharmaceutical supply chain. *Proceeding - 5th International Conference on Computer Sciences and Convergence Information Technology, ICCIT 2010*, 58–63. 10.1109/ICCIT.2010.5711029

Ben-Daya, M., Hassini, E., & Bahroun, Z. (2019). Internet of things and supply chain management: A literature review. *International Journal of Production Research*, *57*(15–16), 4719–4742. doi:10.1080/00207543.2017.1402140

Benatia, M. A., De Sa, V. E., Baudry, D., Delalin, H., & Halftermeyer, P. (2018, March). A framework for big data driven product traceability system. In *2018 4th international conference on advanced technologies for signal and image processing (ATSIP)* (pp. 1-7). IEEE. 10.1109/ATSIP.2018.8364340

Bocek, T., Rodrigues, B. B., Strasser, T., & Stiller, B. (2017). Blockchains everywhere - A use-case of blockchains in the pharma supply-chain. *Proceedings of the IM 2017 - 2017 IFIP/IEEE International Symposium on Integrated Network and Service Management*, 772–777. 10.23919/INM.2017.7987376

Botcha, K. M., & Chakravarthy, V. V. (2019, June). Enhancing traceability in pharmaceutical supply chain using Internet of Things (IoT) and blockchain. In *2019 IEEE International Conference on Intelligent Systems and Green Technology (ICISGT)* (pp. 45-453). IEEE. 10.1109/ICISGT44072.2019.00025

Bryatov, S. R., & Borodinov, A. (2019, May). Blockchain technology in the pharmaceutical supply chain: Researching a business model based on Hyperledger Fabric. In *Proceedings of the International Conference on Information Technology and Nanotechnology (ITNT)* (pp. 21-24). 10.18287/1613-0073-2019-2416-134-140

Chanson, M., Bogner, A., Bilgeri, D., Fleisch, E., & Wortmann, F. (2019). Blockchain for the IoT: Privacy-preserving protection of sensor data. *Journal of the Association for Information Systems, 20*(9), 1271–1307. doi:10.17705/1jais.00567

Chiacchio, F., Compagno, L., D'Urso, D., Velardita, L., & Sandner, P. (2020). A decentralized application for the traceability process in the pharma industry. *Procedia Manufacturing, 42*, 362–369.

Chitre, M., Sapkal, S., Adhikari, A., & Mulla, S. (2019). Monitoring counterfeit drugs using counterchain. *2019 6th IEEE International Conference on Advances in Computing, Communication and Control, ICAC3 2019*. 10.1109/ICAC347590.2019.9036794

Clauson, K. A., Breeden, E. A., Davidson, C., & Mackey, T. K. (2018). Leveraging Blockchain Technology to Enhance Supply Chain Management in Healthcare: An Exploration of Challenges and Opportunities in the Health Supply Chain. *Blockchain in Healthcare Today, 1*(0), 1–12.

Da Xu, L., He, W., & Li, S. (2014). Internet of things in industries: A survey. *IEEE Transactions on Industrial Informatics, 10*(4), 2233–2243. doi:10.1109/TII.2014.2300753

De Aguiar, E. J., Faiçal, B. S., Krishnamachari, B., & Ueyama, J. (2020). A Survey of Blockchain-Based Strategies for Healthcare. *ACM Computing Surveys, 53*(2), 1–27. doi:10.1145/3376915

Dwivedi, S.K., Amin, R., & Vollala, S. (2020b). Blockchain based secured information sharing protocol in supply chain management system with key distribution mechanism. *Journal of Information Security and Applications, 54*.

Hasan, H., AlHadhrami, E., AlDhaheri, A., Salah, K., & Jayaraman, R. (2019). Smart contract-based approach for efficient shipment management. *Computers and Industrial Engineering, 136*(July), 149–159.

Hastig, G. M., & Sodhi, M. S. (2020). Blockchain for Supply Chain Traceability: Business Requirements and Critical Success Factors. *Production and Operations Management, 29*(4), 935–954. doi:10.1111/poms.13147

Haughwout, J. (2018). Tracking medicine by transparent blockchain. *Pharmaceutical Processing, 33*(1), 24–26.

Huang, Y., Wu, J., & Long, C. (2018). Drugledger: A practical blockchain system for drug traceability and regulation. *Proceedings - IEEE 2018 International Congress on Cybermatics: 2018 IEEE Conferences on Internet of Things, Green Computing and Communications, Cyber, Physical and Social Computing, Smart Data, Blockchain, Computer and Information Technology, iThings/Gree.*, 1137–1144. 10.1109/Cybermatics_2018.2018.00206

Hyperledger. (2019). *Case Study: How Walmart brought unprecedented transparency to the food supply chain with Hyperledger Fabric Challenge.* Author.

Jamil, F., Hang, L., Kim, K., & Kim, D. (2019). A novel medical blockchain model for drug supply chain integrity management in a smart hospital. Electronics, 8(5). doi:10.3390/electronics8050505

Jangir, S., Muzumdar, A., Jaiswal, A., Modi, C. N., Chandel, S., & Vyjayanthi, C. (2019). A Novel Framework for Pharmaceutical Supply Chain Management using Distributed Ledger and Smart Contracts. *2019 10th International Conference on Computing, Communication and Networking Technologies, ICCCNT 2019.* 10.1109/ICCCNT45670.2019.8944829

Jha, S., Kumar, R., Chatterjee, J. M., & Khari, M. (2019). Collaborative handshaking approaches between internet of computing and internet of things towards a smart world: A review from 2009–2017. *Telecommunication Systems, 70*(4), 617–634. doi:10.100711235-018-0481-x

Kamble, S.S., Gunasekaran, A., & Sharma, R. (2020). Modeling the blockchain enabled traceability in agriculture supply chain. *International Journal of Information Management, 52*(June).

Khari, M., Garg, A. K., Gandomi, A. H., Gupta, R., Patan, R., & Balusamy, B. (2019). Securing data in Internet of Things (IoT) using cryptography and steganography techniques. *IEEE Transactions on Systems, Man, and Cybernetics. Systems, 50*(1), 73–80. doi:10.1109/TSMC.2019.2903785

Kim, H. M., & Laskowski, M. (2018b). Toward an ontology-driven blockchain design for supply-chain provenance. *Intelligent Systems in Accounting, Finance & Management, 25*(1), 18–27. doi:10.1002/isaf.1424

Kshetri, N. (2018). 1 Blockchain's roles in meeting key supply chain management objectives. *International Journal of Information Management, 39*(June), 80–89. . doi:10.1016/j.ijinfomgt.2017.12.005

Kumar, A., Choudhary, D., Raju, M. S., Chaudhary, D. K., & Sagar, R. K. (2019). Combating counterfeit drugs: A quantitative analysis on cracking down the fake drug industry by using blockchain technology. *Proceedings of the 9th International Conference On Cloud Computing, Data Science and Engineering, Confluence 2019.*, 174–178. 10.1109/CONFLUENCE.2019.8776891

Kumar, R., & Tripathi, R. (2019). Traceability of counterfeit medicine supply chain through Blockchain. *2019 11th International Conference on Communication Systems and Networks, COMSNETS 2019*, 568–570. 10.1109/COMSNETS.2019.8711418

Kumari, K., & Saini, K. (2020). Data handling & drug traceability: Blockchain meets healthcare to combat counterfeit drugs. *International Journal of Scientific and Technology Research, 9*(3), 728–731.

Marbury, D. (2019). How Blockchain Can Reduce Waste, Fraud in Pharmacy. *Drug Topics, 163*(1), 30–31.

Markarian, J. (2018). Modernizing Pharma Manufacturing. *Pharmaceutical Technology, 42*(4), 20–25.

Meyliana & Surjandy. (2019). Success factor of implementation blockchain technology in pharmaceutical industry: A literature review. *2019 6th International Conference on Information Technology, Computer and Electrical Engineering, ICITACEE 2019.*

Molina, J. C., Delgado, D. T., & Tarazona, G. (2019). Using blockchain for traceability in the drug supply chain. *Communications in Computer and Information Science, 1027*, 536–548. doi:10.1007/978-3-030-21451-7_46

Musamih, A., Salah, K., Jayaraman, R., Arshad, J., Debe, M., Al-Hammadi, Y., & Ellahham, S. (2021). A Blockchain-Based Approach for Drug Traceability in Healthcare Supply Chain. *IEEE Access: Practical Innovations, Open Solutions, 9*, 9728–9743. doi:10.1109/ACCESS.2021.3049920

Okoli, C. (2015). A Guide to Conducting a Standalone Systematic Literature Review. *Communications of the Association for Information Systems, 37*(1), 879–910. doi:10.17705/1CAIS.03743

Olson-Hazboun, S. K., Howe, P. D., & Leiserowitz, A. (2018). 'The influence of extractive activities on public support for renewable energy policy'. *Energy Policy, 123*, 117–126. doi:10.1016/j.enpol.2018.08.044

Pandey, P., & Litoriya, R. (2020). Securing E-health Networks from Counterfeit Medicine Penetration Using Blockchain. *Wireless Personal Communications*. Advance online publication. doi:10.100711277-020-07041-7

Papert, M., Rimpler, P., & Pflaum, A. (2016a). Enhancing supply chain visibility in a pharmaceutical supply chain: Solutions based on automatic identification technology. *International Journal of Physical Distribution & Logistics Management, 46*(9), 859–884. doi:10.1108/IJPDLM-06-2016-0151

Patel, K. K., Patel, S. M., & Scholar, P. G. (2016). Internet of Things-IOT: Definition, Characteristics, Architecture, Enabling Technologies, Application & Future Challenges. *International Journal of Engineering Science and Computing, 6*(5), 1–10.

Popay, J., Roberts, H., Sowden, A., Petticrew, M., Arai, L., Rodgers, M., ... Duffy, S. (2006). *Guidance on the conduct of narrative synthesis in systematic reviews. A product from the ESRC methods programme version*. Academic Press.

Premkumar, A., & C, S. (2020). Application of Blockchain and IoT towards. *Die Pharmazeutische Industrie*, 729–733.

Radanović, I., & Likić, R. (2018). Opportunities for Use of Blockchain Technology in Medicine. *Applied Health Economics and Health Policy, 16*(5), 583–590.

Raj, R., Rai, N., & Agarwal, S. (2019). Anticounterfeiting in Pharmaceutical Supply Chain by establishing Proof of Ownership. *IEEE Region 10 Annual International Conference, Proceedings/TENCON*, 1572–1577. 10.1109/TENCON.2019.8929271

Redman, R. (2019). Walmart joins FDA blockchain pilot for prescription drugs. *Supermarket News*, 1–3.

Rejeb, A., Keogh, J. G., & Treiblmaier, H. (2019). Leveraging the Internet of Things and blockchain technology in Supply Chain Management. *Future Internet, 11*(7), 10–11. doi:10.3390/fi11070161

Rotunno, G., Mannarelli, C., Guglielmelli, P., Pacilli, A., Pancrazzi, A., Pieri, L., Fanelli, T., Bosi, A., & Vannucchi, A. M. (2014). Impact of calreticulin mutations on clinical and hematological phenotype and outcome in essential thrombocythemia. *Blood, 123*(10), 1552–1555. doi:10.1182/blood-2013-11-538983 PMID:24371211

Sahoo, M., Singhar, S. S., Nayak, B., & Mohanta, B. K. (2019). A Blockchain Based Framework Secured by ECDSA to Curb Drug Counterfeiting. *2019 10th International Conference on Computing, Communication and Networking Technologies, ICCCNT 2019*. 10.1109/ICCCNT45670.2019.8944772

Saunders, M. N., Altinay, L., & Riordan, K. (2009). The management of post-merger cultural integration: Implications from the hotel industry. *Service Industries Journal*, *29*(10), 1359–1375. doi:10.1080/02642060903026213

Settanni, E., Harrington, T.S., & Srai, J.S. (2017). Pharmaceutical supply chain models: A synthesis from a systems view of operations research. *Operations Research Perspectives*, *4*, 74–95.

Shanley, A. (2017). Real-Time Logistics: Internet of things, advanced analytics, and blockchain solutions such as smart contracts promise to give manufacturers more control over products and supply chains. *Pharmaceutical Technology Europe*, *29*(10), 46–48.

Shanley, A. (2018). FDA Provides More Clarity on DSCSA. *Pharmaceutical Technology Europe*, *30*(11), 36–37.

Shi, J., Yi, D., & Kuang, J. (2019). Pharmaceutical Supply Chain Management System with Integration of IoT and Blockchain Technology. Lecture Notes in Computer Science (including subseries Lecture Notes in Artificial Intelligence and Lecture Notes in Bioinformatics), 11911 LNCS, 97–108. doi:10.1007/978-3-030-34083-4_10

Sinclair, D., Shahriar, H., & Zhang, C. (2019, January). Security requirement prototyping with hyperledger composer for drug supply chain: a blockchain application. In *Proceedings of the 3rd International Conference on Cryptography, Security and Privacy* (pp. 158-163). 10.1145/3309074.3309104

Srivastava, S., Bhadauria, A., Dhaneshwar, S., & Gupta, S. (2019). Traceability and transparency in supply chain management system of pharmaceutical goods through block chain. *International Journal of Scientific and Technology Research*, *8*(12), 3201–3206.

Sunny, J., Undralla, N., & Pillai, V. M. (2020). Supply chain transparency through blockchain-based traceability: An overview with demonstration. *Computers & Industrial Engineering*, *150*, 106895. doi:10.1016/j.cie.2020.106895

Sylim, P., Liu, F., Marcelo, A., & Fontelo, P. (2018a). Blockchain technology for detecting falsified and substandard drugs in distribution: Pharmaceutical supply chain intervention. *Journal of Medical Internet Research*, *20*(9), 1–12. PMID:30213780

Thaul, S. (2015). Pharmaceutical supply chain security. *Securing the Pharmaceutical Supply Chain: Issues and Perspectives*, 1–26.

Ting, S. L., Kwok, S. K., Tsang, A. H. C., & Lee, W. B. (2010). Enhancing the information transmission for pharmaceutical supply chain based on Radio Frequency Identification (RFID) and internet of things. *SCMIS 2010 - Proceedings of 2010 8th International Conference on Supply Chain Management and Information Systems: Logistics Systems and Engineering*.

Tranfield, D., Denyer, D., & Smart, P. (2003). Towards a Methodology for Developing Evidence-Informed Management Knowledge by Means of Systematic Review. *British Journal of Management, 14*(3), 207–222. doi:10.1111/1467-8551.00375

Treiblmaier, H. (2019). Toward More Rigorous Blockchain Research: Recommendations for Writing Blockchain Case Studies. *Frontiers in Blockchain, 2*(May), 1–15. doi:10.3389/fbloc.2019.00003

Tseng, J.-H., Liao, Y.-C., Chong, B., & Liao, S.-W. (2018). Governance on the drug supply chain via gcoin blockchain. *International Journal of Environmental Research and Public Health, 15*(6), 1055. doi:10.3390/ijerph15061055 PMID:29882861

Uddin, M., Salah, K., Jayaraman, R., Pesic, S., & Ellahham, S. (2021). Blockchain for drug traceability: Architectures and open challenges. *Health Informatics Journal, 27*(2). doi:10.1177/14604582211011228 PMID:33899576

Vecchione, A. (2017). Blockchain tech could track pharmacy supply chain. *Drug Topics, 161*(11).

WHO. (2010). *Monitoring the Building Blocks of Health Systems : a Handbook of Indicators and.* WHO.

Wu, H., Li, Z., King, B., Miled, Z. B., Wassick, J., & Tazelaar, J. (2017). A distributed ledger for supply chain physical distribution visibility. Information, 8(4). doi:10.3390/info8040137

Xie, W., Wang, B., Ye, Z., Wu, W., You, J., & Zhou, Q. (2019). Simulation-based Blockchain Design to Secure Biopharmaceutical Supply Chain. *Proceedings - Winter Simulation Conference,* 797–808. 10.1109/WSC40007.2019.9004696

Yadav, A.S., Selva, N.S., & Tandon, A. (2020). Medicine manufacturing industries supply chain management for blockchain application using artificial neural networks. *International Journal of Advanced Science and Technology, 29*(8), 1294–1301.

Yong, B., Shen, J., Liu, X., Li, F., Chen, H., & Zhou, Q. (2020). An intelligent blockchain-based system for safe vaccine supply and supervision. *International Journal of Information Management, 52*, 52. doi:10.1016/j.ijinfomgt.2019.10.009

Zhou, W., & Piramuthu, S. (2014, June). Security/privacy of wearable fitness tracking IoT devices. In *2014 9th Iberian Conference on Information Systems and Technologies (CISTI)* (pp. 1-5). IEEE. 10.1109/CISTI.2014.6877073

Zhou, Y., Cahya, S., Combs, S. A., Nicolaou, C. A., Wang, J., Desai, P. V., & Shen, J. (2019). Exploring Tunable Hyperparameters for Deep Neural Networks with Industrial ADME Data Sets. *Journal of Chemical Information and Modeling, 59*(3), 1005–1016. doi:10.1021/acs.jcim.8b00671 PMID:30586300

Chapter 2
Insights on the Prospects of Multi–Access Edge Computing

Dhaya R.
https://orcid.org/0000-0002-3599-7272
King Khalid University, Saudi Arabia

Kanthavel R.
King Khalid University, Saudi Arabia

ABSTRACT

Edge computing is an open information technology design that is empowering mobile computing and internet of things innovations. Edge computing is the arrangement of the process that is significant because it makes as good as ever ways for mechanical and undertaking level organizations to amplify operational proficiency, improve execution and security, computerize all center business measures, and guarantee consistently on accessibility. The effectiveness of edge computing depends on the assessment of the cleverness of IoT-supported gadgets and the way of clustering our IoT devices. Even though edge computing can give convincing advantages across a huge number of utilization cases, the innovation is a long way from foolproof. Past the conventional issues of organization constraints, a few key contemplations can influence the reception of edge computing. This chapter deals with the viewpoints on the challenges of multi-access edge computing that specially focuses on network bandwidth, distributed computing, latency, security, backup, data accumulation, control and management, and scale.

INTRODUCTION

The capability of edge computing is amazingly high. It has been anticipated that by 2025, an astounding 75 percent of big business information would be produced and handled at "the edge." Put another way, in five years, most big business information could sidestep the cloud. Edge computing engineering permits them to put workers in server farms close to stock trades the world over to run asset escalated calculations as near the wellspring of information as could reasonably be expected. This furnishes them with the most precise and state-of-the-art data to keep their business moving. There is a distinction between

DOI: 10.4018/978-1-7998-8367-8.ch002

Edge Computing and Cloud computing. Edge computing is used to hold occasion delicate data, while distributed computation is exploited to deal with information that isn't term-based. Other than inertness, edge computing is preferential over distributed computing in far-off areas, where there is constrained or nil availability to a brought together part. Edge computing would be the future arrangement of IoT. The utilization of edge computing assists with expanding the accessible data transfer capacity of a nearby organization which can improve different administrations, for example, neighborhood workers and other IoT gadgets, and thusly increment the greatest number of gadgets on a solitary organization (accordingly taking into account more IoT gadgets to be coordinated). In Edge computing, information is the soul of present-day business, giving important business understanding and supporting ongoing authority over basic business cycles and tasks. The present organizations are inundated with an expanse of information, and gigantic measures of information can be regularly gathered from sensors and IoT gadgets working continuously from far-off areas and ungracious working conditions any place on the planet.

Yet, this virtual surge of information is additionally changing how organizations handle computing. The customary computing worldview based on a unified server farm and regular internet aren't appropriate to moving perpetually developing waterways of certifiable information. Data transmission impediments, dormancy issues, and flighty organization disturbances would all be able to plot to debilitate such endeavors. Organizations are reacting to these information challenges using edge-computing design. In the easiest conditions, edge computing stirs several parts of capacity and registers assets out of the focal server farm and nearer to the wellspring of the information ourselves. As opposed to sending crude information to a focal server farm for preparing and investigation, that work is rather performed where the information is created - regardless of whether that is a trade location, a production line ground, rambling usefulness, or crossways a shrewd town. Simply the delayed consequence of that registering work at the edge, for example, constant business experiences, hardware support forecasts, or additional noteworthy responses, is launched reverse to the principle server farm for audit and additional human being teamwork's (Shi et al., 2019).

In customary endeavor computing, information is created at a customer endpoint, for example, a client's PC. That information is obtained crossways a Wide Area Network, for example, the web, throughout the business Local Area network, wherever the information is put away and occupied by venture appliances. Aftereffects of that effort are then passed on the reverse to the customer's point of view. This remaining parts a demonstrated and dependable way to deal with customer worker computing for most run-of-the-mill industry purposes. But the quantity of gadgets associated with the help of the web, and the quantity of information is being created by those gadgets and utilized by organizations, is becoming dreadfully rapidly for conventional server farm frameworks to oblige(Hu et al., 2015). The objectives of the proposed chapter are explained the following things

- To analyze the strategic considerations of edge data centers aiming to improve efficiency.
- To describe and access the challenges of Edge computing and possible solutions.
- To study the edge computing use cases and examples for better understandings towards smart utilization

SCOPE OF THE PROPOSED CHAPTER

The main preferred position of edge computing is its ability to improve network execution by the decrease in inactivity as the handled information is done through IoT in edge computing gadgets. Together edge computing and haze computing are firmly on the ascent for similar careful reasons: an IoT information storm, unquestionably in IIoT (Symeonides et al., 2019). If you get a ton of information similar to the situation when you influence IoT in such start to finish ways or even in explicit exceptionally sensor-serious and accordingly information escalated conditions whereby information is created at the edge which by definition occurs in IoT as your information detecting and assembling gadgets ARE at the edge. Edge processing pushes the knowledge, dealing with power and correspondence limits of an edge gateway or contraption direct into devices like programmable computerization controllers ".Hence it is essential to take care of the difficulties of edge processing in a multi-access climate and this part would fuse the top to bottom examinations as an extension to improve the adequacy of edge computing

HOW DOES EDGE COMPUTING FUNCTION

The Need for Using Edge Computing: Most organizations stock up, oversee, and dissect information on a concentrated stockpiling, ordinarily in a public cloud or private cloud climate. Notwithstanding, customary foundation and distributed computing are not, at this point ready to meet the prerequisites for some genuine applications. For instance, on account of IoT and IoE, a profoundly accessible organization with insignificant idleness is needed to handle a lot of information progressively, which is unimaginable on a conventional IT framework. For this situation, the upsides of edge computing turn out to be more self-evident (Ravi et al., 2005). Figure 1 shows the base of edge computing

Figure 1. Base of edge computing

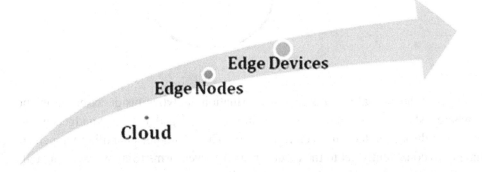

Role of Edge Computing Devices

Edge computing gadgets are the equipment that drives the use of edge computing across different enterprises. They are utilized to achieve various undertakings relying upon the product applications or highlights they're provisioned with and described in figure 2.

Figure 2. Role of edge computing devices

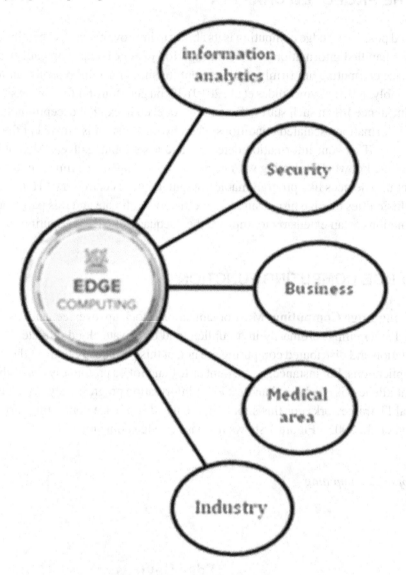

Edge computing additionally disentangles information analytics inside assembling shop floors. In occasions where a shop floor contains many machines and IoT gadgets, edge gadgets gather, cycle, and store information through a decentralized framework. This guarantees handling happens progressively without having to consistently get to the cloud or outer server farms (Satyanarayanan et al., 2009).

The decentralized idea of edge computing likewise implies security is neighborhood to each edge gadget. Subsequently, this fills in as a shield against digital assaults. In circumstances where fruitful penetrates happen, the data situated inside the penetrated edge network is influenced yet not moved to different organizations inside an endeavor's biological system.

In assistance-based businesses, for example, the account and web-based business area, edge-computing gadgets additionally have tasks to carry out. For this situation, an advanced mobile phone, PC, or tablet turns into the edge computing gadget. With these gadgets, workers can be conveyed to distant locales and convey customized administrations to the populace. A model is the utilization of tablets to catch the record subtleties of people and make banking profiles for them without visiting a bank. The caught information would then be able to be moved to the bank's venture network when required (Shi et al., 2016).

In medical services, edge computing gadgets are being conveyed on wearable gadgets and implantable clinical gadgets to helps patients. In the greater part of these circumstances, the gadget is equipped for taking care of biomedical sign handling plans to help gadgets make explicit moves. The joining of edge gadgets in medical care additionally upgrades the conveyance of customized clinical answers for patients.

Producers inside the biomedical business and specialist organizations who own stockrooms can likewise use edge computing gadgets to upgrade shop floor activities. Joining edge gadgets to material taking care of devices or inside explicit segments assists with understanding shop floor traffic, stock administration, and efficiency. The caught information would then be able to be utilized to improve warehousing and accelerate request-handling exercises (Symeonides et al., 2019).

Features of an Edge Computing Way Out

- A key reason for edge computing access is to empower availability with the sensors and actuators. Numerous industry conventions encourage various styles of gadget correspondence. An edge arrangement should uphold the most widely recognized conventions.

    ◦ The capacity to privately run applications is the way to empower nearby information handling. Contingent upon the space, model applications incorporate analytics calculations, edge-based warnings and alerts, symptomatic and checking applications, and some other custom programming code that is executed on the entry way (Vakali & Pallis, 2003).
    ◦ In expansion to nearby handling, a passage ought to be able to store information locally. This is vital to permitting a passage to run self-governing. The blend of neighborhood calculation and nearby stockpiling ought to permit the doorway to work in a disengaged mode.
    ◦ Security should be incorporated into the edge arrangement. An edge arrangement ought to consider authorization- based admittance control, secure encoded correspondence, endorsement the board and the mix into existing security arrangements.
    ◦ Edge computing entry requires an approach to distantly oversee and get to every individual passage. The distant administration highlights ought to permit to distantly begin, stop, arrange, and update a door and the gadgets connected to it.
    ◦ As a final point, the product for an edge arrangement ought to be versatile to various equipment stages

EDGE VS. CLOUD VS. FOG COMPUTING

Both Edge processing and Fog processing offer relative functionalities for pushing both information and information to close by smart stages that are found either on, or near the wellspring of the start of the information, be it be vehicles, motors, speakers, screens, sensors or, siphons(Aazam et al., 2018). Both the advancements impact the force of processing limits inside a local association to perform estimation tasks that may have been finished in the cloud with no issue (Xu, 2014). They can help associations with diminishing their dependence on cloud-based stages for information getting ready and limit, which regularly prompts idleness issues, and can make information - driven decisions quicker(Jain & Singhal, 2016).

Region of Data Processing: The main distinction between distributed computing, Fog figuring, and Edge registering is the area where information handling happens.

- In distributed computing, information is set up on a central cloud specialist, which is by and large arranged far away from the wellspring of information. It occurs on cloud organizations, for instance, Amazon E2C cases.
- Edge registering for the most part happens clearly on the contraptions to which the sensors are related or an entry device that is in the region of the sensors.
- Fog figuring shifts the Edge registering endeavors to processors that are related to the LAN gear or the LAN .so they may be genuinely more unavailable from the actuators and the sensors (Bonomi et al., 2012).
- Along these lines, for Edge figuring, the information is set up on the sensor or contraption itself without moving to somewhere else. Oppositely, in Fog figuring, the information is set up inside an IoT entryway or Fog center points that are arranged in the LAN association.

Allotment Power and Memory Office: Distributed computing can collect unquestionably more information than Fog registering that has the limited dealing with power. The planning power and limit capacities are significantly lesser because of Edge processing, since both of them are performed on the devices or IoT sensor itself (Francis & Madhiajagan, 2017).

Guideline: Distributed computing is generally suitable for the long stretch all around assessment of information. Mist and Edge processing are more sensible for the expedient examination required for constant response. To the extent security, Fog and Edge are a ton of security (Al-Qamash & Soliman, 2018).

- In Fog, the information stays scattered among center points. As such, it is difficult to control information when appeared differently about the united design of Cloud computing (Alrawais et al., 2017).
- In Edge figuring, the information stays on the actual contraption, making it more secure out of the three.
- Along these lines, in the cases, where security is a huge concern, Fog and Edge are ideal.

Since the information is passed on among center points in Fog registering, the get-away is insignificant when diverged from distributed computing, where everything is taken care of in one spot and if anything ends up being awful with it, it cuts down the whole structure. Whether or not one center point goes down in Fog processing, various centers stay operational; making it the right choice for the usage cases that require zero individual time (Dolui & Datta, 2017).Table1 shows the Comparison of Cloud, Edge and, Fog Computing

Table 1. Diffentiate - cloud, edge and fog computing

	Cloud	Fog	Edge
Architecture	centralized	distributed	Decentralized
Data processing	far from the source of information	close to the source of information	Limited data processing
Computing capabilities	bigger	smaller	lower
Analysis	long term	short term	medium
Latency	high	low	low
Connectivity	internet	various protocols and standards	Limited connectivity
Security	weaker	strongest	potential

EDGE ANALYTICS

Edge analytics is a method to deal with information assortment and verify in which a robotized insightful calculation is executed which is shown in figure 3. Edge Analytics is the arrangement, dealing with, and examination of data at the edge of the general public or framework either at or close to a sensor, an association switch or, some other related contraption.

Figure 3. Edge analytics

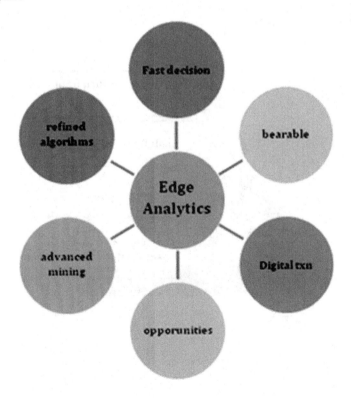

Edge Analytics: Profit

- On-time dynamic
- Removes loft information
- Saves handling and transferring time
- Preserves protection just handled, consistent information shipped off the cloud
- Greater creation scope organization and prescriptive support
- More proficient assistance and guarantee measures
- Lower effect of availability issues

Working Flow of Edge Analytics

The overall work processes of edge analytics instruments follow this example:

- Sensing devices or gadgets at the edge get together the information
- Analytics competence inside the gadgets empower performing investigation at the edge
- On the off chance that the device needs to take any action, it does so contingently upon the outcomes of the examination.
- Relevant data is imparted from the edge to the cloud so associations can see the 10,000 foot see by gathering summarized data from a considerable number of contraptions

Figure 4. Working flow of edge analytics

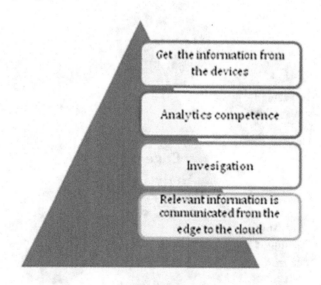

Benefits of Edge Analytics

Benefits of edge analytics comprise:

- quicker, self-ruling dynamic since experiences are distinguished at the information source, fore-stalling dormancy
- Lower cost of focal information stockpiling and the executives since less information is put away midway
- A Lesser rate of information broadcast as more information is conveyed to the focal information stockroom
- Improved security/protection since the most granular information, for example, video film isn't put away or conveyed

Drawbacks of Edge Analytics

We have noticed two normal entanglements to maintain a strategic distance from when associations choose to bother cash analytics (Shi et al., 2016).

- **Security:** Cloud conditions are planned in light of security since breaks on the cloud are very exorbitant for the industry. Notwithstanding, edge security is likewise significant because some edge gadgets settle on choices about the certifiable conduct of machines. Breaks can bring about the damage of hardware, other expensive machine mistakes or if nothing else falsehood.
- **Preservation:** Various edge analytics frameworks split just their yield by means of using the cloud because of data transfer capacity or capacity limitations. At that point, organizations get no opportunity to survey the crude data sources that prompted the examinations that are imparted to the cloud frameworks. Consequently, they need to ensure that data sources are handled with the most recent analytics programming, depending on obsolete models can lead organizations to settle on choices on wrong data (Satyanarayanan, 2017).

Key Challenges

Although edge analytics can be seen as inverse to conventional enormous information analytics, which is acted centralized, it is not here to supplant cloud analytics. Notwithstanding, there are a couple of worries that should be tended to first. Some edge analytics frameworks split just their yield with the cloud because of transfer speed or capacity imperatives. This would confine organizations from looking into the crude data sources that prompted the investigations imparted to the cloud frameworks. Next, at present not all IoT gadgets and edge gadgets can store their information or perform complex preparation and analytics (Zwolenski & Weatherill, 2014). In conclusion, there is as of now no administrative system for edge gadgets all things considered.

Importance of Edge Analytics

- **Saves Time:** In incorporated frameworks, all the gathered information at web associated gadgets is sent in their crude state for the preparing, which is inalienably moderate. Regardless of whether this crude information is important or unclear, prepared, and dissected to remove any esteem it contains. The fundamental point of the utilizing Edge Analytics framework is to sift through the superfluous data before the check, and just the important information goes through higher-request frameworks. The entirety of these outcomes in saving both preparing and transferring time, which makes the muddled insightful stage performed on the cloud considerably more proficient and is an incredible advantage.

- **Reduce Expenses:** Edge analytics in IoT shorten the expense of information stockpiling and the board. It additionally decreases the operational expenses, limits required transmission capacity and diminishes assets spent on information examination. Every one of these variables joins to give huge monetary reserve funds. In most of modern IoT, the information is never at any point dissected, which brings about squandering many data and lost upgrades (Bangui et al., 2018).
- **Preserves Privacy:** Edge Analytics assists with safeguarding protection when touchy or a gadget catches secret data. This delicate data is preprocessed on location and is not transferred to the cloud for preparation. This additional progression implies that lone security agreeable information leaves the gadget for additional examination, and it experiences an anonymizing collection in preprocessing. This delicate substance is saved without missing out on the advantages complex cloud-based examination can offer.
- **Reduced Latency of Data Analysis:** Utilizing Edge Analytics is more powerful to dissect information on the broken hardware and promptly shut it up as opposed to sitting tight for sending information to a focal information analytics climate (Taleb et al., 2017).
- **Connectivity Issues:** Edge Analytics in IoT assists with securing against potential availability blackouts by guaranteeing that restricted or irregular organization networks do not disturb the applications. It comes valuable in far-off areas or decreasing availability costs while utilizing costly innovations like cell (Shi et al., 2016).
- **Reduced Bandwidth Usage: Work** on the backend workers gets diminished, and analytics abilities are conveyed to distant areas changing from crude transmission to metadata.

Table 2. Importance of edge analytics

Domain	Importance
Saves Time	Use less time in the cloud environment
Reduce Expenses	decreases the operational expenses, limits required transmission capacity, and diminishes assets
Preserves Privacy	safeguarding protection in complex cloud-based assessment
Reduced Latency of Data Analysis	Use data analysis tech in reduced latency in analytics climate
Connectivity Issues	Guaranteeing connection in far off areas
Reduced Bandwidth Usage	-use minimum bandwidth with good abilities

EDGE DATA CENTER STRATEGIC CONSIDERATIONS

Conveying edge-computing foundation can be trying for end clients, who should adjust their models and cycles for a more modest, denser climate to deal with more administrations and client information (Rehman et al., 2017). There are numerous regular difficulties revealed by end clients working with edge plans, which is described in figure 5:

Figure 5. Edge data center strategic considerations

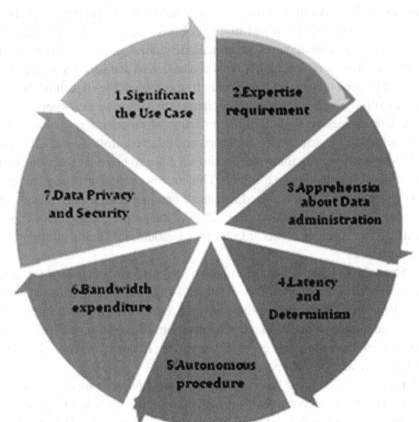

Significant the Use Case: Significant the Use Case: There might be a good thought or idea yet characterizing the utilization case arrives at a boundary. This generally happens when there's a misalignment between IT, tasks innovation prerequisites, and the board. In these circumstances, it's essential to make a stride back and take a gander at the drawn-out procedure of your association. Besides, some suppliers can help you on this excursion. Nonetheless, it's imperative to adjust the framework and business to guarantee that your technique can succeed. From that point, it's vital to work with the correct individuals who can rejuvenate that vision. This carries us to the following point. The responses to three fundamental inquiries encourage the business segment of your edge arranging (Kim et al., 2017).

1.   What is the current server farm structure, and which applications dwell in every office?

2. Who are the "end-clients "to be upheld and what are their particular prerequisites?
3. Where are imminent "end-clients" found, and what number of live in each geographic region?

Expertise Requirement: Regardless of whether an association can characterize a utilization case, they may stall out about working with accomplices who can help them execute the vision. Edge organizations accompany various contemplations around space, thickness, power, the board, availability and excess than a customary server farm. Distinguishing experienced accomplices is basic, and there are a developing number of associations, accomplices and server farm suppliers that can assist with edge arrangements (Jain & Mohapatra, 2019).

Apprehension about Data Administration: End clients should set aside additional effort to characterize information prerequisites and the board strategies Consistence and guideline can be incorporated into edge engineering, however this requires additional safeguards to guarantee information security and control. Despite the fact that there is certainly not a characterized standard on edge computing yet, it's critical to think about the area of the edge, stockpiling frameworks at the edge, how the information will be handled, and who will approach it. Programming characterized arrangements permit you to coordinate with center server farm frameworks and backing amazing information territory strategies, which are necessities for businesses like pharmacy, medical care, and other controlled associations (Abbas, 2018).

Latency and Determinism: Anything that requires a close to constant reaction should be done at or approaches the Edge, even inside to a machine. This incorporates control and continuous examination applications. Anything that does not need a genuine ongoing reaction is a contender to be moved to an off-plant server farm or the Cloud (Ai et al., 2018). Great representations for Cloud applications are information utilized for AI applications or Enterprise Resources Planning information for inventory network booking purposes

Autonomous Procedure: Latency and determinism might be one specialized factor in requiring an Edge arrangement. Another is a network (Bastug et al., 2014). Uniting applications at a brought together server farm, or in the Cloud, can be of incredible advantage to IT. In any case, from a modern control point of view, losing admittance to mechanization applications can have a critical effect. Likewise, with latency and determinism, the results can go from the variety in quality to loss of creation and at last security factors, including death toll(Lopez, 2015).

Bandwidth Expenditure: complete Edge computing procedure is one approach to control bandwidth cost heightening. By channeling information from a plant to an Edge area it is frequently conceivable to channel information nearby and propel just the fundamental data to the Cloud for cutting edge examination and long haul stockpiling. Utilizing an Edge stage as the passage or course to the Cloud empowers a lot simpler observing and control of the bandwidth and association between the Edge and the Cloud (Roman et al., 2016).

Data Solitude and Safety: Data solitude and safety are new matters that should be confronted. Privacy is another issue to numerous associations however, something that has gone to the front line over close to home data as of late (Shi & Dustdar, 2016). While the data privacy laws authorized by numerous nations around the globe are centered on the individual data of people, there are extra factors that organizations ought to consider. These are data residency and data power alongside the laws that oversee admittance to the data.

EDGE COMPUTING USE CASES AND MODELS

Edge computing is an energizing advancement in organizational framework that is simply starting to understand its latent capacity.

Independent Vehicles: While driverless vehicles are not expected to assume control over the expressways at any point soon, the car business has just put billions of dollars in building up the innovation. To work securely, these vehicles should assemble and investigate immense measures of information relating to their environmental factors, headings, and climate conditions, also speaking with different vehicles out and about(Salman et al., 2015). They will likewise have to take care of information back to producers to follow use and support cautions just as the interface with neighborhood city organizations. Edge computing engineering makes it workable for self-sufficient vehicles to gather, cycle, and divides information among vehicles and to more extensive organizations continuously with practically no idleness. Joined with an organization of edge server farms topographically situated to gather and hand-off basic information to regions, crisis reaction administrations, and car producers, edge-empowered vehicles will offer unrivaled dependability without devastating organization frameworks which are briefly defined in figure 6.

Figure 6. Independent vehicles –edge computing

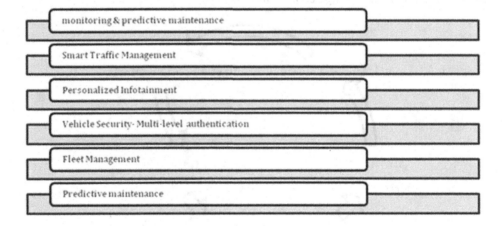

Smart Cities: Metropolitan regions are rapidly turning out to be enormous data gathering focuses, with sensors gathering information on traffic designs, utility utilization, and key foundation consistently. While that information permits city authorities to react to issues quicker than at any other time, the entirety of that data should be gathered, put away, and examined before it very well may be put to utilize. Edge computing design makes it workable for gadgets managing utilities and other public administrations to react to changing conditions close to ongoing is well defined in figure 7. Combined with the rising number of self-ruling vehicles and the always-extending web of things, brilliant urban communities can change how individuals live and use administrations in a metropolitan climate (Tong et al., 2016). Since all edge computing use cases depend upon gadgets gathering information to complete essential handling undertakings, the city of things to come will be able to respond powerfully to changing conditions as they happen.

Figure 7. Smart city –edge computing

Modern Manufacturing: Maybe no industry stands to profit more from IoT gadgets than the assembling area. By fusing information stockpiling and computing into modern hardware, makers can accumulate information that will consider better prescient support and energy effectiveness, permitting them to lessen expenses and energy utilization while keeping up better dependability and profitable uptime is briefly shown in figure 8. Keen assembling strategies educated by progressing information assortment and examination will likewise assist organizations with tweaking creation races to more readily satisfy buyer needs. Edge computing can likewise give extraordinary favorable circumstances to enterprises working where transfer speed is low or non-existent. Seaward oil rigs, for example, can use edge computing design to accumulate, screen, and cycle information on an assortment of ecological components without relying on an inaccessible server farm foundation.

Figure 8. Modern manufacturing – edge computing

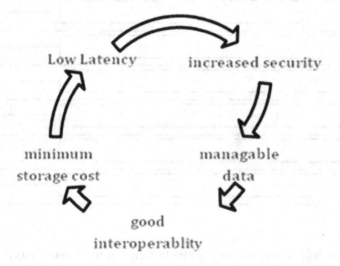

Monetary Sector: Banking establishments are receiving edge computing related to cell phone applications to all the more likely objective administrations to clients. They're additionally consolidating similar standards to give ATMs and booths the capacity to assemble and handle information, making them more responsive and permitting them to offer a more extensive set-up of highlights(Shi et al., 2016). For high-volume account firms managing in hedge reserves and different business sectors, even a millisecond of slack in an exchanging calculation can mean a considerable deficiency of cash is shown in figure 9. Edge computing design permits them to put workers in server farms close to stock trades the world over to run asset escalated calculations as near the wellspring of information as could reasonably be expected. This furnishes them with the most precise and exceptional data to keep their business moving.

Figure 9. Monetary sector – edge computing

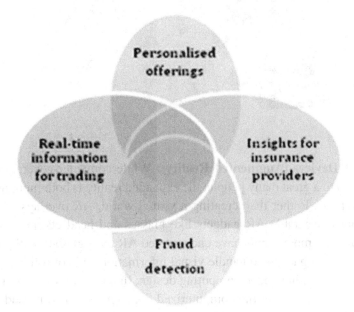

Medical Services: The medical services industry has since quite a while ago attempted to incorporate the most recent IT arrangements; however, edge computing offers to energize additional opportunities for conveying tolerant consideration. With IoT gadgets fit for conveying immense measures of patient-produced wellbeing information, medical care suppliers might approach basic data about their patients continuously as opposed to interfacing with moderate and inadequate data sets. Clinical gadgets themselves could likewise be made to accumulate and handle information over the span of analysis or treatment prescribed in figure 10. Edge computing could have a critical effect on the conveyance of medical care administrations to difficult to-arrive at rustic regions(Bonomi et al., 2012). Patients in these districts are regularly numerous miles from the closest wellbeing supplier and regardless of whether a medical care proficient assesses them on location, they will most likely be unable to get to pivotal clinical records. With edge computing, gadgets could assemble, store, and convey that data progressively and even utilize their handling capacities to suggest medicines.

Figure 10. Health sector – edge computing

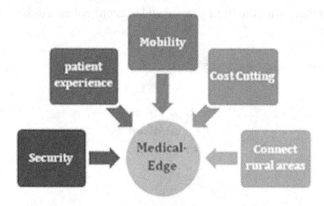

Expanded Reality Devices (Augmented Reality): While computer-generated reality might be a more recognizable term to a great many people, the expanded reality is both more normal and has more commonsense applications. Rather than creating a virtual world, AR overlays advanced components over genuine conditions. Wearable AR gadgets like glasses and headsets are now and then used to make this impact; however, most clients have encountered AR through their cell phone shows. The innovation behind AR expects gadgets to handle visual information and consolidate pre-delivered visual components continuously. Without edge computing design, this visual information would be conveyed back to unified cloud workers where the computerized components could be added before sending it back to the gadget. Edge computing permits IoT gadgets to composite AR shows in a flash, permitting clients to look any place to take in new AR subtleties without managing tacking times. Retail chains are now using AR innovation to add an extra layer of detail to the shopping experience. An AR gadget can undoubtedly show item data and deal cautions that give clients motivation to shop face to face as opposed to utilizing on the web retailers. Edge computing design is fundamental for offering these types of assistance with negligible dormancy.

Artificial Intelligence Virtual Assistants: Among cell phones and AI-controlled menial helpers like Amazon's Alexa and Google's Assistant, the advanced family unit is turning into a completely incorporated organization unto itself. As increasingly more of these gadgets enter homes, there will be a more noteworthy strain on specialist co-op networks as more demands flood into their workers and various types of streaming substance are conveyed to clients. By consolidating edge computing engineering into their organizations, organizations can improve execution altogether and decrease inertness. As opposed to each AI remote helper sending preparing and information solicitations to a brought together worker, they can rather circulate the weight among edge server farms while playing out some computing capacities locally.

CONCLUSION

This chapter presented the viewpoints on the challenges of multi-access Edge Computing that elaborated on network bandwidth, distributed computing, latency, security, backup, data accumulation, control and management, and scale. Later in this chapter, edge computing use cases and examples has been illustrated. As a conclusive remark, it is inferred that MEC figuring alludes to the processing at the edge of an organization. The edge is like a dispersed cloud with nearness near the end client that conveys super-low inertness, dependability, and versatility. Besides, tackle the intensity of the present organizations (like LTE) and the upcoming organization advancements (counting 5G) to convey recently discovered degrees of insight, control, unwavering quality, security, and speed to your organization's design. Furthermore, 5G Architecture View of Edge Computing. Edge processing alludes to finding applications and the universally useful register, stockpiling, and related exchanging and control capacities expected to run them generally near end clients or potentially IoT endpoints. It is believed that the outcome of this chapter would help the researchers who have been undergoing multi-access edge computing.

REFERENCES

Aazam, M., Zeadally, S., & Harras, K. A. (2018). Fog computing architecture, evaluation, and future research directions. *IEEE Communications Magazine*, *56*(5), 46–52. doi:10.1109/MCOM.2018.1700707

Abbas, N. (2018). Mobile edge computing: A survey. *IEEE IOT J.*, *5*(1), 450–465.

Ai, Y., Peng, M., & Zhang, K. (2018). Edge cloud computing technologies for internet of things: A primer. *Digital Communication Network.*, *4*(2), 77–86. doi:10.1016/j.dcan.2017.07.001

Al-Qamash & Soliman. (2018). Cloud, Fog, and Edge Computing: A Software Engineering Perspective. *2018 International Conference on Computer and Applications (ICCA)*. 10.1109/COMAPP.2018.8460443

Alrawais, A., Alhothaily, A., Hu, C., & Cheng, X. (2017). Fog computing for the internet of things: Security and privacy issues. *IEEE Internet Computing*, *21*(2), 34–42. doi:10.1109/MIC.2017.37

Bangui, H., Rakrak, S., Raghay, S., & Buhnova, B. (2018). Moving to the Edge-Cloud-of-Things: Recent Advances and Future Research Directions. *Electronics (Basel)*, *7*(309), 309. Advance online publication. doi:10.3390/electronics7110309

Bastug, E., Bennis, M., & Debbah, M. (2014, August). Living on the edge: The role of proactive caching in 5G wireless networks. *IEEE Communications Magazine*, *52*(8), 82–89. doi:10.1109/MCOM.2014.6871674

Bonomi, F., Milito, R., Zhu, J., & Addepalli, S. (2012). Fog computing and its role in the Internet of Things. *Proc. 1st Ed. MCC Workshop Mobile Cloud Comput.*, 13–16. 10.1145/2342509.2342513

Dolui & Datta. (2017). Comparison of edge computing implementations: Fog computing, cloudlet and mobile edge computing. *Global Internet of Things Summit (GIoTS)*. doi:10.1109/GIOTS.2017.8016213

Francis, T., & Madhiajagan, M. (2017). A Comparison of Cloud Execution Mechanisms: Fog, Edge and Clone Cloud Computing. *Proc. EECSI*, 446-450. 10.11591/eecsi.v4.1032

Hu, Y. C., Patel, M., Sabella, D., Sprecher, N., & Young, V. (2015). *Mobile edge computing—A key technology towards 5G*. ETSI, Sophia Antipolis, France.

Jain, A., & Singhal, P. (2016). Fog computing: Driving force behind the emergence of edge computing. *2016 International Conference System Modeling & Advancement in Research Trends (SMART)*, 294-297. 10.1109/SYSMART.2016.7894538

Jain, K., & Mohapatra, S. (2019). Taxonomy of Edge Computing: Challenges, Opportunities, and Data Reduction Methods. In *Al-Turjman Fields, Edge Computing. EAI/Springer Innovations in Communication and Computing*. Springer. doi:10.1007/978-3-319-99061-3_4

Kim, Kim, & Park. (2017). *A combined network control approach for the edge cloud and LPWAN-based IoT services*. doi:10.1002/cpe.4406

Lopez, P. G. (2015). Edge-centric computing: Vision and challenges. *ACM SIGCOMM Computational Communication Rev., 45*(5), 37–42.

Ravi, J., Shi, W., & Xu, C.-Z. (2005, March). Personalized email management at network edges. *IEEE Internet Computing, 9*(2), 54–60. doi:10.1109/MIC.2005.44

Rehman, M. H., Jayaraman, P. P., Malik, S. R., Khan, A. R., & Gaber, M. M. (2017). RedEdge: A Novel Architecture for Big Data Processing in Mobile Edge Computing Environments. *J. Sens. Actuator Network., 6*(3), 17. doi:10.3390/jsan6030017

Roman, R., Lopez, J., & Mambo, M. (2016). A survey and analysis of security threats and challenges. *Future Generation Computer Systems, 78*, 680–698. doi:10.1016/j.future.2016.11.009

Salman, O., Elhajj, I., Kayssi, A., & Chehab, A. (2015). Edge computing enabling the Internet of Things. *Proc. IEEE World Forum Internet of Things (WFIOT)*, 603–608. 10.1109/WF-IoT.2015.7389122

Satyanarayanan, M. (2017). The Emergence of Edge Computing. *IEEE Computer Society, 50*(1), 30–39. doi:10.1109/MC.2017.9

Satyanarayanan, M., Bahl, P., Caceres, R., & Davies, N. (2009, October/December). The case for VM-based cloudlets in mobile computing. *IEEE Pervasive Computing, 8*(4), 14–23. doi:10.1109/MPRV.2009.82

Shi, W., Cao, J., Zhang, Q., Li, Y., & Xu, L. (2016, October). Edge computing: Vision and challenges. *IEEE Internet of Things Journal, 3*(5), 637–646. doi:10.1109/JIOT.2016.2579198

Shi, W., & Dustdar, S. (2016, May). The promise of edge computing. *Comput, 49*(5), 78–81. doi:10.1109/MC.2016.145

Shi, W., Pallis, G., & Xu, Z. (2019, August). Edge Computing. *Proceedings of the IEEE, 107*(8), 1474–1481. doi:10.1109/JPROC.2019.2928287

Symeonides, M., Trihinas, D., Georgiou, Z., Pallis, G., & Dikaiakos, M. (2019). Query-driven descriptive analytics for IoT and edge computing. *Proc. IEEE Int. Conf. Cloud Eng. (IC2E)*, 1–11. 10.1109/IC2E.2019.00-12

Taleb, T., Dutta, S., Ksentini, A., Iqbal, M., & Flinck, H. (2017). Mobile edge computing potential in making cities smarter. *IEEE Communications Magazine, 55*(3), 38–43. doi:10.1109/MCOM.2017.1600249CM

Tong, L., Li, Y., & Gao, W. (2016). A hierarchical edge cloud architecture for mobile computing. *Proc. IEEE Int. Conf. Computational Communication (INFOCOM)*, 1–9. 10.1109/INFOCOM.2016.7524340

Vakali, A., & Pallis, G. (2003, November). Content delivery networks: Status and trends. *IEEE Internet Computing, 7*(6), 68–74. doi:10.1109/MIC.2003.1250586

Xu, Z.-W. (2014, January). Cloud-sea computing systems: Towards thousand-fold improvement in performance per watt for the coming zetta-byte era. *J. Computational Science Technol.*, *29*(2), 177–181. doi:10.100711390-014-1420-2

Zwolenski, M., & Weatherill, L. (2014). The digital universe: Rich data and the increasing value of the Internet of Things. *Austral. J. Telecommunication. Digit. Econ.*, *2*(3), 47. doi:10.7790/ajtde.v2n3.47

Chapter 3

Achieving Ambient Intelligence in Addressing the COVID–19 Pandemic Using Fog Computing–Driven IoT

Oshin Rawlley

Birla Institute of Technology and Science, Pilani, India

Shashank Gupta

Birla Institute of Technology and Science, Pilani, India

ABSTRACT

In this chapter, the authors present a comprehensive review on how the fog computing-based IoT can be utilized for the outbreak prevention and its existing control systems. The authors have also explained how numerous edge computing devices (e.g., sensors/actuators, RFID systems, webcams, drones, etc.) are playing a key role in controlling this disease using IoT protocols like 6LoWPAN. In addition, the authors also emphasize IoT security attacks and vulnerabilities which are prevalent in the existing infrastructure setup of smart cities. The key aspects of emerging uses of IoT (such as smart retail store automation, smart transportation, smart waste management, etc.) are described that played a key role in controlling this epidemic in the existing infrastructure of sustainable smart cities. Finally, some future research directions are also discussed that highlight the steps in mitigating the effect of this pandemic using fog-enabled IoT and AI techniques.

INTRODUCTION

Data has become an integral part in every walk of life. In today's digital world, technology is the new driving force of different businesses and other applications. This information technology age has started producing enormous amount of data to be handled. According to the reports of International Data Corporation (IDC), the digital data as of now has almost crossed zettabytes in 2010. On a daily basis, 2.5

DOI: 10.4018/978-1-7998-8367-8.ch003

zettabytes data is produced since 2011 (Yousef et.al., 2019). It is anticipated that in near future, by 2020, around 50 billion connected devices will generate new dataFor instance, IoT applications in healthcare showed data of 25k tuples were produced per second by 30 million users (Sarkar et al., 2015).

One of the computing paradigms- cloud computing has proved to be an efficient way which has high power of processing, computing, storage capacity gained much prevalence (Yousef et.al., 2019). All data to be processed is sent to the centralized cloud & further analysis is done. Cloud computing is a centralized paradigm of computing model where all the steps of data pre-processing, post-processing is done in the cloud itself at a principal place. But due to multiplication of devices & its data generated the bandwidth is not considerate in satisfying the latency needs. The bandwidth factor has become a bottleneck in cloud computing (Kharrufa et al., 2019).

The chapter elucidates the various technology paradigms evolving to newer paradigms like fog computing for addressing Covid-19 pandemic by controlling existing systems. The section of "Inception of Covid-19" states the augmentation of fog computing paradigm with the existing models for better identification & tracing of the virus. This chapter produces sufficient background as a knowledge base for establishing the concept of fog technology enabled IoT devices by reaffirming the relevance of fog Computing in Covid-19 & the abstract layers of the connection mechanism.

Inception of Covid-19

The first case was detected with symptoms of pneumonia in Wuhan, China on Dec 08, 2019. Following which many incidents were reported in China by WHO. Figure 1 highlights the timeline of corona virus. Then Europe witnessed the proliferation of the disease & announced its first case on Jan 07, 2020. The sudden escalation led to deaths, the first death in China. Pneumonia affecting people & leading to death raised an alarm all over the world arising the situation of Global red alert & nations declaring national lockdowns in March 2020. Even after lockdown more than 50k deaths were reported. The year 2020 was a mere spectator of the pandemic having no solution to this outbreak. In Jan 2021, medical science was able to administer few drugs to counter the virus with the introduction of vaccinations for Covid-19 all over the world (Rasheed et al, 2020).

It is onerous on the part of apt identification of the disease & is much demanding to address this problem of identification of cases by utilizing some existing technologies. The sudden outbreak of black fungus & white fungus has further fanned the flames of COVID-19 aggravating the pandemic situation to be more intensified. Indeed, there is a need for greater strides to make towards ameliorating the condition. Fog computing frameworks can be augmented to the cloud computing community for fast tracing of the cases. Mobile devices can be made as fog devices with tracing apps installed in them.

Figure 1. Inception of COVID-19

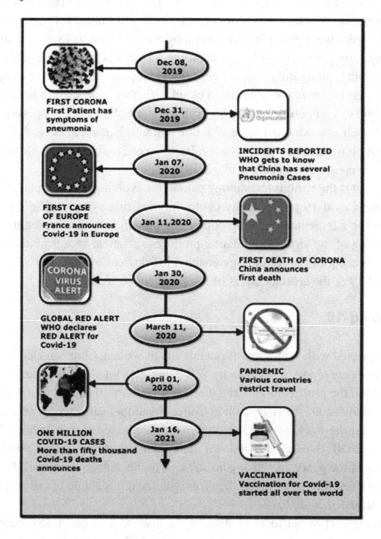

Emergence of Fog Computing-Enabled IoT

Keeping in view the limitations of cloud computing model, there is an essential need for a model which can address issues of bandwidth, ultra-low latency, privacy for geographically dispersed applications. There is an inception of Fog computing paradigm taking charge over existing conventional model. To satiate the needs of the above-mentioned issues Fog computing paradigm has been proposed. To quench the requirement of the connected devices to be in close vicinity of cloud, this model has satisfied the need of the hour.

Figure 2 talks about the stages of Covid transmission levels. The proliferation this disease started from 1 man infecting many more people forming a chain & inflicted population mushrooming rapidly. FC has extended its capabilities by serving as an intermediate interface between cloud & connected devices I.e. the physical devices like sensors, actuators etc. (Sarkar et al. 2015). It has empowered the existing model of cloud computing with its own peculiarity of exhibiting capacity of processing, networking, storage etc. These activities can be carried out along the path as the data transmits from physical world to digital world I.e. from IoT devices to cloud. Many other similar models are mist computing, cloud-lets, edge computing etc. Have come into existence to complement each other & to address the issues together (Chiang et.al., 2016).

Figure 2. Transmission levels of Covid.

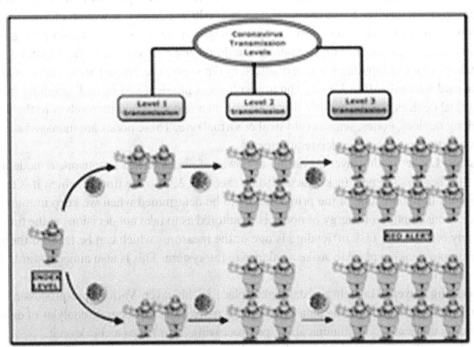

This architecture helps the devices to analyze & locate data with intelligent geographic location hierarchy (Mahmud et al., 2018). It has a layer of network environment which is distributed & has integration with cloud computing & technologies of IoT. FC has seamlessly reduced the bandwidth requirements required for transfer of data. IoT industry is poised to transform many verticals of industry like retail, healthcare, automobile industry. It is a decentralized computing paradigm which does processing of data in decentralized fog nodes (Atlam et al, 2018).

Relevance of Fog Computing in Covid-19

After the Covid-19 upsurge almost every domain of the world has digitized itself across the globe. People have started moving towards more automotive processes, drifting towards cloud-based approach to ensure uninterrupted functioning of the services. FC provides required security features to enable the communication properly in a fog network. In the coming era of sensory world, digitization of almost everything will be dominating the businesses around the world with new disruptive technologies like AI, FC with IoT, ML, blockchain etc. The strength of fog computing is best exhibited in distributing the computing power for faster access, retrieval, analysis of real time data for it to be analyzed & interpreted for masses in Covid-19. It may help in speedy functioning of local places where connectivity & reachability is poor. As fog computing can be a cluster of devices having networking, processing & storage capabilities so these clusters can be installed in far-flung places.

Connection Mechanism in Fog Computing

Fog nodes connect through wireless modes like Bluetooth, 4G, Wi-Fi to provide independent computing, storage & networking services to the users (Yousef et.al., 2019). Also, connection of Fog nodes can be established with the cloud via Internet to fulfill rich requirements of storage & computing resources. The certitude lying in the fact of Fog computing should be emphasized that it should not be construed as a substitute of cloud computing but an expansion of the same. The layered architecture is as follows:

Physical and Virtualization Layer: The lowest layer is physical and virtualization layer. It constitutes of physical devices that are capable of generating data & connecting themselves to the network. It has networking devices, nodes, sensors (physical & virtual) etc. These nodes are managed according to their characteristic qualities & service requirements.

Monitoring Layer: In this layer according to power of nodes & tasks, network & node activity is monitored. It schedules the next task which is to be executed & also the time at which it is to be done. The energy consumption is one of the prime factors to be determined when we keep in mind the state of the sensor. Consumption of energy of nodes is monitored as to take apt decisions at the time of overloading or any other issue. Task offloading is one of the measures which can be taken if there is more energy consumption taking place to strike a balance in the system. This is also aimed towards a greener computing vision.

Preprocessing Layer: Managing of data takes place in this layer. Various pre-processing tasks involving data trimming, standardizing data & filtering is carried out for accurate analysis of data. For the sake of avoiding unnecessary communication, preprocessing layer keeps a check on it.

Storage Layer: Data storage in fog nodes is administered by storage layer. The fog nodes have a temporary storage where data is stored temporarily. This is to cater to the immediate need of computing capabilities like immediate access from the warehouse & speedy processing of the data. Contrarily, storing the data for longer time can be done on cloud, where cloud computing capacities can be milked out at its fullest. As the data reaches to the cloud then the fog nodes can be relieved of holding the same data anymore to avoid redundant sets.

Security Layer: There are many avenues where data sensitivity is a major concern. Domains like healthcare and smart health services has data being generated containing personal & confidential information of patients. Privacy is essential in location-equipped data in some cases. Functions like security 7 privacy are provided for the protection of data before sending it over a public prone channel.

Transport Layer: When the data is ready to leave for processing in the cloud, transport layer takes the charge. This frees the core network of the extra burden by enabling the enhanced services much faster. Nodes of fog are intermediate between the cloud layer & nodes of IoT. Tailored services which aware of their context, more refined provisioning is enabled by Fog. This is because of the less distance from the underlying physical objects. The resulting scenario is fast streaming with high quality is availed by the mobile nodes having low latency (Chifor et al., 2018).

Figure 3. Architecture of fog computing

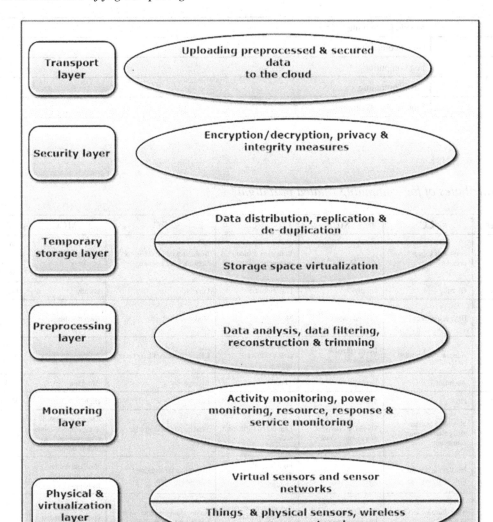

Based on the dependency of constraints put on nodes which are generating data & feedback received from the application or cloud, fog layer can fine tune the communication between the sensor networks, machines, nodes & cloud. This ensures an efficient utilization of all resources like network resources, cloud resources (Yousef et.al., 2019). For instance, in healthcare services, fog layer processes the data according to needs of each application service.

Fog layer can obtain raw data from the medical devices. The layers of fog architecture performs pre-processing tasks on the raw data. This way the overhead of cloud layer is reduced as it would save time & space of the cloud layer to handle the full burden of the data all together. After that, the processed data is transferred to the cloud. Subsequently the fog services transforms the processed data into relevant information. For instance, an application of health care services can alarm the patient when his/her sugar level rises above the threshold level & if his heartbeat is unusual. (Farahani et al., 2018).

Table 1. Usage of fog related paradigms acronyms

MC	Mobile Computing
CC	Cloud computing
FC	Fog computing
EC	Edge computing
MCC	Mobile cloud computing

Table 2. Attributes of fog-computing related paradigms

Attributes	CC	MC	FC	EC	MCC	Mist
Operators	Service of Cloud operators	Organized on its own	Both users & cloud providers	Businesses on local basis & Network infrastructure.	Both users & cloud providers	Businesses on local basis & Network infrastructure.
Type of Service	Globally	Locally	Less globally	Locally	Locally	Locally
Availability of Computing Resources	High in existence	Limited resources	Moderate level	Moderate level	High in existence	Limited resources
Type of Application	Adequate computation	Decentralized & mobile processing	Abundant computation power with less latency	Computation with Less latency	Adequate computation	Decentralized processing on IoT devices
Availability	Abundant	Less	Abundant	Average	Abundant	Less
Latency issues	High	Moderate	Less	Less	High	Moderate
Security	Should be enabled along cloud-to-things continuum	Should be catered on every mobile device	Enabled on participant nodes	Must be provided on edge devices	Should be enabled along cloud-to-things continuum and on mobile devices	Must be provided on IoT devices
Location of Server	Installation done in big dedicated buildings	—	Installed at the dedicated locations or edge	Installed at the dedicated locations or edge	Installation done in big dedicated buildings	—
Internet Connectivity	Must- have for services to function.	Can suffice with low Internet connectivity	Autonomous operation with less Internet connectivity	Autonomous operation with less Internet connectivity	Autonomous operation with less Internet connectivity	Can suffice with low Internet connectivity
Service Access	Done through core	Done through mobile devices	Done via network of connected devices from the edge to the core	Edge	Done through core	Done through IoT devices
Architecture	Hierarchical/ Centralized	Distributed	Hierarchical/ Centralized	Hierarchical/ Centralized	Centralized cloud with decentralized mobile devices	Distributed / Localized
Main Standardization Entity	CSA, DMFT, NIST, OCC, GICTF	MobileInfo	Open-Fog Consortium, IEEE	—	NIST	—

Key Contributions

We have presented a comprehensive review on how the fog computing-based IoT and its enabling technologies facilitates in preventing the outbreak of COVID-19. The primary contributions are as follows:

- We have presented that how FC can be utilized in helping data & networking problem in this Covid pandemic.
- We have introduced layered architecture of FC & in addition we have presented a comparative analysis of FC & its related computing paradigms.
- The major important capabilities like networking, communication, storage & computing technologies, privacy and security protection, management of resources are described to address real time issues of data access & analysis like in Covid-19, & also break the Covid-19 crisis & ensure deployment.
- The emerging usecases of fog computing driven IoT that plays a key role in mitigating and controlling this outbreak epidemic are also explained for the sustainable smart cities infrastructure.
- In addition, some future research directions are also discussed that elaborates the preventive measures in controlling the effect of this unprecedented epidemic using Fog-enabled IoT and AI applications.

Outline of the Chapter: Section II discusses about Internet of Things in Smart related environment. IOT Protocols are described in Section II. To gain a thorough understanding of fog computing, in Section 3, we will see IoT security technologies. Next, in Section IV, we describe our use cases which are emerging in real life. In Section V, we present Future research directions in this field. Finally, Section VI concludes the chapter.

Figure 4. Technology enabler for fog computing.

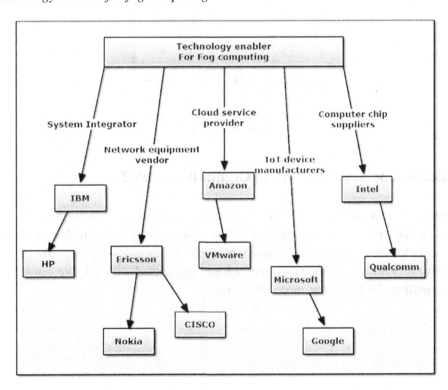

FOG-ENABLED IOT INFRASTRUCTURE IN COVID-19

The evolution of IoT can be depicted by many phases as shown in Fig. 5. The use of RFID has initiated IoT which is gaining popularity in retail, logistics, healthcare, pharmaceutical industry. In any IoT system we got three things i.e sensing, processing & communication. For IoT to scale we have less power to be able to run communications over the network typically over long distances. ZigBee, Bluetooth5, RFID are important to enable communication between these devices. IoT can be observed as a globally established network of connected devices building a a sensory digital world. In this sensory network computing takes place in the form of data processing, networking, communication amongst the devices, technologies for information processing etc. One of the technologies of IoT is explained as follows.

Figure 5. Technology evolution

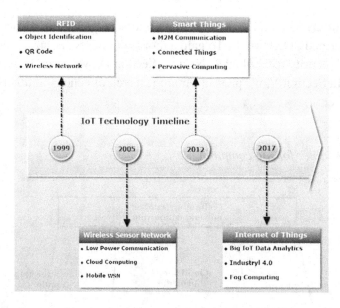

Technologies Associated with IoT in Combating COVID-19

RFID is the principal technology for IoT. It allows to transmission of identification information through microchips to a reader via a wireless communication. Furthermore, other technologies like barcode scanners, cloud computing, smart phones & social networks etc are extensively used in support of IoT to form an extensive network. Fig. 6 shows the technologies associated with IoT. We can see a little detail of the RFID technology further in the next subsection.

Figure 6. Technologies associated with IoT in mitigating Covid-19

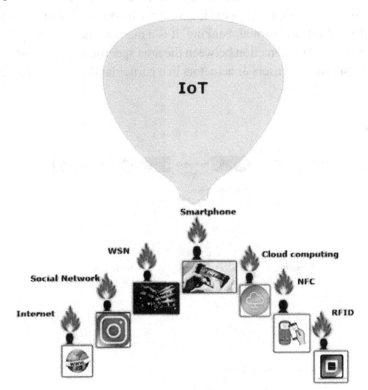

RFID System

Figure 7 shows 2 main components of RFID system namely a tag reader & radio signal transponder(tag). The structural description of the tag consists of a chip & an antenna. The chip reads the object & stores its unique identity while the antenna allows the chip to do communication with the tag reader through radio waves. Radio frequency is generated by the tag reader for identification of the objects via radio waves reflected from the tag. RFID sends tag numbers to the tag reader through radio waves as depicted in the diagram below. Then that number is passed to a particular computer application called ONS i.e.. Object-Naming Services. It looks up the details of tag from the database, details like the name of manufacturer, location of manufacturing, time of manufacturing etc.

IoT Markets

A mushrooming growth of tangible devices are connecting to the network & are proliferating at an unparalleled rate perceiving the esscence of Internet of things. An important instance can be HVAC (Heating, Ventilation, and Air Conditioning) & thermostats control & monitoring systems powering smart homes. IoT has proved its worth in other domains also by playing role in improving quality of life. These domains include applications like transport system, health emergency response system. Tangible objects are powered to sense, perceive, interpret, and take decisions by having them communicate with each other. They coordinate with each other to share information & make decisions. There are area specific applications called as vertical markets. While horizontal markets, have analytic services & ubiquitous computing forming area independent services. IoT vertical markets include oil industry, agriculture, retail, finance etc. Like real estate, hospital, banking. It is a market where all people belong to the same sector/industry. Fig. 8 shows the interaction between the area specific applications i.e., vertical markets & domain independent services. Sensors & actuators in a particular domain contact each other directly.

Figure 7. RFID system

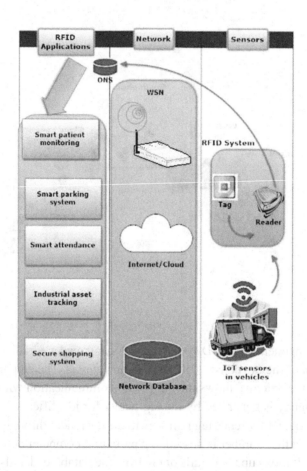

IoT Elements

In the world's burgeoning economy, many sectors will be digitized & may expect cognitive solutions for smarter systems. These systems will be expected to infuse in the intelligence that IoT systems require for independent functioning. For human like intelligence there some fundamental elements of the intelligent IoT system. Fig 9 presents 6 principal elements representing the functionality of the IoT. We list below the understanding of the elements.

Identification

This step is important in identifying the IoT objects. Their services are synchronized with their demands. uCode (ubiquitous codes) & EPC (electronic product codes) are the various methods which are used for identification. It is critical to address an IoT device in differentiating the address of its object ID. Here Object ID signifies a nomenclature. For e.g. Temp for a temperature sensor. Address of the object refers to the location which is within the communication network. There are various other methods of addressing like IPV4, IPV6 etc. It ascertains a mechanism for compression over IPv6 headers. This leads to a solution for low power wireless network which uses IPv6 addressing. There should be a significant difference between the address of the object & its identification, as the methods of identification are not unique globally. Therefore, addressing helps in identifying the objects uniquely. Hence network comprising of objects may use public IPs, & private ones are not used. We can conclude that the methods of identification can be a good base for providing a crisp identity for every object in the network (Letaief et al., 2019, Hu & Dhelim, 2017).

Figure 8. The overall picture of IoT emphasizing the vertical markets and the horizontal markets

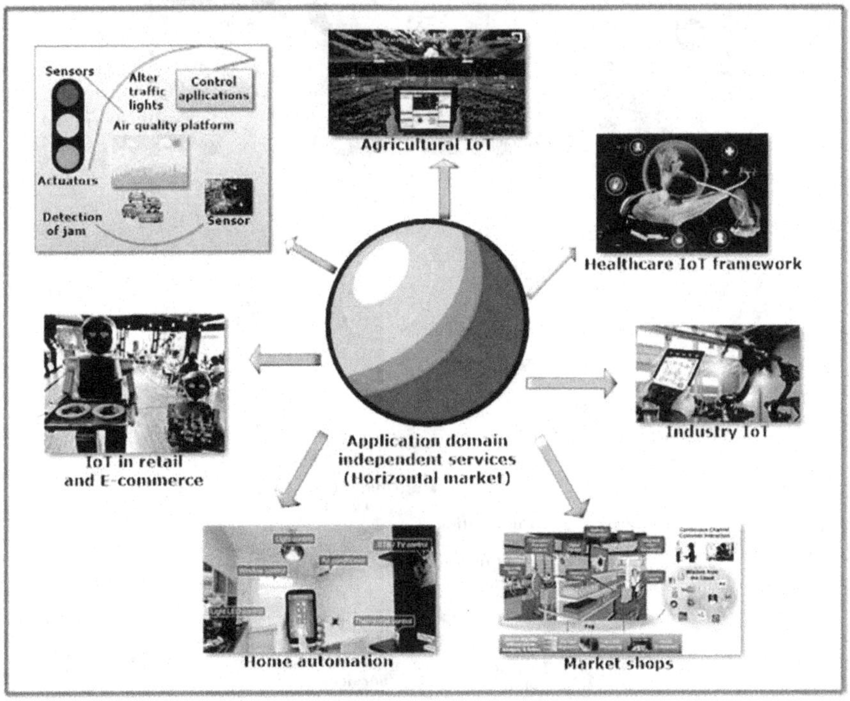

Figure 9. IoT elements

Services

Figure 10. IoT services

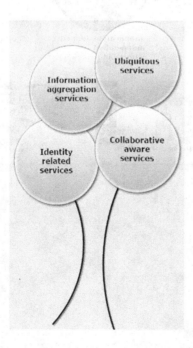

IoT services are divided into 4 domains namely: Collaborative aware services, identity related services, Ubiquitous services, Information aggregation services. Fig. 10 depicts the same.

The IoT Architecture

There are multiple IoT architectures, one of being the 3-layered architecture. We have also elaborated a brief description of 5-layered architecture of IoT. Figure 11 shows the layers with examples of relevant devices. 3-layered architecture consists of following 3 layers: Application layer, Network layer, Perception layer

Figure 11. 3- layer Architecture of IoT

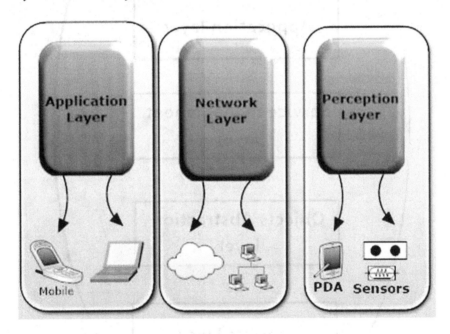

Other architecture is a basic 5- layered architecture having layers like object layer, object abstraction layer, service management layer, application layer, business layer (Naha & R. K., Garg, 2018). It can be seen as an extension of the above 3-layered architecture. A brief elaboration is provided in the below section. A diagrammatic arrangement of the layers is illustrated in Figure 12. Figure 13 highlights the overall functionality of middleware (Hu & Dhelim, 2017, Al-Turjman et al., 2019, Hu & Dhelim, 2017).

Figure 12. 5-layered architecture

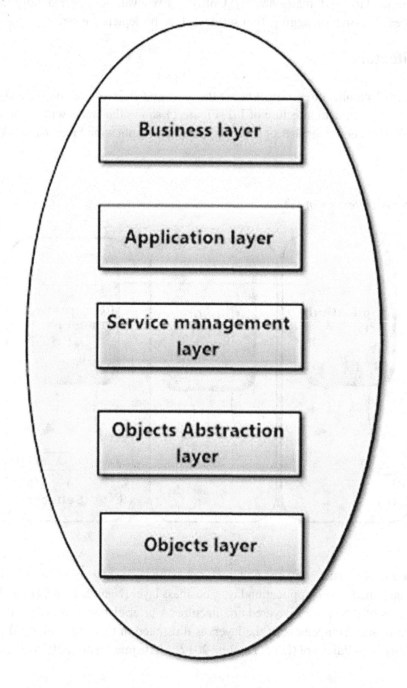

Figure 13. Middleware

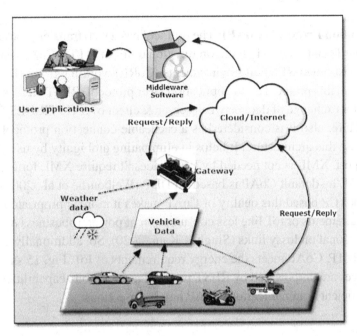

IOT PROTOCOLS

We present 4 types IoT protocols which may constitute an IoT application. Not necessarily these protocols should work collaboratively to deliver an IoT application for combating COVID-19. In the subsequent sections, we present an elaborative overview of the protocols lying in the respective categories with their functionalities. Fig.14 shows the categorization & subsequent sections has elaborative description of the same .

Figure 14. IoT protocols

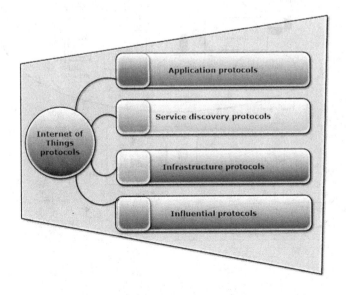

APPLICATION PROTOCOLS

Constrained Application Protocol (CoAP): The protocol has a web transfer protocol. It depends upon Representational State Transfer (REST) lying on functionalities of HTTP. CoAP was brought into existence by the IETF Constrained RESTful Environments (CoRE) working group (Kharrufa et al., 2019). Applications of IoT uses this protocol as an application layer protocol. REST has easier ways of communication established for exchange of data between server & client over HTTP. REST counts on stateless client-server architecture, also it is considered as a cacheable connection protocol. Social network & mobile applications use this architecture. It helps in eliminating ambiguity by using methods of HTTP like put, delete, get, post. XML is not needed by REST doesn't require XML for exchanging messages. Differently from REST, by default CoAP is based on UDP (Welbourne et al., 2009).

Since CoAP is not TCP based this quality of CoAP makes it more appropriate for IoT applications. There are certain requirements of IoT like less consumption of power, robustness & operational in noise surroundings & operational on lossy links (Singh & Kaur, 2020). So, additionally, by modifying few of these operations of HTTP, CoAP meets the energy requirements of IoT. Fig. 15 shows CoAP structure. Tiny embedded devices are empowered by REST protocol as it exhibits capabilities like less computation, low power & efficient communication. CoAP has 2 subsections:

- Messaging layer
- Request/Response layer

To detect duplicates message IDs are used. RST message is sent when there is a miss of message or communication lag occurs. CoAP provides some key features listed in fig. 16

Figure 15. CoAP (constraint application protocol)

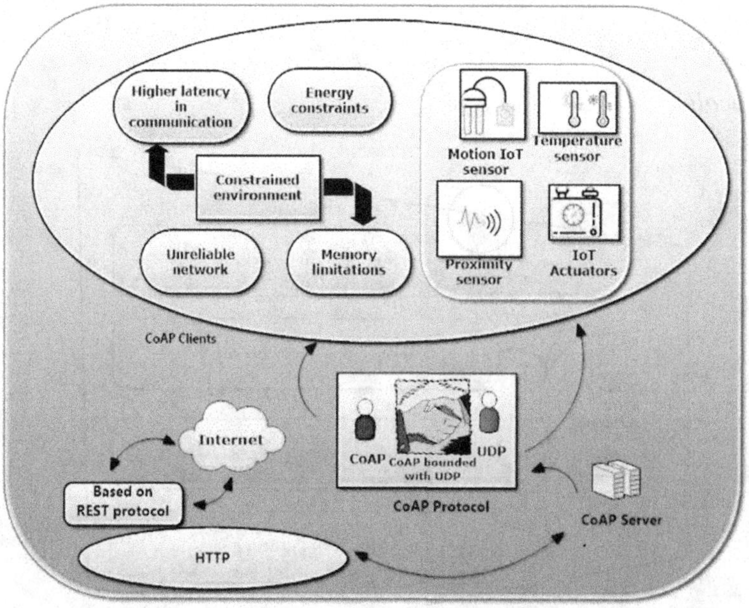

Message Queue Telemetry Transport (MQTT): It is a message protocol whose aim is to connect embedded devices, middleware, applications to network. Different mappings like one-one, many-many, one-many are used by the connection step. This empowers MQTT protocol be an optimal option for communication between IoT & M2M. Since MQTT is based on TCP protocol, so for resource constrained devices, it is suitable as it uses less bandwidth & unreliable links (Kharrufa et al., 2019). For maintaining prominent levels of QoS, it has 3-level hierarchy of QoS specifications.

Figure 16. Features of CoAP

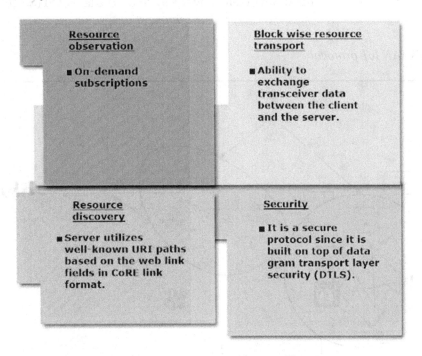

Extensible Messaging and Presence Protocol (XMPP): XMPP is a standard for instant messaging & facilitates multi-purpose communication, video chatting, voice calling etc. It was developed to support distributed messaging mechanism, a spam free with full security protocol. This protocol allows users to chat with each other through instant messages regardless of the OS used. Applications of IM are used by XMPP for authentication of the messages exchanged & establishes better access, privacy controls, strengthens compatibility & end- to end encryption among other protocols. Textual communication poses a challenge by involving a big overhead on the network. The remedy to this challenge is that XML stream of data is compressed (Rabah et al., 2018).

Service Discovery Protocols

Due to increased no. Of connected devices & the need for high scalability pushes to the direction of maintaining robust mechanisms of resource management. These mechanisms will be able to record & register the resources & their services in an efficient way (Kharrufa et al., 2019). The most prominent protocols in this category are DNS-SD, DNS-SD & mDNS i.e., DNS Service Discovery, DNS Service Discovery & multicast DNS, respectively. These protocols have the capability of discovering all services & resources that are given by devices of IoT.

Other Influential Protocols

Apart from the conventional features, protocols & standards there are other factors that contribute to the operational framework of IoT applications. Interoperability among devices & secure transmission of data & other operations should be considered for any IoT system to be accepted (Saleem et al, 2019).

Figure 17. 6LoWPAN IoT protocol

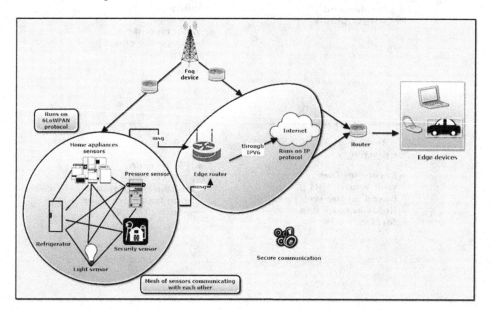

IOT SECURITY TECHNOLOGIES

Various areas of application are driven by the development of IoT systems. These applications are divided on their network accessibility type, their heterogenous nature, scope, involvement of user, scale & repeatability (Ni, J. & Zhang, 2018). There are many techniques of security existing in this taxonomy as shown in the below table III. Often, used techniques of security are listed in coordination with their application domain like:

- Authorization
- Trust establishment
- Authentication
- Exhaustion of resources.

Table 3. Summary of different IoT security technologies

State-of-the-Art	Interest area	Technology implemented	Aim	Pros	Cons
2013	Intelligent environment	**Platform used**- Aneka for implementing cloud	Investigate current trends of IoT applications. Need for interlaced technologies	System & storage resources are used in combination with cloud (public, private)	Hybrid clouds may compromise security along with personality vault.
2014	Applications limited to single-authorities	**Attribute based encryption** (ABE) scheme is availed (based on elliptic curve cryptography)	Reduction in overhead of communication and complexity of computation Cater privacy and security problems in IoT	The encryption technique (ABE) can be used in broadcast encryption & cipher-text-based access control.	Inaccessibility to attribute. Less scalability
2015	Data analytics, mining.	Recent version of **Shamir's secret** sharing scheme.	Escalate data scalability Lessen complexity of key management in cryptographic algorithms Increase reliability feature in data.	Successful achievement in using Shamir's secret scheme.	Inefficient when generates unnecessary computational overheads. Robustness is compromised when one of the component of hardware fails.
2016	Health industry	**Fog computing**	(Resource management & estimation) Build a model of resource estimation for fog computing customers.	Enables deliverance of real time data. Induces cloud technology properties in edge devices.	Latency is high.
2015	Smart energy meter	For safe channel establishment **light weight scheme** is exploited.	Control privacy in fine grained information generated from sensors. Secure communication of information and defending the protection content	Interdependence of security and privacy of sensor data is influenced. Encourage less resource consumption by offering E2E service with adaptive & enhanced security.	Sensitive to multiple security scenarios (i.e. can take 1 scenario)

Architecture

There is no architecture which has been universally accepted. In context field of authorization & authentication many types of research are done on different architectures of IoT exposing them to different application domains & diversified scenarios (Hu & Dhelim, 2017). Table IV provides a summary of existing IoT architectures and application domains (Pham et al., 2020).

Table 4. Different IoT security architecture types and application domains.

Applicative domain	State-of-the-art	Design	Goal
Smart city	Gaur et.al	Smart city model	Moderating the interaction between communication technologies & sensor edge devices(remote).
	Chakrabarty et.al	Black SDN model	Catering to the prone areas in conventional IoT systems.
Smart environment	Valdivieso	SDN	Remove rigidity in conventional IoT networks
Smart grid	Vucinic et.al	Object security architecture (OSCAR)	To address E2E security & access control by building a scalable model of IoT.
Smart transportation	Ramao et.al	SOA- Service oriented architecture.	Introduce secure services for IoT middleware. Infer analysis of security services structure to be implemented on middleware (IoT).
Commercial organizations	Vishvakarma et.al	Conceptual organizations framework (COF)	To formulate 2 IoT architectures: 5-layered model, 3-layered cloud-centric architecture, autonomic-oriented. Address certain vulnerabilities in IoT systems.

Discussion on Possible Attacks Posed by Threats and Vulnerabilities of IoT

IoT has crept in all walks of our life. Many technologies like cloud, RFID, NFC, WSNs have evolved &are utilized by IoT networks (Singh & Kaur, 2020). The essential base of the IoT model is M2M functionality on which itis based on. Furthermore, IoT is applicable on other areas like health, retail, smart city etc. So, these interconnected devices should interact with each other along with communication with human beings. The communication path & link should be highly protected & robust to get the users believe in the reliability of the system.

1. Hardware Threats

Some of the examples of hardware devices of IoT are sensors, tags of RFIDs, Bluetooth, and ZigBee. Unique identity & automatic identification are the main functionalities of the RFID tags. These perform a fast information exchange through wireless communication between readers & tags. Other, potential threats can be spoofing, counterfeiting, DoS, tracking, repudiation etc. ZigBee is a small size, low power technology. It comprises of a microcontroller, a protocol, & a radio. It is inexpensive & consumes less power. However, vulnerability is high in these devices also involving attacks like KillerBee, hacking, Scapy, key exchange etc. Bluetooth technology is threatened by eavesdropping, car whisperer, bluebugging, bluejacking, DoS etc as it allows to connect 2 devices wirelessly (Goudarzi et al., 2020).

2. B. Network Threats

Wireless & wired medium of communication both are exposed to the attacks & threats posed by the network. But these IoT deployments in various fields invite threats like fake detections of malicious attacks, DoS, manipulating information which costs reliability of the management. SG is also exposed to trust issues amongst conventional power devices, physical security, security of the customer etc. In health domain, users have their mart health cards which has important & confidential information about them (Amanullah et al., 2020). The patient's security & his privacy comes to stake when it faces attacks like theft, internal attacks, other unintentional intrusions & cyber-attacks. A brief description about attacks is presented below:

a. **DoS**: IoT devices are rendered inaccessible to the users who intend for use & service through transient interruptions & delay. Other DoS attacks include collision, creepy internal attacks, & jamming.

b. **Eavesdropping**: Itis a form of attack which is done electronically. It can be done on wired or non-wired channels. Continuous listening of the message transferred or sniffing of the message is done in this attack.

c. **Device endpoint**: Active hackers or attackers can easily intrude IoT driven smart applications like traffic light manipulation, street light, smart meters, health card blocking & sniffing data etc. After extracting information from these smart objects, it is exploited & malicious intentions disrupt the working & reliability of the systems (Zhou et al., 2018).

d. **Counterfeiting attacks**: Counterfeiting refers to imitating the contents or forging them to his own use. Devices like lighting systems, smart wearables are vulnerable to these attacks as they have light weight security & are fragile to threats. The content is duplicated or modified for further exploitation & cripples the system.

e. **MitM attack:** These attacks challenges security & privacy of the data. Countering solutions like lightweight cryptography protocols are adopted tp provide security for secure communication over the network. The bird's eye view of the potential attacks & vulnerabilities with their threats are tabulated in Table V.

Communication

Communication means exchanging information among different IoT devices & layers of IoT. The most crucial factor of any system is securing its users data & maintaining standards for their confidentiality to make the system robust & reliable (Lin et al., 2017). With shooting number of connected devices in IoT & with their great potentials oozing we can sense some inconsistencies in security. The end users are not satisfied with the unreliable services as their data is compromised. There are few potential threats in each layer which should be addressed & are listed in the below table VI.

Table 5. Analysis of the possible attacks posed by threats and vulnerabilities to the IoT hardware, network infrastructure, and smart application environment.

IOT Hardware	Specs	Threats	Advantages	Susceptibility	Intrusion
RFID	Automatic tracking-identification	Denial of service, repudiation	Enables progress tracking in livestock, automobiles, inventory management.	Corruption, deletion, alteration.	Passive attacks-sniffing, eavesdropping
ZigBee	Low power, low cost mesh network, delivers less latency communication.	Packet manipulation	Low latency, secure data connection, radio, small size	Hacking	Scapy, key exchange, KillerBee.
Bluetooth	Wireless streaming, frequency hopping spectrum.	Man-in the-middle, DoS, eavesdropping	Low power, handles Both data & voice.	Bluejacking, bluesnarfing	Blueborn, bluebugging
Sensors node	WSN components, actuators	Jamming, collisions, exhaustion	Cost-efficient, high latency, flexible.	Tampering, flooding (Dos attack)	Data integrity attack, sybil attack
Network infrastructure					
Wireless	Satellites, transmitters, receivers, radio communication	Data leaks, false configurations, sniffs, rogue access	High scalability, mobility, flexible in access.	Loss of signal, hacking	Protocol tunnelling, Dos, man-in-the-middle attack, war dialling.
Wired	Hub, router, cables, adapters	Hacking, manipulation	More reliable, greater security	Hijacking, signal tampering	Passive attacks, weak link.
Smart city application					
Smart city	Development using Inclusive technology, safety & improved mobility & accessibility	Data leakage, privacy compromise, spoof communication	Structured cities, efficient utilities, e-governance aiding in proper regulation	Fake news dissemination by amplifying attacks, Reading IoT devices communicating private data, cyber-kinetic attacks	Breach in access, ransom attacks by hijacking smart meters
Smart grid	EMS, smart meters	User security	Reliable, independent of tampering, cost-efficient	Data insecurity, interoperability issue leading to data loss.	Cyber attacks
Healthcare	Automated billing, patient monitoring, ful inventory management etc.	Physical devices burnout, aging infrastructure	Preservation of privacy, enhanced responsiveness towards patients.	Hacking of data as there is enormous amount to exploit.	Cyber-attack, internal attack.
Smart transportation	Automated traffic management, speed monitoring cameras, car identification (inbuilt face-recognition), security CCTV.	Network attacks, stalking through passive network attack.	Reduced congestion, energy efficient management	Security compromise	Cyber attacks

Continued on following page

Table 5. Continued

IOT Hardware	Specs	Threats	Advantages	Susceptibility	Intrusion
Smart transportation	Automated traffic management, speed monitoring cameras, car identification (inbuilt face-recognition), security CCTV.	Network attacks, stalking through passive network attack.	Reduced congestion, energy efficient management	Security compromise	Cyber attacks

Table 6. Summary of security threats within each IoT layer

S.No.	Layers	Threats
1.	Physical Layer	Eavesdropping, micro probing, tamper attacks, electrical glitches, jamming.
2.	Link Layer	Message replay, Denial of service (DoS), collision of packets, exhaustion, meta-data attacks.
3.	Network Layer	Black holes, network spoofing, mislead routing, homing, traffic jamming, malware/virus.

EMERGING USE CASES IN IoT

In this section we present different scenarios representing the deployment of Fog computing paradigm with IoT (Krishnamoorthy et al., 2021). These are real time case scenarios which are common to see in today's world due to ubiquity of IoT in life. The following use cases are presented:

- Smart Retail Store Automation
- Smart waste management
- Smart Water Management
- Smart transportation

Smart Retail Store Automation

In the coming future times, the retail experience of a customer can be drastically changed & improved by introducing IoT automated activities in the store. As depicted in Fig. 18 the whole cycle of purchasing-selling is infused by technology & fog computing paradigms are adopted to ease out the time taking activities. With improved machine learning methods & system intelligence any shopping can be automated with supports like automatic checkout-check-in, scanning, automatic payment gateways & methods etc. Also express self-shopping is being promoted in many malls where the dresses can be tried on virtually (without physically touching them). A selection can be made virtually only & the selected piece can be sent for billing at the billing counter avoiding long queues (Al-Garadi et al, 2020). This satisfies the vested interest of the customers & improves the overall shopping experience. This way entire inventory management processes can be regulated (Krishnamoorthy et al., 2021). Orders can be placed effectively with less communication & human interference. Such type of retail experiences aim to cut down operational costs with automated management & customers may get prompt responses to their needs.

Figure 18. Smart retail automation

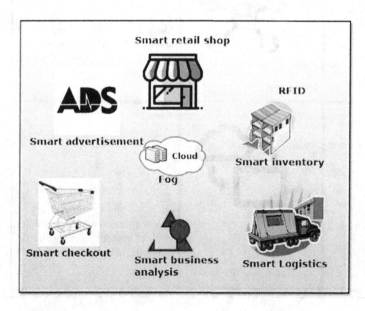

Smart Waste Management

We will explain the working of sensing in waste management. In a developed city there are many offices which are interested in smart management of waste like various manufacturing plants, recycling units, heath care units etc. Sensor data is used to ensure optimized collection of garbage from various places. This way fuel saving strategies can also be implemented to save energy & fuel for further use. Also, recycling units extract information from sensors to monitor the amount of waste generated & coming in the units for next level of processing. This helps in optimizing other internal processes more appropriately (Goudarzi et al., 2020). Fig.19 shows the process flow of the system. The motive of different sensors installed on different objects; bins are to keep a track of the amount of waste is dumped into it. These sensors also gather other data also like the levels of garbage bins are maintained or not, if it is full an alarm is alerted to send information to the centre to empty the bins.

Figure 19. Smart waste management

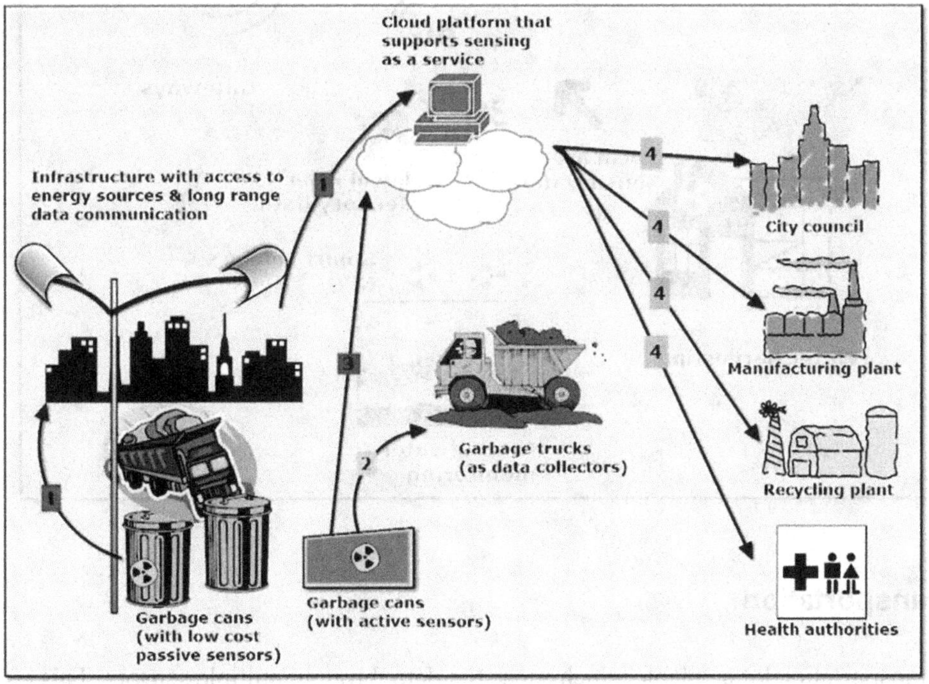

Smart Water Management

Water management is holding prime importance in various aspects for it to be utilized efficiently. Smart cities have a robust water management system with proper plans implemented for its smooth functioning. The critical elements of any water management system in a smart city are treatment which is environment friendly, cost-effective, transportation which is energy saving (Raj et al., 2021). This smart water system monitors the overall consumption of the water of the city, localities. This way future predictions of efficient water usage can be done. For example, Fig. 20 illustrates the water needs in the form of water harvesting, monitoring of ground water. This will depend on the support of Fog computing model involving smart meters, gateways of fog, short-long range communications, wireless sensors, LTE, 4G like communication protocols etc. After all these steps, an actionable plan for efficiently regulating the water flow & reducing loss in water is expected in smart city water management system (Lin et al, 2017).

Figure 20. Smart water management

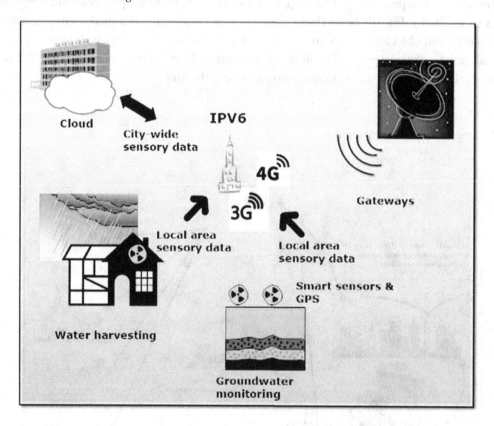

Smart Transportation

There is a transportation kit available which sense the data through multiple sensors. This kit has communication technology like 3G/4G with wireless sensors (Perera et al., 2017). An application which does data processing of the data gathered from the sensors. Algorithms are employed to analyse the data & deduce information from the data, based on which further prediction of can be done. Fig.21 shows distinct aspects of smart city including smart transport system having smart traffic management.

Figure 21. Smart city and transport

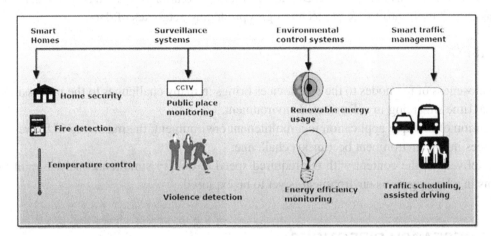

Enabling Technologies

Realization of the concept of IoT into this digital world can be made viable by integrating various enabling technologies (Al-Fuqaha et al., 2015). Here, in this section we will elaborate some of them. In our vision we attempt to give an extensive survey of relevant technologies. We also elucidate the role of these technologies in the IoT system.

Identify, Sense, Communicate: Technologies like wireless communication are pushing forth the digital economy manifolds with the long-term vision of enabling devices with capabilities of identifying objects, sensing data, & communicating amongst each other (Al-Fuqaha et al., 2015). Essential components of IoT system can be RFIDs. It has RFID tags & readers. Also, these are uniquely identified by identifiers. These can be applied to animals or even on humans. These readers enable transmission through the network by initiating a process signal. For real time monitoring of the objects, RFIDs can be used. It seamlessly conjoins physical world with the virtual reality. Hence, it can be used in wide variety of applications like health & safety. RFID are passive tags.

Trends in Fog Computing in Covid-19

- The FC market is anticipated to shoot at CAGR of 68%. The forecast period is starts from 2021 to 2026. The FC market has started making a mark in the digital market.
- It has enlarged the scope of cloud computing & transformed it to edge technology to cater real time analysis of data & accelerate time constrained services.
- For e.g. The most featured companies are IBM Corporation, Dell, Intel Corporation, Amazon web services etc.
- The fog nodes are installed in the close vicinity of the end devices to give a smart processing environment virtually & speedily.
- Smart meters have come into existence for keeping a record of electricity consumption.
- The fog computing market has risen in North America. The open fog consortium is a web of educational institutions & high tech companies which has a vision of promoting & standardizing the

fog computing in varied capacities. Due to enormous generation of data in North American region it has delved itself into IoT & 5G technologies producing zetabytes of data.

Issues in FC

- The closeness of fog nodes to the end devices brings in many challenges to the processing of data & real time streaming in a distributed environment.
- Execution of multiple application in a multitenant environment, the managing of the resources & services in fog environment becomes a challenge.
- The delivery of the content with the required speed & quality simultanaeously in multiple platforms in a heterogenous environment is yet to be explored.

FUTURE RESEARCH DIRECTIONS

FC is the new vogue in the marketplace, & it is such an evolving technology that soon it will reach to the standards of market adoption. It will be able to support low-latency & time critical applications. Many firms & organizations like Open Fog Consortium i.e., Open Fog are important initiatives taken by Cisco, Microsoft, ARM, Intel, Princeton University, Dell etc (Mukherjee et al., 2018). In November, 2015. Some of the contributing members are Shanghai Tech University, Hitachi, Foxconn, ZTE & General Electric. Innovation Digital world is accelerated with the blend of wireless technology like IoT, 5G, embedded AI etc. These provide robust & prompt architectures with high interoperability.

Future scope: The FC market has great business agility. It can be said that it will maximize the utilization of network bandwidth. Improved interconnectivity & machine-machine interaction will be ubiquitous with optimal operational cost. Enhanced quality of services will attract more crowd & potential companies to leverage this technology for better data activities.

Covid Scenario: FC will provide future digitization in crisis times like Covid by enabling prompt responses, immediate data retrieval from the local nodes & even fast analysis in localized clusters without actually reaching to higher level of cloud (Lalmuanawma et al., 2020). We can create connected experiences by garnering data from distributed devices & analysing them. This will help in improving individual experiences. We can modernize the existing IT by having remote controlled infrastructure with technology of microcloud computing or fog computing. This will help in performing real time diagnosis enabling over the air updates to flow. This will also help in reducing the operational cost & facilitate faster services. However, some open issues still exist in this budding computing paradigm. In this section, we present some of future issues & challenges in research. Also, we attempt to view the future directions of this research (Tuli et al., 2020). Figure 22 depicts few relevant challenges of FC research. We list out issues as following:

- Deployment issue
- Platform related issue
- Communication Between Different Layers
- Security & Privacy

Deployment Issues

OpenFog is referred to as N-tier environment in context of deployment (Kumar et al.,2020). But also, this fact should be addressed that introducing many levels in layers of fog computing would defeat the purpose of this new paradigm i.e. low latency (Swapnarekha et al., 2020). It may cause high delay in delivering services & responding to the end users. So based on the use case, number of layers to be involved can be decided. Decisions related to deployment can be taken based on factors like capability of the fog device, sensors count, amount of task, task type etc. Still, it is necessity to see to the fulfillment of these requirements. During deployment scaling of resources & application is vital.

Figure 22. Future research issues in Fog Computing-enabled IoT in Combating Covid-19

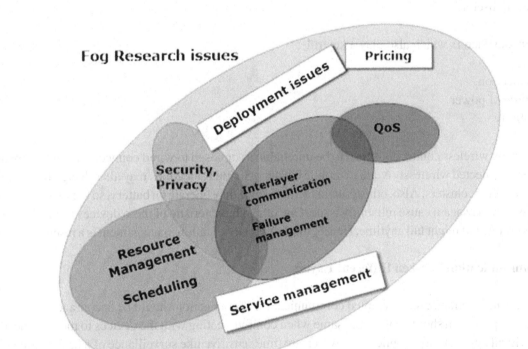

Platform Related Issues

1. **Resource Management**

The resources come from most diverse sources. This contributes in the variety of different hardware & manufacturers. Due to such heterogenous & dynamic resources in FC paradigm performance issues may arise. As an example, a system which depends on staff group o do some ordinary stuff like email or documenting some work can be a part of Fog & can also be made into a Fog device. This way we can conclude that fog resources are dynamic. Resource management or prediction is necessary as when the task undertaken by fog devices is over, the status may change as it may be set free for other application. Fog aims to utilize the resources which are idle. Therefore, resource allocation & management can be an incredibly challenging task (Gluhak et al., 2011).

2.   Failure Management

The probability of the failure of a fog device is high. Due to its distributed arrangement, there is lack of proper management. The management is not completely centralized because of which faults occur. Therefore, fog devices fail for reasons listed:

a.   Issue in hardware
b.   Software discrepancy
c.   Fault in user activity

Miscellaneous factors which also play a key role:

a.   Connection
b.   Source of power
c.   Mobility

Also, many wireless connections tend to be unreliable as opposed to wired connections. In fog, many devices are connected wirelessly & are in mobile clusters. So, their locations may also change frequently into some different clusters. Also, other crucial factor is since they operate on battery, so batteries may fail anytime which may again cause reliability issue. One other characteristic of these devices is that they are battery powered and might fail anytime. Hence, the complexity of failure management is a research issue.

3.   Communication between Different Layers

Seamless interaction & uninterrupted communication & connection should be encouraged in an any network. Fog paradigm should ensure the same when communicating with the devices to meet the needs of time-critical applications. Applications which are time sensitive like surveillance of a health care unit or control of an autonomous car may be inflicted with great harm if connection failure occurs. Even if the centralized connection to cloud fails, the intermediate layers should be operational & should serve full time connectivity. Therefore, cross layer functionality & connectivity in cloud, IoT devices, Fog devices are delicate & crucial factors to be dealt with (Sheth et al, 2020).

4.   Security and Privacy

The location, manufacturing, ownership of the fog devices is different in many aspects. The heterogeneity of these devices gives birth to security & privacy issues (Goudarzi et al., 2020). These devices are administered by different operators. Users will be less interested to adopt this computing model if their privacy is compromised in any way. Therefore, security of the communication & privacy of the user is an extensive research issue in fog computing. As devices are decentralized, so accordingly the management of fog devices & monitoring should also be distributed in different clusters to ensure speedy & parallel operation of all small networks of fog.

Internet of Things Fighting against Covid-19

Figure 23 represents various layers- Perception, network, fog and cloud layer. The perception layer has IoT devices connected to home and hospital environments. Those devices are connected to other the wireless devices in the network layer. These models are integrated with Fog and ML-DL approaches for C-19 symptoms, quarantine surveillance, tracking the contacts and maintaining the social distancing between individuals. The cloud layer is helpful in predicting the coronavirus. The technological advances are made in Cloud and fog layers (Bhattacharya et al., 2021). These technologies include Big data, ML, DL. They together mingle with IoT and provide solution more effectively to solve C-19 problems (Lopez et al; 2012).

Figure 23. Prevention and control of the pandemic COVID-19 using Internet of Things (IoT)

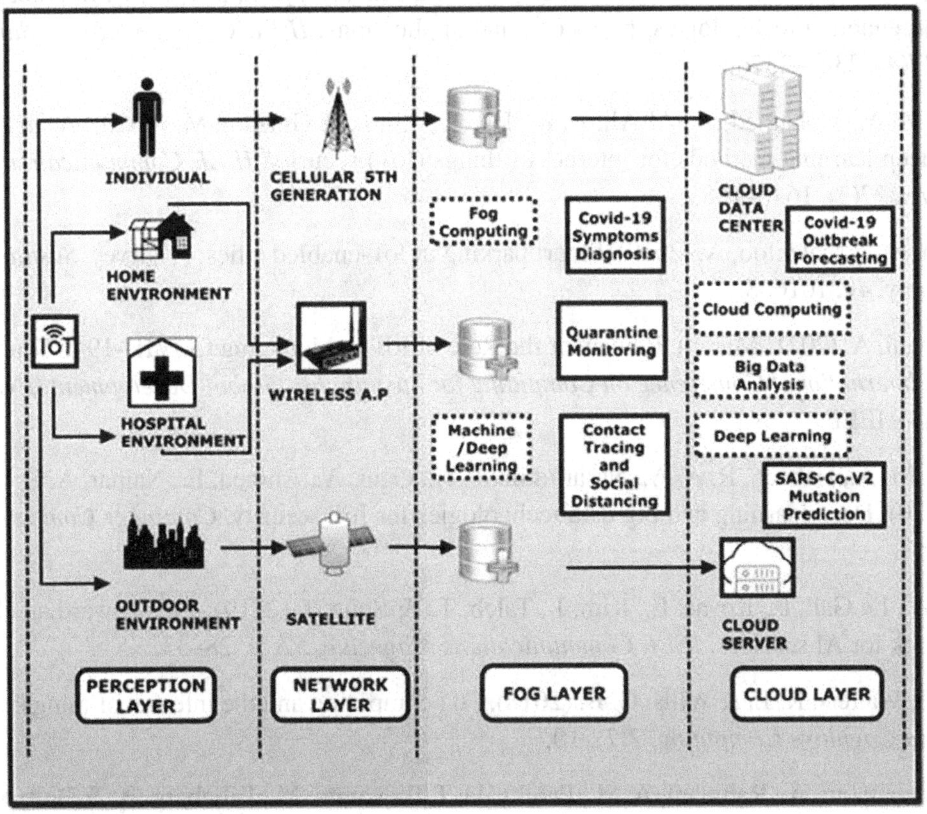

CONCLUSION

We anticipate that FC will accelerate prompt responses & awareness amongst the nodes to exchange information. In emergency conditions like in this COVID-19 pandemic, it will efficiently manage the resources near to the smart wearables monitoring health & give processed data for further analysis in localized zones. Also, there would be less bandwidth issues by distributing the load among the fog nodes. Data of the patients is very sensitive, so it is easy for the fog computing to be able to monitor small personalized clusters. Ultimately, organizations that adopt fog computing gain deeper and faster insights, leading to increased business agility, higher service levels, and improved safety & seamless communication. The accuracy and precision of latency-sensitive applications and discovery of drug and vaccines related to this epidemic needs to be accomplished with fog computing as a part of future work, since this infrastructure platform works only on optimized bandwidth consumption and improving the latency.

REFERENCES

Al-Fuqaha, A., Guizani, M., Mohammadi, M., Aledhari, M., & Ayyash, M. (2015). Internet of things: A survey on enabling technologies, protocols, and applications. *IEEE Communications Surveys and Tutorials, 17*(4), 2347–2376.

Al-Garadi, M. A., Mohamed, A., Al-Ali, A. K., Du, X., Ali, I., & Guizani, M. (2020). A survey of machine and deep learning methods for internet of things (IoT) security. *IEEE Communications Surveys and Tutorials, 22*(3), 1646–1685.

Al-Turjman, F., & Malekloo, A. (2019). Smart parking in IoT-enabled cities: A survey. *Sustainable Cities and Society, 49*, 101608.

Almuhammadi, A. (2021, March). Review of the Role of IoT in Managing COVID-19 in Saudi Arabia. In *2021 8th International Conference on Computing for Sustainable Global Development (INDIACom)* (pp. 439-444). IEEE.

Amanullah, M. A., Habeeb, R. A. A., Nasaruddin, F. H., Gani, A., Ahmed, E., Nainar, A. S. M., ... Imran, M. (2020). Deep learning and big data technologies for IoT security. *Computer Communications, 151*, 495–517.

An, J., Li, W., Le Gall, F., Kovac, E., Kim, J., Taleb, T., & Song, J. (2019). EiF: Toward an elastic IoT fog framework for AI services. *IEEE Communications Magazine, 57*(5), 28–33.

Atlam, H. F., Walters, R. J., & Wills, G. B. (2018). Fog computing and the internet of things: A review. *Big Data and Cognitive Computing, 2*(2), 10.

Azimi, I., Anzanpour, A., Rahmani, A. M., Pahikkala, T., Levorato, M., Liljeberg, P., & Dutt, N. (2017). HiCH: Hierarchical fog-assisted computing architecture for healthcare IoT. *ACM Transactions on Embedded Computing Systems, 16*(5s), 1–20.

Bhattacharya, S., Maddikunta, P. K. R., Pham, Q. V., Gadekallu, T. R., Chowdhary, C. L., Alazab, M., & Piran, M. J. (2021). Deep learning and medical image processing for coronavirus (COVID-19) pandemic: A survey. *Sustainable Cities and Society, 65*, 102589.

Chiang, M., & Zhang, T. (2016). Fog and IoT: An overview of research opportunities. *IEEE Internet of Things Journal, 3*(6), 854-864.

Chifor, B. C., Bica, I., Patriciu, V. V., & Pop, F. (2018). A security authorization scheme for smart home Internet of Things devices. *Future Generation Computer Systems, 86*, 740–749.

Dastjerdi, A. V., Gupta, H., Calheiros, R. N., Ghosh, S. K., & Buyya, R. (2016). Fog computing: Principles, architectures, and applications. In *Internet of things* (pp. 61–75). Morgan Kaufmann.

Farahani, B., Firouzi, F., Chang, V., Badaroglu, M., Constant, N., & Mankodiya, K. (2018). Towards fog-driven IoT eHealth: Promises and challenges of IoT in medicine and healthcare. *Future Generation Computer Systems, 78*, 659–676.

Gams, M., Gu, I. Y. H., Härmä, A., Muñoz, A., & Tam, V. (2019). Artificial intelligence and ambient intelligence. *Journal of Ambient Intelligence and Smart Environments, 11*(1), 71–86.

Gluhak, A., Krco, S., Nati, M., Pfisterer, D., Mitton, N., & Razafindralambo, T. (2011). A survey on facilities for experimental internet of things research. *IEEE Communications Magazine, 49*(11), 58–67.

Goudarzi, M., Wu, H., Palaniswami, M., & Buyya, R. (2020). An application placement technique for concurrent IoT applications in edge and fog computing environments. *IEEE Transactions on Mobile Computing, 20*(4), 1298–1311.

Hu, P., Dhelim, S., Ning, H., & Qiu, T. (2017). Survey on fog computing: Architecture, key technologies, applications and open issues. *Journal of Network and Computer Applications, 98*, 27–42.

Kharrufa, H., Al-Kashoash, H. A., & Kemp, A. H. (2019). RPL-based routing protocols in IoT applications: A Review. *IEEE Sensors Journal, 19*(15), 5952–5967.

Krishnamoorthy, S., Dua, A., & Gupta, S. (2021). Role of emerging technologies in future IoT-driven Healthcare 4.0 technologies: A survey, current challenges and future directions. *Journal of Ambient Intelligence and Humanized Computing*, 1–47.

Kumar, A., Sharma, K., Singh, H., Naugriya, S. G., Gill, S. S., & Buyya, R. (2021). A drone-based networked system and methods for combating coronavirus disease (COVID-19) pandemic. *Future Generation Computer Systems, 115*, 1–19.

Lalmuanawma, S., Hussain, J., & Chhakchhuak, L. (2020). Applications of machine learning and artificial intelligence for Covid-19 (SARS-CoV-2) pandemic: A review. *Chaos, Solitons, and Fractals*, 110059.

Letaief, K. B., Chen, W., Shi, Y., Zhang, J., & Zhang, Y. J. A. (2019). The roadmap to 6G: AI empowered wireless networks. *IEEE Communications Magazine, 57*(8), 84–90.

Lin, J., Yu, W., Zhang, N., Yang, X., Zhang, H., & Zhao, W. (2017). A survey on internet of things: Architecture, enabling technologies, security and privacy, and applications. *IEEE Internet of Things Journal, 4*(5), 1125–1142.

López, T. S., Ranasinghe, D. C., Harrison, M., & McFarlane, D. (2012). Adding sense to the Internet of Things. *Personal and Ubiquitous Computing, 16*(3), 291–308.

Mahmud, R., Kotagiri, R., & Buyya, R. (2018). Fog computing: A taxonomy, survey and future directions. In *Internet of everything* (pp. 103–130). Springer.

Mukherjee, M., Shu, L., & Wang, D. (2018). Survey of fog computing: Fundamental, network applications, and research challenges. *IEEE Communications Surveys and Tutorials, 20*(3), 1826–1857.

Naha, R. K., Garg, S., Georgakopoulos, D., Jayaraman, P. P., Gao, L., Xiang, Y., & Ranjan, R. (2018). Fog computing: Survey of trends, architectures, requirements, and research directions. *IEEE Access: Practical Innovations, Open Solutions, 6*, 47980–48009.

Ni, J., Zhang, K., Lin, X., & Shen, X. (2017). Securing fog computing for internet of things applications: Challenges and solutions. *IEEE Communications Surveys and Tutorials, 20*(1), 601–628.

Perera, C., Qin, Y., Estrella, J. C., Reiff-Marganiec, S., & Vasilakos, A. V. (2017). Fog computing for sustainable smart cities: A survey. *ACM Computing Surveys, 50*(3), 1–43.

Pham, Q. V., Nguyen, D. C., Huynh-The, T., Hwang, W. J., & Pathirana, P. N. (2020). *Artificial intelligence (AI) and big data for coronavirus (COVID-19) pandemic: A survey on the state-of-the-arts.* Academic Press.

Rabah, K. (2018). Convergence of AI, IoT, big data and blockchain: A review. *The Lake Institute Journal, 1*(1), 1-18.

Raj, M., Gupta, S., Chamola, V., Elhence, A., Garg, T., Atiquzzaman, M., & Niyato, D. (2021). A survey on the role of Internet of Things for adopting and promoting Agriculture 4.0. *Journal of Network and Computer Applications*, 103107.

Rasheed, J., Jamil, A., Hameed, A. A., Aftab, U., Aftab, J., Shah, S. A., & Draheim, D. (2020). A survey on artificial intelligence approaches in supporting frontline workers and decision makers for COVID-19 pandemic. *Chaos, Solitons, and Fractals*, 110337.

Saleem, T. J., & Chishti, M. A. (2019). Deep learning for Internet of Things data analytics. *Procedia Computer Science, 163*, 381–390.

Sarkar, S., Chatterjee, S., & Misra, S. (2015). Assessment of the Suitability of Fog Computing in the Context of Internet of Things. *IEEE Transactions on Cloud Computing, 6*(1), 46–59.

Sharma, M. (2021). Drone Technology for Assisting COVID-19 Victims in Remote Areas: Opportunity and Challenges. *Journal of Medical Systems, 45*(9), 1–2. doi:10.100710916-021-01759-y PMID:34322759

Sheth, K., Patel, K., Shah, H., Tanwar, S., Gupta, R., & Kumar, N. (2020). A taxonomy of AI techniques for 6G communication networks. *Computer Communications, 161*, 279–303.

Singh, P., & Kaur, R. (2020). An integrated fog and Artificial Intelligence smart health framework to predict and prevent COVID-19. *Global Transitions, 2*, 283-292.

Singh, S. K., Rathore, S., & Park, J. H. (2020). Blockiotintelligence: A blockchain-enabled intelligent IoT architecture with artificial intelligence. *Future Generation Computer Systems, 110*, 721–743.

Swapnarekha, H., Behera, H. S., Nayak, J., & Naik, B. (2020). Role of intelligent computing in COVID-19 prognosis: A state-of-the-art review. *Chaos, Solitons, and Fractals, 138*, 109947.

Tuli, S., Tuli, S., Tuli, R., & Gill, S. S. (2020). Predicting the growth and trend of COVID-19 pandemic using machine learning and cloud computing. *Internet of Things*, *11*, 100222.

Welbourne, E., Battle, L., Cole, G., Gould, K., Rector, K., Raymer, S., ... Borriello, G. (2009). Building the internet of things using RFID: The RFID ecosystem experience. *IEEE Internet Computing*, *13*(3), 48–55.

Yousef pour, A., Fung, C., Nguyen, T., Kadiyala, K., Jalali, F., Niakanlahiji, A., ... Jue, J. P. (2019). All one needs to know about fog computing and related edge computing paradigms: A complete survey. *Journal of Systems Architecture*, *98*, 289–330.

Zhang, P., Zhou, M., & Fortino, G. (2018). Security and trust issues in fog computing: A survey. *Future Generation Computer Systems*, *88*, 16–27.

Zhou, W., Jia, Y., Peng, A., Zhang, Y., & Liu, P. (2018). The effect of iot new features on security and privacy: New threats, existing solutions, and challenges yet to be solved. *IEEE Internet of Things Journal*, *6*(2), 1606–1616.

Zikria, Y. B., Afzal, M. K., Ishmanov, F., Kim, S. W., & Yu, H. (2018). A survey on routing protocols supported by the Contiki Internet of things operating system. *Future Generation Computer Systems*, *82*, 200–219.

ADDITIONAL READING

Ahanger, T. A., Tariq, U., Nusir, M., Aldaej, A., Ullah, I., & Sulman, A. (2021). A novel IoT–fog–cloud-based healthcare system for monitoring and predicting COVID-19 outspread. *The Journal of Supercomputing*, 1–24.

Dong, Y., & Yao, Y. D. (2021). IoT platform for COVID-19 prevention and control: A survey. *IEEE Access: Practical Innovations, Open Solutions*, *9*, 49929–49941.

Garg, L., Chukwu, E., Nasser, N., Chakraborty, C., & Garg, G. (2020). Anonymity preserving IoT-based COVID-19 and other infectious disease contact tracing model. *IEEE Access: Practical Innovations, Open Solutions*, *8*, 159402–159414.

Jahmunah, V., Sudarshan, V. K., Oh, S. L., Gururajan, R., Gururajan, R., Zhou, X., ... Acharya, U. R. (2021). Future IoT tools for COVID-19 contact tracing and prediction: A review of the state-of-the-science. *International Journal of Imaging Systems and Technology*, *31*(2), 455–471.

Kumar, K., Kumar, N., & Shah, R. (2020). Role of IoT to avoid spreading of COVID-19. *International Journal of Intelligent Networks*, *1*, 32–35. doi:10.1016/j.ijin.2020.05.002

Kumar, M., Nayar, N., Mehta, G., & Sharma, A. (2021). Application of IoT in Current Pandemic of COVID-19. *IOP Conference Series. Materials Science and Engineering*, *1022*(1), 012063.

Mukherjee, R., Kundu, A., Mukherjee, I., Gupta, D., Tiwari, P., Khanna, A., & Shorfuzzaman, M. (2021). IoT-cloud based healthcare model for COVID-19 detection: An enhanced k-Nearest Neighbour classifier based approach. *Computing*, 1–21.

Pandya, S., Sur, A., & Kotecha, K. (2020). Smart epidemic tunnel: IoT-based sensor-fusion assistive technology for COVID-19 disinfection. *International Journal of Pervasive Computing and Communications*.

Rahman, A., Hossain, M. S., Alrajeh, N. A., & Alsolami, F. (2020). *Adversarial examples–security threats to COVID-19 deep learning systems in medical IoT devices*. IEEE Internet of Things Journal.

Siripongdee, K., Pimdee, P., & Tuntiwongwanich, S. (2020). A blended learning model with IoT-based technology: Effectively used when the COVID-19 pandemic? *Journal for the Education of Gifted Young Scientists*, *8*(2), 905–917.

Yousif, M., Hewage, C., & Nawaf, L. (2021). IoT Technologies during and beyond COVID-19: A Comprehensive Review. *Future Internet*, *13*(5), 105.

KEY TERMS AND DEFINITIONS

Artificial Intelligence (AI): It is a computational intelligence established through computing machines that further includes perception and emotionalism.

COVID-19: A contagious infection caused by SARS-CoV-2 to humans.

Deep Learning: It is a part of ML that is based on ANN with enhanced supervised/unsupervised learning.

Edge Computing: It is a distributed computing model which has brought computation nearer to the application layer nodes for enhancing the response time.

Fog Computing: It is a virtual cloud that acts as an intermediary between the physical layer of IoT devices and cloud data centres.

Internet of Things: It is a network of outgrowing connected objects that fetch and communicate the data between physical layer nodes.

Machine Learning (ML): It is the study of certain rigorous techniques which escalates the performance by gaining experience and via utilization of several data.

Sustainable Smart Cities: An infrastructure of connected cities deployed with IoT sensors/actuators with emerging technologies.

Chapter 4
Elaborative Investigation of Blockchain Technology in Intelligent Networks

Dhaya R.

(iD) https://orcid.org/0000-0002-3599-7272

King Khalid University, Saudi Arabia

Kanthavel R.

King Khalid University, Saudi Arabia

ABSTRACT

The fifth generation (5G) network advancement focus is to help mixed upright applications by associating heterogeneous gadgets and machines with extreme upgrades regarding high quality of administration, extended organization limit, and improved framework throughput regardless of significant difficulties like decentralization, straightforwardness, dangers of information interoperability, network protection, and security weaknesses. The challenges and limitations of other intelligent 5G internet of networks (5G IoTs) are also to be met by using blockchain technology with the integration of cloud computing and edge computing technologies. In this chapter, the authors render an elaborated analytics of the empowering of blockchain technology in intelligent networks that include 5G networks and 5G-based IoT. The solutions for the spectrum management, data sharing, security, and privacy in 5G networks will also be analyzed. It is believed that the proposed chapter would definitely be useful for the researchers in the field of blockchain in intelligent networks.

INTRODUCTION

Blockchain has been actually made and viably used first for Bitcoin computerized capital. Blockchain gives security, mystery, and data decency with no untouchable relationship in the control of the trades, and likewise, it makes entrancing assessment locales, especially from the perspective of particular

DOI: 10.4018/978-1-7998-8367-8.ch004

troubles and hindrances (Kaushik et al., 2017). Most of the expounding on this advancement fixates on uncovering and improving the obstructions of blockchain from insurance and security perspectives.

Man-made awareness (AI) and AI (ML) figuring's may be the enhancement that blockchain models ought to be used in more applications, for instance, Industry 4.0, Internet of things, domestic structures, Secures, crypto chips, and so forth Blockchain is a conveyed data base course of action that keeps a continually creating summary of data records that are insisted by the centers checking out it. The data is recorded in an openly available report, including the information of each trade ever wrapped up. It is a decentralized game plan where AI and ML estimations may expect different parts to confirmation security in a beneficial manner (Dinh & Thai, 2018). In spite of the way that blockchain is apparently a fitting response for driving trades using computerized types of cash, it has some specific incites that ought to be tended to. High uprightness of trades and security of centers are required to prevent attacks, and AI may offer a response, especially when it is used in distant sensors. Far off crypto chips may be a response for some coordination issues, and ML counts may be used on them also. Blockchain gives off an impression of being tangled, and it surely can be, yet its focal thought is in reality extremely clear. A blockchain is a sort of data base. To have the choice to grasp blockchain, it serves to at first understand what a data base truly is. An informational index in the form of variety of data can be taken care of digitally on a PC system and informational indexes is characteristically coordinated by chart association in the direction of considering more straightforward looking and filtering for unequivocal information (Aste et al., 2017).

The differentiation between someone using an accounting page to store information instead of a data base has been given as follows: Spreadsheets are proposed for one individual, or a bit of social occasion of group, to accumulate and right to use restricted proportions of data. On the other hand, an informational index is proposed to house generally greater proportions of data with the intention to be cleaned, and controlled rapidly to convince users. Colossal data bases accomplish this by accommodating information on laborers which are completed of historic PCs (Litke et al., 2019). The laborers at a time are created by means of voluminous amount of PCs to encompass the processing command and limit significant intended for certain customers to get into the data base concurrently. At the same time as an accounting page or data base possibly will be available to many individuals, it be regularly controlled through a industry and directed via an assigned person who have full oversight above to see the statistics inside of it. One key differentiation between a blockchain and normal data base is the manner wherein the infor- mation is coordinated. A BC assembles message within social events, in any case considered squares so as to grasp setting of data. Squares contain assured limit limits and, once packed, have been secured against the as of late crammed square, outline a sequence of information identified by "blockchain."

Every innovative data which pursues with the intention of recently further obstruct is requested keen on an as of late outlined square so as to similarly be included. Data base constructions embed in to its information into bench however a blockchain, similar to its title proposes arrangement interested in ir- regularities to facilitate jointly. This constructs it with the objective to every BC have been data bases yet not every informational collections have been BCs and this structure in like manner intrinsically creates an irrevocable plan of figures after the completion in a distributed environment. Exactly as soon as a square is crammed it is unchangeable in order to transform into spitted schedule. Every square in the sequence is known an accurate instance stamp once the chain is included. This chapter presents the Elaborative investigation of Blockchain Technology in intelligent networks in three main sections namely Features, advantages, disadvantages and need of Blockchain for Intelligent Networks, Integration of 5G networks with Blockchain along with Potential of 5G network using Black chain technology and finally the Role of Blockchain in 5G- IoT.

NEED OF BLOCKCHAIN FOR INTELLIGENT NETWORKS

Coming up next are the highlights of the Blockchain innovation. BC is a specific kind of data collection.

- BC supplies data in open area which have been then attached jointly.
- As novel data approaches in it is moved out to be keen on another square. At the point when the square is stacked up in the midst of information joined on the preceding square that builds the information integrated inside consecutive request (Alkadi et al., 2020).
- Dissimilar sorts of data is being taken care of BC yet the broadly perceived employ so far-off is while a record intended for trades.
- For Bitcoin's purpose, BC as a form of distributed manner and no individual or social even t have managed relatively, every customer aggregately hold be in charge of.
- Decentralized BCs are constant, that infers the data noted is permanent.

Figure 1. Significant properties of blockchain

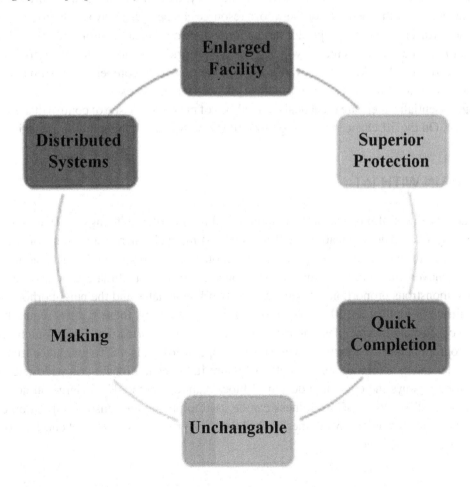

Figure 1 shows the features of blockchain. These highlights will give us some significant properties of Blockchain

Enlarged Facility: This is the first and a significant element of Blockchain. The most exceptional thing about this Blockchain innovation is that it expands the limit of the entire organization. On account of the explanation that there are a ton of PCs cooperating which in complete offers an extraordinary force then not many of the gadgets where the things are unified.

Superior Protection: Blockchain innovation has a superior security in light of the fact that there isn't so much as a solitary possibility of closing down of the framework. Indeed, even the most significant level of the monetary framework is liable to get hacked. Bitcoin in the second hand had never been hacked. the explanation is that the blockchain network is made sure about by various PCs called hubs and these hubs affirm the exchange on this organization

Unchangeable: Making unchanging records is one of the primary estimations of Blockchain. Any data set that is incorporated is exposed to get hacked and they require trust in the outsider to keep the data set secure. Blockchain like Bitcoin keeps its records in an endless **condition of sending force.**

Quick Completion: Customary financial frameworks can be moderate, as they require a ton of settlement time which typically requires days to continue. This is one of the primary motivation behind why these financial foundations need to redesign their financial frameworks. We can take care of this issue by the methods for Blockchain as it can settle cash move at super quick paces. These eventually save a ton of time and cash from these foundations and give comfort to the buyer too.

Distributed Systems: Decentralized innovation enables you to store your resources in an organization which further access by the methods for the web, a resource can be in any way similar to an agreement, a record and so forth Through this proprietor has an immediate command over his record by the methods for a key that is connected to his record which gives the proprietor an ability to move his resources for anybody he needs. The Blockchain innovation ends up being a truly compelling instrument for decentralizing the web. It has the ability to acquire huge changes the enterprises

Making: Essentially, there are great deals of methods of printing an issue of control that we can tackle by Blockchain. On the off chance that you go toward the west and ask them do they trust innovation.

BLOCKCHAIN WITH IoT

The quick advancement of blockchain development and the Internet of Things (IoT) are felt all during our time by day lives. The applications will agitate existing cycles across grouping of organizations including manufacturing, trading, transportation, the money related region and clinical administrations. Despite these movements security remains a top concern for the IoT climate as it uncovered various contraptions, monstrous proportions of data, store network associates and the neighborhood general to security infiltrates (Gupta et al., 2018). With IoT gadgets multiplying, these gadgets regularly come up short on the confirmation principles important to protect client information. Basic foundation will be harmed if programmers enter through the expansive scope of IoT gadgets. To guarantee trust, verification and normalization across all components of IoT are fundamental for far and wide selection. Here are a few different ways the circulated design of blockchain can help address large numbers of these security and trust difficulties: BC usefulness can be used to pursue the sensor information evaluation and delay repetition by way of any another wicked data. The figure 2 shows the benefit of Blockchain and IoT in combined together.

Figure 2. Benefit of blockchain and IoT in combined together.

- The IoT Deployments of device are marvelous, and suitable evidence is appropriate to provide IoT tool ID, endorsement and dependable protected information move.
- Instead of encountering a recluse to develop confidence, the exchange data within IoT devices anyway a BC.
- A scattered record takes out a singular wellspring of disillusionment inside the organic framework, protecting an IOT device's data from changing.
- Blockchain engages device self-rule (sagacious agreement), particular character, and uprightness to support circulated correspondence by killing specific bottlenecks and weaknesses.
- The association and action costs of IoT can be reduced through blockchain since there is no agent.
- IoT devices are clearly addressable with blockchain, giving a foundation set apart by related contraptions for researching purposes.
- BC-based IOT measures have been suitable to disentangle trade measures, humanizing user knowledge and bring about enormous expenses.

BLOCKCHAIN CHARACTERISTICS, ADVANTAGES AND DISADVANTAGES

For the entirety of its multifaceted nature, BC probable as a distributed sort unbounded information. As of more vital customer insurance and expanded security to cut down handling charges and fewer blunders, blockchain innovation might just see applications past those illustrated previously(Gochhayat et al., 2020). In any case, there are likewise a few inconveniences.

Pros

- Improved precision by taking out human commitment in the affirmation
- Cost diminishes by clearing out outcast check
- Distribution formulates it difficult to adjust
- Communication have been protected, confidential, and capable
- See-through development
- Provide a monetary other decision and scheme to deal with ensuring singular in order for inhabitants of states by means of uncertain.

Cons

- Noteworthy development charge identified by taking out bitcoin
- Short trades each moment

- The past of usage in unlawful behavior
- Directives
- Favorable conditions of Blockchain
- The exactness of the Chain

BC business system have been attested through an organization by hundreds ofs PCs. This disposes of essentially every individual consideration by check cycle, achieving the fewer individual missteps and a precise evidence of data. Whether or not a PC of any organization was in the direction of submitting a processing error, the bungle can simply be completed to the reproduction of the BC.

Impact of Blockchain

The impacts of Blockchain are debated in a detailed manner as follows:

Cost Reductions: Regularly, a client disburses a depository to affirm a trade, a legitimate authority to symptom a manuscript, or a nun to play out matrimony. BC executes the necessity designed for outcast affirmation and, in the midst of it, their connected expenditure. Industry people cause a little charge at whatever point they recognize portions using Mastercards, for example, since banks and portion getting ready associations need to deal with those trades. Bitcoin, of course, doesn't comprise an essential force and has restricted trade charges (Zou et al., 2020).

- **Decentralization:** BC doesn't accumulate whichever data in a central region. Taking everything into account, the BC has been recreated and increased across an organization of PCs. At no matter what position an extra square is supplementary to the BC, each PC on the organization revives its BC to reproduce the modification. By distribution of that data from corner to corner an organization, relatively than taking care of it in single middle data base, BC ends up being harder to meddle by. If a reproduction of the BC cuts down heavily influenced by a developer, simply a lone reproduction of the data, to a certain extent than the complete organization point is done.
- **Productive Communication:** Trades put from side to side a essential power that can require up to a certain days to resolve. When you try to store a watch out for a particular night, then you might not in fact perceive resources in your record in anticipation of the next morning. While money related associations work for the duration of business duration, 5 days out of each week, BC is operational by 24 hours consistently, 7 days of the week, and one year. Trades are done because possible be seen while secure after several hours because of significant intended for cross-line deal, that ordinarily obtain any more considering time-locale issues and the way that all social affairs ought to certify portion taking care of.
- **Private Transactions:** Various blockchain networks fill in as open data bases can see an overview of the organization's trade history. Despite the way that customers can get to experiences concerning trades, they can't get to perceiving data on the subject of the customers creating individuals who trades. It has been a regular wrong insight that BC networks similar to bitcoin have been secretive while without a doubt of its characterization. With the intention, where a user divulges trades, their exceptional code named a public key, has been documented on the BC, to a certain extent than their own data. In the event that someone has completed a Bitcoin buy on a trade which necessitates recognizable proof after that the individual's character is as yet connected to their

blockchain address, yet an exchange, in any event, when attached to an individual's name, doesn't uncover any close to home data (Naz & Lee, 2020).

- **Secure Transactions:** At the point when a trade is recorded, its realness ought to be affirmed by means of the BC set-up. An enormous numbers of PCs competitions en route for attesting that the nuances to procure the ones which are correct. Subsequent to a PC has affirmed the trade to a new to the BC block. Every square on the blockchain contains it's possess stand-out hash, close by the exceptional hash of the square previous to it. Exactly when the information on a square is adjusted into several ways, so as to square's hashcode modifications regardless to the hashcode on the square subsequent to it and this mistake composes it staggeringly hard for the sequence happening the BC to be altered exclusive of become aware of.

- **Straightforwardness:** The larger part BCs are out and out open foundation programming and this suggests that everyone could see its system to empower analysts to overview advanced types of cash like Bitcoin for security. This manner suggests, no veritable master in Bitcoin is able to adjust. Thus, anyone can prescribe switches or climbs to the scheme. But predominant organization customers have the same opinion that the novel type of the system with the renewal is good enough.

- **Banking the Unbanked:** The significant feature of blockchain and Bitcoin are the capacity, identity, sexual orientation and social foundation. As per the world bank, almost 2 billion grown-ups with the intention of not comprising financial balances or any methods for putting away their cash or wealth.5 Nearly these people live in non-industrial nations where the economy is at its outset and completely reliant on money. These individuals frequently bring in little cash that is paid in actual money. They at that point need to store this actual money in concealed areas in their residences or spaces of livelihood send-off the theme to theft or superfluous brutality (Peters et al., 2015). Inputs to a bitcoin folder can be put away on a bit of document, a modest PDA, or even retained if important. For the vast majority, almost certainly, these alternatives are more effectively covered up than a little heap of money under a sleeping cushion. Blockchains of things to come are additionally searching for answers for not exclusively be a unit of record for abundance stockpiling, yet additionally to stock up clinical reports, possessions datas, and an assortment of additional legitimate agreements.

- **Disservices of BC:** As there have been tremendous expected increases to the BC an immense confrontation in terms of allocation. The hindrances to the development of BC nowadays have not been particular. The certified troubles are authoritarian, for the the majority element in order to try also countless times of BC programming plan and back-end programming expected to organize BC to present industry organizations. At this point a segment of the dispute is disturbing the overall progression of broad blockchain choice.

- **Innovation Rate:** In spite of the way that blockchain can get a decent arrangement on trade costs, development are distant as of at no cost. The "confirmation of employment" system that bitcoin is to make use to support trades, for example, putting away huge proportions of processing power. Disregarding the expenses of taking out bitcoin, customers carry on driving out of bed their force statement to affirm trades of BC. Since, at what time diggers append a square to the bitcoin BC, they have been repaid through adequate bitcoin to formulate their moment and power valuable. With respect to blockchain that don't use advanced cash, regardless, diggers ought to be paid or regardless, helped to favor trades. A couple of answers for the problems of BC are starting to happen and hence, bitcoin farmhouses are building to make use of solar power, bounty combustible chat as of profound earth boring districts, or power from wind ranches (Al-Jaroodi & Mohamed, 2019).

- **Speed Ineffectiveness:** The ideal pertinent assessment of Bitcoin intended for the expected inadequacies of BC. Bitcoin's structure needs approximately certain proceedings to put in one more square. Next to that price, it has been reviewed that the blockchain organization could basically supervise around seven do businesses intended for each second (TPS). Thus far other advanced monetary standards, for instance, Ethereum acts in a way that is in a way that is enhanced than bitcoin, they are up till now incomplete by BC.

- **Criminal Behavior:** Despite the fact that grouping lying on the BC network shields customers commencing slashes and jam insurance, it similarly considers unlawful deal and action.

INTEGRATION OF 5G NETWORKS WITH BLOCKCHAIN

The Blockchain Provides high security for 5G organizations drew in with decentralized records. Blockchain ensures about the 5G organizations by outfitting disseminated trust models with high access approval, thusly empowering 5G frameworks to secure themselves and guarantee information protection. The ramifications of combining the two advancements can confront different difficulties (Klessig et al., 2016). To meet the complete 5G assumptions, there are a ton of primary and specialized angles that should be investigated. Clear administrative systems should be characterized and found for the usage of different arrangements like shrewd agreements. Likewise, in particular, the versatility of Blockchain should be improved to manage a high number of gadgets, as each gadget should have kind locations. Additionally, noxious gadgets can make confusion inside the network, hence confining the progression of development. The incorporation of Blockchain with 5G can give another definition to the creating society.

It is not just blockchain innovation that is exclusively changing the 5G networks. It wouldn't be reasonable on the off chance that we do exclude other arising innovations like distributed computing, NFV (Network Function Virtualization), D2D interchanges to give some examples. Yet, without a doubt, Blockchain opens the chance for putting away and overseeing information on 5G networks by means of its distributed record. Blockchain can be viewed as a key empowering agent guaranteeing security and network executives, and there is no denying the way that Blockchain will inspire the generally advanced portable administrations. In any case, a huge transformation in the versatile network society is yet to be predicted. With developing Blockchain, advance yourself as well. For moment refreshes about blockchain news and confirmations, look at Blockchain Council.

Characteristics and Challenges of Blockchain Technology Based Fifth Generation Networks

The outline for a critical attributes of BC innovation that are necessary to its latent capacity.

- Fraud discovery and anticipation
- No outsider contribution
- Operates trustless
- Decentralized stockpiling
- Making computerized cash secure

- Transparent yet made sure about
- Processing execution
- Trust in the trustless world

As 5G is headed to be conveyed across the world, interfacing all the heterogeneous gadgets and machines. The world is getting obsessed with its rapid, decreased inertness, and expanded network limit, and can hardly wait to profit of such extraordinary availability (Mafakheri et al., 2018).
In any case, there are a couple of moves that should be tended to and can't be disregarded.

- Excessive human traffic can cause clog and over-burden.
- Depending upon the quantity of passages, low throughput settlement takes place.

POTENTIAL OF 5G NETWORKS USING BLACK CHAIN TECHNOLOGY

As Blockchain is unchanging and follows decentralized exchange records, it can offer monstrous correspondence without breaking security, hence keeping up dependability among associations and organizations. As we as a whole know about the attributes of blockchain innovation, it is straightforward how these highlights empower the turn of events and change of 5G networks (Mistry et al., 2020). The fifth-age 5G innovation is the following huge stage in the business of broadcast communications that will be presented soon. With regards to modern and completely fledged innovation, Blockchain and 5G are the most talked about and advertised advancements that are hitting the commercial center. The majority of the organizations and associations have just received this arising innovation while few are yet to take an action. It is intriguing to sort out how Blockchain can affect the media transmission industry and what are the difficulties that innovation will confront while changing.

- **Decentralized Approach:** Blockchain innovation doesn't include any outsider or supporters of play out the exchanges; along these lines, it is a decentralized framework that dispenses with the prerequisite of believed outer experts in the 5G networking. The decentralizing methodology further dispenses with bottleneck issues, in this way proficiently upgrading administration conveyance (Shafee, 2020).
- **Blockchain-An Immutability Feature:** Blockchain empowers unchanging nature for 5G network administrations which permit the shared information and asset exchanging to be recorded permanently importance there is no adjustment or change of information.
- **Permitting Localized Availability:** We know about the straightforwardness that blockchain offers and the joining of Blockchain into 5G permits specialist co-ops and customers with full access where an approved individual can follow and check the exchanges.
- **Cost-Saving Methodology:** Blockchain follows the shared strategy, and consequently it eliminates the outsider understanding prompting cost decreases while fabricating better coordination and trust levels among accomplices and furthermore saving time and clashes.
- **Security-The Prime Factor:** Blockchain utilizes cryptography that implies all the data is encoded and made sure about. The mix of Blockchain with the 5G can change security by giving distributed trust models, in this way making 5G fit for shielding themselves from security penetrating. Decentralized Blockchain utilizes helter kilter cryptography and different hash calculations which

helps in securing the characters of the clients. Blockchain can empower the gadgets to be enrolled with their blockchain address; consequently, there is no doubt about personality misfortune (Global Mobile Suppliers Association, 2015).

How Blockchain will Solidify 5G Inspired Services

5G is the current wireless network standard that promises to deliver more than the customary increase in speed as with previous generation networks. Predicted to be at least 100 times faster than 4G and having a higher capacity to accommodate a myriad of connected devices, 5G will be radically different from other generations – something it has in common with modern blockchain tech. Yet, what truly distinguishes this highly anticipated light-speed mobile network is its significantly reduced latency in the transfer and sharing of huge datasets. Consequently, these characteristics of 5G will spur a rethinking of the IoT. A community of compact and low-powered devices can be easily connected via 5G. While data may flow in real-time, thanks to the heightened connectivity due to 5G, it needs to travel through secured means such as encryption or blockchain-powered solutions (Liyanage et al., 2018).

Blockchain, as an immutable, distributed ledger, has already outgrown the singular context of cryptocurrencies. Various organizations have been making big strides on non-crypto applications of blockchain, which will be discussed below and will further support the materializing fifth-generation mobile network. Blockchain will bring security and standardization to various 5G applications, for example, the development of autonomous vehicles. Autonomous vehicles rely on massive heaps of data to be transmitted between the vehicle, a central operating system, and its surrounding environment during development. There are a plethora of devices, sensors, and gadgets embedded in the vehicles and across the environment; it's of paramount importance to ensure the data is kept safe from the hands of hackers. Besides the streams of data exchange bolstered by 5G's ultra-speed, tech giants such as IBM and digital-first automakers are recognizing the significance of blockchain in managing, storing, and transferring vital digital records for automobiles. Additionally, projects like the Mobility Open Blockchain Initiative (MOBI) indicate the major role blockchain will play in the autonomous vehicles sphere but also contribute to supporting 5G applications in the industry. With 5G on the rise, SMEs are eager to get a slice of this next-gen mobile network, and more processes will migrate to the cloud and online; hence, data security and verification are essential(Popovski et al., 2018). As an example, Boeing enlisted blockchain to power the sale of airplane parts, replacing its predominantly paper-based certificates. Essentially, the distributed ledger technology (DLT) will include all parties from the manufacturer, distributor, and seller in the sales of airplane parts, adding more transparency to the key details and transaction history. Researchers have consistently been exploring and analyzing the capabilities of blockchain to potentially empower 5G applications, from spectrum supervision, information sharing and organization virtualization, asset the executives to obstruction the board, unified learning, protection, and security arrangement.

BLOCKCHAIN ON EDGE AND CLOUD COMPUTING

Blockchain and edge processing have a fascinating reliant relationship. Edge computing is a distributed process that can give a framework to blockchain hubs to store and check exchanges. Then again, blockchain could empower a genuinely open distributed cloud commercial center. Then again, Blockchain is a morally sound online record of financial exchanges that can be customized distinctly through approval from each gathering included(Yang et al., 2019). The information is overseen through a bunch of PCs that are not possessed by any single gathering, so the information submitted isn't corruptible. A cloud is something that we can access through the web. It is where we can get the information on the web. Then again, blockchain is an encoded framework that utilizes various styles of encryption and hash to store information in secured data sets. Edge figuring can serve to cut down IT foundation costs, for instance in facilitating. Not exclusively does information not need to go as far, there's less equipment required, which thus is additionally of gigantic advantage to the climate. Most sites are fabricated utilizing arrangements, for example, WordPress or Wix which thusly are facilitated on mists like Amazon AWS or Microsoft Azure. Very soon sites will be assembled utilizing programming arrangements that are facilitated tense networks, at a small amount of the expense of customary cloud-based administrations. The table 1 shows the difference between EC & CC.

Table 1. Differentiate EC and CC

Edge Computing(EC)	Cloud Computing(CC)
Edge Computing is viewed as ideal for tasks with outrageous dormancy concerns. In this manner, medium scale organizations that have spending constraints can utilize edge registering to save monetary assets.	CC more appropriate for manage activities and associations which manage huge information stockpiling
A few unique stages might be utilized for programming, all having distinctive runtimes.	Real writing computer programs is more qualified in mists as they are by and large made for one objective stage and uses one programing language.
Edge Computing requires a hearty security plan including progressed confirmation strategies and proactively handling assaults.	It requires to a lesser degree a powerful security plan.

In any case, quite possibly the most energizing territories where the innovation is required to have a genuine effect is encouraging the advancement of shrewd urban communities. Around the globe there are numerous urban communities that are now utilizing sensors to computerize things, for example, street lamps turning on and off to save power, stopping, squander the board, and in any event, shopping. In specific pieces of China, canister covers will just open on facial acknowledgment prompting more proficient waste administration. Before long you will have the option to stroll into a bistro, plunk down and have an espresso, and essentially leave with installment being consequently taken from your ledger. The quantity of the two urban areas and savvy advances are developing quickly and at such a speed that the cloud just won't have the option to adapt at the speed and figuring limit required. It isn't difficult to see the legitimacy of the forecasts of a huge number more associated gadgets turning into a reality and the dramatic measure of information that should be overseen. This IoT expansion will be served by a horde of innovations. We accept edge figuring will have a key impact in the manner information is prepared, overseen, and put away, and the manner in which we see this event rapidly is on the off chance that we can permit individuals to loan their extra processing ability to turn into a piece of the new cloud.

ROLE OF BLOCKCHAIN IN FIFTH GENERATION IOT

Development of Blockchain will be useful in after hundreds of Crores of related contraptions, allow the treatment of trades and harmonization among strategy; consider immense speculation assets to IoT industry makers. In an IoT organization, the blockchain can keep an absolute documentation of the verifiable background of adroit strategy. IoT and blockchain are cooperating as one to make the world a superior associated place. Instances of IoT and blockchain remember everything from record security for modern IoT gear to blockchain being utilized as a strategy to track-and-follow IoT-empowered steel trailers. Blockchain, which is generally natural for bitcoin and Ethereum, offers a fascinating answer for IoT security. The blockchain contains solid securities against information altering, locking admittance to the Internet of Things gadgets, and permitting bargained gadgets in an IoT network to be closed down.

IoT innovation permits unmistakable objects of ordinary use to have the option to associate with the web to communicate information by means of calculations and serve proprietors better. The world is as of now seeing a multiplication of savvy gadgets like TVs, furniture things, vacuum cleaners, etc. As of now, there are savvy homes, which are totally worked by in-constructed calculations. Assessments by the Fraunhofer Institute place possible keen home investment funds at 40% taking everything into account, an objective that applies to the business as much as property holders. Thoughts of savvy urban areas are not a long way from being acknowledged, by the same token. Savvy urban communities dream past the reducing of discharges and energy expenses, assessed by McKinsey to improve drive times by a potential 15-20% and crisis administration reaction times by 20-35% with the assistance of intelligent streets. As referenced before, 5G would give a road to these shrewd homes, keen urban areas, and a lot more savvy gadgets to understand their actual potential.

Once there is level ground for shrewd gadgets, particularly low-fueled ones to flourish, at that point IoT would get a gigantic lift. Since it would turn out to be more helpful to work these gadgets, there would be a lot a greater amount of them and even a lot more individuals to promptly receive it. The world is arriving at a level where it is hard to live as an individual without admittance to the web. Truth be told, the UN has since 2016 proclaimed admittance to the web as a basic liberty. Notwithstanding, while the marriage of 5G and IoT as of now vows to be a happy one, there are as yet authentic concerns particularly in the zones of security and protection. That is the place where blockchain comes in. Numerous individuals today are in any event mindful of virtual monetary forms today like Bitcoin, Ethereum, Swisscoin, Litecoin, etc. However, a couple truly has a grip of the innovation behind it: Blockchain. Blockchain is a shared, decentralized information base stage for putting away squares of exchange information connected together in chains – thus the name. The decentralized idea of blockchain implies it is impervious to most security issues. Its significant level encryption gives more noteworthy assurance from hacking than the customary customer worker framework. That is the thing that makes online exchanges and installments utilizing virtual monetary forms are so secure(Stanciu, 2017).

IoT and 5G together have incredible potential however which must be acknowledged by injecting the blockchain innovation. While 5G gives an availability cover to IoT gadgets and exchanges, blockchain handles security and guarantees the insurance of client and exchange information. Furthermore, truly, this trinity would be extremely solid as each part reinforces the other. The web of abilities would get an enormous lift with the presentation of blockchain. Recently, a Chinese specialist did the world's first 5G far off a medical procedure on the cerebrum of a patient who was a few miles away utilizing robots. A greater amount of this is relied upon to occur as we see significantly better medical care conveyance around the world. Security around there is, for evident reasons, fundamental and blockchain executed in medical care would make distant cycles considerably more secure(Zheng et al., 2018) .

Moreover, the foreseen 5G-persuaded monstrous expansion in appropriation of brilliant gadgets implies that the blockchain would have within reach, unquestionably more information than previously. This information is an extraordinary push towards globalization in innovation.

CONCLUSION

This chapter presented the Elaborative investigation of Blockchain Technology in intelligent networks. By its content structure, at first Black chain features, characteristics, integration aspects with 5G and potential impact and challenges have been analyzed and secondly Potential of 5G network using Black chain technology was taken in to account for the interpretation. Finally the Blockchain on Edge and Cloud Computing and Role of Blockchain in 5G-IoT also have been assessed and discussed in a detailed way by considering the points of the security aspects, decentralization and interoperability. From the studies it is inferred that as a conclusion, 5G, IoT and blockchain all need and effect each other to flourish in this globalized world. There is no halting 5G and IoT now, except to trust that architects and blockchain engineers will figure out how to address or go around the foreseen its adaptability issues so the three innovations can arrive at their brought together potential.

REFERENCES

Al-Jaroodi, J., & Mohamed, N. (2019). Blockchain in industries: A survey. *IEEE Access: Practical Innovations, Open Solutions*, 7, 36500–36515. doi:10.1109/ACCESS.2019.2903554

Alkadi, O., Moustafa, N., & Turnbull, B. (2020). A Review of Intrusion Detection and Blockchain Applications in the Cloud: Approaches Challenges and Solutions. *Access IEEE*, 8, 104893–104917. doi:10.1109/ACCESS.2020.2999715

Aste, T. D. M. T., Tasca, P., & Di Matteo, T. (2017). Blockchain Technologies: The Foreseeable Impact on Society and Industry. *Computer*, *50*(9), 18–28. doi:10.1109/MC.2017.3571064

Dinh, T. N., & Thai, M. T. (2018). AI and Blockchain: A Disruptive Integration. *Computer*, *51*(September), 48–53. doi:10.1109/MC.2018.3620971

Global Mobile Suppliers Association. (2015). *The Road to 5G: Drivers, applications, requirements and technical development*. Global Mobile Suppliers Association.

Gochhayat, S. P., Shetty, S., Mukkamala, R., Foytik, P., Kamhoua, G. A., & Njilla, L. (2020). Measuring Decentrality in Blockchain Based Systems. *Access IEEE*, 8, 178372–178390. doi:10.1109/ACCESS.2020.3026577

Gupta, Y., Shorey, R., Kulkarni, D., & Tew, J. (2018). The Applicability of Blockchain in the Internet of Things. *10th International Conference on Communication Systems & Networks (COMSNETS)*. 10.1109/COMSNETS.2018.8328273

Kaushik, A., Choudhary, A., Ektare, C., Thomas, D., & Akram, S. (2017). Blockchain – Literature Survey. *2nd IEEE International Conference On Recent Trends in Electronics Information & Communication Technology (RTEICT).* 10.1109/RTEICT.2017.8256979

Klessig, H., Ohmann, D., Reppas, A. I., Hatzikirou, H., Abedi, M., Simsek, M., & Fettweis, G. P. (2016). From immune cells to self-organizing ultra-dense small cell networks. *IEEE Journal on Selected Areas in Communications, 34*(4), 800–811. doi:10.1109/JSAC.2016.2544638

Litke, A., Anagnostopoulos, D., & Varvarigou, T. (2019, January). Blockchains for supply chain management: Architectural elements and challenges towards a global scale deployment. *Logistics, 3*(1), 5. doi:10.3390/logistics3010005

Liyanage, M., Ahmad, I., Abro, A. B., Gurtov, A., & Ylianttila, M. (2018). *A Comprehensive Guide to 5G Security.* John Wiley & Sons. doi:10.1002/9781119293071

Mafakheri, B., Subramanya, T., Goratti, L., & Riggio, R. (2018). Blockchainbased Infrastructure Sharing in 5G Small Cell Networks. *14th International Conference on Network and Service Management (CNSM).*

Mistry, I., Tanwar, S., Tyagi, S., & Kumar, N. (2020). Blockchain for 5Genabled IoT for Industrial Automation: A Systematic Review, Solutions, and Challenges. *Mechanical Systems and Signal Processing, 135*, 106382. doi:10.1016/j.ymssp.2019.106382

Naz, S., & Lee, S. U.-J. (2020). Why the new consensus mechanism is needed in blockchain technology? *Blockchain Computing and Applications (BCCA) Second International Conference on*, 92-99.

Peters, G., Panayi, E., & Chapelle, A. (2015, November). Trends in cryptocurrencies and blockchain technologies: A monetary theory and regulation perspective. *J. Financial Perspect., 3*(3), 1–25.

Popovski, Trillingsgaard, Simeone, & Durisi. (2018). 5G Wireless Network Slicing for eMBB, URLLC, and mMTC: A communication-theoretic view. *IEEE Access, 6*(55), 765–779.

Shafee, A. (2020). Botnets and their detection techniques. *Networks Computers and Communications (ISNCC) International Symposium on*, 1-6.

Stanciu, A. (2017). Blockchain based distributed control system for edge computing. In *2017 21st International Conference, on Control Systems and Computer Science (CSCS)*, (pp. 667–671). IEEE. 10.1109/CSCS.2017.102

Yang, R., Yu, F. R., Si, P., Yang, Z., & Zhang, Y. (2019). Integrated blockchain and edge computing systems: A survey, some research issues and challenges. *IEEE Communications Surveys and Tutorials, 21*(2), 1508–1532. doi:10.1109/COMST.2019.2894727

Zheng, Z., Xie, S., Dai, H.-N., Chen, X., & Wang, H. (2018). Blockchain challenges and opportunities: A survey. *International Journal of Web and Grid Services, 14*(4), 352–375. doi:10.1504/IJWGS.2018.095647

Zou, Y., Meng, T., Zhang, P., Zhang, W., & Li, H. (2020). Focus on Blockchain: A Comprehensive Survey on Academic and Application. *Access IEEE, 8*, 187182–187201. doi:10.1109/ACCESS.2020.3030491

Chapter 5
A Proposed Approach for Building a SARS–COV–2 Watch in the IoT Network

Maissa Daoud
University of Sfax, Tunisia

ABSTRACT

Considering the conditions that we are living in since 2020 and the cases of death caused by covid, all the researchers of the world have participated in defending humanity from this epidemic. Like all these people, the author has thought about what she cannot reduce but to specify the number of cases in an environment thanks to this project called "SARS-COV-2 watch," and this measures the temperature of the owner and also informs him in the case of someone close to him at a distance less than one meter who is infected. The proposed SARS-COV-2 watch design consists of a case to place all components, a metal cap to conduct heat into the main temperature sensor, an LCD screen to display the temperature data, and a button to activate the temperature conversion and display it on the LCD screen. In order to inform the watch wearer that there is someone around him with high temperature, the author integrated a vibrating module. This small vibrating motor is ideal for projects with haptic feedback.

INTRODUCTION

The Covid-19 crisis has upended our healthcare systems and forced most states to rethink how they operate. Faced with saturated hospitals and emergency departments in the midst of the health crisis, telemedicine has seen a sudden interest and small success (Chakkarwar, & Tamane, 2020; Mnaoui, Najoua, & Ouajji, 2020). Indeed, several months before the health crisis and the containment measures, consultations via telemedicine, i.e. an appointment with a doctor by videoconference, represented a very marginal percentage of medical consultations. Patients preferred to travel to their doctor's office even though remote medical consultations are reimbursed by the Health Insurance (Chen, 2021; Harris, 2020). However, the health crisis has completely changed the situation. Indeed, the containment measures, the recommendations of social distancing and the overloaded hospitals encouraged the French to

DOI: 10.4018/978-1-7998-8367-8.ch005

resort more and more to remote consultations to prevent the risks of contamination, to allow to target more quickly the patients "at risk" and to avoid the faster circulation of the virus. (Crisostomo, Balida, & Gustilo, 2020) Connected health devices such as watches, thermometers or glucose meters are not the only levers of action for connected medicine (Garg, & Dave, 2019; Hindrayani, Fakhruddin, Prismahardi Aji, & Safitri, 2020). In fact, some more infected countries have implemented additional technologies to help health services and patients fight the Coronavirus pandemic. For example, the city of Wuhan, the first Covid-19 cluster, has implemented connected robots to distribute medicines to infected patients, helping to limit the circulation of the virus in the territory (Gawade, & Joshi, 2020; Hameed, 2021; Muladi, et al., 2020).

New technologies related to medicine and health and their development can significantly improve patient management, monitoring and treatment of diseases (Gupta & Johari, 2019; Khant, & Patel 2021; Qjidaa, et al. 2020). The Internet of Things (IOT) is one of the most used technologies to solve the problem of distance between people existing in the same place (Miladinovic, & Schefer-Wenzl, 2018; Rahim, & Iqbal, 2020).

The IoT network is used to provide an object with connectivity to the Internet to allow the feedback of information. Different communication protocols are available on the market to do this. Not all of them have the same characteristics. For companies that are getting into IoT, choosing the most suitable communication network for their uses can thus become a Chinese puzzle. They have to take into account the network coverage, the battery life of the objects, the communication distance or the service cost. Connected objects allow for real-time and on-demand tracking and identification of tools, equipment and medications. Being able to have instant information about a patient can often be decisive. IOT applications allow the user to interact with others to maintain and build relationships. For example, connected objects could automatically trigger messages to our friends to let them know what we are doing and where we are. There are also some IOT systems allowing an operator or a user to report a malfunction. If it is interesting at the end of an airport service to ask a user his level of satisfaction, it is even more useful for the improvement of the service, to allow to signal a lack of soap, paper, or a problem of smell (Saini, 2019; Saini, Agarwal, Varshney, & Gupta, 2018; Soumya, Shanmugam, Saini, & Kumar, 2020; Kumari, & Saini, 2021).

It allows to connect several existing systems in spaced locations to exchange information and measurements or to execute orders (Thepade, & Jadhav, 2020; Yadav, & Vishwakarma, 2019). Based on existing connected systems, the researchers in the technology field noticed that sensors in connected watches could potentially reveal coronavirus contamination even before the first symptoms of Covid-19 are reported (Thepade, Chaudhari, Dindorkar, & Bang, 2020). It is largely the temperature sensor that indicates whether a rise in temperature is significant enough to indicate the presence of the virus (Varun, & Nagaraj, 2021; Vishwakarma, Upadhyaya, Kumari, & Mishra, 2019). For the proposed watch, I used a temperature sensor to measure the temperature of its wearer, a GPS module to detect high temperature people around the target, and a vibrator module to alert the target of a high temperature person near him.

In this chapter, a detailed approach will be presented to cite each step in the design of this proposed watch. Also, I will describe each of the connections between the above-mentioned components and the arduino micro card, as well as the codes and software used to realize this project.

DESCRIPTION OF THE PROPOSED SARS-COV-2 WATCH

The proposed SARS-COV-2 (Figure 1) watch design consists of a case to place all components, a system on chip, a metal cap to conduct heat into the main temperature sensor, an LCD screen to display the temperature data and a button to activate the temperature conversion and display it on the LCD screen.

Figure 1. SARS-COV-2 watch

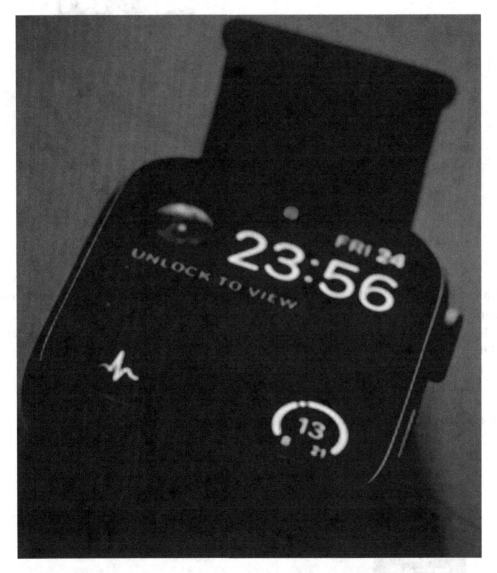

Choice of the System on Chip

In this project, we used an Arduino board to control the entire system process. It is a control unit based on the ATmega AVR microcontroller (Yamanoor, & Yamanoor, 2017; Parthornratt, Burapanonte, &

Gunjarueg, 2016). Arduino is an open-source hardware platform and very useful for project development. There are many types of Arduino boards like Arduino UNO, arduino mega, arduino pro mini, Lilypad etc. available on the market. The arduino micro card is my choice for this project. It is presented in Figure 2.

Figure 2. Arduino micro card

With a size of 1.8 x 4.8 cm, the Micro bears its name well and is one of the smallest microcontrollers on the market (Figure 3). At the other end of the spectrum, the arduino Mega 2560 card measures about 10.2 x 5.3 cm, which is about 6 x the size of the Micro. Somewhere in between these two extremes, you will find the Uno and its dimensions of 6.9 x 5.3 cm. The price of the Micro is usually around $19-25 while the Uno is around $20-23, and the Mega 2560 costs between $36 and $39.

Figure 3. Comparison with the existing Arduino UNO cards

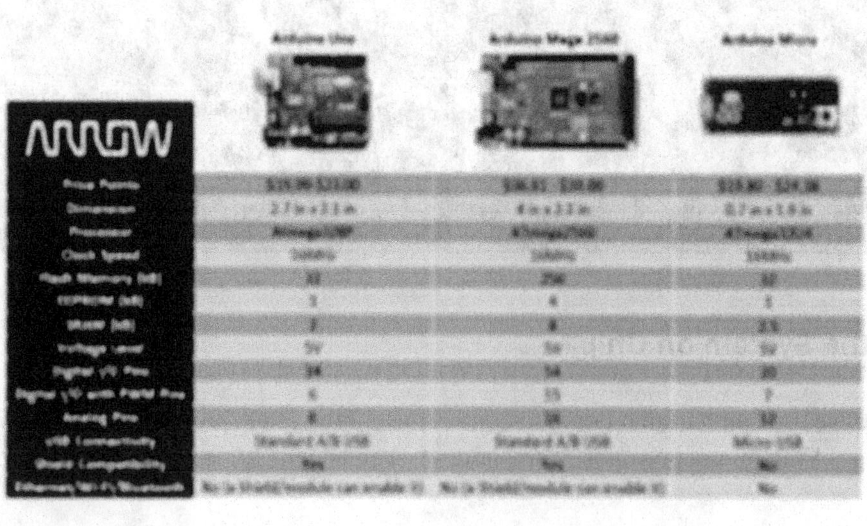

Choice of the LCD Screen

The role of the tactile display of the proposed watch is to display the temperature measurements captured by the LM35 sensor and processed by the arduino micro board. it also displays the phrase "keep the distance!" in case of detection of a person close to the wearer of the watch from a distance less than 1m. The Figure 4 show the tactile LCD screen module.

Figure 4. LCD screen module

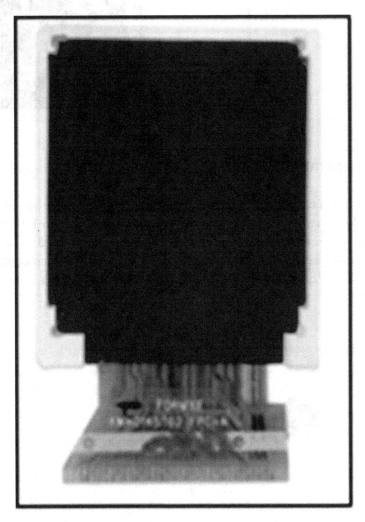

To connect the screen to the arduino board, you have to install the OLED screen libraries. First of all, we start by installing the Adafruit GFX library " and then the SSD1306.h library. The Connection of the LCD screen module with the Arduino uno card is presented in Figure 5.

Figure 5. Connection of the LCD screen module with the Arduino uno card

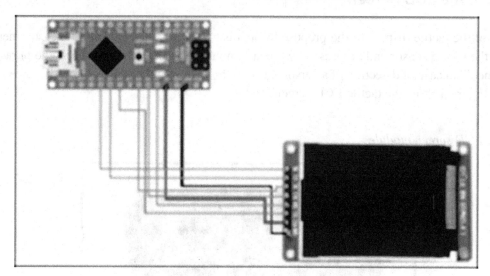

Choice of the Temperature Sensor

For temperature detection, I chose the LM35 sensor. It is a 3-pin temperature sensor that gives 1 degree Celsius at each 10 mVolt change. This sensor can detect a temperature up to 150 degrees Celsius. The first digital pin of the lm35 sensor is Vcc, the second is the output and the third is the ground. The LM35 is the simplest temperature sensor and can be easily interfaced with any microcontroller (Nasution, & Harahap, 2020; Liu, Ren, Zhang, & Lv, 2011). The LM35 sensor datasheet summary is displayed in Figure 6.

Figure 6. LM25 temperature sensor

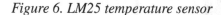

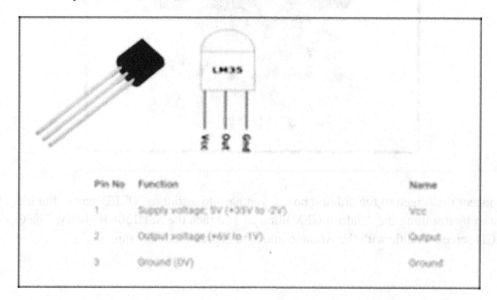

An LM35 temperature sensor is used to detect the ambient temperature, which gives a temperature of 1 degree for every 10 mV change at its output pin. You can easily check this with a voltmeter by connecting Vcc to pin 1 and ground to pin 3 and the output voltage to pin 2 of the LM35 sensor. For example, if the output voltage of the LM35 sensor is 250 m volts, it means that the temperature is about 25 degrees Celsius. The Connection of the LM35 temperature sensor with the Arduino uno card is shown in Figure 7.

The circuit diagram for a digital thermometer using Arduino and the LM35 temperature sensor is shown in the Figure 8. Make the connections carefully as shown in the diagram. Here, the 16x2 LCD unit is directly connected to arduino in 4-bit mode. The data pins of the LCD, namely RS, EN, D4, D5, D6, D7, are connected to arduino digital pin 7, 6, 5, 4, 3, 2. A temperature sensor LM35 is connected to arduino analog pin A0, which generates temperature of 1 degree Celsius at each output change of 10 mV at its output pin.

Figure 7. Connection of the LM35 temperature sensor with the Arduino uno card

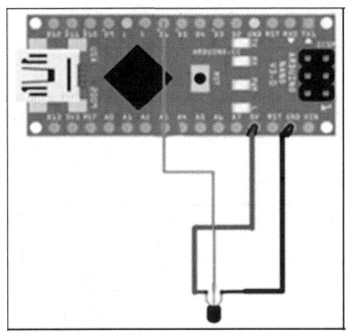

Figure 8. Connection of the LM35 temperature sensor and LCD screen module with the Arduino uno card

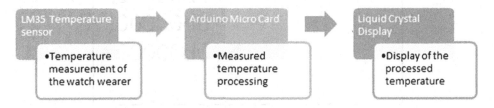

LM35 Arduino Code and Explanation

First, we include the library for the LCD unit, then we define the data and control pins for the LCD and the temperature sensor as shown in Figure 9.

Figure 9. Library of LCD module and declaration of the temperature sensor pin in the main code

```
#include<LiquidCrystal,h>
LiquidCrystal lcd(7,6,5,4,3,2);

#define sensor A0
```

After getting the analog value on the analog pin, we read this value using the analog read function and store this value in a variable. And then convert the temperature values. In this case, the degree symbol is created using the method of personalized character as presented in Figure 10.

Figure 10. Method of personalized character

```
byte degree[8] =
           {
               0b00011,
               0b00011,
               0b00000,
               0b00000,
               0b00000,
               0b00000,
               0b00000,
               0b00000
           };
```

The code of the connection of the temperature sensor and the OLED screen with the arduino board is presented in the following Figure.

Figure 11. Main code of the connection of the LCD module and the temperature sensor

The Human Detection System

For the detection of other people around the watch wearer, I have chosen the Nano GPS 2 Click module. It has the smallest GPS module with an integrated patch antenna. It is the smallest multi-constellation antenna module in the world allowing high performance in many applications. The Nano GPS module is displayed in Figure 12.

Figure 12. Nano GPS module

Despite its size, the Nano GPS 2 Click offers superior sensitivity and exceptional performance, with a first correction time (TTFF) of less than 1 second, high accuracy of less than 2.5 m and tracking sensitivity down to -165 dBm. An overview of the connection of the Nano GPS module with the Arduino uno card is presented in Figure 13.

Figure 13. An overview of the connection of the Nano GPS module with the Arduino uno card

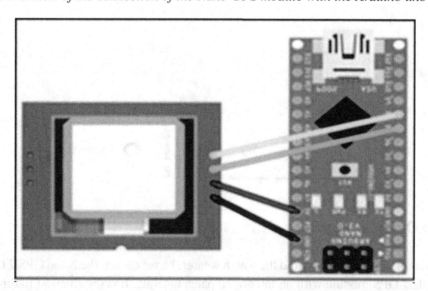

In order to inform the watch wearer that there is someone close to him at a distance less than one meter, I integrated a vibrating module. This small vibrating motor is ideal for projects with haptic feedback. Totally encapsulated in a metal disc, it will be easy to use and to embark. Two wedges allow to feed it and to manage the power of the vibration (blue for the negative and red for the positive). It works between 2V and 5V, the higher the voltage, the stronger the vibration will be. If you want to decrease the current to drive it directly with an Arduino pin, you can put in series a resistor from 100 ohm to 1 kOhm, but it is rather advisable to use a transistor. The Vibrating module is presented in Figure 14.

Figure 14. Vibrating module

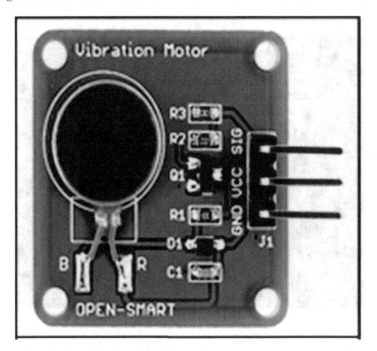

To realize the connection of the vibrating module with the arduino board; Connect the VCC pin of the vibrating module in the 3.3v pin, the SIG Pin of vibrating module in the D6 Pin and the Ground Pin of the vibrating module in the Ground Pin of the Arduino-Micro board. The Real Connection of the Vibrating module with the Arduino uno card is presented in Figure 15.

Figure 15. Connection of the Vibrating module with the Arduino uno card

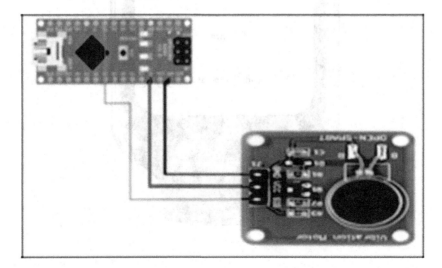

After the pinning of the two modules GPS and vibrator with the arduino board, it is necessary to test their performance, for this end we should upload the following code (Figure 16) in the arduino board.

Figure 16. Main code of the connection between the vibrating module, nano GPS module and the Arduino uno card

```
1    digitalWrite(VIBRATE_PIN, LOW);
2
3    const GPS = require('GPS');
4    Seriall.setup(9600,{rx:14 ,tx:15});
5    GPS.connect(Seriall, data-> {
6      print(data);
7      if (!GPS.rx.begin()) {
8        void vibrate() {
9          Serial.println("Vibrate");
10         digitalWrite(VIBRATE_PIN, HIGH);
11
12         delay(200);
13         digitalWrite(VIBRATE_PIN, LOW);
14         Serial.println("End Vibrate");
15
16       }
17     }
18       )
```

Figure 17. Display measurement when the distance is less than 1m, the distance is greater than 1m.

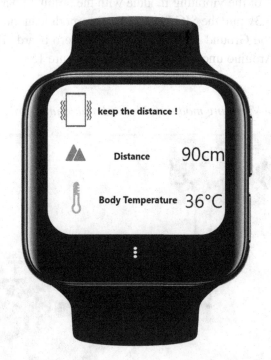

Figure 18. Display measurement when the distance is greater than 1m.

MEASUREMENT DISPLAY

The proposed watch displays all the time the temperature measurements measured by the LM35 sensor and the distance, between the wearer and another person close to him, measured by the Nano GPS module. If the distance between the proposed watch wearer and a person near him/her is less than 1m, the display of the watch will show "keep the distance!" as shown in Figure 17. otherwise, nothing will be displayed (Figure 18).

CONCLUSION

This chapter present an approach to realize a SARS-COV-2 watch. This one measure the body temperature of the owner of the proposed watch and the location of a person close to him, in an instantaneous way. It displays by the tactile screen module the measured temperature and the distance to a person near him. if the measured distance is less than one meter, the watch vibrates and displays the sentence "Keep the distance!".

FUTURE RESEARCH DIRECTIONS

As perspectives, we can add several options to the proposed watch, for example the measurement of the heartbeat and the measurement of oxygen in the blood if the wearer of the watch is a covid sufferer. We can also add the option "ask for help" if the wearer is in a severe situation such as dizziness or intensive tiredness.

REFERENCES

Chakkarwar, V., & Tamane, S. (2020). Social Media Analytics during Pandemic for Covid19 using Topic Modeling. *IEEE International Conference on Smart Innovations in Design, Environment, Management, Planning and Computing (ICSIDEMPC)*, 279-282. 10.1109/ICSIDEMPC49020.2020.9299617

Chen, D. (2021). All-round and Accurate Online Education Model amid COVID19. *IEEE/WIC/ACM International Joint Conference on Web Intelligence and Intelligent Agent Technology (WI-IAT)*, 713-717. 10.1109/WIIAT50758.2020.00109

Crisostomo, A. S. I., Balida, D. A. R., & Gustilo, R. C. (2020). K- means Clustering of Online Learning Profiles of Higher Education Teachers and Students Amid Covid19 Pandemic. *IEEE International Conference on Humanoid, Nanotechnology, Information Technology, Communication and Control, Environment, and Management (HNICEM)*, 1-5. 10.1109/HNICEM51456.2020.9400036

Garg, H., & Dave, M. (2019). Securing IoT Devices and SecurelyConnecting the Dots Using REST API and Middleware. *International Conference on Internet of Things: Smart Innovation and Usages (IoT-SIU)*, 1-6. 10.1109/IoT-SIU.2019.8777334

Gawade, P., & Joshi, P. S. (2020). Personification and Safety during pandemic of COVID19 using Machine Learning. *IEEE International Conference on Electronics, Communication and Aerospace Technology (ICECA)*, 1582-1587. 10.1109/ICECA49313.2020.9297555

Gupta, A. K., & Johari, R. (2019). IOT based Electrical Device Surveillance and Control System. *IEEE International Conference on Internet of Things: Smart Innovation and Usages (IoT-SIU)*, 1-5. 10.1109/IoT-SIU.2019.8777342

Hameed, K. (2021). An Approach to design Human Assisting Prototype Robot for providing Fast and hygienically secure environment to Clinical professionals in order to fight against COVID19 in Hospitals, *IEEE International IOT, Electronics and Mechatronics Conference (IEMTRONICS)*, 1-7. 10.1109/IEMTRONICS52119.2021.9422658

Harris, R. M. (2020). Data Warehousing and Decision Support System Effectiveness Demonstrated in Service Recovery During COVID19 Health Pandemic. *IEEE International Conference on Open Source Systems and Technologies (ICOSST)*, 1-5. 10.1109/ICOSST51357.2020.9333019

Hindrayani, K. M., Fahrudin, T. M., Prismahardi Aji, R., & Safitri, E. M. (2020). Indonesian Stock Price Prediction including Covid19 Era Using Decision Tree Regression. *IEEE International Seminar on Research of Information Technology and Intelligent Systems (ISRITI)*, 344-347. 10.1109/ISRITI51436.2020.9315484

Khant, S., & Patel, A. (2021). COVID19 Remote Engineering Education: Learning of an Embedded System with Practical Perspective. *IEEE International Conference on Innovative Practices in Technology and Management (ICIPTM)*, 15-19. 10.1109/ICIPTM52218.2021.9388360

Kumari, R., & Saini, K. (2021). Advanced Automobile Manufacturing: An Industry 4.0. *15th INDIACom*, 899-904. DOI: doi:10.1109/INDIACom51348.2021.00161

Liu, C., Ren, W., Zhang, B., & Lv, C. (2011). The application of soil temperature measurement by LM35 temperature sensors. *IEEE Proceedings of International Conference on Electronic & Mechanical Engineering and Information Technology*, 1825-1828. 10.1109/EMEIT.2011.6023459

Miladinovic, I., & Schefer-Wenzl, S. (2018). NFV enabled IoT architecture for an operating room environment. *IEEE World Forum on Internet of Things (WF-IoT)*, 98-102. 10.1109/WF-IoT.2018.8355128

Mnaoui, Y., Najoua, A., & Ouajji, H. (2020). Analyzing COVID19 Crisis in North Africa: Using Health Indicators. *IEEE International Conference on Electronics, Control, Optimization and Computer Science (ICECOCS)*, 1-5. 10.1109/ICECOCS50124.2020.9314612

Muladi. (2020). Development of The Personnel Monitoring System Using Mobile Application and Real-Time Database During the COVID19 Pandemic. *IEEE International Seminar on Research of Information Technology and Intelligent Systems (ISRITI)*, 371-376. 10.1109/ISRITI51436.2020.9315377

Nasution, T. H., & Harahap, L. A. (2020). Predict the Percentage Error of LM35 Temperature Sensor Readings using Simple Linear Regression Analysis. *IEEE International Conference on Electrical, Telecommunication and Computer Engineering (ELTICOM)*, 242-245. 10.1109/ELTICOM50775.2020.9230472

Parthornratt, T., Burapanonte, N., & Gunjarueg, W. (2016). People identification and counting system using raspberry Pi (AU-PiCC: Raspberry Pi customer counter). *IEEE International Conference on Electronics, Information, and Communications (ICEIC)*, 1-5. 10.1109/ELINFOCOM.2016.7563020

Qjidaa, M. (2020). Early detection of COVID19 by deep learning transfer Model for populations in isolated rural areas. *International Conference on Intelligent Systems and Computer Vision (ISCV)*, 1-5. 10.1109/ISCV49265.2020.9204099

Rahim, Z. A., & Iqbal, M. S. (2020). Malaysia Chapter on University Roles to Support the Frontliners during COVID19 Pandemic. *International Conference on Assistive and Rehabilitation Technologies (iCareTech)*, 5-9. 10.1109/iCareTech49914.2020.00013

Saini, K. (2019). Recent Advances and Future Research Directions in Edge Cloud Framework. *International Journal of Engineering and Advanced Technology*, 9(2), 439–444. Advance online publication. doi:10.35940/ijeat.B3090.129219

Saini, K., Agarwal, V., Varshney, A., & Gupta, A. (2018). E2EE For Data Security For Hybrid Cloud Services: A Novel Approach. *IEEE International Conference on Advances in Computing, Communication Control and Networking*, 340-347. 10.1109/ICACCCN.2018.8748782

Soumya, R. J., Shanmugam, R., Saini, K., & Kumar, S. (2020). Cloud Computing Tools: Inside Views and Analysis. *International Conference on Smart Sustainable Intelligent Computing and Applications*, 382-391.

Thepade, S. D., Chaudhari, P. R., Dindorkar, M. R., & Bang, S. V. (2020). Covid19 Identification using Machine Learning Classifiers with Histogram of Luminance Chroma Features of Chest X-ray images. *IEEE Bombay Section Signature Conference (IBSSC)*, 36-41. 10.1109/IBSSC51096.2020.9332160

Thepade, S. D., & Jadhav, K. (2020). Covid19 Identification from Chest X-Ray Images using Local Binary Patterns with assorted Machine Learning Classifiers. *IEEE Bombay Section Signature Conference (IBSSC)*, 46-51. 10.1109/IBSSC51096.2020.9332158

Varun, S. S., & Nagaraj, R. (2021). Covid19 tracking algorithm and conceptualization of an associated patient monitoring system. *International Conference on Trends in Electronics and Informatics (ICOEI)*, 1549-1553. 10.1109/ICOEI51242.2021.9452910

Vishwakarma, S. K., Upadhyaya, P., Kumari, B., & Mishra, A. K. (2019). Smart Energy Efficient Home Automation System Using IoT. *IEEE International Conference on Internet of Things: Smart Innovation and Usages (IoT-SIU)*, 1-4. 10.1109/IoT-SIU.2019.8777607

Yadav, P., & Vishwakarma, S. (2019). Application of Internet of Things and Big Data towards a Smart City. *IEEE International Conference On Internet of Things: Smart Innovation and Usages (IoT-SIU)*, 1-5. 10.1109/IoT-SIU.2018.8519920

Yamanoor, N. S., & Yamanoor, S. (2017). High quality, low cost education with the Raspberry Pi. *IEEE Global Humanitarian Technology Conference (GHTC)*, 1-5. 10.1109/GHTC.2017.8239274

Chapter 6
Blockchain Implementation Using Python

Saugata Dutta
Galgotias University, India

Kavita Saini
Galgotias University, India

ABSTRACT

This chapter covers an introductory overview of blockchain using Python code. This chapter will give a basic understanding of using Python codes in development of blockchain. The chapter throws light on beginner-level blockchain creation which will help in understanding developing an advance blockchain project using Python codes. This chapter covers basic building blocks which will help in creating various functions and methods to enhance the blockchain in terms of security. This will also help students in creating advanced level of Python program in creating better mining algorithms, better queue management, enhanced and secured transactions, consensus algorithm, wallets, and accounts.

PREFACE

The motivation for this writing is originally triggered for my passion into network security and data leak prevention. Due to innovation of latest technology and at the same time rise in breach of digital security, there are greater needs for a technology which has high rate of data security, tamper proof and data leak prevention. With a hope to achieve this success, blockchain technology claim to produce a same effect of data security, needless to say that using this technology, data tampering is immutable where the entire information is stored in blocks and hashed. The use of this technology is not restricted only to cryptocurrencies but being used in other industries like logistics, supply chain, healthcare and so on. This chapter discuss an introduction to blockchain using python code. The change in the outlook and market trends due to the usage of this technology which is future proof with high level of data security without the involvement of any central authority.

DOI: 10.4018/978-1-7998-8367-8.ch006

It is my interest to find out those latest trends in blockchain technology, future developments and a platform to use in various platforms. In reality, the success credit goes to everyone who was involved to make this writing a success.

INTRODUCTION TO BLOCKCHAIN

Blockchain can be said as a public ledger which is distributed across systems irrespective of geographical locations. The ledger is stored and updated across many systems across the world. The man behind the blockchain technology is Satoshi Nakamoto. The white paper of blockchain was submitted in 2009 where the technology exhibits peer to peer, decentralization, consensus algorithm and use of technology without the intervention of any third party. Initially the technology was exclusively meant for bitcoin but on later stage the functionality extended to every line of business with its attribute of high security, append only, decentralized network and most importantly does not require any third party approval (Jena et al., 2019). The usage of currency is not new and had been in vogue since medieval period. The common method of transactions during ancient times were barter method, as the settlements were done in exchange of items of same corresponding value like metals, precious stones etc. Advent of development, the transactions took a drastic change with introduction of coins and notes. The centralized authority is responsible for generation of these currencies and has full control over it. The government, regulatory body has a strong hold on these currencies and has full authority on circulation. These currencies are fixed and doesn't decline with period. During recent times, introduction of floating currencies made transactions easy and quite faster. However these transactions which involves, record keeping, identification and verification, transfers are centrally managed. Information technology has made life easy with users to execute transaction at any point in time but however the cyber threat is a challenge. The vulnerabilities are still there and has already made a footprint of losses globally. The transactions are centrally managed and non-visible. Data and transactions can be modified, tampered, spoofed with well orchestration of IT vulnerabilities and loop holes. In fact the data can be a threat from an internal traitor as well. There are various other factors and ways of violating critical data which is centrally managed. The Blockchain technology which during its manifestation stage introduced Bitcoin to start a parallel economy claim to solve these problems. Blockchain uses decentralized and distributed network along with distributed ledger which doesn't require any intervention of third party or centralized authority to approve or manage. Bitcoins currency is said to be the mother of cryptocurrencies and was the first currency introduced using the blockchain technology (Jena et al., 2020). The ledger copy of bitcoin is already shared among the nodes and each nodes holds the same copy of this distributed ledger. The sender uses private and public key to sign and encrypt the transaction to send to a receiver. These transactions can be authenticated with the public key by anyone but can only be deciphered with the sender's private key. A group of people known as "Miners" known for validating transactions and accumulate these transactions with other transactions into a block for which they are paid some rewards. This process is also known as mining. After the mining process, once the block is generated and the shared ledger is updated to all nodes, the receiver is said to have received the amount. These transactions are transparent and cannot be modified or tampered. Bitcoin, digital cryptocurrencies invention was an innovation, however the blockchain technology has evolved these years with different types of consumptions. Industries has started finding ways to use this secured technologies in various forms such that the data remains secured, un-tampered, decentralize and no control of any party. Ethereum, an open source cryptocurrency and blockchain platform, has progressed in use of smart contracts, in fact an inventor. The use of smart contracts has been accepted and used by mass and granted as an acceptable tools where one can create self-executable contracts on a blockchain platform. These contracts has no intervention or control of any parties(Kumari & Saini, 2019). Proof of stake discovery has made easy in creation of blocks. The validators are selected on the basis of more mining power or currency they hold to validate block transactions. This has few advantages over the traditional proof of work algorithm like saving on power consumptions which is the most common issues and more secured in terms of 51% attack. Proof of stake validators doesn't receives reward while they are given transaction fee. The next achievement in the field of blockchain technology is scaling. As the blockchain transactions increases there are performance degradation and storage related issues. In order to counter these issues various ways are being explored like sharding, sidechains, proof of stake, block compressions, hybrid consensus etc. (Kavita, 2018). Thus blockchain is an evolving technology which deals with the transactions in a secured way with the use of decentralized networking, hashing, and cryptography including reward mechanism. Blockchain can be said as a digital disruption and a new innovative foundation for researchers, scientist and engineers. There are few significant components of successful blockchain operations such as appropriate trustworthiness standards for individual transactions, robust cryptographic and hashing mechanism, system preparedness and reward mechanism to motivate miners (Saini et al., 2018).

BLOCKCHAIN DESIGN

Blockchain as the name says, it's a chain of blocks. Blockchain is a distributed ledger built from a chain of blocks. A block consists of multiple transactions and block header. Block header are used to differentiate blocks and helps in creating the chain.

A block header consists of

- **Timestamp**: The time stamp specifies the time of block creation
- **Version:** Specifies the version number of the blockchain
- **Merkle Root**: Blocks are connected with each other through hash values. Every block will have transactions. It can be one transactions or thousands and there should be a root hash of the block. This is achieved by Merkle tree. A tree will have root, branches and leaves. The end nodes are called leaves, the nodes in between roots and leaves are called branches and in the top is roots. Imagine having a block consists of 8 transactions. So calculating hash of each transactions will have eight hashes. So we will calculate hash value of first and second, third and fourth, fifth and sixth and so on till eighth. Here we will combine the hash of first, second, third and fourth and then fifth, sixth, seventh and eighth. Finally we will combine a hash of first to eighth which will be the root hash or merkle root.

Figure 1. Merkle root

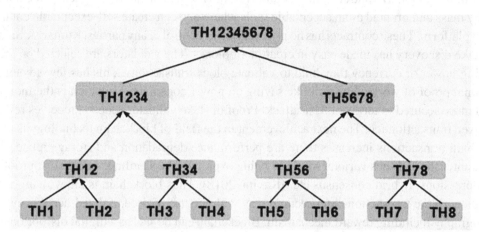

- **Difficulty Target:** It is a number which controls the time taken to add a new block to the chain
- **Nonce:** Nonce which is "number only used once" is added to the hashed block and when it is rehashed meets the criteria of difficulty target.
- **Previous Hash:** Hash of the previous block

These are some critical components of blockchain functioning.

    Genesis Block: The first block is known as genesis block. The previous hash value of genesis block is 0 as it is the first block.

Figure 2. Connected blocks in blockchain

```
tran_2 = Transaction(
    Joseph,
    lara.identity,
    4.0
)
tran_2.tx_signature()
transactions.append(tran_2)
tran_3 = Transaction(
    Betty,
    Sam.identity,
    8.0
)
tran_3.tx_signature()
transactions.append(tran_3)
```

Cryptography: It means secret writing. Here the sender encrypts the message with a public key. The encrypted data also known as cipher text cannot be read unless decrypted. The encrypted data is decrypted at receivers end with a private key.

Digital Signature: It is used for authentication and integrity sometimes. If a data is sent, it must be authenticated from the right user. Here the data is encrypted with the sender's private key and re-encrypted with receiver's public key. At the receiver end it is decrypted with receiver's private key and re-decrypted using sender's public key.

Hashing: Hash is a function which takes any random length of data and converts into a fixed length output. This is used to check the integrity of the data, if changed, the fixed output data value will change.

Consensus: As blockchain is a distributed ledger and each node will have a copy of this ledger. When a block is added, all nodes should come to consensus that all have the same copy of the blockchain. So with a consensus algorithm, nodes can agree on a particular state of blockchain. On the basis of consensus algorithm, it can be decided which node can add the block in the blockchain.

Proof of Work: The node which solves the mathematical puzzle, will add the block to the blockchain and in return will receive some rewards. The nodes are usually mining nodes. The mathematical puzzle requires lots of power and time and requires specific hardware to solve this puzzle. Once the puzzle is won, the block can be added to the chain. This whole procedure is known as Proof of work.

So to sum up, blockchain works in the principle of adding blocks in chain which are connected to each other through hashing mechanism. In blockchain, data cannot be manipulated and cannot be tampered with. The block consists of transactional data and block header which stores timestamp, version, merkle root, difficulty target, nonce and previous hash (Dutta & Saini, 2019). The reason it is said to be secured because if the data is modified, the hash value will change. So let's assume there are four blocks and data is modified on the second block, as soon as the same is done the hash value of the second block is changed which will affect the third block. The third block hash value needs to be regenerated which again affect the hash will value of the next block that is fourth. This continues to go on. As the number of blocks in the blockchain is humungous, it is nearly impractical to change all corresponding blocks because of proof of work, which requires a mathematical puzzle to be solved to generate a block and takes a certain period of time. Blockchain is also said to be a trustless technology in terms that there is no central control or authority. As an example a transaction in blockchain, A as sender and B as receiver. A sends some coins to B. The transaction to miners will be digital address of B, digital signature, public key and amount. Hence this transactions along with other transactions are mined. The difficulty target may be the number of 0's to be measured valid. A nonce number is added in the block and are tried randomly until the miners find a valid hash which satisfies the consensus criteria. The miner who wins this race is said to be successfully mined the block. The block is then added to the chain for which the miner is rewarded.

PYTHON LIBRARIES FOR BLOCKCHAIN

In order to create a blockchain code using python, there are many libraries that needs to be imported. Python libraries consists of literals, built in functions and exceptions. It is a library of modules which can be used in python code when one requires it. "json" is an inbuilt package in python to work with json data similarly "string" package consists constants, classes and various strings operations which will works once it is imported in the Python file. As an example, "crypto" and "crypto.Hash" packages can be used to sign and hash the transactions.

Figure 3. Python libraries

```
class User:
    def __init__(self):
        random-key = Crypto.Random.new().read
        self._private_key = RSA.generate(1024, random-key)
        self._public_key = self._private_key.publickey()
        self._auth_signer = PKCS1_v1_5.new(self._private_key)

    @property
    def identity(self):
        return
binascii.hexlify(self.public_key.exportKey(format='DER')).decode('ascii')
```

STARTING WITH BLOCK AND TRANSACTION CLASS

The blockchain is a chain which can be attributed as a list. The elements in the list are separated by comma. One can access elements of the list while the index starts with 0. The blocks will hold values and each block will be connected by hash. Blocks will store transaction values. The first block is the genesis block which has no previous hash. The block class will have attributes and will have couple of arguments. Self is always required to represent the instance of the class, index, previous hash of the block, transaction items of the block, nonce and time. Time function will provide the current time. The constructor body will have instance attributes for example the transactions instance attribute is created by calling self.transactions in the constructor and so on.

Figure 4. Block class

```
Joseph = User()
Lara = User()
Betty = User()
Sam = User()
```

In this chapter, a simple example of financial transaction between a sender and recipient is illustrated. A transaction class is created where an amount is sent to receivers address.

Figure 5. Transaction class

```
l_hash = ""

Lara = User()

tran_1 = Transaction (
    "Genesis",
    lara.identity,
    2.0
)


block-user0 = block-user()


block-user0.p_hash = None
Nonce = None

block-user0.transactions.append (tran_1)

d_value = hash (block-user0)
l_hash = d_value
```

Time variable is created to store the transaction time. Parameters like sender, receiver and amount are actually stored in the instance variables. Here we create a dictionary object which will have all these four variables such that it can be accessed from a single point.

Figure 6. Dictionary object

```
lst_val = []


def disp_bchain (self):
    print ("Qty of blocks: " + str(len (self)))
    for a in range (len(lst_val)):
        temp_bl = lst_val[a]
        print ("block # " + str(a))
        for transactions in temp_bl.transactions:
            display_transaction (transactions)
            print ('')
    print ('')
```

As genesis is the primary block, there is a check if sender is the creator of the first transaction in genesis block and some value is assigned in the identity field else the address of the sender is assigned. This dictionary object will be signed by the private key of the sender with built in SHA algorithm. A method named tx_signature is created.

Figure 7. Signature method

```
lst_value.append (user-block0)

disp_bchain(lst_val)
```

A transaction queue can be declared where transactions can be appended here. This is a global list variable.

Figure 8. Transaction Queue

```
block = block-user()
for j in range(5):
    prov_transaction = transactions[lst_transaction_index]

validate transaction

if valid

    block.transactions.append (prov_transaction)
    lst_transaction_index += 1


block.p_hash = l_hash
block.Nonce = mine (block, 2)
digest = hash (block)
lst_val.append (block)
l_hash = digest
```

An example of a digital crypto transaction is as follows, here the sender named John has transferred an amount of 2 coins to Ria. Here the public key of Ria is addressed. Tx_signature method is invoked to get the senders private key while it is signed by calling the method, once the transaction object is created.

Figure 9. Transaction example

```
def sha256(message):
    return hashlib.sha256(message.encode('ascii')).hexdigest()
```

More transactions can be added to the transactions queue. As an example below:

Figure 10. Transactions

```
def mine(MyMessage, difficulty=2):
    assert difficulty >= 2
    Myprefix = '11' * difficulty
    for j in range(1000):
        digest = sha256(str(hash(MyMessage)) + str(j))
        if digest.startswith(Myprefix):
           print ("after " + str(j) + " repeatations found nonce: "+ digest)
        return digest
```

USER CLASS

The user class generates public and private keys with the help of built in python RSA algorithm. The values are kept in the instance variable and should not be lost as it holds the key. The public key is utilized as an identity for users. A property named identity is declared which returns the public key as an HEX representation.

Multiple users can be created as follows:

Figure 11. User class

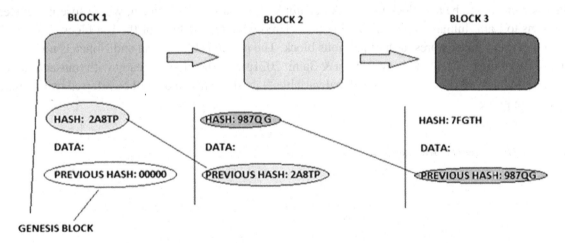

Figure 12. Users

```
from hashlib
import json
import random
import string
import binascii
import pylint
import numpy as np
import pandas as pd
import pylab as pl
import logging
import time
import collections
import requests
import Crypto
import Crypto.Random
from Crypto.Hash import SHA
from Crypto.PublicKey import RSA
from Crypto.Signature import PKCS1_v1_5
```

CREATING THE FIRST GENESIS TRANSACTION

Genesis block is the first block in the blockchain which does not contains any previous hash. A block class is created and be as "block-user0". An example of a transaction is taken, where Joseph transfers 2.0 coins to Lara. Initially a global variable is declared which is the hash of the last block, keeping in mind that every block stores hash of previous block. The previous block hash and Nonce is none in the first block of the blockchain always (Dutta & Saini, 2021a). As the block is ready with transaction, it is hashed and hash value is stored in the global variable "l_hash". This value will be referred by the miner for mining process.

Figure 13. First genesis transaction

```
class block-class:
    def __init__(self, myindex, transactions, timestamp, p_hash, nonce=0):
        self.myindex = index
        self.transactions = transactions
        self.timestamp = timestamp
        self.p_hash = previous_hash
        self.nonce = nonce
```

CREATING AND LISTING THE BLOCKCHAIN

A list variable is created to store the entire blockchain "lst_val". The entire contents of the blockchain can be displayed by creating a method called "disp_bchain". The contents will increase in due course of time, but considering as an example, this method list the number of blocks and the contents. A "for" loop is created for iteration and values are temporarily stored in the variable "temp_bl". All transactions are retrieved from iteration in "for" loop and display all transactions eventually.

Figure 14. Creating and displaying the blockchain

```
def __init__(self, sender, receiver, amount):
    self.sender = sender
    self.receiver = receiver
    self.amount = amount
    self.time = datetime.datetime.now()
```

ADDING THE BLOCKS TO THE CHAIN

Adding the block to the blockchain will use append to the list variable "lst_val". The genesis block is now attached in the chain and blockchain contents are displayed when the function "disp_bchain" is called.

Figure 15. Append the list variable

```
def dict_obj(self):
    if self.sender == "G-block":
        identity = "Genesis"
    else:
        identity = self.sender.identity

    return Dict({
        'sender': identity,
        'receiver': self.reciever,
        'amount': self.amount,
        'time' : self.time})
```

For the block class "block-user", an instance is created. Five transactions are selected. Miners validates and confirms transactions before it is added in the blockchain. This process holds true when the hash created by the sender equals to the hash calculated by miner using public key of sender. The index of the last transaction is increased such that the next miner can start with the next transaction to validate. Here in theis example five transactions are added, hashed and mined with difficulty level of 2. The block created is added to the blockchain and the global variable "l_hash" is re-initialize for next use.

Figure 16. Adding blocks to the blockchain

```
def tx_signature(self):
    private_key = self.sender._private_key
    auth_signer = PKCS1_v1_5.new(private_key)
    hash = SHA.new(str(self.dict_obj()).encode('utf8'))
    return binascii.hexlify(auth_signer.sign(hash)).decode('ascii')
```

MINERS AND MINING

Mining is a significant process in public blockchain. The validation and verification of transactions and adding those transactions in the block is done by miners (Dutta & Saini, 2021b). A digest is generated for proof of work in mining process.

Figure 17. SHA 256 hash

```
transactions = []
```

SHA 256 is a hash function which can take any inputs and produces a 256 bits output. If there is integrity of the data. This function takes message and produces hexadecimal digest output. One can develop own mining function like generate a hash of a message which can start with two "1s". The difficulty level specification relies on the number of "1s". If the difficulty level is 3 then the prefix of "1s" will be three e.g. "111", while if the difficult level is 2 then the prefix of "1s" will any change in the input, the output will change. This is also a one way process because one cannot generate the input from the output. SHA 256 is best suited for checking the two e.g. "11". In this example, difficulty level of 2 is specified which means the prefix should have two "1s".

Figure 18. Mining function

```
tran_1 = Transaction(
    John,
    Ria.identity,
    2.0
)

signature = trans_1.tx_signature()
```

Here the message and the difficulty levels are two parameters for mining and the difficulty level is greater than and equal to "2". The variable "j" is added with new numbers and added to the message and the digest value changes. If the digest value condition is satisfied, the loop will end returning the digest value.

SCOPE

Here in this chapter, an introductory overview of blockchain is covered using python code. This chapter will give you a basic understanding of using python codes in further development of a blockchain project. The chapter throws light on basic blockchain creation using python codes and will help you in developing advance blockchain development. You can add various other functions and methods to enhance the blockchain in terms of security. Using advanced level of python you can create better mining algorithms, better queue management, enhanced and secured transactions, consensus algorithm, wallets and accounts. This chapter doesn't include interface for clients, server implementation, mining interface, rewards distribution and other enhanced features to run a blockchain project and is beyond the scope of this chapter.

ACKNOWLEDGMENT

The success and final outcome of this chapter required a lot of guidance and assistance from many people and I am extremely privileged to have got this. All that I have done is only due to such supervision and assistance and I am extremely thankful to them.

REFERENCES

Dutta & Saini. (2019). Evolution of Blockchain Technology in Business Applications. *Journal of Emerging Technologies and Innovative Research, 6*(9), 240-244.

Dutta, S., & Saini, K. (2021a). Securing Data: A Study on Different Transform Domain Techniques. *WSEAS Transactions on Systems And Control, 16*. doi:10.37394/23203.2021.16.8

Dutta, S., & Saini, K. (2021b). Statistical Assessment of Hybrid Blockchain for SME Sector. *WSEAS Transactions on Systems And Control, 16*. doi:10.37394/23203.2021.16.6

Jena, Shanmugam, Dhanaraj, & Saini. (2019). Recent Advances and Future Research Directions in Edge Cloud Framework. *International Journal of Engineering and Advanced Technology, 9*(2). doi:10.35940/ijeat.B3090.129219

Jena, S. R., Shanmugam, R., Saini, K., & Kumar, S. (2020). Cloud Computing Tools: Inside Views and Analysis. *International Conference on Smart Sustainable Intelligent Computing and Applications under ICITETM2020*, 382-391.

Kavita. (2018). A Future's Dominant Technology Blockchain: Digital Transformation. *IEEE International Conference on Computing, Power and Communication Technologies 2018 (GUCON 2018)*. doi:10.1109/GUCON.2018.8675075

Kumari, K., & Saini, K. (2019). CFDD (CounterFeit Drug Detection) using Blockchain in the Pharmaceutical Industry. *International Journal of Engineering Research & Technology, 8*(12), 591-594.

Saini, K., Agarwal, V., Varshney, A., & Gupta, A. (2018). E2EE For Data Security For Hybrid Cloud Services: A Novel Approach. *IEEE International Conference on Advances in Computing, Communication Control and Networking (IEEE ICACCCN 2018)*. 10.1109/ICACCCN.2018.8748782

Chapter 7
An End–to–End Video Content Encryption Module for HLS Video Streaming

Kazim Rizvi
Vellore Institute of Technology, India

Bhavisha J. Dholakia
Vellore Institute of Technology, India

Aditya Kaushik
Vellore Institute of Technology, India

Aswani Kumar Cherukuri
https://orcid.org/0000-0001-8455-9108
Vellore Institute of Technology, India

Chandra Mouliswaran S.
Vellore Institute of Technology, India

ABSTRACT

For an individual or a small organization, protecting and securing content could be a new and challenging task. The existing options do not completely fulfill the demands for today's content consumption and security while providing a good customer experience. The authors came across this problem of content security as a small group while building an application and tried to find a simple solution to secure content for playback on Android, so that the end users would be able to stream seamlessly and without any hindrance caused due to the enhanced security. They explore the way of securing video content through AES and using HLS to enable streaming of those video files over the internet. At the client's end, they have used Google's exoplayer to decrypt the data and play it directly after authentication and authorization. They performed a comparative analysis of the current models with the given model of securing content. Overall, with the aim to create an end-to-end module, they show how all the elements interact and work together as a system to provide protection against external threats.

DOI: 10.4018/978-1-7998-8367-8.ch007

INTRODUCTION

Nowadays, the most popular type of content being consumed is videos. With around 1 billion hours of video content being watched from only YouTube, and based on the studies (https://www.bento4.com/documentation/mp42hls/) showing us that 32 percent of the total people consuming video content on a daily basis and 72 percent of the total videos coming from a video website or app, we can clearly state that the security of the content becomes a priority and in the near future, with the introduction of various social video applications such as tiktok, this demand is going to rise very high. In this kind of a situation, security is always an integral part. Small startups and individuals who cannot invest in building huge architectures need a simple solution to ensure the safety and security of the content in their applications.

One of the best ways of securing data is using cryptography to make it accessible to only those people who are authorized to do so. For this project, we explored various symmetric encryption algorithms based on their speed and efficiency and found that AES outperformed compare to all others in case of encryption as well as decryption. (Chakraborty, Dev & Naganur, 2015).

The comparative study between symmetric and asymmetric encryption provides us the details about the difference between the two types of algorithms on the basis of speed, complexity, nature, vulnerabilities etc. (Kumar, Munjal & Sharma, 2011; Maqsood, Ahmed, Ali & Shah, 2017). In terms of security, speed, effectiveness and possible attacks the comparison between symmetric algorithms, Princy (2015) have showed good results for blowfish and AES. After analysis of these studies we concluded that, in this case, AES would be the right algorithm for the encryption and decryption of huge files because of the lesser decryption time which eventually would result in a better user experience while providing security at the same time.

HLS stands for HTTP Live streaming protocol. It has been developed by Apple (https://developer.apple.com/streaming/) and was released in 2009. HLS protocol divides the video content into chunks of small videos that are further streamed over HTTP. One of the main features of HTTP streaming protocols like HLS and DASH is adaptive bitrate streaming which enables the user to stream at different bitrates depending on the client's bandwidth (Jain, Shrivastava & Moghe, 2020). They allow multiple types of content consumption methods such as VOD and Live. Additional features of the HTTP streaming protocols include switching streams, ad insertion and variable segmentation (Jugović & Banduka, 2017). The HLS works by downloading the master playlist once and then fetching the adapted streams. The delay between the client and server during an HLS live stream can be optimized using open source software such as FFmpeg (Kuchta & Miklošík, 2017). For the conversion of simple mp4, mpeg, etc video files to multiple segmented streams of .ts files and a manifest.m3u8 file, we can use libraries like Bento and FFmpeg (https://www.bento4.com/documentation/mp42hls/).

DRM (Digital Rights Management) is an approach to securing digital content and preventing unauthorized access. The basic need for a model of DRM includes encryption which provides the supplier to put constraints on the consumption of data (Mushtaq et al., 2017).The architecture of DRM involves a DRM server in between the client and the publisher which acts as a medium for authentication and sharing data between the two parties (Oyman & Singh, 2012). The comparison of multiple DRMs allows us to check their support on various client platforms and the type of content they deliver (Princy, 2015). The DRM model can be used for multiple applications too, such as in the healthcare industry, hence allowing our architecture to have a wide range of possible use cases in the real world (Sheppard, Safavi-Naini & Jafari, 2009).

Exoplayer is an extensive and multipurpose library used in android devices for video playback and streaming. It is developed by google and is expanding its support for other platforms such as flutter, etc. The exoplayer library can be used for the implementation of HTTP streaming protocols such as HLS and DASH including the adaptive bitrate streaming (Singh, 2013). This project implements the exoplayer library in android.

With the combination of HLS and AES-128 we have proposed this system to ensure security and a better user experience (Sodagar, 2011). However, AES can be tweaked a bit to provide a better security which can be done as a future work.

Table 1. Analysis of the literature.

S. No.	Title	Author	Year	Abstract
1.	Cooperative Server-Client HTTP Adaptive Streaming System for Live Video Streaming (Han, Go, Noh & Song, 2019).	Sangwook Han, Yunmin Go, Hyunmin Noh and Hwangjun Song.	2019	The authors proposed an agreeable server–client HTTP versatile streaming framework that can give great video to clients utilizing a live video web-based feature. To accomplish this, the server adaptively signifies the section encoding bitrates dependent on the k-means clustering technique for the assessed data transmission of the clients. The client demands a fragment from the server by thinking about the assessed transmission capacity, the video quality change, and the cradled playback time. They directed a reenactment to check the presentation of the proposed DASH framework. The reproduction results demonstrated that the proposed framework can give excellent video higher transmission capacity usage and stable video quality contrasted with the current DASH framework.
2.	User Friendly Digital Rights Management System Based on Smart Cards (Lee & Lee, 2009).	Narn-Yih Lee and Tzu-Yi Lee	2009	The creators improve the convention proposed by Sun et al's. DRM framework dependent on the smart card. The strategy utilizes diverse encryption keys to give protection and security. Purchasers can utilize their own keen cards openly on any agreeable physical gadget. Each advanced substance can be played in both on-line and disconnected situations. Besides, it makes the buyer play similar advanced substance on agreeable gadgets without paying at least multiple times. Subsequently, the proposed framework is very appealing and easy to use.
3.	A Digital Rights Management Model for Healthcare (Sheppard, Safavi-Naini & Jafari, 2009).	Nicholas Paul Sheppard, Reihaneh Safavi-Naini and Mohammad Jafari	2009	Digital rights management can be joined with thoughts from electronic assent and work process based admittance control to authorize security strategies that consolidate the necessities of medical care specialists with the wants of patients. Digital rights management broadens conventional access control frameworks with assurance that perseveres all through incorporated information bases, singular medical services offices, and different associations that have a need to get to medical services data. The medical services can be transformed if we are able to use the DRM in this field.

Continued on the following page

Table 1. Continued

S. No.	Title	Author	Year	Abstract
4.	From AES-128 to AES-192 and AES-256, How to Adapt Differential Fault Analysis Attacks on Key Expansion (Floissac & L'Hyver, 2011)	No´emie Floissac and Yann L'Hyver	2011	Through this paper, authors consider variation of DFA assault on AES-128 to the variations AES192 and AES-256. They recognize two fundamental parts in the variation: the first comprises in broadening the first assault and the subsequent one in recreating this assault on a front round. The variation of the DFA on Key Expansion with this technique is more mind boggling than the DFA on state and each assault must be considered as a particular case. For this sort of DFA, they propose three principle issues to be understood to acquire enough round key bytes so as to uncover the underlying key. On account of the C. H. Kim and J. Quisquater's assault, they prevail with regards to adjusting the first assault by utilizing two explicit stunts. Their transformation requires 16 couples for both 192-piece and 256-piece keys variations relating to the twofold of AES-128 number of required couples.
5.	Strengthening digital rights management using a new driver-hidden rootkit (Tsaur, 2012).	Woei-Jiunn Tsaur	2012	In this article, researchers propose another driver-covered up rootkit for reinforcing the DRM in securing against the illicit appropriation and utilization of copyrighted digital sight and sound substance. The proposed new driver-covered up rootkit with five tricks dependent on DKOM has effectively evaded the notable rootkit finders, and hence can be utilized to keep unapproved clients from eliminating the rootkit of disguising the digital right management programming by utilizing hostile to rootkit devices. The examination is significant for expanding the security of the DRM programming, and can be an incredible motivation to DRM programming producers to viably improve the current strategies of ensuring against the illicit circulation and utilization of copyrighted digital mixed media content. Besides, this examination additionally rouses safeguards to viably strengthen the genuine uses by the covertness stunts of the proposed modern rootkit.
6.	An Implementation of the AES cipher using HLS (Meurer, Mück & Fröhlich, 2013)	Rodrigo Schmitt Meurer, Tiago Rogério Mück and Antônio Augusto Fröhlich	2013	In this paper, the authors have investigated diverse hardware executions of the AES utilizing HLS. They built up an elite programming usage that necessary just little change to be effectively incorporated to hardware. By investigating various HLS mandates and memory apportioning advancements they lessened the zone involved by the plan while additionally diminishing the quantity of cycles important to scramble a square. In spite of empowering the quick plan space investigation of hardware miniature models, the HLS cycle required adjustments on the source code to produce effective hardware. This yields in any event two distinctive base AES usage: one focusing on programming, and one focusing on hardware. Considering a situation wherein the AES could be actualized as hardware or programming, keeping up two unique usages for a similar segment can be blunder inclined and lead to useful findings.

Continued on the following page

Table 1. Continued

S. No.	Title	Author	Year	Abstract
7.	Digital rights management with ABAC implementation to improve enterprise document protection (BudimanBadarsyah & Rosmansyah, 2014)	BudimanBadarsyah and Yusep Rosmansyah	2014	DRM is one of the interesting issues in information security today that can give ideal insurance from robbery of licensed property in the digital media content. Through seclusion of the 4 pillars of DRM, we can alter as per the necessities of the association. And with an end goal to improve execution, particularly as far as the dispersion of archives/information/data, an open ecological association to all partners in an association can give adequacy in dynamic in a brief timeframe. At that point an entrance control that bolsters the receptiveness of information/data without eliminating the security turns into a significant achievement key that cannot be dodged. Expected with the execution of ABAC in big business DRM, clients can all the more effectively perform information conveyance both in the formal and arranged with simpler, open and safer way.
8.	AES Implementation for RFID Tags: The Hardware and Software Approaches (Hongsongkiat & Chongstitvatana, 2014)	Thanapol Hongsongkiat and Prabhas Chongstitvatana	2014	The two frequency ranges in which AES encryption is generally utilized are low frequency range (LF, 120-150 kHz) and high frequency range (HF, 13.56 MHz). These two applications have various requirements as far as encryption time. The LF applications expect encryption to complete inside a couple hundred RF cycles, In HF applications, AES preparing time can be up to a few thousand RF cycles. The product AES program is executed dependent on our exclusive instruction set. The asset use of the program can fit in the microcontroller. The preparing time additionally meet our determination for high-frequency RFID applications. Two strategies to accelerate the microcontroller preparing time are additionally proposed.
9.	Enhancing AES algorithm with arithmetic coding (Mukesh, Pandya & Pathak, 2013).	Patel Sanket Mukesh, Morli S Pandya and Shreyas Pathak	2013	This article helps us to understand how AES can be strengthened. The input data used in the paper is either 128 or 256 bits in AES. By using MATLAB the sequence is encoded, encrypted, decrypted and decoded sequentially. Before encryption compression of data has been done by arithmetic coding in MATLAB. Error detection and correction capabilities are proved to be high. This paper has high future improvements in the field of network security and shows much promise. This particular strategy can be used for multiple other protocols and much more efficient compressing techniques can be used before encryption.
10.	DES and AES performance evaluation (Bhat, Ali & Gupta, 2015).	Bawna Bhat, Abdul Wahid Ali and Apurva Gupta.	2015	Nowadays utilization of digital data trade is expanding step by step in every field. Information security plays very significant job in putting away and sending the data. At the point when we send a mixed media data, for example, sound, video, pictures and so forth over the system, cryptography gives security. In cryptography, we encode data before sending it and decipher it on accepting, for this reason, we utilize numerous cryptographic calculations. AES and DES are most usually utilized cryptographic calculations. AES gives the encryption to make sure about the data before the transmission and DES additionally gives security as AES. In this paper we talked about AES and DES and their correlation utilizing MATLAB programming. We think about their outcome based on avalanche effect, re-enactment time and memory required by AES and DES. As compared to DES, AES provides a better security, even though it utilizes much more time when it comes to computation.

Continued on the following page

Table 1. Continued

S. No.	Title	Author	Year	Abstract
11.	Automated monitoring of HTTP live streaming QoE factors on Android STB (Kovacevic, Kovacevic, Stefanovic & Novak, 2015)	Marko Kovacevic, Branimir Kovacevic, Dejan Stefanovic, Sebastian Novak	2015	This paper proposes a framework for automated monitoring of elements that impact Quality of Experience of media player on Android STB. Media player uses HTTP live web based convention where the video is isolated into little portions (chunks) and encoded in different quality levels (portrayals). In light of the organization conditions media player application chooses which video fragments to download, causing exchanging between the diverse video quality levels. These quality switches, along with elements, for example, introductory postponement, video slowing down, synchronization of sound and video, sway the end-client Quality of Experience. The framework introduced in this paper is planned for automated monitoring of these components, so as to help content suppliers to confine reasons for low QoE and to fix them simpler. Proposed framework presents an expansion of the framework for automated discovery testing of Android STBs by including modules for estimating and identification of variables that impact HLS, for example, recurrence of changing video quality levels, playback introductory deferral, video slowing down, outline drops, sound/video synchronization. Framework encourages content suppliers to confine reasons for low QoE and to fix them simpler.
12.	Adaptive bitrate transcoding for power efficient video streaming in mobile devices (Hemalatha, Yadav & Ramasubramanian, 2015)	K. Hemalatha, Praveen Kumar Yadav and N. Ramasubramanian	2015	Power consumption by video application relies upon factors like organization load, signal quality, data transfer capacity and it tends to be improved through heuristics-based streaming. The work introduced here adventures versatile bitrate spilling to decide the ideal bitrate for accessible transfer speed. The determination of ideal bitrate guarantees quality conveyance of video just as the ideal power consumption of the gadget. Moving Picture Expert Group - Dynamic Adaptive Streaming over HTTP (MPEG-DASH) has been utilized for executing the exchanging between the bitrates. The fifteen bitrates chose for encoding are nearer to the mean worth which is accessible for streaming. The methodology has been tried on an Android based tablet more than thirty recordings to check the reliance of the variables on one another. This is the significant way to deal with set up a connection among bitrate and power consumption for video web based. The outcome acquired shows a 14 level of power-sharing with least buffering and great nature of administration.
13.	Digital Signature Security in Data Communication (Rahim et. al., 2018).	Rahim et. al.	2018	Authenticity of access in very information are very important in the current era of Internet-based technology, there are many ways to secure information from irresponsible parties with various security attacks, some of technique can use for defend attack from irresponsible parties are using steganography, cryptography or also use digital signatures. Digital signatures could be one of solution where the authenticity of the message will be verified to prove that the received message is the original message without any change, Ong-Schnorr-Shamir is the algorithm are used in this research and the experiment are perform on the digital signature scheme and the hidden channel scheme.

Continued on the following page

Table 1. Continued

S. No.	Title	Author	Year	Abstract
14.	An AES Cryptosystem For Small Scale Network (Arom-oon, 2017)	Ukrit Arom-oon	2017	This paper was finished with the usage of the ECB-AES calculation with 128-bit, 192-bit and 256-bit keys running on Free RTOS. The Free RTOS was utilized for managing tasks and resources in the time imperatives. Plaintexts was encoded and then unraveled to the first plaintexts. The encryption productivity was tested dependent on UAV messages, and the outcomes were demonstrated that the MCU can handle all messages without loss. The deferrals and throughput for cryptosystem were tested.
15.	Secure Implementation for Video Streams Based on Fully and Permutation Encryption Techniques (Elshamy et al., 2017)	Ahmed M. Elshamy, Aziza I. Hussein, Hesham F. A. Hamed, Hamdy M. Kelash, M. A. Abdelghany and Ahmad Q. Alhamad	2017	This article discusses a video stream encryption method based on Henon Chaotic Map and Optical phase modulation. This process is carried by splitting the video into frames and converting the color 3D images to grayscale 2D and provides good result in encryption quality metrics.
16.	Secure H.264 Video Coding Using AES/CFB/PKCS5 Padding Encryption on Various Video Frames (I, P, B) (Adiguna, 2016)	Tahta Adiguna	2016	This paper discusses the process of encrypting H.264 video coding along with comparing different algorithms for the purpose of encryption. The idea discussed is to encrypt various video frames (I, P, B). It uses the NAL (Network Abstraction Layer) unit during the encryption of I, P and B frames of the video.
17.	Look Ahead: A DASH Adaptation Algorithm (Belda, De Fez, Arce & Guerri, 2018)	Román Belda, Ismael De Fez, Pau Arce and Juan Carlos Guerri	2018	This article has demonstrated that the immediate bitrate variability of video substance is a key factor for DASH variation calculations. Indeed, even in consistent bandwidth conditions, which would give enough bandwidth to a un-interrupting playback at the normal video bitrate, not considering this data about momentary video fragment bitrate can prompt slows down during the video playback. The paper has introduced a calculation called Look Ahead which considers the fluctuation of the bitrate to compute the best portrayal level so as to evade interferences. Results demonstrate that both the number and term of video playback slows down (rebuffering) are profoundly diminished, contrasted with the versatile calculation utilized by ExoPlayer and the Müller and SARA calculations, to the detriment of somewhat diminishing the normal video quality.
18.	Accelerating the AES Algorithm using OpenCL (Sanida, Sideris & Dasygenis, 2020)	Theodora Sanida, Argyrios Sideris and Minas Dasygenis	2020	Cryptography plays a significant function in every field these days as we have to secure a wide range of data, be it literary or media. With the expansion in the size of the document/content the general encryption measure requires a ton of assets so the general time taken is obliged inside as far as possible. For this reason, this paper assesses the distinction in the proficiency of scrambling information utilizing CPU versus GPU. Since significantly different assignments today are being performed by the GPUs, for example, cryptocurrency mining, video/picture handling, and so forth, this paper attempts to implement the same for encryption and decryption
19.	A robust computational DRM framework for protecting multimedia contents using AES and ECC (Hassan, Tahoun & ElTaweel, 2020).	Heba El-Rahman Hassan, Mohamed Tahoun and Gh.S. ElTaweel	2020	The article discusses the use of AES-256 for the encryption and decryption of multimedia content and ECC-256 for the encryption and decryption of shared keys to create a DRM framework to guarantee confidentiality, authentication, data integrity and non-repudiation. The architecture is based on a cloud server and takes the advantage of cloud computing to build an end to end solution. The result system proposes high performance in terms of protecting author's rights, ownership of the content and to prevent illegal activities.

Continued on the following page

Table 1. Continued

S. No.	Title	Author	Year	Abstract
20.	Image Encryption Based on AES and RSA Algorithms (Alsaffar et. al., 2020)	Alsaffar, Dalia Mubarak, Atheer Sultan Almutiri, Bashaier Alqahtani, Rahaf Mohammed Alamri, Hanan Fahhad Alqahtani, Nada Nasser Alqahtani, and Azza A. Ali.	2020	This investigation in this paper expects to do a comparison between Advanced Encryption Standard (AES) and Rivest-Shamir-Adleman (RSA) encryption calculations in image encryption utilizing MATLAB. The examination is done in the terms of testing image encryption quality for every calculation. Along with this, dissecting the histogram and connection results are also examined. The outcomes demonstrated that AES calculation has a superior image encryption quality with more convergent segments in the histogram. Besides, AES calculation connection coefficient will in general be nearer to the zero, in this manner a more grounded relationship.

BACKGROUND

The background talks about the ways and the mediums which inspired us to take up this topic. Here, we have discussed the literature survey, which enables us to get in depth information about the already existing papers and how the existing research has been going on in the domain of exoplayer, HTTP Adaptive streaming along with using various other ways which ensure security.

We have also talked about problem definition and contributions of the work in the same section.

With this detailed literature analysis, we formulate the problem as encrypting Video content using AES-128 along with conversion to HLS format and streaming encrypted data through a server for secured live decryption and playback on the client device using Exoplayer. The literary sources utilized for the literature review have helped us understand the existing frameworks and models for video streaming. With this in mind, we have done critical analysis of these models and understood their downsides. Hence, we have proposed a new model which not only provides security, but also can be utilized to give flexibility to our model.

SOLUTIONS AND RECOMMENDATIONS

Proposed Model

Detailed Architecture

We are trying to replace the current video streaming method with an AES-128 encrypted video streaming method that will provide security and authentication to copyright videos on websites, apps, etc., and will prevent them from misuse/piracy. We are trying to achieve that by creating an HLS encrypted video and then sharing it over a server which will then be decrypted and played live on client's device.

Figure 1. Phase 1 - Encryption and conversion to HLS

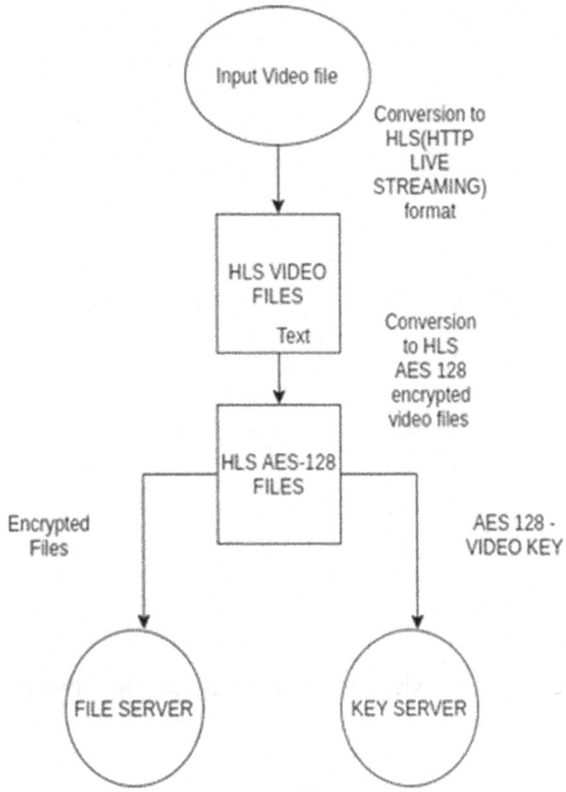

Encrypt the Videos

Figure 1 depicts the first phase of the architecture which is converting the video into AES-128 encrypted HLS files. The process starts with first converting the files into HLS and then encrypting them using a 128 bit randomly generated key. The next step is to save the encryption key to the KEY server and the encrypted file to the FILE server. This key will be further used to decrypt the videos in the client's device.

Decrypt and Playback

Figure 2 depicts the second phase of the implementation which consists of retrieving the data on the client's device and playing the encrypted videos. In this situation, both the client and a server already possess a shared key called USER KEY. The above depicted process can be divided into the following steps:

1. The user requests for the video file to be played on the client's device
2. The client device requests the File server for the encrypted data
3. The File server responds with the requested data
4. The client requests the Key server to obtain the key for the particular video file
5. The Key server encrypts the VIDEO KEY using the USER KEY, using AES, to share it over the network safely, and sends it to the client
6. The client receives the data and decrypts it using the same USER KEY to obtain the VIDEO KEY
7. The final VIDEO KEY is used to play the encrypted video files

Figure 2. Phase 2 – Retrieving the key and decrypting the file

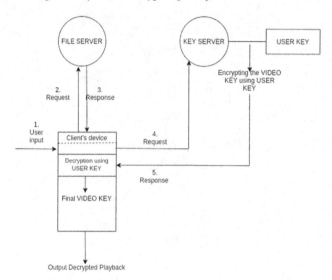

FUNCTIONALITY

The implementation of the complete model can again be divided into two parts:

Server Side

The first step is to convert the video into HLS and encrypt them. For this process, we can use open source software such as FFmpeg or Bento. It takes a video as an input and outputs HLS converted videos containing the manifest m3u8 file. We can also configure it to encrypt the input file at the same time.

To encrypt and convert the input file to HLS using bento we use the following command:

```
mp4hls -o. /output --encryption-key = {16 char hexadecimal key} ./input.mp4
```

16 characters of hexadecimal = 32 bytes = 256 bits

Client Side

The implementation of the client's end in this implementation requires the creation of an android application. Exoplayer is a video player library created by Google and is used in this project for the playback of videos. It is a Java based library and uses the Cipher class of Java to perform encryption decryption operations on the segmented file. It has a wide support of video codecs and types and can be configured to decrypt the videos and play them in real time.

Figure 3. Client side implementation (Exoplayer)

The main code to set up the exoplayer is shown in Figure III. It requires two additional custom classes to be built to a) redirect custom requests to the servers b) retrieve the file data through HTTP that are implemented as CustomDataSourceFactory.java and DefaultHttpDataSource.java.

Exoplayer comes with in-built classes for HLS based on the Cipher class of java that we have used for this implementation.

EXPERIMENTAL RESULTS

Server Side

Figure 4 depicts the input video which goes through the process of conversion and encryption.

As shown in Figure 5, segmented output files generated after encryption and conversion to HLS. These files are segmented into chunks of 10 second videos and then encrypted. This feature of HLS allows smooth streaming over the internet and reduces lag. The manifest file is stream.m3u8 and is the one which is passed to the player. The manifest file contains the information about the chunked files and along with their order of playback.

Figure 4. Input video

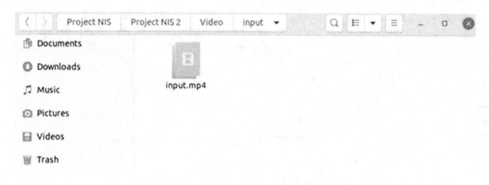

Figure 5. Encrypted and segmented HLS output files

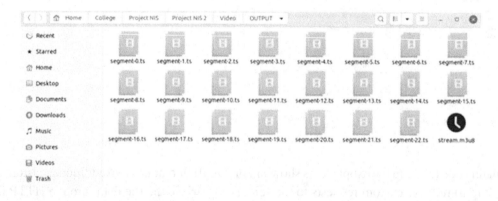

Client Side

Figure 6. Decryption of incoming data

The Android app in Figure 6, with the help of the exoplayer library, decrypts the incoming data from the File server using the VIDEO KEY and plays it to the user in real time. The user experiences no lag in terms of usage as the video is decrypted during playback.

ANALYSIS

Comparison with the Literature

Currently we have a number of solutions for the purpose of securing digital content. These solutions fall in one of the following categories that:

1. Provide good user experience but poor security
2. Provide good security but poor user experience
3. Have restrictions in the architecture/system
4. Are complicated or difficult to implement

Our solution provides both, a way to have security and a good user experience. It becomes more suitable than the previous solutions for the current businesses needs and hence becomes a possible simple solution for today's requirements. The model is simple to understand and implement, hence it can be incorporated into different business solutions as well.

The security of the model is dependent on the security of the AES-128 algorithm as we have used it while encrypting the files as well as while sharing the keys. When it comes to the user experience, it is evident from the demonstration video that there isn't any lag or delay during the playback.

Comparison with the Current Industry Standard

The current standard for protecting Digital Content is known as DRM which stands for Digital Rights Management. It tries to control the use, modification and sharing of copyright content. It can include the usage of technologies such as encryption, authentication, regional lockout, etc.

Currently most of the big companies like Netflix, Prime Video, etc use proprietary DRMs that use licensing servers in between to authorize users to be able to watch content. For example, some proprietary DRMs are Widevine by Google, FairPlay by Apple and PlayReady by Microsoft. The architecture of DRM uses certification that is needed to be installed in the device by the manufacturer. For example, all the Android devices require to have Google's widevine L1 certificate to be able play HD and above quality content. Devices not possessing this certificate would not be able to play high quality videos.

Our solution is platform independent and flexible and simple to implement as compared to the existing ones. It provides the flexibility to have complete control on the authorization, usage and other features of the architecture. It does not restrict the quality of the content on any device but allows the businesses to decide that.

CONCLUSION

As the world becomes completely digital, it is extremely crucial to make our systems more secure so that we can prevent malicious access of our private content. In such a scenario, it is hence the need of an hour to secure our digital content and make the already existing frameworks better and more flexible as the time progresses. Flexibility also becomes an important factor because the change in advancement of technology is increasing for the better every day; hence we need to come up with solutions which are flexible so that it can be used on all the devices, be it older or newer ones. Therefore, this particular framework can prove to be just the right one at this time. However, DRM, which is utilized by big companies like Amazon and Netflix, is more stable and established at the moment. For the future work, we believe that there is a huge scope to improve our current model which can make it more secure and stable.

REFERENCES

Adiguna, T. (2016). Secure H. 264 Video Coding using AES/CFB/PKCS5 padding encryption on various video frames (I, P, B). In *2016 10th International Conference on Telecommunication Systems Services and Applications (TSSA)* (pp. 1-5). IEEE.

Alsaffar, D. M., Almutiri, A. S., Alqahtani, B., Alamri, R. M., Alqahtani, H. F., Alqahtani, N. N., & Ali, A. A. (2020). Image Encryption Based on AES and RSA Algorithms. In *2020 3rd International Conference on Computer Applications & Information Security (ICCAIS)* (pp. 1-5). IEEE.

Arom-oon, U. (2017). An AES cryptosystem for small scale network. In *2017 Third Asian Conference on Defence Technology (ACDT)* (pp. 49-53). IEEE. 10.1109/ACDT.2017.7886156

Belda, R., De Fez, I., Arce, P., & Guerri, J. C. (2018). Look ahead: a DASH adaptation algorithm. In *2018 IEEE International Symposium on Broadband Multimedia Systems and Broadcasting (BMSB)* (pp. 1-5). IEEE.

Bento documentation for conversion from mp4 to HLS. (n.d.). https://www.bento4.com/documentation/mp42hls/

Bhat, B., Ali, A. W., & Gupta, A. (2015). DES and AES performance evaluation. In *International Conference on Computing, Communication & Automation* (pp. 887-890). IEEE. 10.1109/CCAA.2015.7148500

BudimanBadarsyah, I., & Rosmansyah, Y. (2014). Digital rights management with ABAC implementation to improve enterprise document protection. In *2014 8th International Conference on Telecommunication Systems Services and Applications (TSSA)* (pp. 1-6). IEEE.

Chakraborty, P., Dev, S., & Naganur, R. H. (2015). Dynamic http live streaming method for live feeds. In *2015 International Conference on Computational Intelligence and Communication Networks (CICN)* (pp. 1394-1398). IEEE. 10.1109/CICN.2015.333

Elshamy, A. M., Abdelghany, M. A., Alhamad, A. Q., Hamed, H. F., Kelash, H. M., & Hussein, A. I. (2017). Secure implementation for video streams based on fully and permutation encryption techniques. In *2017 International Conference on Computer and Applications (ICCA)* (pp. 50-55). IEEE. 10.1109/COMAPP.2017.8079738

Exoplayer documentation. (n.d.). https://exoplayer.dev/hls.html

FFMPEG documentation. (n.d.). https://ffmpeg.org/ffmpeg-formats.html

Floissac, N., & L'Hyver, Y. (2011). From AES-128 to AES-192 and AES-256, how to adapt differential fault analysis attacks on key expansion. In *2011 Workshop on Fault Diagnosis and Tolerance in Cryptography* (pp. 43-53). IEEE. 10.1109/FDTC.2011.15

Han, S., Go, Y., Noh, H., & Song, H. (2019). Cooperative server-client http adaptive streaming system for live video streaming. In *2019 International Conference on Information Networking (ICOIN)* (pp. 176-180). IEEE. 10.1109/ICOIN.2019.8718151

Hassan, H. E. R., Tahoun, M., & ElTaweel, G. S. (2020). A robust computational DRM framework for protecting multimedia contents using AES and ECC. *Alexandria Engineering Journal, 59*(3), 1275–1286. doi:10.1016/j.aej.2020.02.020

Hemalatha, K., Yadav, P. K., & Ramasubramanian, N. (2015). Adaptive bitrate transcoding for power efficient video streaming in mobile devices. In *2015 3rd International Conference on Signal Processing, Communication and Networking (ICSCN)* (pp. 1-5). IEEE. 10.1109/ICSCN.2015.7219825

HLS Article by Apple Inc. (n.d.). https://developer.apple.com/streaming/

Hongsongkiat, T., & Chongstitvatana, P. (2014). AES implementation for RFID Tags: The hardware and software approaches. In *2014 International Computer Science and Engineering Conference (ICSEC)* (pp. 118-123). IEEE. 10.1109/ICSEC.2014.6978180

Jain, N., Shrivastava, H., & Moghe, A. A. (2020). Production-ready environment for HLS Player using FFmpeg with automation on S3 Bucket using Ansible. In *2nd International Conference on Data, Engineering and Applications (IDEA)* (pp. 1-4). IEEE.

Jugović, D., & Banduka, M. L. (2017). Extending and integration of HLS software support in Android based systems. In *2017 25th Telecommunication Forum (TELFOR)* (pp. 1-4). IEEE.

Kovacevic, M., Kovacevic, B., Stefanovic, D., & Novak, S. (2015). Automated monitoring of HTTP live streaming QoE factors on Android STB. In *2015 IEEE 1st International Workshop on Consumer Electronics (CE WS)* (pp. 72-75). IEEE. 10.1109/CEWS.2015.7867159

Kuchta, M., & Miklošík, A. (2017). Evolution of digital video consumption patterns. *Communication Today, 8*(2), 58–69.

Kumar, Y., Munjal, R., & Sharma, H. (2011). Comparison of symmetric and asymmetric cryptography with existing vulnerabilities and countermeasures. *International Journal of Computer Science and Management Studies, 11*(03), 60–63.

Lee, N. Y., & Lee, T. Y. (2009). User friendly digital rights management system based on smart cards. In *2009 Fifth International Conference on Intelligent Information Hiding and Multimedia Signal Processing* (pp. 869-872). IEEE. 10.1109/IIH-MSP.2009.130

Maqsood, F., Ahmed, M., Ali, M. M., & Shah, M. A. (2017). Cryptography: A comparative analysis for modern techniques. *International Journal of Advanced Computer Science and Applications, 8*(6), 442–448. doi:10.14569/IJACSA.2017.080659

Meurer, R. S., Mück, T. R., & Fröhlich, A. A. (2013). An Implementation of the AES cipher using HLS. In *2013 III Brazilian Symposium on Computing Systems Engineering* (pp. 113-118). IEEE. 10.1109/SBESC.2013.36

Mukesh, P. S., Pandya, M. S., & Pathak, S. (2013). Enhancing AES algorithm with arithmetic coding. In *2013 International Conference on Green Computing, Communication and Conservation of Energy (ICGCE)* (pp. 83-86). IEEE. 10.1109/ICGCE.2013.6823404

Mushtaq, M. F., Jamel, S., Disina, A. H., Pindar, Z. A., Shakir, N. S. A., & Deris, M. M. (2017). A survey on the cryptographic encryption algorithms. *International Journal of Advanced Computer Science and Applications, 8*(11), 333–344.

Oyman, O., & Singh, S. (2012). Quality of experience for HTTP adaptive streaming services. *IEEE Communications Magazine, 50*(4), 20–27. doi:10.1109/MCOM.2012.6178830

Panda, M. (2019). Text And Image Encryption Decryption Using Symmetric Key Algorithms On Different Platforms. *Int. J. Sci. Technol. Res, 8*(09).

Princy, P. (2015). A comparison of symmetric key algorithms DES, AES, Blowfish, RC4, RC6: A survey. *International Journal of Computer Science and Engineering Technology, 6*(5), 328–331.

Rahim, R., Pranolo, A., Hadi, R., Nurdiyanto, H., Napitupulu, D., Ahmar, A. S., . . . Abdullah, D. (2018). Digital Signature Security in Data Communication. doi:10.2991/icedutech-17.2018.34

Sanida, T., Sideris, A., & Dasygenis, M. (2020). Accelerating the AES Algorithm using OpenCL. In *2020 9th International Conference on Modern Circuits and Systems Technologies (MOCAST)* (pp. 1-4). IEEE.

Sheppard, N. P., Safavi-Naini, R., & Jafari, M. (2009). A digital rights management model for healthcare. In *2009 IEEE International Symposium on Policies for Distributed Systems and Networks* (pp. 106-109). IEEE. 10.1109/POLICY.2009.8

Singh, G. (2013). A study of encryption algorithms (RSA, DES, 3DES and AES) for information security. *International Journal of Computers and Applications, 67*(19).

Sodagar, I. (2011). The mpeg-dash standard for multimedia streaming over the internet. *IEEE MultiMedia, 18*(4), 62–67. doi:10.1109/MMUL.2011.71

Tsaur, W. J. (2012). Strengthening digital rights management using a new driver-hidden rootkit. *IEEE Transactions on Consumer Electronics, 58*(2), 479–483. doi:10.1109/TCE.2012.6227450

Chapter 8
The Industry 4.0 for Secure and Smarter Manufacturing

N. S. Gowri Ganesh
https://orcid.org/0000-0001-9627-0416
Malla Reddy College of Engineering and Technology, India

N. G. Mukunth Venkatesh
Panimalar Engineeting College, Chennai, India

ABSTRACT

Industry 4.0 and smart manufacturing are expected to transform current practices into new milestones of exponential growth with high intensity of velocity, scope, and system impact. Technological advancements in the fields such as artificial intelligence, internet of things (IoT), blockchain technology, and cyber physical systems have resulted in a breakthrough in capturing the potential to boost income levels and an improvement in the quality of life of various sectors of people worldwide. A continuous stream of input data generated by IoT devices can assist to closely monitor an industry's various production phases. Edge computing and AI process these data at the end node, while blockchain technology provides a distributed secure data environment for both financial and non-financial applications. Security measures must be built into all manufacturing systems, allowing for failsafe production and cyber threat protection. In this chapter, the authors look at how these technologies can be used in a variety of scenarios to boost productivity in the industry and its environmental elements.

INTRODUCTION

Contemporary industry has witnessed major impetus from the early 18th century due to the impact of great innovations in technology. The ultimate goal in each phase of the industry changes is to improve the efficiency of manufacturing reducing the wastage resulting into more production. Industry 4.0 or the 4th industrial revolution also sometimes referred to as Industrial Internet of Things (IIOT) in the manufacturing sector is the conglomeration of physical production and technology with that of smart digital technology using AI and machine learning, big data, cloud computing, IoT, blockchain Technol-

DOI: 10.4018/978-1-7998-8367-8.ch008

ogy, cyber physical systems and Edge computing. Always Industry works in tandem with the desired process, partners, products and the people. The challenge in the day to day operations of the company is to produce effective output to maintain the connectedness and obtain the insights of the real time data across all these entities. The interconnectivity is possible for the smart manufacturing in Industry 4.0 with these Industrial IoT devices connected to the cloud working with the assistance of Artificial Intelligence and is secured with the aid of blockchain technology. A continuous stream of input data generated by IoT devices can assist to closely monitor an industry's various production phases. The sensors at these locations can be linked to applications that can provide a visual representation of the operations. These applications are capable of not only presenting the data as it is in sequence towards being insightful, but also of displaying intelligence by predicting the output in the future in order to make the necessary decisions using the appropriate machine learning algorithms. Edge computing and artificial intelligence process these data at the end node and intermediate node levels, while blockchain technology provides a distributed secure data environment for both financial and non-financial applications. Blockchain technology is now a tried-and-true method for tracking goods in logistics. It is critical in smart manufacturing to discern among machine health tracking, predictive maintenance, and production scheduling. Deep learning algorithms are used in smart factories to control machines using time-series data. Edge computing in smart manufacturing has thus proven to improve processing time for the machine environment with a large number of tasks. Traditional manufacturing plants were not designed to work in conjunction with cybersecurity arrangements. When these industries transition to the new paradigm of IoT devices with IP-based systems, they are more likely to be attacked by hackers. There is a greater risk of cybercrime, which can result in unauthorized remote access, theft of intellectual property, data manipulation, signal interference, and data loss. Security measures must be built into all manufacturing systems from the start, allowing for failsafe production and cyber threat protection. Because manufacturing equipment has a long life cycle, it is also critical that the solutions chosen have built-in flexibility and advanced over-the-air updating solutions to prevent threats today and in the future. A suitable secure architecture can generate, distribute, and authenticate devices in order for them to interact with users and applications

BACKGROUND

Industry4.0 was first coined in 2011 by three engineers: Henning Kagermann (physicist and one of the founders of SAP) (Henning Kagermann, 2011), Wolfgang Wahlster (professor of artificial intelligence), and Wolf-Dieter Lukas (physicist and senior official at the German Federal Ministry of Education and Research) in the german language 'Industrie4.0' in an industrial fair at Hannover Messe. Since then, the term Industrie 4.0 has sparked a vision of a new Industrial Revolution and has sparked a vigorous, ongoing debate about the future of work, and hence society, among the German public. In 2013, Industry4.0 manifesto("Recommendations for Implementing the Strategic Initiative INDUSTRIE 4.0. Final Report of the Industrie 4.0 Working Group," n.d.) was prepared by German National Academy of Science and Engineering (acatech). The discussion around this future vision eventually extended to other countries, with public awareness peaked in 2016 when the World Economic Forum met in Davos under the banner Mastering the Fourth Industrial Revolution. Industry 4.0-related issues are addressed and developed by the Public-Private Partnership (PPP) for Factories of the Future (FoF). The evolution of Industry4.0 is described as application of inventions and discoveries from time to time as tools and techniques with the objective for producing goods in large numbers, less production cost, less time eventually resulting in lower product cost.

Industry1.0: Earlier to the 18th century essential goods like food, cloth and non essential goods like weapons, tools were manufactured by hand or with the aid of animals. It represents a move from an agrarian and artisanal economy to one dominated by machines, and it has had a substantial impact on industries such as mining, textiles, glass, and agriculture due to many inventions like steam engine, spinning jenny and water wheel. James Hargreaves devised the spinning jenny, a multi-spindle spinning frame, in 1764 or 1765 in England. The gadget cut down on the amount of time it took to make cloth. It aided in the establishment of the cotton industrial system. Improvements in transportation and communication, reliance on new energy sources, such as coal, the use of new raw materials, such as steel, and division of labor and worker specialization are all elements that have grown in significance.

Industry2.0: Mass production and the usage of electricity were two significant elements of the second industrial revolution (1871–1914). It happened as a result of massive railroad and telegraph networks that allowed people and ideas to travel more quickly. Manufacturing was also revolutionized during World War I, which lasted from 1914 to 1918.

Industry3.0: Electronic equipment and information technology systems were major characteristics of the third industrial revolution. As a result, manufacturing plants have rapidly transitioned from analog to more digital systems. At this time, automation software made its debut, taking over many of the menial duties traditionally performed by people. The mass manufacture and widespread usage of digital logic, MOS transistors, and integrated circuit chips, as well as their derivative technologies, such as computers, microprocessors, digital cellular phones, and the Internet, are the focal points of this phase. Industry 3.0 is still extant, with the majority of factories in this stage of development.

Industry4.0: Cyber-physical systems are a crucial component of this revolution. Four design principles have been highlighted as essential to Industry 4.0. 1)Interconnectivity: Machines, devices, sensors, and people can link and communicate with each other via the Internet of Things, or the Internet of People (IoP) 2) Transparency of information – Industry 4.0 technology offers operators with a wealth of data on which to base their judgments. 3) Technical aid refers to the ability of systems to aid humans in making decisions and solving problems, as well as the ability to assist humans with difficult or dangerous activities. 4) Decentralized decision-making – the ability of cyber physical systems to make intelligent decisions and perform tasks as independently as possible. Since the introduction of Industry 4.0 in Germany, numerous related concepts or initiatives, such as the Industrial Internet in the United States, Made in China 2025, Industry 4.1J in Japan, and Manufacturing Industry Innovation 3.0 in South Korea, have been launched in various nations or regions.

INDUSTRY4.0 AND ITS ADOPTION OF TECHNOLOGIES FOR SMART MANUFACTURING

Smart manufacturing is a new paradigm that uses digital innovation to make work smarter and more connected, resulting in increased speed and flexibility in production. In the present scenario, natural resource extraction, excessive waste creation, and global warming are all well-known issues in the industries. In this regard, recent searches have shown how a circular model for reusing waste improves the entire supply chain for manufacturing products, while many have focused on the influences of technological innovations in the domain of manufacturing, optimization processes, and scheduling problems to resolve the issue of industrial pollution and resource waste. In the perspective of Industry4.0, a Smart Factory is a manufacturing solution that delivers such flexible and adaptable production processes that will tackle problems that arise on a production facility with dynamic and fast changing boundary conditions in the world of increasing complexity. This approach may be related to automation, which is defined as a mixture of software, hardware, and/or mechanics. On the other hand, it could be viewed from the standpoint of collaboration between various industrial and nonindustrial partners, with the smartness stemming from the creation of a dynamic organization. Smart products are those that can perform calculations, store data, interact with others, and connect with their surroundings. Industry 4.0 provides a better collaborative value (smarter services and processes) by bringing together new and expanded skills and skills in a supply network using new technology, particularly information and communication technology. Smart manufacturing, the use of Cyber Physical Systems (CPS) for production, i.e. embedded actuators and sensors, computing device networks, and connecting machines to the value chain, are all key components of Industry 4.0. Smart manufacturing includes technologies such as smart sensors, IoT, cloud computing, Blockchain Technology and Big data. Autonomous robots, augmented reality, additive manufacturing, cybersecurity, and horizontal and vertical integration are other technologies mentioned in the Industry4.0 recommendations document. The figure (Figure 1: Adoption of technologies in Industry4.0 for smart manufacturing) indicates the adoption of technologies in Industry4.0. Industrial Artificial Intelligence technologies are mostly used to help intelligent manufacturing. Despite the fact that the corresponding research is still in its early stages, IAI is gaining traction, undergoing rapid technical improvement, and making significant progress in applications. Smart devices, such as IoT and CPS, have now established themselves as a global paradigm capable of radically transforming any industry equipped with sensing, identification, remote control, and automated control capabilities. Because they rely on expensive centralized servers that are similarly costly to build and maintain, it is especially suitable for Industry 4.0 applications with medium and heavy user and computational loads. Blockchain may add value by facilitating the transformation from the Internet of Information to the Internet of Value, as well as the construction of a true peer-to-peer sharing economy, by replacing centralized servers with decentralized servers and evolving the existing Internet.

Figure 1. Adoption of technologies in industry 4.0 for smart manufacturing

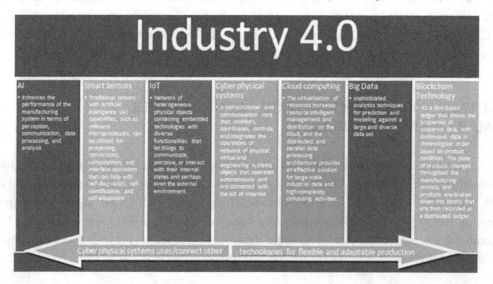

Cyber Physical Systems

Cyber Physical Systems (CPS) platforms emerge as a result of the strategic effort Industry4.0, which will support collaborative industrial business processes and the accompanying business networks which defines the features of smart factories and smart product life cycles. They are based on the Internet as a communication medium and comprise computation and storage capacity, mechanics, and electronics. CPS connects the virtual and physical worlds to form a network of intelligent objects that can communicate and interact with each other. Systems in which cyber and physical systems are strongly integrated at all sizes and levels are known as cyber-physical systems. Cyber refers to discrete, logical, and switched computation, communication, and control. Physical systems are natural and man-made systems that are regulated by physics rules and operate in real time. The first stage in designing a Cyber-Physical System application is obtaining precise and trustworthy data from machines and their components. Sensors may collect data directly, or data may be collected from controllers or corporate manufacturing systems. Data must be used to derive relevant information, such as evaluating health value, estimating remaining usable life, and so on. In this architecture, the cyber level serves as the core information hub. To construct the machines' network, information is pushed to it from every linked machine. The level of cognition generates a full understanding of the monitored system. The correct presentation of gained knowledge to expert users supports the accuracy of the results.

CPS(Gill, n.d.) is a computational core integrates, monitors, and/or controls the activities of physical, biological, and engineering systems. The computing core is typically an embedded system that requires real-time response and is dispersed. A cyber-physical system's behavior is a completely integrated blend of computer (logical) and physical action. CPS(Greer et al., 2019) has six common characteristics as referred to in the figure (Figure 2: Characteristics of CPS systems) they are hybrid systems, hybrid methods, control, component classes, Time, Trustworthiness .

Figure 2. Characteristics of CPS systems

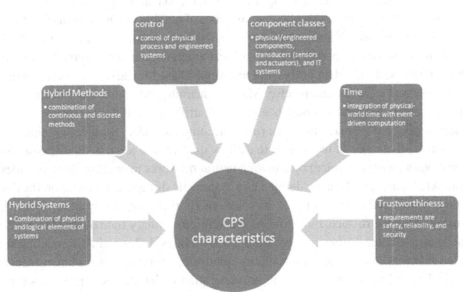

From design through assembly and operation, the Manufacturing Execution System IT solution is now a critical component. Static manufacturing lines (with established sequences) characterize today's automotive sector, making it difficult to reconfigure for new product versions. Dynamic manufacturing lines emerge as a result of Industrie 4.0. Vehicles are transformed into smart products that travel autonomously from one CPS-enabled processing module to the next in the assembly shop. The layers of interaction between items in CPS(Plakhotnikov & Kotova, 2020) are as follows: 1. Smart Connection Level 2. Data-to-Information Conversion Level 3. Cyber Level 4. Cognition Level 5. Configuration Level. A large amount of data is created during the functioning of cyberphysical systems. Processing such "big data" necessitates the use of specialized technologies. Artificial intelligence methods must be used to improve the performance of all components of cyberphysical systems.

Artificial Intelligence, Smart Sensors and IoT

Smart manufacturing has emerged as a method of utilizing advanced intelligence systems to enable a dynamic reaction to changing product demand as well as real-time optimization across the whole value chain. Through interconnectivity, cloud computing, and big data, Industry 4.0 of intelligent manufacturing in the production process achieves vertical system integration. In response, the entire factory's internal elements connected and worked with one another, allowing it to carry out individualized production while also adjusting product productivity and resource conservation.

Artificial Intelligence (AI): AI is a branch of computer science concerned with the creation of data processing systems that fulfill functions traditionally associated with human intelligence, such as reasoning, learning, and self-improvement. AI technologies can be considered as enablers for systems to perceive their surroundings, analyze data, and solve complicated issues, as well as learn from experience to increase their ability to do specific tasks from an industrial standpoint. Artificial Intelligence (AI) has made tremendous progress in a variety of domains, including image processing, natural language processing, and speech recognition. The rise of a new generation of AI technologies has offered smart factories with new possibilities and challenges. To a significant extent, AI can be applied to smart manufacturing. The use of AI in smart factories has resulted in a number of notable changes, including the following:

AI-enabled smart devices, such as machine vision, are more accurate and reliable; 2) collaborative mechanisms with autonomous decision-making and reasoning functionalities demonstrate more sensible dynamic characteristics; and 3) data processing techniques based on advanced AI algorithms, such as deep learning, are more effective and precise. Machine learning, which includes deep learning, is part of artificial intelligence. Machine learning is a subset of artificial intelligence that comprises advanced statistical methods that enable machines to learn and accomplish tasks. Machine learning includes deep learning as a subset. It is made of techniques that allow machines to learn to do difficult tasks (such as object recognition in images or voice) by allowing neural networks to analyze large volumes of data.

Industrial AI: Industrial AI can be defined as a systematic discipline focusing on the development, validation, deployment and maintenance of AI solutions (in their varied forms) for industrial applications with sustainable performance. Industrial AI is a multidisciplinary field of study that includes fields like machine learning, natural language processing, and robotics. Industrial AI's enabling technologies can be divided into five categories: data, analytics, platform, operations, and human-machine interaction. In the field of industrial manufacturing, incorporation of intelligence in the machines/machine components is an unavoidable development. Deep integration of AI with sophisticated manufacturing technologies provides a comprehensive solution for improving product quality and efficiency, raising company service levels, and significantly lowering energy usage. Industrial AI is concerned with the technologies of defect detection, remaining useful life prediction, and quality inspection in the sphere of industrial monitoring. Industrial Artificial Intelligence (Industrial AI) opens up options in manufacturing, with the goal of rapidly enhancing quality, composition, and essence. People's experience can be quickly accumulated and passed on by standardizing a person's workflow with data and establishing a better reference and interaction with data, for example. Data may be used to make implicit problems in manufacturing systems apparent, allowing equipment health to be transparently maintained, process parameters to become more stable, and overall efficiency to be better coordinated and maximized.

AI is quickly evolving, particularly in the field of deep learning. In the McKinsey Global Institute paper (Chui et al., 2018) in April of 2018, it looked at over 400 applications from 19 industries and 9 business activities, as well as their economic potential. The deployment of artificial neural networks is referred to as AI technology in the report. Feedforward neural networks, recurrent neural networks, and convolutional neural networks are the three primary forms of neural networks. Other common machine learning algorithms include decision tree algorithms (which use tree structure to build decision models), regression algorithms (which predict continuous values), classification algorithms (which predict discrete values with prior knowledge of classification), clustering algorithms (which predict discrete values without prior knowledge of classification), and ensemble learning (which predicts discrete values without prior knowledge of classification) (integrating several learning models). Other machine learning technologies are classified into two categories: generative adversarial networks (GANs) and deep reinforcement learning (DRL).

After seeing and possibly feeling a few instances of things like wood, humans are able to interpret the concept of a wood. From then on, he can recognize any wood, even if it is shaped differently or has different colors or textures than the wood he has previously seen. This is a tremendously powerful capacity that humans take for granted because our brains do it so well naturally. Artificial neural networks (ANNs)(Lemley et al., 2017) are capable of learning something about what they observe and then generalizing that information to new examples (or specimens). An input layer, an output layer, and one or more so-called hidden layers are essential in neural networks. These layers are made up of nodes, sometimes known as neurons that are connected to succeeding and prior layers in a variety of ways. Axons receive input from other neurons, and dendrites transfer information to other cells in the biological model. In a neural network, this relates to the input and output connections. The soma is the body of a biological neuron, and it can determine when and what to transmit based on a variety of factors. The activation function, which is seen in artificial neurons, works in a similar way. A classification task is the process of determining which category a piece of data belongs to. Generalization is the ability to classify previously unseen examples. ANNs are particularly useful in problems when the desired output cannot be predicted ahead of time. Training refers to the process of teaching our network. The training set is a collection of data that we believe is sufficiently representative for our network to learn from. The validation set is the set of data on which we base our model's evaluation during training. The task is the skill that we want our network to learn. When an ANN isn't sufficiently trained to do this, we term it underfitting, which suggests the network didn't learn the training set well enough. Overfitting is the inverse of this, when the network learns the training set so well that it can't be applied to data it hasn't seen before. Neural networks can perform two types of learning: 1) supervised learning, in which the data is labeled or annotated in some way, and the job is to learn to match the data to the labels; and 2) unsupervised learning, in which the data is not labeled and the neural network learns to find relationships between data. The weights are updated and the way the loss changes over time is measured using training algorithms. Gradient descent optimizers are commonly used to do this. Back propagation is a technique for propagating error information from the last layer to the first layer in order to adjust the weights, and it's commonly confused with training. Learning rules are techniques that can be used to improve the performance of a network.

Analog-to-digital conversion is the process of converting analog inputs into digital data. This changes the information's state from continuous to discrete. In the process, some information is lost. Although that information isn't always necessary for interpreting the underlying analog signal, we could lose essential data, like high-frequency information, in some cases. We often refer to a piece of data, such as an image, as a sample in digital processing. The representation of these samples in a high-dimensional space, where each unit (or pixel in the case of images) is regarded to be positioned on a specific axis, with the range of potential values being the size of that axis, is handy but computationally expensive. A vector, which is a point in a 10,000-dimensional space, would be used to represent a 100 x 100 pixel image. This area is referred to as the feature space. We aim to limit the number of dimensions to only those that are necessary for the work at hand, or we adapt the way these features are represented. To accomplish a task in the typical pattern recognition technique, we divide our process into two steps: feature generation and feature selection. The former creates new features from the pixel space, whilst the latter lowers the feature space's dimensionality. Morphological, Fourier, and wavelet transforms are examples of feature generating techniques that provide more relevant features for certain applications. Principal component analysis and linear Fisher discriminant are examples of feature selection methods. Instead of attempting to lower the dimensions, a recent strategy based on sparse mapping argues for growing the dimensions with the purpose of reflecting more abstract aspects. This sparse mapping approach is used by convolutional layers, which are a major component of deep learning. The convolution operator is used by convolutional layers.

On two functions, the convolution operator is applied. The signal from the sample space is one, and the filter, which is applied to the sample, is the other. Convolutions are implemented as matrix multiplications on the GPU. Deep neural networks are typically composed of one or more convolutional layers, each of which is followed by a pooling (max-pooling) operation. Convolutional, pooling, and unpooling layers are frequently put between two convolutional layers in fully convolutional networks.

The real value of AI applications that can be realized with AI technology is the ability to create systems with increased degrees of autonomy and the value-added that comes with it. The general condition of a system can be described using autonomy levels. Intelligence is required to evolve the system to a certain level of autonomy. Artificial intelligence (AI) is a technological means of achieving a certain amount of autonomy. The general impact of AI-based autonomy(Klaus Ahlborn, Gerd Bachmann, Fabian Biegel, Jörg Bienert, Prof. Dr. Svenja Falk, n.d.) of an industrial process can span from no autonomy (Level 0: no AI programming), to partial autonomy (Levels 1 to 4: AI programming is used; human intervention is still required in the process), to full autonomy (Level 5: AI programming replaces every form of human intervention).

Smart Sensors: Smart sensors (Pech et al., 2021) interpret aggregated data from manufacturing processes in real time, allowing machines and other smart devices to self-determine. Intelligent sensors can be used as a multi-component measurement device that is self-calibrating, self-optimizing, and simple to incorporate into the environment for high connection. Intelligent sensors can also produce multidimensional data information and have process intelligence. Sensors in the Internet of Things can proactively monitor a device and send out notifications if it deviates from set criteria; this is referred to as facilities management. The main characteristics of Sensors are Sensitivity, connectivity, robustness and automatic diagnostics. The relationship unit change between output and input is known as sensitivity. Smart sensors, such as those used in IoT devices, are wireless and rely on the internet and, in most cases, the cloud. Low power consumption, automatic diagnostics, calibration, and the capacity to interpret and share data in real time are all features of intelligent sensors. Solid welds, seals, potting, chemical compatibility, secured wires, and other situational protection are all examples of robustness. Automatic diagnostics are concerned with the ability to make decisions or take action-based control activities. Sensors used in maintenance rely on the internet, smart grids, and blockchain technology. In smart factories, sensors are primarily used for control, with a focus on processes.

The establishment of vertical networks that connect smart manufacturing systems with design teams, suppliers, and the front office is what Industry 4.0 is all about. Identifying and monitoring objects in smart factories is accomplished by employing barcodes, QR codes, and RFID tags on labels or tags. Smart labels have evolved into complex context-aware tags with embedded modules that utilize wireless communications, energy-efficient displays, and sensors. Smart labels can detect and react to their surroundings in addition to identifying them.

The security of stored data from sensors is the current safety challenge. Aside from the sensors that collect data, which are a physical requirement for the Industry 4.0 idea, data sovereignty is critical.

Internet of Things: Kevin Ashton invented the term "Internet of Things" to describe a massive network of digitally connected products and machinery. The term "Industrial Internet of Things (IIoT)" is sometimes used to describe the application of IoT in industry. Remote sensors, independent of industry or company size, collect data created by machines (and increasingly, humans) to improve efficiency, encourage better decision-making, and build competitive advantages in the IIoT framework.

Cloud Computing, Big Data and Blockchain Technology

Cloud computing: The cloud computing establishes the connectivity of the numerous systems involved in the manufacturing process, upon which Industry 4.0 is founded, doubles the data created in real time from multiple sources and formats, which must be stored and analyzed using modern algorithms and technologies. In general, a smart factory employs important technologies such as IIoT, Big Data, and cloud computing from the physical resource layer, network layer, and data application layer. Industrial Internet of Things (IIoT) should accommodate new protocols and data formats at the network layer. The cloud platform should be able to assess the semantics of various data at the data application layer. As a result, the method employs cloud computing and big data as two primary technologies. Industry 4.0 considers both of these to be essential requirements. There is latency time in the cloud due to the enormous volumes of data handled, which might influence the performance of the production process. It is feasible to employ "Fog Computing" to tackle this problem. The processing power for data analysis and control operations based on high volumes of data collected through Internet of Things is referred to as fog computing (IoT).

Big Data: Big Data approaches enable the analysis of massive amounts of data created in an Industry 4.0 production ecosystem. Real-time sensor data, machine logs, and manufacturing process data are examples of big data in smart factories, which have a high volume, multiple sources, and considerable value. Advanced, historical, predictive, and descriptive analysis techniques can be used to examine the state and functioning of machines used in manufacturing processes, control, and monitoring. Data from multiple sources, such as the production unit, the enterprise, customer feedback and product request systems, and so on, is collected and analyzed to aid in real-time decision making for smart manufacturing. Manufacturers today want their customers to provide their comments and personal perspectives on the items they use or plan to use, so that they may focus their product design to appeal to a wide range of customers. Big data analysis will aid the manufacturer in identifying the current status and causes of product failures in real time, as well as encouraging customers to buy their products by better understanding their purchasing habits and requirements.

Blockchain: A blockchain is a series of connected blocks that can be used to store and transfer data in a distributed, transparent, and tamper-proof manner. Each block contains data and uses pointers to connect to other blocks. Such connections safeguard the blockchain's integrity and resistance to tampering. A blockchain transaction is made up of several steps. A network node or a user requests a new transaction first. The transaction is then written down in block format or structure. The index, time-stamp, data, previous hash, and current block hash make up the block structure. Blockchain systems(Raj et al., 2020, p. 9) are classified as public, private, or consortium. Industry 4.0-based applications can be seamlessly integrated with blockchain. It makes use of smart contracts, which do away with the need for paper contracts and regulate the network by consensus. Smart Contracts are a mechanism that allows transactions to be completed without the involvement of a third party, making them irreversible and traceable. The shared ledger should not be tampered with or updated for any of the records on the network. The integrity of the saved data is ensured as a result of this. Transactions should only be updated when all of the network's verified users agree using consensus techniques. A block of transactions is broadcast to all of the network's peer nodes. The SHA-256 technique is used by the blockchain network to generate a unique hash. Each block in the blockchain is linked to the previous block's hash, resulting in an impenetrable network of transactions. If a transaction is attempted to be appended, it must be validated by network nodes or smart contracts, and consensus must be reached. This immutable record cannot be changed; instead, it can only be appended to block of transactions, resulting in a safe and dependable decentralized system.

Other Technology Enablers of Industry 4.0

The spectrum of applications for 5G technologies(Sasiain et al., 2020) like Networks Functions Virtualization (NFV) and Software Defined Networking (SDN) is expanding, and Industry4.0 is adapting them. SDN and NFV will enable organizations to move away from static solutions based on dedicated hardware and toward more cost- and resource-effective virtualization and softwarization mechanisms, as well as improve service accessibility, reusability, and lifecycle management, and provide highly granular service isolation at the data and performance levels.

Software Defined Networking (SDN): Traditional computer networks are unprepared to adjust to continual changes in network flow, which carries a large number of devices and information. In terms of management, performance, and scalability, traditional networks have been constrained in comparison to other technologies. SDN is appropriate for large-scale and high-speed computing because the data-forwarding layer (switches and routers, for example) is separated from the control layer (controller or operating system). It can control all network traffic from various sources (MAC address, IP address, port number, etc.) in several ways using different protocols such as Internet Protocol version 6 (IPv6) and Internet Protocol version 4 (IPv4). The operating system, which coordinates with the application layer to conduct various functions such as intrusion detection, load balancing, routing, and so on, is part of the control layer. The SDN architecture enables a controller to manage a diverse set of data plane resources and provides the ability to scale. SDN can also address many of the issues of Industry 4.0, thanks to its versatility, which is one of its primary qualities, as well as the increased energy efficiency that can be achieved through device connection. Because Industry 4.0 is known for its ability to communicate effectively, as well as its flexibility and self-management, the SDN has a lot to offer.

Network Functions Virtualization (NFV): NFV is a four- to seven-layer Open System Interconnection (OSI) reference model that enables functional virtualization; it includes network nodes, routers, firewalls, Intrusion Detection and Prevention System (IDPS), and load balancers. Virtualization technology is currently utilized in networks to handle packet delivery, routers, data transfer, and other network activities, and is controlled by network hardware and software. Virtual resources (such as CPU, memory disk, and network interfaces) are exposed as physical resources by NFV architecture, and each virtual service or virtual service component is assigned a specified portion of these virtual resources on demand. Virtual services can be deployed in a standalone mode regardless of the hardware server they are assigned to.

SMART MANUFACTURING

Smart manufacturing, which is also the cornerstone of the smart factory, lies at the heart of modern production and manufacturing in terms of digitalization. Massive terminal devices and facilities are digitalized and connected in the smart manufacturing process using information technologies (IT) such as radio frequency identification (RFID), WiFi, ZigBee, and 5G. The continual contact and interoperation of various devices generates a massive data stream with a variety of data processing needs, such as enormous data volume, unstructured data type, and minimal time delay. Manufacturing, computing, virtualization, communication, data management, and other technologies are all integrated into smart manufacturing. Because of the interoperability of multiple technologies, the scope of smart manufacturing technologies has expanded, resulting in cost-effectiveness, time-savings, easy configuration, improved understanding, quick reaction to market demand, flexibility, and remote monitoring.

Machine speed prediction can be used in smart factories to dynamically change production processes based on various system variables, improve production throughput, and reduce energy consumption. Authors(Essien & Giannetti, 2020) developed an end-to-end model for multistep machine speed prediction in this research, which was inspired by recent deep learning work in smart manufacturing. A deep convolutional LSTM encoder–decoder architecture is used in the model. In a smart manufacturing process, the Deep ConvLSTM autoencoder architecture was used to predict machine speed. As a result, the computational demand and training time are lowered.

Smart manufacturing's digitalization encourages the virtualization of manufacturing processes, which leads to cloud manufacturing services. Blockchain technology(Lee et al., 2020) can be used to speed up the validation and transaction of services. A service transactional block is formed when a manufacturing service is inquired and purchased. A transaction block of this type will be broadcast and validated by other peer-to-peer organizations. The transaction block is then added to the blockchain of transactions. The above transaction blockchain operational mechanisms build smart contracts between numerous interactive business partners, with the core protocols facilitating, verifying, and enforcing contract performance or negotiation. By enabling the identification, distribution, and validation of critical relevant data in a distributed manner, blockchain technology can be utilized to increase data integrity and eliminate data transmission hazards. Blockchain technology can be used to determine the source and destination of a data flow, as well as evaluate and confirm the data package's completeness and ensure the integrity of response command data. The use of edge computing in smart manufacturing is much more than just a way to supplement cloud computing. Because of its inherent ease of communication and high scalability, it is critical for the development of smart manufacturing. Virtualization technologies, such as virtual machines and virtual containers, are critical to the proper operation of edge computing because they allow the concurrent processing of numerous separate activities at the same time.

Due to the vast size and strong coupling of modern process industries, the impact of a little flaw could be greatly magnified. As a result, it's critical to keep an eye on the status of the operation and take the appropriate maintenance steps to ensure the safety of industrial processes. In order to create effective multivariate statistical process monitoring (MSPM) models, recent approaches have tried to use past information that is customized to continuous manufacturing processes. Model predictive control (MPC) (Shang & You, 2019) is a well-known and well-established approach in advanced industrial process control that is based on a precisely known mathematical model to characterize system behaviors and determine optimal control sequences in the near future. In these circumstances, combining mechanistic models with data analytics and machine learning, which have shown considerable promise in dealing with unknowns, is a promising strategy. Their applications can be divided into two types based on their functionality. First one entails fitting existing past data into prediction models for unknowns, allowing the uncertainty to be split into the deterministic part, which is known in advance, and the stochastic part, which represents prediction errors. The unsupervised learning of the distribution of uncertainty is the second area of data analytics and machine learning applications in MPC.

Edge devices can be used to run intelligent software packages to support manufacturing activities of production equipment in smart factories in the Industry 4.0 era. However, when this type of edge device faces a sudden high-computation (SHC) job that cannot be completed by the edge device itself within the needed time frame, it may fail to perform planned features in a timely manner. As a result, ensuring that an edge device can efficiently execute SHC jobs in order to offer manufacturing services to equipment in a timely manner is a critical and difficult issue for smart manufacturing. A new manufacturing behavior-based map–reduce work offloading strategy is proposed(Chen et al., 2018) in a research contribution. To begin, a distributed job processing architecture is created to enable remote edge devices to work together to finish a SHC job in order to support manufacturing. Following that, a map–reduce program structure is created so that a SHC job may be easily separated into numerous sections that can be done in parallel by the specified edge devices, with each device processing a part. Then, in order to achieve high offloading efficiency, a mechanism for picking appropriate edge devices to finish the SHC job is presented, which takes into account historical manufacturing characteristics of each edge device.

To enable smart production, tool health monitoring and maintenance scheduling are essential. Using partial least squares and exponentially weighted moving-average for feature selection and model construction, this study aims to develop a data-driven framework that monitors and predicts tool health by analyzing status data collected from sensors, and thus derive the optimal maintenance strategy for smart production. Indeed, the proposed(Chien & Chen, 2020) method can deal with equipment multicollinearity and efficiently process data.

Challenges in Smart Manufacturing

Based on different variable dependencies, smart manufacturing systems encounter safety problems, lack of system integration, lack of return on new technology investment or financial problems when erecting new intelligent production systems and/or upgrading current industries by smart production technology.

Sharing information over the internet necessitates data and information security at numerous stages across the system, including global unique identity and end-to-end data encryption. As a result, each network node should be safeguarded from external threats and data exploitation. Compatibility issues between current and new devices cause a slew of issues in the adoption of smart manufacturing technology. Old machinery controlled by certain communication protocols may be obsolete, while new gadgets may use a different protocol. Interoperability refers to the capacity of different systems to communicate data and information regardless of the hardware or software vendor. Operational, systematical, technical, and semantic interoperability are the four stages of I4.0 interoperability. The differences in transmission bandwidth, operational frequency, mode of communication, hardware capabilities, and other factors determine the system's interoperability restrictions. The additional expenditure that should be made to embrace newer technology is weighed against the production losses that would occur during an upgrade, as well as the time required to recover the investment with existing system income. This influences the adoption of newer technology.

SECURE MANUFACTURING

Confidentiality, integrity, and availability are three fundamental components of information and data security in IT systems. Confidential information should be kept safe from those who are not allowed to see it. The integrity of information is a critical factor in determining the data's validity. Without falling into the hands of unauthorised persons, data should always be available to the intended parties.

In addition to the introduction of low-cost devices with Internet connectivity capabilities, the rapid evolution of a new type of low-cost technology that offers endless application possibilities while presenting the ability to be controlled over the Internet has resulted in the rapid evolution of a new type of low-cost technology. Such devices constitute the Internet of Technology (IoT). As IoT technology grew in popularity, the range of applications began to expand into the industrial sector. As the number of industrial devices using IP for communication increased, these devices began to enter the IT network domain. Operational Technology (OT) equipment might now be connected to an IT network router or switch and controlled through the Internet. Industry 4.0 and the Internet of Things (IoT) are two approaches that are transforming present Web correspondence into a Machine-to-Machine (M2M) premise. Essentially, the Internet of Things (IoT) is a collection of interconnected figuring devices, mechanical and advanced machines, articles, creatures, or individuals that have been given unique identifiers and the ability to exchange data over a network without requiring human-to-human or human-to-PC communication. Smart Manufacturing as prescribed by Industry 4.0, like any other set of interconnected systems, is vulnerable to both internal and external threats, especially given the complexity and evolving protection-evasion mechanisms accessible in the cyber-sphere. Smart Factory depends on advanced technologies like cyber physical systems, Internet of Things (IoT) technology to provide a link between digital and physical environments, as well as improvements to those digital environments through increased usage of cloud services, data analytics, and machine learning. Furthermore, as an organization adopts new Industry 4.0 technologies, the number of attack surfaces grows, and the following unexpected number of attacks or points of attacks grows as well, depending on the number of extended systems and the attack surfaces specific to them. Smart manufacturing capabilities are based on levels of technical sophistication, integration, and automation far beyond those of conventional manufacturing processes; there will be new vulnerabilities, and the lack of clarity on security is doubly concerning. Security is a dynamic process that necessitates a variety of solutions to deal with ever-changing assaults. Vulnerabilities will always exist, regardless of how well prepared you are, and attackers will try to uncover them by attacking the system. To combat this, it's vital to pay attention to the dynamic behavior and assess whether it's aberrant. Despite all of the security mechanisms in place, successful attacks will continue to occur. When an incident occurs, the ability to respond safely, bring the system back to a safe state, and continue operations as soon as feasible is critical.

Cyber Attacks in Industries

Cyber-attacks offer not only the traditional corporate challenges of intellectual property theft and data theft, but also the potential of infiltration into operations, resulting in complete plant closure, quality flaws that can go unnoticed, and implications affecting human lives.

Attackers got access to a steel factory in Germany at the end of 2014. The attackers used spearphishing and social engineering techniques to acquire access to the control network through the corporate network, according to a report issued by the German Federal Office for Information Security. As a result of manipulating various control components, the attackers were able to do unidentified but enormous physical damage to the system, allowing them to take control of the blast furnace. The skill sets necessary to carry out this attack went beyond information security and included industrial control systems and manufacturing processes. Havex/Dragonfly, a Remote Access Trojan (RAT)(*News from the Lab Archive : January 2004 to September 2015*, n.d.) used to infiltrate industrial control systems such as SCADA, PLC, and DCS utilized in the energy sector, was discovered in 2014.

An attack on Ukraine's power infrastructure(Tuptuk & Hailes, n.d.) occurred in December 2015. Attackers used a variety of strategies, including malware and denial of service, to put the electrical distribution infrastructure in a bad state, resulting in power disruptions.

According to the Ponemon Institute's 2019 Cost of a Data Breach Report(*What's New in the 2019 Cost of a Data Breach Report*, 2019), the average cost of a data breach in the industrial sector is $5.2 million. It could be a lot worse. Many manufacturing industries were particularly heavily struck by the WannaCry ransomware assault in May 2017, with several vehicle makers shutting down operations for days. The overall amount of money lost was in the billions of dollars.

Effect of Cyber Attack

Companies have already been identified as profitable targets by cyber attackers. Manufacturing companies' most valuable assets are their Information Technology (IT), Operations Technology (OT), and managerial assets. System logs, network access details, and network structure are all examples of IT assets. SCADA systems and system configuration are examples of OT assets. Customer and staff data, as well as internal communications, are among the management assets. Direct attacks from malicious people and/or software can put Industrial Control Systems (ICS) at jeopardy. Control systems such as Supervisory Control and Data Acquisition (SCADA), process control systems, distributed control systems, and CPS or Programmable Logic Controllers (PLC) are examples of industrial ICS. As the number of connected devices grows, so does the potential for cyber-attacks. Attackers can readily identify entry holes into enterprise networks or through hyper-connected devices, particularly if they are insecure or obsolete. The source of the cyber-attack could be internal or external. An internal source, such as an operator with physical access to a data port, or an external source, such as an outside communication channel or a wireless transmission, can both be used to launch a cyber-attack.

These are some of the possible outcomes of an attack.

1. **Theft of Information**: Hackers who obtain access to Industrial Control Systems (ICS) can acquire access to data about the production environment, as well as information about products (e.g. blueprints, sketches, specs, and other creative works) and the production itself (orders and capabilities). This could result in not only the revealing of sensitive business information, but also the breakdown of confidentiality agreements with other parties.

2. **Damage to the System**: Ransomware is a major issue, particularly when it comes to systems with weak (default) passwords or credentials that have been reused across multiple platforms and have thus been vulnerable to attackers. Using brute-force assaults, such passwords can be easily guessed. The attackers then demand a payment in order to restore access to the computers.

3. **Damage to the Product**: End-products can potentially be tampered with by attackers causing minor but sometimes disastrous modifications. Steel blocks, for example, that should be manufactured to exact specifications can be altered so that a straight cut deviates by a few centimetres, compromising the durability of an airplane or an automobile. Such damages may appear insignificant at first glance, yet they can be very powerful in destroying a company's reputation or trustworthiness.

Security Concerns

The most significant security concerns that an industry 4.0 factory faces can be divided into the following categories.

1. **Cyber espionage**: Cyber espionage, often known as cyber spying, is a form of cyberattack in which an unauthorized user tries to acquire access to sensitive or confidential data or intellectual property (IP) for commercial, competitive, or political gain. It is a term that refers to Industry 4.0 is vulnerable to cyber threats because of its smart and networked corporate operations. Industry 4.0 has become a favorite target for well-organized cyber hackers looking to steal critical information and intellectual property. Black Vine is one of these organizations, which focuses on the aerospace, energy, and healthcare industries. Social engineering is used in cyber espionage attacks to elicit activity or obtain information from the target in order to advance the assault. These approaches frequently use human emotions like enthusiasm, curiosity, empathy, and fear to motivate people to act rapidly or rashly.

2. **Distributed Denial of Service (DDoS)**: It is a cyber assault that seeks to render a system unavailable. The unavailability of some equipment in a production setting can be disastrous.

3. **Watering hole**: Malicious actors can infect genuine websites frequented by the victim or others affiliated with the target with malware for the express aim of compromising the user.

4. **Spear-phishing**: Hackers use phishing emails, SMS, and phone calls to target specific persons in order to obtain login credentials or other sensitive information.

5. **Zero-day exploits**: Cybercriminals use zero-day exploits to take advantage of an undisclosed security vulnerability or software issue that has yet to be discovered and patched by the program developer or the customer's IT team.

6. **Inside actors or insider threat:** An insider threat occurs when a threat actor persuades an employee or contractor to reveal or sell information or system access to an unauthorized third party.

7. **Advanced persistent threats (APT):** APT are a type of cyberattack that has evolved over time. They're carried out by organizations with a lot of experience and money. The idea is to use vulnerabilities to infiltrate the victim's network and remain undetected for an extended length of time. It is a sophisticated, long-term cyberattack in which an intruder creates an unnoticed presence in a network in order to steal critical data over time. An APT assault is a well-planned and executed attempt to infiltrate a specific organization and elude existing security measures for an extended period of time.

8. **Malware:** It is a harmful intrusion that can infect individual computers or the entire network of a business.

9. **Pretexting:** In this type of assault, smart lies are used in the emails, presenting as a requirement for sensitive information to complete a key assignment. They're made to entice victims into giving personal information, which can lead to identity theft or malware installation.

10. **Scareware:** In this type of threat, victims are bombarded with false alerts and threats that are aimed to infect the target's computer with malware via ostensibly genuine pop-ups.

There are currently a slew of methods available to identify and combat DDoS attacks. These solutions are divided into two groups for analysis: signature-based and anomaly-based solutions. Signature-based solutions use the signature of each DDoS attack to identify it. DDoS attack signatures are maintained in a database. Anomaly-based solutions are those that learn about the network's "typical" behavior.

Reasons for Attack

The following are the main reasons why industrial devices are hacked:

1. Devices that have been left unattended for an extended period of time (weeks or months) without receiving security or anti-virus updates;

2. There are a significant number of obsolete controllers in ICS networks that were created before CyberSecurity was a concern;

3. Due to the existence of various paths from multiple ICS networks, CyberSecurity threats can enter and evade CyberSecurity protections.

4. Malware spreads quickly due to numerous ICS networks that are still configured as a flat network with no physical or virtual isolation from neighboring networks.

Implications of an Attack and Incident Response

The implications of an attack on a smart manufacturing system may extend beyond damage to an industrial process: people may be injured, and the environment or the plant may be harmed. When an attack occurs, the response and recovery time should be as quick as possible to minimize potential losses, such as productivity, equipment, and reputation. Naturally, this necessitates having the resources in place prior to the attack, as well as having suitable policies and guidelines in place to allow the responsible persons to act quickly and efficiently. Within the industry, consistent event management methods such as documentation, awareness and training, and responses must be created. Once data about an incident has been gathered, it is vital to analyze the data and document the conclusions. SDN and NFV enable automatic incident response for a variety of industrial threats, allowing for the immediate detection and temporary replacement of failed systems with virtual implementations of those systems. SDN and NFV are technologies that help with the following: 1) network visibility, 2) network capabilities (enables better management of network traffic flows), and 3) network function deployment and control via software rather than particular hardware middleboxes.

Prevention of Cyber Attack

Although threat opponents are frequently sophisticated and can employ advanced technology in their operations, protecting against these attacks is not hopeless. Many cybersecurity and intelligence tools are available to help enterprises better understand their adversaries, their attack methodologies, and the tradecraft they apply on a regular basis.

1. **Coverage of Sensors**: What you don't see can't be stopped. To minimize blind spots that might constitute a safe haven for adversaries, organizations should implement technologies that give their defenders full visibility across their environment.
2. **Technical Intelligence**: It is a term used to describe a person's ability Use technical intelligence, such as indications of compromise (IOCs), to enrich data and feed it into security information and event management (SIEM). This adds intelligence to event correlation, perhaps emphasizing events on the network that would have gone unreported otherwise. Implementing high-fidelity IOCs across many security systems improves situational awareness, which is critical.
3. **Threat Intelligence**: It is the study of threats. Consuming narrative threat intelligence reports is a surefire way to get a clear picture of threat actor behavior, tools, and tradecraft. Threat intelligence aids in the profiling of threat actors, campaign tracking, and malware family tracking. These days, it's more critical to understand the context of an attack than it is to simply know that one occurred, which is where threat intelligence comes in handy.

Security Aspects for Industry4.0

The utilization of next-generation smart manufacturing equipment, sensors, and processes is one of Industry 4.0's core characteristics, and the attack vectors used by cyber attackers must be evaluated in the context of the Industry 4.0 environment. Sensors utilized in the Industry 4.0 environment often contain some of the most recent technical breakthroughs and can typically work as small sub-systems within the larger context of the manufacturing information architecture. Unfortunately, security is seen as a secondary issue in many of these next-generation technologies. There are a number of distinct security issues that Industry 4.0 faces, each with its own set of characteristics that necessitate careful attention to its underlying mechanisms in order to be effectively addressed. Following are some of the security aspects that are addressed in the smart manufacturing scenarios.

Anamoly Detection Techniques: Critical actionable information may be derived from underlying abnormalities or irregular patterns to aid human decision-making and limit potential risk in a variety of real-world data-driven applications, including fraud detection, cyber security, medical diagnostics, and industrial manufacturing. A network diffusion-based anomaly detection technique(Dong et al., 2021) for rapidly and effectively capturing aberrant event sequences For each potential event sequence, an anomaly score is produced that quantifies its "rareness" in relation to normal profiles. The path pattern creation component creates anomalous event sequence patterns.

Cognitive Digital Twins: Digital twins are now being used by businesses to monitor, evaluate, and imitate physical assets and processes. Digital twins are mostly used for I status monitoring, ii) simulation, and iii) visualization in smart manufacturing. Cognitive digital twins(Intizar Ali et al., 2021) are extensions of existing digital twins with communication, analytics, and intelligence capabilities. To further evaluate and cognitively interpret the abnormalities, the cognitive digital twin can interact with the operational environment and digital twins of products, as well as ongoing processes. All past anomalies recognized and associated remedial measures are gradually added to a factory-level knowledge base.

Cooperative Safety Assurance: Subsystems create a system of systems in a collaborative scenario, and the safety cases for the entire system can be formed by composing the safety cases of the participating subsystems to give overall safety guarantees. This study(Kabir, 2021) examines the Internet of Things (IoT) paradigm in cooperative system safety assurance using a hypothetical case to demonstrate the possible usage of IoT to provide CPS safety assurance.

Protected Areas: Modern corporate security(Kiss et al., 2019, p. 0) necessitates a comprehensive information security setup that includes both logical and physical controls. Aside from logical controls, physical information security creation is also required. In some cases, industrial secrets or sensitive technological data escapes IT systems and appears in formats that are directly readable by humans. Protected areas are defined locations where sensitive, important data or information may be heard or seen in an auditory or visual manner. The goal is to prohibit unauthorized users from accessing the data and information shown in this protected area and to make third-party acquisition impossible.

Security Compliance: Moving to Industry 4.0(Pereira et al., 2017) is a massive undertaking with ramifications in many aspects of today's industrial industry, including security. The majority of industrial organizations aren't entirely aware of the security threats associated with the Industry 4.0 paradigm's adoption. They usually only deal with security issues when a major incident occurs. As a result, businesses must embrace the establishment of a strategy to implement and manage the security compliance processes that Industry 4.0 necessitates.

Isolation of Services: The use of NFV and SDN technologies in industrial networks(Garcia et al., 2018) promotes innovation by allowing the deployment of new services and applications while utilizing existing physical infrastructure. Because they offer isolation between distinct services at the computing and networking levels, NFV and SDN provide security.

Defense-in-Depth: The idea of defense-in-depth(Jansen & Jeschke, 2018), as defined by the international standard IEC/ISA-62433, was discussed as a multilayer method for security industrial control systems, incorporating three measures: technological, organizational, and human-centered. At the plant, network, and system levels, this idea necessitates security controls.

Plant security uses doors, code cards, and other means to secure physical access to essential components. This is usually governed by procedures and norms, such as cyclic risk assessments and the adoption of suitable security safeguards. The goal of network security is to safeguard production networks from unauthorized access at network connections. The security of automation systems and controls at the device level against unwanted access is part of system integrity.

IT/OT Convergence: The guidelines for developing a secure smart factory concentrate on how to secure low-power, low-cost IIoT devices is discussed in this article(Mantravadi et al., 2020). In comparison to traditional information technology (IT) systems, the manufacturing environment has extra problems, particularly given the convergence of IT and operational technology (OT) systems. The combination of IT systems used for data-centric computing with OT systems used to monitor events, processes, and equipment and make adjustments in enterprise and industrial operations is known as IT/OT convergence. In terms of cybersecurity, it has been discovered that a factory's IT/OT link is a weak point.

Dynamic Watermarking: Because sensor measurements or other information flowing through the communication network may be intercepted and manipulated en route, cybersecurity becomes a risk. Consider the difficulty of determining whether a sensor is reporting accurate plant output measurements. On top of their nominal actuation instruction, the actuation nodes superimpose a small hidden random "excitation signal." The name dynamic watermarking comes from the fact that this secret excitation can be thought of as a type of "watermarking" in the signal domain for the dynamical (control) system.

Security of CAD File: The security and validity of CAD files is a fundamental concern in the Digital Manufacturing. The appearance of a part 3-D printed from a design file incorporating such security features will differ from the onscreen portrayal. Imaging methods such as tomography, radiography, and ultrasonic imaging can read interior marks such as serial numbers, bar codes, and QR codes. The sliced codes can be orientated in such a way that they appear in the CAD/STL files, but slicing will delete them, leaving a solid part with no sign of the code.

ML Techniques for GIS Insulation Flaws: The classification of GIS insulation flaws is one of the most difficult tasks. In online monitoring of the gas-insulated switchgear (GIS) state, powerful machine learning algorithms are used to detect cyber-attacks. IoT architecture(Elsisi et al., 2021) based on extreme gradient boosting (XGBoost), a machine learning technique, can depict all flaws in the GIS with different warnings, as well as efficiently reveal cyber-attacks on networks.

Application of Blockchain in Industry: The next generation of cybersecure industrial applications could benefit from blockchain technology(Fernández-Caramés & Fraga-Lamas, 2019). Smart contracts can offer security, trust, immutability, disintermediation, decentralization, and a greater level of automation to Industry 4.0 technology. To automate data exchanges inside factories and interact with suppliers and clients, horizontal and vertical integration are required. The manufacturer publishes offers for the design of the switching supply in the blockchain based on Multichain, while the engineers examine and analyze such offers to see if they compete for the suggested incentive.

FUTURE RESEARCH DIRECTIONS

The future growth of smart manufacturing using Artificial Intelligence is expected to focus on four aspects: robustness, generalization, interpretability, and analyzability, according to experts. The first two are aimed at increasing the applicability of Industrial Artificial Intelligence technology in real-world scenarios. AI algorithms, in particular, should be resistant to uncertainties arising from systems, data, and the environment. Furthermore, they are projected to be usable in a variety of areas for tasks such as monitoring, prediction, and diagnosis. Industrial manufacturing, as a field that stresses risk assessment, necessitates causality analysis for model reasoning and decision making.

In comparison to the issue of functionality, the issue of security in smart manufacturing receives much too little attention. The danger is that if systems are launched too soon, they may be functional but extremely vulnerable to attackers. Fundamental research that allows us to examine and evaluate the security of smart industrial systems is urgently needed. There are no traces on which to test new intrusion detection systems for smart industrial systems. Work in the direction of using machine learning algorithms to generate attacks in order to improve intrusion detection systems could have a significant impact on secure manufacturing. To allow researchers to conduct tests, good testbeds and simulators for smart manufacturing that are near to reality are essential.

CONCLUSION

Smart devices, such as IoT, Smart Sensors and CPS with the adoption of artificial intelligence, blockchain technology, have now emerged as a universal paradigm that has the potential to radically disrupt any industry that has sensing, identification, remote control, and automated control capabilities. The Internet and interconnected devices form the technological foundation of Industry 4.0, which focuses on process control with less human interventions and smart judgments, which has a tremendous impact on the worldwide market. This chapter covered the smart manufacturing system and its associated technologies, as well as newly presented paradigm and their impact on smart manufacturing technology, as well as related standardizations and challenges. In the security aspect, various attacks, the reasons for the attacks, the outcomes of the attacks and prevention of attacks are also discussed.

ACKNOWLEDGMENT

This article received no specific grant from any funding agency in the public, commercial, or not-for-profit sectors.

REFERENCES

Ahlborn, Bachmann, Biegel, Bienert, & Falk. (n.d.). *Technology Scenario 'Artificial Intelligence in Industrie 4.0.'* Academic Press.

Chen, C.-C., Su, W.-T., Hung, M.-H., & Lin, Z.-H. (2018). Map–Reduce–Style Job Offloading Using Historical Manufacturing Behavior for Edge Devices in Smart Factory. *IEEE Robotics and Automation Letters*, *3*(4), 2918–2925. doi:10.1109/LRA.2018.2847746

Chien, C.-F., & Chen, C.-C. (2020). Data-Driven Framework for Tool Health Monitoring and Maintenance Strategy for Smart Manufacturing. *IEEE Transactions on Semiconductor Manufacturing*, *33*(4), 644–652. doi:10.1109/TSM.2020.3024284

Chui, M., Manyika, J., Miremadi, M., Henke, N., Chung, R., Nel, P., & Malhotra, S. (2018). *Notes from the AI frontier. Insights from hundreds of use cases.* McKinsey & Company.

Dong, B., Chen, Z., Tang, L.-A., Chen, H., Wang, H., Zhang, K., Lin, Y., & Li, Z. (2021). Anomalous Event Sequence Detection. *IEEE Intelligent Systems*, *36*(3), 5–13. doi:10.1109/MIS.2020.3041174

Elsisi, M., Tran, M.-Q., Mahmoud, K., Mansour, D.-E. A., Lehtonen, M., & Darwish, M. M. F. (2021). Towards Secured Online Monitoring for Digitalized GIS Against Cyber-Attacks Based on IoT and Machine Learning. *IEEE Access: Practical Innovations, Open Solutions*, *9*, 78415–78427. doi:10.1109/ACCESS.2021.3083499

Essien, A., & Giannetti, C. (2020). A Deep Learning Model for Smart Manufacturing Using Convolutional LSTM Neural Network Autoencoders. *IEEE Transactions on Industrial Informatics*, *16*(9), 6069–6078. doi:10.1109/TII.2020.2967556

Fernández-Caramés, T. M., & Fraga-Lamas, P. (2019). A Review on the Application of Blockchain to the Next Generation of Cybersecure Industry 4.0 Smart Factories. *IEEE Access: Practical Innovations, Open Solutions*, *7*, 45201–45218. doi:10.1109/ACCESS.2019.2908780

Garcia, D., Astorga, J., & Jacob, E. (2018). Innovating at the Connected Industry: SDN and NFV Experiences and Lessons Learned. *2018 IEEE 26th International Conference on Network Protocols (ICNP)*, 245–246. 10.1109/ICNP.2018.00035

Gill, H. (n.d.). *From Vision to Reality: Cyber-Physical Systems*. Academic Press.

Greer, C., Burns, M., Wollman, D., & Griffor, E. (2019). Cyber-physical systems and internet of things (NIST SP 1900-202; p. NIST SP 1900-202). National Institute of Standards and Technology. doi:10.6028/NIST.SP.1900-202

Henning Kagermann. (2011, April 1). *Industrie 4.0: Mit dem Internet der Dinge auf dem Weg zur 4. industriellen Revolution - ingenieur.de*. Ingenieur.de - Jobbörse Und Nachrichtenportal Für Ingenieure. https://www.ingenieur.de/technik/fachbereiche/produktion/industrie-40-mit-internet-dinge-weg-4-industriellen-revolution/

Intizar Ali, M., Patel, P., & Breslin, J., Harik, R., & Sheth, A. (2021). Cognitive Digital Twins for Smart Manufacturing. *IEEE Intelligent Systems*, *36*(2), 96–100. doi:10.1109/MIS.2021.3062437

Jansen, C., & Jeschke, S. (2018). Mitigating risks of digitalization through managed industrial security services. *AI & Society*, *33*(2), 163–173. doi:10.100700146-018-0812-1

Kabir, S. (2021). Internet of Things and Safety Assurance of Cooperative Cyber-Physical Systems: Opportunities and Challenges. *IEEE Internet of Things Magazine*, *4*(2), 74–78. doi:10.1109/IOTM.0001.2000062

Kiss, M., Breda, G., & Muha, L. (2019). Information security aspects of Industry 4.0. *Procedia Manufacturing*, *32*, 848–855. doi:10.1016/j.promfg.2019.02.293

Lee, C. K. M., Huo, Y. Z., Zhang, S. Z., & Ng, K. K. H. (2020). Design of a Smart Manufacturing System With the Application of Multi-Access Edge Computing and Blockchain Technology. *IEEE Access: Practical Innovations, Open Solutions*, *8*, 28659–28667. doi:10.1109/ACCESS.2020.2972284

Lemley, J., Bazrafkan, S., & Corcoran, P. (2017). Deep Learning for Consumer Devices and Services: Pushing the limits for machine learning, artificial intelligence, and computer vision. *IEEE Consumer Electronics Magazine*, *6*(2), 48–56. doi:10.1109/MCE.2016.2640698

Mantravadi, S., Schnyder, R., Møller, C., & Brunoe, T. D. (2020). Securing IT/OT Links for Low Power IIoT Devices: Design Considerations for Industry 4.0. *IEEE Access: Practical Innovations, Open Solutions*, *8*, 200305–200321. doi:10.1109/ACCESS.2020.3035963

News from the Lab Archive: January 2004 to September 2015. (n.d.). Retrieved June 23, 2021, from https://archive.f-secure.com/weblog/archives/00002718.html

Pech, M., Vrchota, J., & Bednář, J. (2021). Predictive Maintenance and Intelligent Sensors in Smart Factory [Review]. *Sensors (Basel)*, *21*(4), 1470. doi:10.339021041470 PMID:33672479

Pereira, T., Barreto, L., & Amaral, A. (2017). Network and information security challenges within Industry 4.0 paradigm. *Procedia Manufacturing*, *13*, 1253–1260. doi:10.1016/j.promfg.2017.09.047

Plakhotnikov, D. P., & Kotova, E. E. (2020). The Use of Artificial Intelligence in Cyber-Physical Systems. *2020 XXIII International Conference on Soft Computing and Measurements (SCM)*, 238–241. 10.1109/SCM50615.2020.9198749

Raj, P., Saini, K., & Surianarayanan, C. (2020). *Identification of Blockchain-Enabled Opportunities and Their Business Values: Interoperability of Blockchain. In Blockchain Technology and Applications*. Auerbach Publications. doi:10.1201/9781003081487

Recommendations for implementing the strategic initiative INDUSTRIE 4.0. Final report of the Industrie 4.0 Working Group. (n.d.). *Acatech - National Academy of Science and Engineering*. Retrieved June 6, 2021, from https://en.acatech.de/publication/recommendations-for-implementing-the-strategic-initiative-industrie-4-0-final-report-of-the-industrie-4-0-working-group/

Sasiain, J., Sanz, A., Astorga, J., & Jacob, E. (2020). Towards Flexible Integration of 5G and IIoT Technologies in Industry 4.0: A Practical Use Case. *Applied Sciences (Basel, Switzerland)*, *10*(21), 7670. doi:10.3390/app10217670

Shang, C., & You, F. (2019). Data Analytics and Machine Learning for Smart Process Manufacturing: Recent Advances and Perspectives in the Big Data Era. *Engineering*, *5*(6), 1010–1016. doi:10.1016/j.eng.2019.01.019

Tuptuk, N., & Hailes, S. (n.d.). *The cyberattack on Ukraine's power grid is a warning of what's to come*. The Conversation. Retrieved June 21, 2021, from https://theconversation.com/the-cyberattack-on-ukraines-power-grid-is-a-warning-of-whats-to-come-52832

What's New in the 2019 Cost of a Data Breach Report. (2019, July 23). *Security Intelligence*. https://securityintelligence.com/posts/whats-new-in-the-2019-cost-of-a-data-breach-report/

KEY TERMS AND DEFINITIONS

Artificial Intelligence (AI): AI is an area of computer science concerned with the development of data processing systems that perform functions usually associated with human intellect, such as reasoning, learning, and self-improvement.

Cyber-Attack: A cyber-attack is an occurrence that has an adverse effect on an organization's operations, assets, or individuals through unauthorized access, disclosure, denial of service (DoS), information manipulation, or any other means. Active mode and passive mode attacks are two types of attacks.

Cyber-Physical Systems (CPS): CPS is a new generation of technologies with integrated computational and physical capabilities capable of interacting with humans in a variety of new ways.

Horizontal and Vertical System Integration in Industry 4.0: Interconnection between organizations and suppliers is critical for speedy and timely delivery in today's fast-paced industry. To speed up the manufacturing process, the engineering department must be closely connected to the production department. This mechanism is provided by Industry4.0, which connects all of these units.

Industrial IoT (IIoT): IIoT is a network of machines, computers, and people that enables intelligent industrial operations employing advanced data analytics for transformative business outcomes, and it is changing the landscape for businesses and individuals alike.

Industry 4.0: Industry 4.0 refers to the application of cutting-edge concepts such as CPS, M2M, and IoT to build a smart, self-managing, and dynamic manufacturing process.

Internet of Things (IoT): IoT is a scenario in which every object or "thing" has a sensor and can communicate its state with other things and automated systems in the environment. Each object is a node in a virtual network that transmits a significant amount of data about itself and its surroundings on a continual basis.

Software-Defined Networking (SDN): SDN is a networking paradigm that allows network managers to manage network services by abstracting higher-level functions.

Chapter 9
Advanced Associated Defence in a Cloud IoT Environment

Ambika N.

(iD) https://orcid.org/0000-0003-4452-5514

St. Francis College, India

ABSTRACT

IoT is a dispersed stage that bolsters the improvement of disseminated IoT applications. Subsequently, it gives an IoT computerization framework that encourages both the foundation definition and the framework arrangement. This framework incorporates programming arrangement devices to send administrations and applications everywhere on the IoT figuring framework. The previous work accepts that the model breaking time is longer than the model update time frame. The engineering approach comprises two sections: industrial IoT gadgets and their cloud worker. The cloud worker comprises two modules. The assault screen module records the most recent assault data for Industrial IoT gadgets as per their areas or types. The module deals with a library comprising of all the revealed assault plans. When the assault screen module recognizes some new assault for a gadget, it will require the instrument to download the relating assault plot with the end goal of ill-disposed retraining. The enhanced suggestion improves availability by 8.54% and security by 9.54%.

INTRODUCTION

The Internet of Things (IoT) (Ambika N., 2020) (Atzori, Iera, & Morabito, 2010) is presently generally utilized in different spaces. It includes intelligent structures (Akkaya, Guvenc, Aygun, Pala, & Kadri, 2015), power networks, diversion, transportation (Masek, et al., 2016), and medical services (Elhoseny, Shankar, Lakshmanaprabu, Maseleno, & Arunkumar, 2018). It is conjecture to assume a critical part in future specialized insurgencies. Its usage is probably going to increment dramatically throughout the next few years. Numerous IoT gadgets can be effortlessly focused on by interruption. They are associated with outside assets at the organization layer, and they don't have an appropriate security guard. The aggressor bargains the organization layer and acquires command over an IoT gadget (Nagaraj, 2021). IoT gadgets give numerous chances to aggressors to agreement them. It uses vindictive messages, arrange-

DOI: 10.4018/978-1-7998-8367-8.ch009

ment assaults, and forswearing of administration assaults among different kinds of assault. The instrument for assault location is isolated. It underpins the canny preparing and investigation of information and dynamic in a self-ruling way by connecting such devices as information handling joins specialized gadgets and sensors.

Cloud processing (Aceto, Botta, Donato, & W., 2013) (Ambika N., 2019) fills the front end in the IoT. It permits end clients to utilize the whole scope of administrations upheld over the web to do their normal figuring activities. It additionally gives elite, unwavering grades and pervasiveness to the IoT. Such assignments include cloud-based assault recognition in the IoT. It is a unified assault discovery framework. It performs inadequately because of the overheads brought about by putting away and preparing information from a consistently more number of gadgets. It suggests that the current cloud-based assault identification system can't tackle the assault location issue.

The previous work (Song, Liu, Wei, Wang, Tao, & Chen, 2020) accepts that the model breaking time is longer than the model update time frame. The engineering approach comprises two sections Industrial IoT gadgets and their cloud worker. The Deep Neural Networks dwelled in Industrial IoT gadgets are answerable for the Deep Neural Networks development for opposing antagonistic models. At first, all the instruments share similar Deep Neural Networks. They communicate in various conditions. They experience diverse information models and various sorts of assaults. The uneven characters make the combined learning the best answer for total distinctive guard abilities. The cloud worker comprises two modules. The assault screen module records the most recent assault data for Industrial IoT gadgets as their areas or types. The module deals with a library comprising of all the revealed assault plans. When the assault screen module recognizes some new assault for a gadget, it will require the instrument to download the relating assault plot with the end goal of ill-disposed retraining. The combined protection model age module intermittently gathers gadget slope data and totals them to accomplish a refreshed model with better heartiness. At that point, the module will dispatch the recently framed model to all the associated Industrial IoT gadgets with the end goal of model synchronization. During the execution of an Industrial IoT device, the gadget keeps a cushion to hold the nature models. For a particular period, all the Industrial IoT gadgets retrain and synchronize in a united adapting way. This cycle comprises three stages. Every device produces comparing ill-disposed models locally to shape a retraining set, whose components are sets of nature models and relating antagonistic models. In the subsequent advance, the nearby adversarial preparing measure occasionally transfers the recently accomplished angle data from Industrial IoT gadgets to the cloud worker for the model update and synchronization. The model produces by the combined protection approach and conveys each associated Industrial IoT gadget.

The work has some pitfalls. The software attacks download by the deployed IoT devices. The assaults can make the gadgets behave abnormally(if they get compromised). Hence keeping the machines safe from intruders is necessary. The devices collect the attack data. The suggestion enhances security by using two kinds of devices. The illegitimate bits are loaded into the dynamic devices. The same is communicated to the cloud. The cloud generates the prediction model and updates the same to the static instruments. The devices are secure by 9.54% and increase availability by 8.54% compared to the previous contribution. The chapter has four divisions. The second segment summarizes the proposal suggested by other authors. The third section details the proposal and compares the work with the previous contribution. The fourth division concludes the chapter.

LITERATURE SURVEY

Many authors have provided their suggestions regarding the considered domain. The section summarizes the same. A Deep blockchain system (Alkadi, Moustafa, Turnbull, & Choo, 2020) distinguishes digital assaults and ensures the information in the cloud. The deliberate design incorporates four primary parts. They are elements inside a cloud network situated in the blockchain network. These substances are relied upon to have enough cloud administrations to give them client elements. The protection conservation-based Blockchain and savvy contract layer are not the same as a customary cloud network as it fuses a consortium blockchain. This element is repeated and put away in various hubs of the multi-cloud organization, including inside the Central Coordinator, server farms, or individual hosts. The proposition is comparative information design to Bitcoin construction. Mining new squares remunerate along the way toward adding a block to the blockchain. The Central Coordinator goes about as a SIEM apparatus to store detection system review logs and cautions. The various sources undergo investigation and separation. It is related to recognizing ordinary and abnormal occasions. It would empower network overseers to quickly relieve dangers and increment security mindfulness for members inside cloud organizations. The Coordinated identification framework element organizes the confirmation of casings running on the cloud exchange organization and further guarantees the predetermined principles. They comprise numerous recognition frameworks conveyed on huge appropriated organizations or individuals. It distinguishes facilitated cyber attacks and forestalls conceivable unlawful activities. The role of the discovery framework is to upgrade the general location exactness of a solitary detection system hub. It connects assault proof over different sub-organizations.

The security setting meeting layer (Choi & Choi, 2019) decides the security setting by utilizing the security information conveyed from the distributed computing layer and the IoT layer. It uses the setting surmising module. It uses the data characterized in the cosmology to decide the security setting. The security setting the board layer is a module that gathers security setting data. It creates setting data by gathering security information of the IoT gadgets. It delivers a security occasion in the setting surmising module. The deduction motor and rule of the executive's module covers question age and security setting philosophy into a web cosmology language to induct the security setting metaphysics. The setting deduction module changes over the got security setting data into a question type. It refers to the setting philosophy and planned derivation rules. After surmising the security setting data, a reaction strategy is accommodated. It gives a security setting to the security reaction module. In a force IoT-Cloud climate, the security setting reasoned module comprises a surmising motor and metaphysics storehouse. A triple interpreter, question overseer, and reasoned have a place with the surmising motor and connect with the cosmology storehouse.

The utilization of savvy medical services frameworks (Alhussein, Muhammad, Hossain, & Amin, 2018) is an interconnected brilliant city climate. It empowers occupants and clinical specialists to utilize intelligent sensor gadgets and cloud and psychological IoT mindful advancements of their electronic wellbeing records. Through shrewd wearable innovation and correspondence, patients can consistently refresh their wellbeing-related information. The psychological framework breaks down knowledge progressively and plays out the best activity to offers assistance to patients. The transferred information dissects by clinical staff individuals gives help and counsel to the concerned patients. The sort of patient ward medical care checking is fundamental for medical care. It accomplishes its significant goals, for example, low medical services cost. The neighborhood layer sends the signals from the IoT gadgets layer to a facilitating layer comprising heterogeneous gadgets. It is either worn by patients or installed in city conditions, for example, brilliant homes, clinical focuses, workplaces, or autos. These sensor gadgets can likewise speak with one another utilizing short-range correspondence. The LAN interface layer is shrewd correspondence conventions for short-to medium-range correspondence and interconnection between devices. The facilitating layer contains heterogeneous intelligent gadgets, for example, cell phones, tablets, individual advanced right hand, PCs, or workstations, which gather information to prepare locally. These gadgets have the preparing capacity to distinguish general wellbeing irregularities through devoted applications or projects. Medical issues can incorporate irregular pulse, pulse, or internal heat levels. It sends the same to the cloud for preparation through the WAN interface. The cloud includes the cloud director, server farm, highlight extraction worker, location worker, and characterization worker. The cloud administrator initially confirms whether an occupant is a part of a savvy medical care supplier. The cloud supervisor is liable for checking the personality of all partners in the shrewd medical care framework. The cloud director controls the information stream to and from the different workers and oversees correspondence, stockpiling, and various assets. The cloud chief sends the information to the intellectual motor. It utilizes multimodal knowledge includes EEG, mental and physiological learning, and decides if the patient necessities crisis care.

It is a Semi-Supervised Fuzzy C-Means strategy (Rathore & Park, 2018). It incorporates a Semi-directed Fuzzy CMeans with the Extreme Learning Machine classifier to help proficient assault identification in IoT. The semi-administered bunching strategy depends on utilizing various kinds of earlier learning to upgrade grouping performance. It permits information to highlight divergent classes with a few tiers of participation and offers extra theoretical improvement in a grouping. Along these lines, it gives a more sensible approach to treat examples, and it can likewise distinguish inevitable exceptions. The initial course means the first target capacity to find the concealed space structure, and the subsequent term considers titled information to characterize the information structure. The calculation depends on exact danger minimization. The quantity at the yield layer of SLFNs is controlled by arbitrarily allotting the loads and predispositions to the info and shrouded layer. For example, the Support Vector Machine gives better speculation execution at a quicker learning speed. It first trains the classifier on the marked dataset to create the prepared model. The classifier utilizes the shrouded hubs and the sigmoid actuation work as a concealed hub yield work.

The framework (Tian, Luo, Qiu, Du, & Guizani, 2019) has data readiness, perception, and activities. URLs gathered from edge gadgets of the cloud will be first shipped off data planning, the prepared information contributes to Feature Discriminator and Data Discriminator for discovery. Activities will react as per the outcomes from Discernment. Information Preparation changes over crude URLs gathered from edge gadgets into portrayals. The crude URLs will be decoded and brought down in Processing and encodes information in an uncommon organization in learning standardization. The addressed information ships off Data Discriminator. It fits the contributions of the Feature Discriminator. The knowledge will likewise be changed over into vectors in the component portrayal. Separation is liable for recognizing ordinary URL demands and Anomalous URL demands containing web assaults. We proposed different models in our framework. Activities play out a reaction when all discriminators settle on a similar choice. It will react as indicated by the outcomes from the Comprehensive option. Moves will make a typical reaction if a URL is distinguished as expected.

Fog expects to start to finish insurance against aggressors in the cloud-to-things continuum. The dependability of the correspondence in the general framework commences with making sure about individual hubs. The assault location framework (Diro & Chilamkurti, 2018) assumes a crucial part in the climate as a safeguarding instrument. The engineering uncovers that the preparation and discovery work is performed on every core. The planning center registers and appropriates the update of models and boundaries to each hub. This plan gives the component that apportioning information put away, prepared, and tried at a solitary detect, the cloud. It disperses calculations, controls, and information put away on nearby hubs. Every hub recognizes the interruption of close by IoT gadgets while it trades learned encounters with neighbor hubs through an organizer hub.

The fog hubs (Diro & Chilamkurti, 2018) are liable for preparing models and facilitating assault discovery frameworks at the edge of the conveyed mist organization. The planning ace hub ought to be set up for community boundary sharing and streamlining. It gives independence to nearby assault locations. It uses neighborhood preparation and boundary advancement. The expert core refreshes the boundaries of every agreeable hub. It spreads the subsequent update back to the specialist hubs.

PROPOSED WORK

The previous work (Song, Liu, Wei, Wang, Tao, & Chen, 2020) accepts that the model breaking time is longer than the model update time frame. The engineering approach comprises two sections Industrial IoT gadgets and their cloud worker. The Deep Neural Networks dwelled in Industrial IoT gadgets are answerable for the Deep Neural Networks development for opposing antagonistic models. At first, all the instruments share similar Deep Neural Networks. They convey in various conditions. They experience diverse information models and various sorts of assaults. The uneven characters make the combined learning the best answer for total distinctive guard abilities. The cloud worker comprises two modules. The assault screen module records the most recent assault data for Industrial IoT gadgets as their areas or types. The module deals with a library comprising of all the revealed assault plans. When the assault screen module recognizes some new assault for a gadget, it will require the instrument to download the relating assault plot with the end goal of ill-disposed retraining. The combined protection model age module intermittently gathers gadget slope data and totals them to accomplish a refreshed model with better heartiness. At that point, the module will dispatch the recently framed model to all the associated Industrial IoT gadgets with the end goal of model synchronization. During the execution of an Industrial IoT device, the gadget keeps a cushion to hold the nature models. For a particular period, all the Industrial IoT gadgets retrain and synchronize in a united adapting way. This cycle comprises three stages. Every device produces comparing ill-disposed models locally to shape a retraining set, whose components are sets of nature models and relating antagonistic models. In the subsequent advance, the nearby adversarial preparing measure occasionally transfers the recently accomplished angle data from Industrial IoT gadgets to the cloud worker for the model update and synchronization. The model produces by the combined protection approach and conveys each associated Industrial IoT gadget.

The Drawbacks of the Previous System

- The software attacks are downloaded by the deployed IoT devices. The assaults can make the gadgets behave abnormally (if they get compromised). Hence keeping the devices safe from intruders is necessary.
- The devices collect the attack data rather than sensing the data.

Assumptions

- The IoT devices deployed are liable to attacks. They can get compromised and introduce different kinds of attacks.
- The devices are loaded with a prediction model. The attacks introduced by the intruder either partially/completely match with the behavior of the adversary. Hence the mapping between the communicating bits and prediction model provides the intention of the communicating party.
- Two kinds of IoT devices are deployed –
  - Static IoT devices that sense the environment and provide processed data to the host machines (cloud). They are also programmed to record the occurrence of the attack by verifying with the prediction model.
  - A dynamic device that moves from one location to another sampling the data.
  - Both the devices sync w.r.t to their location.

Role of Static Devices

The motionless and dynamic nodes are 3:1 in ratio. The static devices are installed in the environment to sense the same. These devices make a comparison of the communicating bits with the prediction model. If it senses that the device is illegitimate, it messages the mobile device about the same. This device maintains the count of occurrence of the attack, time of the attack, and its sample data(some bits of communication).

Responsibility of Dynamic Devices

The dynamic devices after receiving the message from the motionless device. This gadget moves to the location of the static device and communicates with the intruder. It collects the sample from the same and communicates with storage (cloud).

The rest of the functionality is similar to (Song, Liu, Wei, Wang, Tao, & Chen, 2020).

Analysis of the Proposal

The suggestion enhances security by using two kinds of devices. The illegitimate bits load into the dynamic devices. The same is communicated to the cloud. The cloud generates the prediction model and updates the same to the static devices. The work is simulated using NS2. Table 1 represents the settings made in the simulated environment.

Table 1. Setting in the simulated environment

Parameters used	Explanation
Dimension of the network	200 m* 200m
Number of static nodes	15
Number of dynamic devices	3
Number of adversaries	4
Length of data communicated	750 bits
Length of sampled bits	10 bits
Size of prediction module	100 kb
Number of rules in the prediction module	200
Total simulation time	60 s

Security

The static devices are secure compared to the previous work (Song, Liu, Wei, Wang, Tao, & Chen, 2020), as these devices are not involved in collecting the attack bits. The devices are secure by 9.54%. Figure 1 represents the same.

Figure 1. comparison of both the work w.r.t security

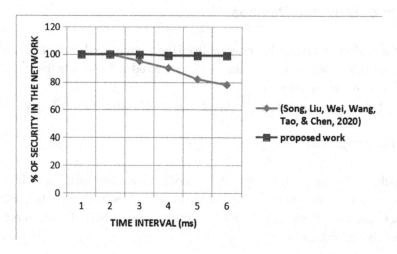

Availability

The previous work (Song, Liu, Wei, Wang, Tao, & Chen, 2020)installs the software (attack bits). It will be involved in processing the same. The devices are installed to sense the environment and take some appropriate measures on time. Hence their availability is a necessity. The contribution has two kinds of devices installed. One set performs the regular activity along with listing the attack bits. The second category of devices samples the attack bits and communicates to the cloud. Comparing with the previous

Figure 2. System availability representations

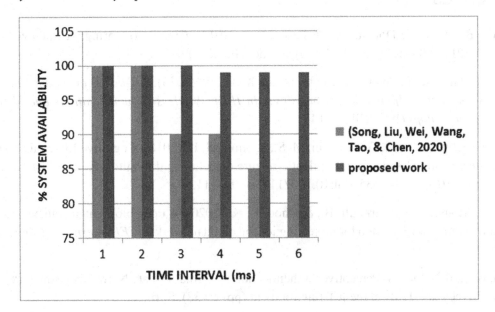

work (Song, Liu, Wei, Wang, Tao, & Chen, 2020), the proposal increases availability by 8.54%. Figure 2 represents the same.

CONCLUSION

IoT comprises different things having personalities, physical and virtual ascribes. It is flawless and safely coordinated into the Internet. IoT portrays by craziness peaky traffic, extraordinary heterogeneity of gadget structure, capacity, and inertness prerequisites, just as the outrageous geographic dispersion of framework from the cloud to the gadget, the purported cloud-to-thing continuum. The conventional model is distributed computing. It works out considerably unexpected financial and specialized standards evaluating IoT, with unified capacity and handling in the cloud and related economies of scale from unifying these capacities in multi-inhabitant server farms.

The previous work accepts that the model breaking time is longer than the model update time frame. The engineering approach comprises two sections Industrial IoT gadgets and their cloud worker. The cloud worker comprises two modules. The assault screen module records the most recent assault data for Industrial IoT gadgets as their areas or types. The module deals with a library comprising of all the revealed assault plans. When the assault screen module recognizes some new assault for a gadget, it will require the instrument to download the relating assault plot with the end goal of ill-disposed retraining. The enhanced approach improves the earlier by increasing availability by 8.54% and security by 9.54%. The suggestion enhances security by using two kinds of devices. The illegitimate bits are loaded into the dynamic devices. The same is communicated to the cloud. The cloud generates the prediction model and updates the same to the static devices.

REFERENCES

Aceto, G., Botta, A., de Donato, W., & Pescapè, A. (2013). Cloud monitoring: A Survey. *Computer Networks, 57*(9), 2093–2115. doi:10.1016/j.comnet.2013.04.001

Akkaya, K., Guvenc, I., Aygun, R., Pala, N., & Kadri, A. (2015). *IoT-based occupancy monitoring techniques for energy-efficient smart buildings. In IEEE Wireless Communications and Networking Conference Workshops (WCNCW)*. IEEE.

Alhussein, M., Muhammad, G., Hossain, M. S., & Amin, S. U. (2018). Cognitive IoT-cloud integration for smart healthcare: Case study for epileptic seizure detection and monitoring. *Mobile Networks and Applications, 23*(6), 1624–1635. doi:10.100711036-018-1113-0

Alkadi, O., Moustafa, N., Turnbull, B., & Choo, K. K. (2020). A deep blockchain framework-enabled collaborative intrusion detection for protecting iot and cloud networks. *IEEE Internet of Things Journal,* 1–12.

Ambika, N. (2019). Energy-Perceptive Authentication in Virtual Private Networks Using GPS Data. In Security, Privacy and Trust in the IoT Environment (pp. 25-38). Springer.

Ambika, N. (2020). Encryption of Data in Cloud-Based Industrial IoT Devices. In S. Pal & V. G. Díaz (Eds.), *IoT: Security and Privacy Paradigm* (pp. 111–129). CRC Press, Taylor & Francis Group.

Atzori, L., Iera, A., & Morabito, G. (2010). The internet of things: A Survey. *Computer Networks, 54*(15), 2787–2805. doi:10.1016/j.comnet.2010.05.010

Choi, C., & Choi, J. (2019). Ontology-based security context reasoning for power IoT-cloud security service. *IEEE Access: Practical Innovations, Open Solutions, 7*, 110510–110517. doi:10.1109/ACCESS.2019.2933859

Diro, A., & Chilamkurti, N. (2018). Leveraging LSTM networks for attack detection in fog-to-things communications. *IEEE Communications Magazine, 56*(9), 124–130. doi:10.1109/MCOM.2018.1701270

Diro, A. A., & Chilamkurti, N. (2018). Distributed attack detection scheme using deep learning approach for Internet of Things. *Future Generation Computer Systems, 82*, 761–768. doi:10.1016/j.future.2017.08.043

Doukas, C., & Maglogiannis, I. (2012). Bringing IoT and Cloud Computing towards Pervasive Healthcare. 6 international conference on innovative mobile and internet services in ubiquitous computing.

Elhoseny, M., Shankar, K., Lakshmanaprabu, S. K., Maseleno, A., & Arunkumar, N. (2018). Hybrid optimization with cryptography encryption for medical image security in Internet of Things. *Neural Computing & Applications,* 1–15. doi:10.100700521-018-3801-x

Masek, P., Masek, J., Frantik, P., Fujdiak, R., Ometov, A., Hosek, J., Andreev, S., Mlynek, P., & Misurec, J. (2016). A Harmonized Perspective on Transportation Management in Smart Cities: The Novel IoT-Driven Environment for Road Traffic Modeling. *Sensors (Basel), 16*(11), 1872. doi:10.339016111872 PMID:27834796

Nagaraj, A. (2021). Introduction to Sensors in IoT and Cloud Computing Applications. Bentham Science Publishers. doi:10.2174/97898114793591210101

Rathore, S., & Park, J. H. (2018). Semi-supervised learning based distributed attack detection framework for IoT. *Applied Soft Computing*, *72*, 79–89. doi:10.1016/j.asoc.2018.05.049

Song, Y., Liu, T., Wei, T., Wang, X., Tao, Z., & Chen, M. (2020). Fda3: Federated defense against adversarial attacks for cloud-based iiot applications. *IEEE Transactions on Industrial Informatics*, 1–8. doi:10.1109/TII.2020.3005969

Tian, Z., Luo, C., Qiu, J., Du, X., & Guizani, M. (2019). A distributed deep learning system for web attack detection on edge devices. *IEEE Transactions on Industrial Informatics*, *16*(3), 1963–1971. doi:10.1109/TII.2019.2938778

Chapter 10
Recent Trends in Block Chain Technology:
Challenges and Opportunities

Kannadhasan S.

https://orcid.org/0000-0001-6443-9993

Cheran College of Engineering, India

R. Nagarajan

Gnanamani College of Technology, India

ABSTRACT

Blockchain is a peer-to-peer (P2P) distributed ledger technology that provides openness and confidence for a new age of transactional applications. The fundamental fabric for bitcoin is blockchain, which is a design pattern made up of three core elements: a distributed network, a public ledger, and digital transactions. Digital transactions are recorded in a public ledger by members of the distributed network. Members of the network run algorithms to test and validate the planned transaction before adding it to the network. The latest transaction is applied to the public ledger if a number of the network participants believe that the transaction is legitimate. In minutes or seconds, changes to the public ledger are mirrored in all copies of the blockchain. A transaction is immutable after it has been added and cannot be reversed or deleted. No one user of the network has the ability to tamper with or change data, and everybody in the network has a full copy of the blockchain. Blockchain is a peer-to-peer (P2P) network of nodes made up of network members.

INTRODUCTION

Blockchain has become recognised as the distributed ledger for all transactions and solved the double-spend issue by integrating peer-to-peer infrastructure with public-key cryptography after it was first conceptualised as a central feature to facilitate transactions in the digital currency – Bitcoin. A blockchain, literally, is a network of knowledge blocks that records Bitcoin transactions; of course, there are

DOI: 10.4018/978-1-7998-8367-8.ch010

strict laws that regulate how to check the block's authenticity to ensure that it cannot be changed or vanish. Blockchain technology refers to the algorithms and computing infrastructure for generating, adding, and utilising blocks. The double-spend dilemma is solved by blockchain technologies using public-key cryptography, in which each individual is given a private key and a public key is exchanged with all other users. The basic concept behind blockchain is that it is a distributed ledger that contains records of transactions that are exchanged by participants. None each of these transactions is validated by a plurality of the system's users, illegitimate transactions are unable to pass mutual scrutiny. A record can never be changed once it is generated and approved by the blockchain. Existing blockchain research has primarily concentrated on device performance, stability, and novel applications. One of the most critical problems for blockchain is performance (Abbott, 2000; Allenby, 2012; Almeida et al., 2015; Antonopoulos, 2014; Ansell & Gash, 2007). To build a new transaction record on the blockchain, a very strict authentication procedure is needed, which results in a substantial delay in validation period and waste of computational resources.

A transaction currently requires about 10 minutes to be authenticated. Thousands of nodes are now working to process and validate transfers. These problems severely restrict the scope of blockchain implementations. As an alternative, Since IoT devices which have to deal with limited computing capacity or low strength, existing blockchain approaches are typically not appropriate for the Internet of Things (IoT) network. As an innovative platform, blockchain has been hailed as a new way to address the demands of individuals, technology, and organisations. For a contract, trust has become a critical function that blockchain may offer. People could be able to share their assets without fear of violating their privacy thanks to modern confidence structures emerging from Blockchain. The blockchin technology allows for open, peer-to-peer, and coalition-based business group organisation. The Bitcoin framework has served as a realistic model of a decentralised enterprise under which no single government is in charge of the system's problem and management. The peer-to-peer relationships between nodes in the blockchain framework are peer to peer. Furthermore, blockchains have the ability to organise, vote, and shape coalitions. The blockchain system's technical components include trustless computation, smart contracts, and network stability (Dubovitskaya et al., 2017; Kblaw et al., 2016; Mylrea & Gourisetti, 2017; Strobel et al., 2018; Yaji et al., 2018).

In a shared blockchain scheme, to reach a consensus. People may not have to care about the confidence problem of smart contracts, because an entity will be autonomous dependent on the autoexecution of codes. These functions are based on network reliability, which allows users to put their faith in the device while conducting business transactions. Researchers should conduct three stages of analysis to resolve the problems of blockchain implementation in a market environment: logical, prescriptive, and descriptive levels. Currently, market analysis in blockchain is mostly focused on the conceptual stage, which conceptualises blockchain technologies in business, and the prescriptive level, which details blockchain business implementations.

For health care and information technology, this is an interesting moment (IT). Health care is seeing a groundbreaking transition to disease prevention and management that combines a particular patient's genetic profile, diet, and climate, thanks to advancements in genetic science and precision medicine. Simultaneously, technological advancements have resulted in vast libraries of health records, resources for tracking health data, and increased people's involvement in their own health care (How Blockchain Can Fight Fraud, 2019; Kolias et al., 2017; Kshetri, 2017; Trautman & Ormerod, 2016; Yeoh, 2017). In the area of health IT, combining these advances in health care and information technology will result in revolutionary reform.

BLOCKCHAIN TECHNOLOGY

Blockchain technology has the potential to solve the existing interoperability problems in health IT systems and become the technological norm that allows patients, health care professionals, health care agencies, and medical researchers to safely exchange electronic health records. Each network participant keeps an identical copy of the blockchain and participates in the network's collaborative phase of validating and certifying cryptographic transactions. A blockchain can hold any sort of data or digital asset, and the network that implements the blockchain determines what type of data is held in each transaction. To ensure authenticity and consistency, data is secured and digitally signed. Blocks are used to organise transactions, and each block incorporates a cryptographic hash of the previous block in the blockchain. The blocks are placed in a chronological sequence. Bitcoin is a cryptocurrency trading network that is built on open-source cryptographic protocols and has proved to be extremely safe. Although the names behind certain Bitcoin transactions remain secret, the network promotes openness by allowing everyone to view balances and transactions on every Bitcoin address on the blockchain.

The Bitcoin public blockchain is unsuitable for a health blockchain that needs privacy and regulated, auditable access due to a lack of data privacy and robust security. Furthermore, for large-scale and commonly used blockchain implementations, the Bitcoin standard for block size and maximum amount of transactions per second raises scalability issues. Privacy, stability, and scalability issues will be addressed by private and consortium-led blockchains. These blockchains, on the other hand, will present unique problems because they are not vendor neutral and do not adhere to transparent principles. The customer would have complete say of how his data was transmitted and would have full access to it. The consumer must designate who may query and write data to his blockchain and grant a collection of access permissions. The customer will be able to see who has authorization to view his blockchain via a smartphone dashboard feature. The customer will now see an audit list of who has accessed his blockchain, as well as where and what data has been accessed. The consumer will be able to grant and revoke access permissions to any person with a unique identification using the same dashboard.

Permissions for access management will be more open than "all-or-nothing" permissions. The consumer will create specific, informative transfers describing who has access, how long they have access for, and what kinds of data they may access. The consumer will change his or her permissions at any time. Access management rules will be automatically maintained on a blockchain as well, with only the customer having the ability to modify them. This creates a transparent atmosphere in which the consumer has complete control of what data is gathered and how it is transmitted. After being given access to a user's health records, a health care company searches the blockchain for the user's details and uses the digital signature to authenticate it. To interpret the health details, the health care professional may use a personalised best-of-breed programme.

Blockchain can operate on commodity hardware that is readily available and stable. Commodity hardware delivers the most useful computation for the least sum of money. The hardware is built on open specifications and is made by a variety of companies. For health and genomic science, it is the most cost-effective and reliable design. Excess blockchain hardware capacity may be exchanged with health researchers, allowing for quicker medication and treatment exploration. Interoperability issues in the wellbeing IT environment are often addressed through blockchain technologies. Open APIs can be used by health IT applications to connect and share data with the health blockchain. The best practises in the sector are used to create open APIs. They are simple to use and will minimise the need for complicated point-to-point data integrations between the various systems. Patients, health care providers, and analysts will be able to use a single shared data source to collect reliable, correct, and detailed patient health data. Patients' smartphone apps, wearable sensors, EMRs, records, and photographs are only some of the health data streams that blockchain data systems paired with data lakes may help. The data systems are adaptable and extensible, and they would be able to handle any potential data that becomes usable.

The amount of data generated by low-cost mobile devices and wearable sensors is the at an exponential pace. Cost-effective high scalability is provided by distributed architectures built on commodity hardware. Cost-effective commodity hardware can be quickly introduced to support the elevated load as more health data is added to the blockchain. Built-in error tolerance and catastrophe recovery are another benefit of blockchain's distributed design. Data is spread through a number of servers in various locations. There is no common point of collapse, and a catastrophe affecting both areas at the same time is impossible. For cryptography and data security, blockchain uses common algorithms and protocols. These innovations have been thoroughly examined and deemed safe, and they are commonly utilised in a variety of industries and government agencies is shown in Figure 1.

Blockchain technology systems will be ideal for collecting data from wearable devices and mobile phones, providing valuable insight into care complications and benefits, as well as patient-reported results. Furthermore, by integrating health data from smartphone apps and wearable sensors with data from conventional EMRs and genomics, medical researchers may be able to further differentiate individuals into subpopulations who react well to a particular medication or are more vulnerable to a certain disease. Patients would be more engaged with their own health treatment and enforcement would definitely increase once they have regular, customised health records. Furthermore, allowing doctors to collect more regular data (e.g., daily blood pressure or blood sugar measurements rather than only when a patient shows up for an appointment) will increase individualised care and specialised medication schedules focused on outcomes/treatment effectiveness.

Figure 1. Block chain technology

Continuous availability and connectivity to real-time data will be ensured via blockchain. Hospital service management and clinical care in emergency response conditions will benefit from real-time data access. Researchers and public policy resources will be able to track, isolate, and accelerate reform for environmental factors that affect public health using real-time data. Epidemics, for example, may be reported and controlled early. The blockchain's real-time availability of mobile app and wearable sensor data will allow constant, 24-hour surveillance of high-risk patients and spur the development of "smart" apps that would alert caregivers and health professionals if a patient crossed a crucial threshold for intervention. Early intervention recovery services could be coordinated by care teams reaching out to the patient. A health care blockchain will likely encourage the development of a new breed of "smart" applications for health providers that will mine the most recent medical research and develop personalised treatment paths, with both the health provider and the patient having access to the same information and being able to engage in a collaborative, educated discussion on the best-case treatment options based on research findings.

APPLICATIONS OF BLOCK CHAIN TECHNOLOGY

Blockchain has many implementations in a variety of areas, with agriculture being one of the most exciting. Food protection by provenance traceability, database systems, agro-trade, banking, seed registration, and insurance are all examples of blockchain applications in agriculture. As a result, the aim of this paper is to study blockchain applications in agriculture from all major databases, ranging from Web of Science to Scopus. According to the report, although there are several blockchain-based applications in agriculture, only a few countries have grasped it, with China leading the way, led by the United States, Italy, India, and Spain. This paper also examines emerging developments in blockchain science in agriculture and offers recommendations for potential research. Blockchain is the most talked-about topic in today's environment, and it is also regarded as one of the most destructive inventions to date. Blockchain is a public ledger that is decentralised and unaltered cryptographically. It is used to document the past of digital transactions (IBM, Hyperledger). In a blockchain scheme, each participant (stakeholder) keeps a copy of all previous transactions that have ever been processed via the system. However, no one party/node owns the machine, indicating that it is not centralised. This model of decentralised structure establishes a basis of confidence since all operation in the system is transparent and auditable by all stakeholders. For any transaction to take place, a consensus algorithm must be followed, which ensures that a majority of nodes must consent on the matter in order for it to be validated and approved. Furthermore, since a blockchain-based framework does not need a mediator or third party for transactions, settlement costs are reduced. This transactions are often permanent, eliminating the need for every public or private entity to serve as a middleman, resulting in a more effective method. The members concerned do not need to trust each other since the structure and code are foolproof.

Consider a village with a limited number of residents where a deal must be made between two individuals or groups. All in the village gathers on a shared forum for this exchange, which takes place in front of everyone. All should keep a record of this exchange in their notebook. Now, in the future or at any moment, none of the two parties involved in the transaction will say any incorrect details or dispute the transaction since everybody in the village has the original note. In order to falsify the information, the fraudster will then have to alter the notice on everyone's copy in the village, which is impossible in practise. Assume that these transactions take place through machines, and that each of the villagers has their own machine where the record is kept. Furthermore, these transfers are encrypted, authenticated, and validated by anonymous approvers (also called as miners). This is how it works in a real-world blockchain environment, where all data/records are held in blocks and everybody on the network has a copy.

Any new transactions are introduced to the new stack, which is connected to the previous ones. Since it is cryptographically protected, it cannot be tampered with. Figure 1 depicts the detailed operation of a blockchain-based method, which can be illustrated in six simple measures. In phase one, a transaction is demanded, and in step two, it is broadcast to all related networks.

The groundwork for a modern form of monetary settlements is being laid by blockchain technology, which has the ability to disrupt the global fiat monetary system. Bitcoin, a newly created cryptocurrency that has sparked global interest and anticipation, is built on the blockchain's operational features. Rather than relying on a centralised infrastructure, blockchain technology distributes a database through a network of interconnected data networks. A blockchain is a computing data system that stores all transactions that have occurred since the blockchain's inception. This arrangement is copied and exchanged among all networked computers that participate. When a new transaction is submitted, it is batched with other transactions to form a "stack," and is then regularly added to the front of the blockchain as the most recent "block" of transactions. The network of participating computers updates their blockchain to match the agreed blockchain until the "block" is acknowledged by a plurality of machines.

The benefits of blockchain are many. To begin with, it is currently a peer-to-peer network with no single point of failure. If one node fails, the remaining nodes can continue to function, ensuring the system's availability and viability. Second, nearly all of the data is digital and can be used in a variety of applications. Third, since all transactions on the Blockchain are transparent to all users, auditability and confidence are improved. Fourth, making modifications to the Blockchain is exceedingly complex, because if it were to arise, it would be apparent to all other users, and if not validated, it would be removed from the block. The scope for blockchain to be used is undeniable. "Blockchain has the power to transform the way we purchase and sell, engage with government, and check the validity of everything from land deeds to organic vegetables," according to Goldman Sachs. It blends the transparency of the internet with the reliability of cryptography to provide a quicker, more secure way for anyone to validate key details and build trust." While a large number of companies are working on blockchain initiatives, it does not appear that full-scale deployment is yet taking place. When early adopters share their success stories, this would most certainly shift. One part of deployment that is yet to be decided is whether the gain can exceed the expense. Since the complete utility of blockchain technologies cannot be achieved without input from relevant third parties, comprehensive replacement of legacy applications and processes is currently not feasible. This creates a conundrum for implementers who wish to venture past the exploratory stage: will substantial capital investments be justified for a technology that has little use right now? The most probable programmes to be implemented would be those of a precise and limited focus, allowing for straightforward and prompt follow-up and review.

To process electronic payments, Internet commerce has come to depend almost entirely on financial entities acting as trustworthy third parties. Although the scheme is adequate for certain purchases, it also suffers from the trust-based model's inherent flaws.

Since financial firms cannot prevent mediating conflicts, completely non-reversible transactions are not feasible. The expense of settlement raises transaction rates, reducing the minimum transaction amount and eliminating the likelihood of minor informal purchases, as well as a larger cost in the lack of right to allow non-reversible purchases for non-reversible services. The need for confidence grows as the likelihood of reversal grows. Customers should be suspicious of merchants who pester them for more details than they want.

A certain amount of fraud is assumed to be inevitable. This expenses and transfer risks can be eliminated in person when utilising actual currencies, but there is no way to allow transfers without a trustworthy party via a messaging system. An electronic payment mechanism focused on cryptographic evidence rather than confidence is required, enabling any two willing parties to interact directly with each other without the involvement of a trustworthy third party. Sellers will be protected from theft by transactions that are computationally impossible to cancel, and consumers will be protected by standard escrow mechanisms is shown in Figure 2. We suggest a solution to the double-spending issue in this article, which uses a peer-to-peer distributed timestamp server to produce statistical evidence of transaction chronological order. As long as honest nodes jointly control more CPU power than any cooperating community of attacker nodes, the device is stable.

A blockchain is a 'distributed archive of documents, or public ledger, of all transactions or digital events that have been completed and exchanged by participating parties.' It allows peer-to-peer transactions, excluding external parties from the equation (for example, banks/financial institutions/states in the conventional style of currency exchange) and maintaining accountability and cost effectiveness. The application of this technology in cryptocurrency payments is the most current and contentious case that has been linked to it.

A Blockchain may be completely transparent or completely private. As in the case of common decentralised blockchains such as Bitcoin, Ethereum, Litecoin, and others, the former is totally free for anyone to participate, i.e. everyone may access the network, apply to transact, or participate in the consensus phase. The above is a permissioned network that operates on an invite-only basis and centralises write permissions with a single entity/organization. As a result, it is not really decentralised, and it limits the amount of participants in a contract as well as the authentication phase. A Consortium Blockchain exists anywhere between a completely decentralised public Blockchain and a single highly trustworthy individual paradigm with a private block chain. It is a combination between the two forms of Blockchains and is partly decentralised, with the consensus mechanism regulated by a pre-selected collection of nodes. For example, in a coalition of thirty organisations, it could be pre-determined that each block must be signed by sixteen of the chosen representatives in order for it to be legitimate. BMW, GM, Ford, and Renault, along with other partners, recently unveiled the Mobility Open Blockchain Initiative (MOBI), a consortium blockchain network aimed at making mobility safer, greener, and more accessible.

Figure 2. Applications of block chain technology

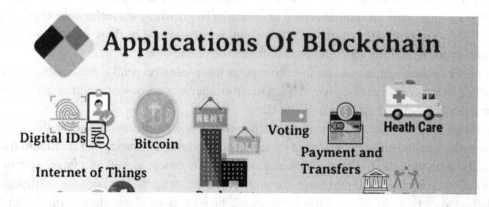

The fundamental foundation of any contract is confidence, whether it is the transacting entity, banks/financial entities acting as intermediaries, or the state acting as regulator. This confidence is established in the digital environment by demonstrating identity (authentication) and permissions (authorisation). Each user has one private and one public cryptographic key under Blockchain technology, similar to a university's public and private IP address. The university's users will see the private IP, whilst the public IP is provided to the network and can be used by other users. Similarly, one signs cryptocurrencies sent to another with his or her private key to their public key, and he or she receives cryptocurrencies sent to his or her address with his or her public key. A digital signature is formed by two keys working together, and the information sent/received is part of a block. When an individual authorises a transaction using a secret key they own and the block chain confirms it, it becomes part of the public ledger (in the case of a completely public blockchain) and everybody (all blockchain participants) will see what value is being transacted.

The anonymity of the transaction is maintained, though, by maintaining the transactor's identification private, i.e., the participants can see the money is being exchanged but no details connecting the transaction to someone. The following diagram better illustrates the privacy model: In addition, blockchain is touted as an incorruptible, irrefutable, and irreversible database of transactions. It has a competitive advantage over conventional trading mediums by providing unrivalled protection advantages. If a hacker was to get through a single block in a Blockchain, they'd have to get through any of the preceding blocks as well, all the way back to the beginning of the Blockchain's existence. They'd have to do that on all of the network's ledgers at the same time, which might number in the millions. As a result, blockchain records details in such a way that any alteration to the blockchain, such as inserting, deleting, or modifying data, is almost impossible to go undetected by other blockchain users. For example, every update to a bitcoin blockchain must be validated by 51 percent of all users in the network through a consensus process, which is unlikely to happen since they have little reason to act on the chain's "old" blocks.

VARIOUS SECTORS IN BLOCKCHAIN TECHNOLOGY

Blockchain technology is a very recent concept. According to Wikipedia, it is "a continuously growing list of documents, known as squares, that are bound and anchored using cryptography." We would discern a delegate analysis of flow issues in blockchain research and discuss potential implications as well as our recommendations in this document. Although blockchain isn't well known, it is rapidly evolving as a platform, and it is a highly discussed topic throughout the current media. However, since media trends often do not correspond to study patterns, this is also a useful exercise in determining how slants in academic, peer-reviewed research distributions cover a slanting topic. In the not-too-distant past, there were few scholarly publications on blockchain; nevertheless, this is quickly changing. In this article, we will present a diagram of recent topics in academic publications, as well as three key questions about blockchain. We'll begin with a definition of blockchain. We then describe the approach we used to collect our data and go on to explore the topics we discovered. This is followed by a discussion of why blockchain is essential and how it is currently used, as well as our recommendations. We wrap up with an overview and several thoughts on the potential and need of possible blockchain science. We plan to respond to the following questions in their entirety: What exactly is a square chain? What are certain square chain classifications and patterns? What are the social and mechanical consequences of the new technology? What would happen to square chain in the end? Then we're asked, "What makes these investigations so important?" What value do they have? To continue, let's go back to the beginning. The square chain was first discovered in a paper titled "Bitcoin: A Peer-to-Peer Electronic Cash System" by an unknown developer who went by the moniker "Bitcoin." What distinguishes the blockchain champion is that the record isn't claimed or saved by a single entity, but rather each trade led has a copy of the exchange's points of interest saved on each PC that took part in the exchange.

"A table of three lines, where each line speaks to a specific exchange, the main segment stores the exchange's timestamp, the second portion stores the exchange's points of interest, and the third segment stores a hash of the current exchange in addition to its subtle elements in addition to the hash of the previous exchange," according to the blockchain. Parties seeking to validate this knowledge will gaze it toward any point by including a time stamp and the past exchange, and because it tells the past exchange, it becomes possible to trace the background without breaking a sweat. There is some precautions in place to prevent others who were not a part of the exchange from taking part in the survey. The hash, also known as section three, is a distorted sequence of letters and numbers that is used to hide facts regarding the trade. Since each exchange's hash will then be used to differentiate the previous exchange's hash, it's almost impossible for misrepresentation to occur. Through each transaction containing a receipt for the previous trade, amounts may be tracked all the way back to the beginning. An feature that would make each bookkeeper's job easier so there would be no further miscounted amounts or missed receipts. Any exchange is a time-stamped screen capture that someone with the appropriate permissions will view when stowing away on show. However, blockchain invention isn't limited to money; since any transaction in the ledger is only a string esteem, trades can be easily tracked. Cook County, Illinois, has started using blockchain technology to manage land deeds when they change hands. The blockchain is essentially a linked network of knowledge squares.

During our preliminary analysis, we came across an article that looked at the ebb and flow of blockchain exploration. By the way they talk, it seems that they could only find a total of 41 peer-reviewed publications at this time. One of the most intriguing points they make at the outset of the report is that 80% of the papers they find focused on the usage of blockchain for Bitcoin, a digital currency. Despite the fact that focusing solely on digital currencies was a strong possibility for such a survey, they chose to focus on advanced blockchain issues such as stability, implementation, adaptability, and so on. They also discovered that the research was mostly focused on blockchain security and privacy, as well as identifying limitations. They offer an overview of the technique they used for their precise mapping analysis after a broad prologue to blockchain – which is quite similar to what we are improving the situation in this current investigation. Their four study questions are: ebb and flow explore themes, blockchain implementations, ebb and flow look at cracks, and potential directions for blockchain. They began by laying out the directories they used to find their writing, followed by a diagram of their screening process. They were able to extract watchwords and details from edited compositions at that stage. They regarded the origins – business or the scholarly community – as well as the geographic region, in addition to themes and development dates. They also called the components of the production: gathering, workshop, diary, book section, and so on. Finally, three distinct paper types were identified: blockchain study, blockchain update, and blockchain implementation. Most of this theory was laid out in large data flow charts and graphs. Defense, squandered assets, ease, safety and keen contracts, cryptographic ways of currency, and dependability were all found to be important themes in the blockchain writing throughout their audit. They discovered that the bulk of the research focused on improving new blockchain advancements, with a significant portion focusing on encryption and privacy concerns. Surprisingly, so few of the research focused on other topics, such as simplicity of usage and squandered money. Surprisingly, a lot of the research at the time was based on Bitcoin. Different money-related benefits of blockchain engineering are debated in Depending on Blockchain.

The developers begin by using a bank and all of the funds that are essentially squandered as a result of putting away and reflect all trades themselves. argue that using fewer items, such as hard drives to hold records or the extra power required to maintain the system going, not only costs banks more money than using a blockchain-based record, it often results in fewer assets being used. As a result, nature will benefit and there will be fewer electronic pollution and vitality use. Furthermore, the cost of a blockchain exchange has shown to be more manageable as the average of strength consumption per exchange has decreased (estimated as Wattage over Gigahash every second, or the measure of power that one billion little assignments devours). If the scope of invention broadens, the innovation becomes more profitable. This power consumption was estimated at 0.69 W/GHps in October 2014, and nearly two years later, in September 2016, it was down to 0.099 W/GHps, a paltry 14% of the vitality cost. Another researcher, Tranquillini, focuses on the potential of blockchain engineering in the financial industry rather than the technology itself. He uses a previous article published in Harvard Business Review by professors Benjamin Edelman and Damien Geradin on the use of blockchain developments in the buyer merchandise sector as a foundation to show an assault on the capability of those advances in the securities business – on which he is an expert. He looks at emerging concerns about the health and soundness of European monetary systems, as well as government regulation. His essay is something of an outlet for his academic thoughts on the potential of such creativity to be incorporated into the socio-administrative controls of European gauges in the securities industry. All things considering, he keeps a deliberate detachment from a particular goal and decides that putting such an idea into action will be difficult.

When we go on in time, blockchain would be the most relevant technology for higher education. They alert about what could inevitably happen if such technology is not implemented, but they also urge us to investigate the vast possibilities of how blockchain technology might enhance the condition of higher education. They describe four places of higher education where innovators can focus: student data, pedagogy, prices, and instructional models (or the meta-university). The definition of meaning is central to their argument, and the internet is severely constrained in this regard. We may exchange records over the internet, but we're exchanging versions of documentation and archives, not the originals. They find out that the blockchain can be used to hold almost every kind of data or knowledge that is valuable to humanity. It can be used to preserve any of a person's data throughout the course of their whole lives. This technology will and will be used to document educational milestones in the process of How, according to them. When technology such as blockchain become more associated with work and careers in the twenty-first century, they often clarify how higher education would be forced to adapt or lose its importance. Although transition is difficult for higher education organisations, they contend that the shift to blockchain would compel them to find new ways to remain effective.On the surface, the two seem to be at odds with how the government can treat revenue, so it seems to be a strange similarity. They contend, though, that this technology is beneficial to Libertarians because it removes capital from the government's hands and places it in the hands of the citizens. This encourages the government to play a smaller part. In such a scheme, loans will not need to be vetted by a financial institution. As a consequence, the government will not be liable for any erroneous purchases. This is analogous to the Federal Deposit Insurance Corporation's current position (FDIC). For the same purposes, undermining the government's financial foundations and government-backed insurance will allow people more influence. This might lead to increased banking openness, ensuring that everyone receives equal care. Under a particular scenario, blockchain's capacity to act as a database might allow for the proper tracking and logging of laboured hours in a decentralised manner. Manipulation would be even harder to get away with, encouraging people to ensure that anyone else should function was doing so.

We are now seeing mainstream acceptance of blockchain technologies due to its strong appeal. Given that virtually every industry employs a kind of agile record-keeping, it is fair to anticipate this technology to be extended to a broad variety of applications, some of which have been pointed at in previous pages, such as the possibility for a smart city, whilst others are either in progress or have yet to be found. Furthermore, because of the peer-to-peer aspect of the technology and the fact that any stakeholder has access to their own block of the ledger, falsifying details or cooking the books has never been easier. This in itself has the ability to boost customer confidence in these latest technical disruptions. Since the underpinnings of any emerging technology are not fully known, it is impossible to predict how broadly the technology would be implemented. Future studies should look at these issues and emerging technologies, as well as the technology's acceptance rates. Further research will reveal what improvements (if any) in efficiency have been reported for those that have adopted blockchain. Studies may also look at the reasons why this technology hasn't caught on, as well as customer trust levels. Furthermore, as technology advances, potential research will be able to shed light on some protection vulnerabilities that were not originally identified. Blockchain has exploded in prominence, gaining traction in virtually every sector from banking and healthcare to schooling to community planning. It all began with some uploaded code by an unknown programmer with the intention of building a new currency network. Finally, blockchain technology seems to have the ability to revolutionise processes that maintain track of the existence of objects through a greatly enhanced, open ledger mechanism, in addition to improving tasks in existing industries.

The transaction is deemed true if the consensus of nodes decides on its legitimacy. Any of the nodes are referred to as "miners." They function on the next block with specialised hardware. Miners combine all usable transactions from the transaction pool into a new nominee block. A proof of work concept is used to mine a block of Bitcoin. That is, the data from the nominee block is used to generate a random hash value. To correctly estimate a hash value, you'll need a lot of computing power that can measure millions of values in a second. A given complexity goal must be met by the correct hash value. This number is derived from all block metadata, including the previous block's hash. This is the most important aspect of Blockchain stability. If anyone attempts to alter a previous transaction, the hash value of the block containing the transaction must be recalculated.

Both hash values for subsequent blocks must be determined again as well. This is impossible because more than half of a network's nodes are hostile. A new block is broadcast to the network when it is produced. Both nodes obtain the block and verify it, as well as all of the transactions included within it. If it's true, both nodes add it to their local Blockchain as the next block. The pool is then cleared of transactions that are part of the generated block. According to the findings, the majority of studies have concentrated on one or a few specific areas of Blockchain deployment. To our knowledge, no studies have looked at the consistency criteria and solutions for Blockhain implementations in depth. This form of research will aid in the identification of consistency standards that can be incorporated into modern Blockchain applications. Furthermore, these studies can be useful in determining how various Blockchain characteristics and current problems can influence the consistency of Blockchain systems.

We performed a literature review for this study to see what level of support there is in the written literature about the consistency criteria for Blockchain implementations. Blockchain is a decentralised ledger mechanism that ensures the confidentiality of transaction records. It is well regarded as the infrastructure that powers the Bitcoin cryptocurrency. When the Bitcoin cryptocurrency was first launched, blockchain technology was utilised for the first time. Bitcoin is now the most widely adopted platform based on Blockchain technologies. Bitcoin is a decentralised digital money payment mechanism based on the Blockchain public transaction ledger. The most important characteristic of Bitcoin is that the currency's value can be maintained without the intervention of any company or government. The Bitcoin network's amount of transactions and users is continuously growing. In addition, common currency conversions, such as KRW, EUR, and USD, occur often in currency exchange markets. As a result, Bitcoin has attracted the interest of a variety of cultures and is becoming the most common digital currency based on Blockchain technology. The shared key infrastructure (PKI) system is used for Bitcoin. The consumer only has one set of public and private keys in PKI. The public key is used in the user's Bitcoin wallet address, while the private key is used to authenticate the user. The sender's public key, various receiver's public keys, and the value exchanged make up a Bitcoin transaction. The transaction will be published in a block in around ten minutes. A previously written block is then added to this latest block. Both blocks, including details about each transaction, are maintained on the users' nodes' disc drive. Each node stores details regarding all Bitcoin network transactions and uses previous blocks to verify the validity of each new transaction. Checking the correctness of transactions rewards the nodes. This approach is known as mining, and it is supported by Proof-of-Work, one of the most important principles of Blockchain technology. A agreement occurs between all nodes when all transactions are successfully verified. The latest blocks are connected to the previous blocks, and they are all aligned in a single chain. The distributed ledger technique used for Bitcoin is called Blockchain, and it consists of a series of blocks.

The Bitcoin blockchain is a decentralised management strategy for releasing and exchanging money for Bitcoin currency consumers. This method will endorse a shared registry of all Bitcoin transactions that have ever been completed, without requiring the involvement of a third party. The benefit of Blockchain is that if the evidence has been validated by all nodes, the decentralised database cannot be changed or erased. This is why Blockchain's data integrity and protection features are well-known. Blockchain technologies may be used for a variety of purposes. It may, for example, build a cloud service environment for digital contracts and peer-to-peer data exchange. The data confidentiality of the Blockchain technique is one of the reasons why it is being used in other services and applications. There are several technological obstacles and drawbacks of blockchain technologies that have been found.

In this part, the fundamentals of blockchain. We agree that understanding the core concept behind blockchain technology and the fundamentals of how it operates is critical to evaluating and analysing the effects it can have. We would not go through technological depth, but rather focus on the most critical characteristics of blockchain, as well as its benefits and drawbacks in terms of financial sectors. Blockchain first appeared in 2009, when Satoshi Nakamoto, an unknown individual or group of people, introduced the cryptocurrency Bitcoin. Bitcoin is a digital money that is "mined" by people using apps to solve mathematical problems on machines all around the world. Bitcoin's core code is called blockchain. It's important to realise that blockchain and Bitcoin are not the same thing. Consider blockchain to be an operating system similar to Windows or Macintosh, with Bitcoin being only one of the programmes that will work on it. Despite technical advancements (such as telephone lines, credit card networks, and the internet) that have rendered trade quicker, more reliable, and more trustworthy, many business transactions remain inefficient, costly, and fragile. (2018, IBM) Blockchain may be the key to make business transactions more cost-effective, reliable, safe, and stable, as it aims to deter bribery, improve confidence and accountability, and save time and money by replacing intermediaries. While we are looking at the potential uses of finance and accounting with blockchain technology (also known as distributed ledger technology), it is important to note that blockchain is not a financial platform in and of itself. Blockchain isn't an accounting forum, a journal entry service, or a substitute for accounting apps, according to Smith . However, blockchain expands on the concept of standard double entry accounting by "adding a third entry" that validates both sides of a transaction in the same block. In a typical dealing case, all sides maintain their own ledgers and logs of the transaction.

CONCLUSION

In next generation networks, blockchain is a technology that redefines confidence. It promotes the concept of handling some kind of transaction without the use of a middleman. Mediators, including companies and states, often appear as key bodies that collect, handle, and store transactions. Much of our confidence in a scheme comes from the mediators, who are obligated to process transactions using proper business reasoning. Mediators have complete power of data protection and privacy. The confidence in Blockchain-based applications is decentralised. Users should only have faith in the mechanism and the smart code that is exchanged by all participants. Blockchain is a distributed blockchain that runs on a peer-to-peer network from a technological standpoint. Since any node in the network is on the same level as the others, this P2P network serves as the system's backbone. While nodes may take several different types, there is no central authority node. Per node keeps a copy of the Blockchain locally.

REFERENCES

Abbott, F. (2000). Distributed Governance at the WTO-WIPO: An Evolving Model For Open-Architecture Integrated Governance. *Journal of International Economic Law*, *3*(1), 63–81. doi:10.1093/jiel/3.1.63

Allenby, B. R. (2012). *The Theory and Practice of Sustainable Engineering* (1st ed.). Pearson Prentice Hall.

Almeida, V., Getschko, D., & Afonso, C. (2015). The Origin and Evolution of Multistakeholder Models. *IEEE Internet Computing*, *19*(1), 74–79. doi:10.1109/MIC.2015.15

Ansell, C., & Gash, A. (2007). Collaborative Governance in Theory and Practice. *Journal of Public Administration: Research and Theory*, *18*(4), 543–571. doi:10.1093/jopart/mum032

Antonopoulos, A. (2014). *Bitcoin Security Model: Trust by Computation*. O'Reilly-Radar. Retrieved from http://radar.oreilly.com/2014/02/bitcoin-security-model-trust-by-computation.html

Dubovitskaya, A., Xu, Z., Ryu, S., Schumacher, M., & Wang, F. (2017). *Secure and Trustable Electronic Medical Records Sharing using Blockchain*. arXiv preprint arXiv:1709.06528.

How Blockchain Can Fight Fraud Based on Know-Your-Customer Data. (2019). Available: https://www.nasdaq.com/articles/how-blockchain-can-fight-fraud-based-know-your-customer-data-2019-02-11.

Kblaw, Azaria, Halamka, & Lippman. (2016). A Case Study for Blockchain in Healthcare. "MedRec" prototype for electronic health records and Medical research data. Proceedings of IEEE Open & Big Data Conference, 13.

Kolias, C., Kambourakis, G., Stavrou, A., & Voas, J. (2017). DDoS in the IoT: Mirai and other botnets. *Computer*, *50*(7), 80–84. doi:10.1109/MC.2017.201

Kshetri, N. (2017). Can blockchain strengthen the internet of things? *IT Professional*, *19*(4), 68–72. doi:10.1109/MITP.2017.3051335

Mylrea, M., & Gourisetti, S. N. G. (2017). Blockchain for small grid resilience:Exchanging distributed energy at speed, scale and security. *Resilience Week*, (Sep), 18–23.

Strobel, V., Ferrer, E. C., & Dorigo, M. (2018). Managing byzantine robots via blockchain technology in a swarm robotics collective decision making scenario. *Proc.17th Int. Conf. Auto. Agents MultiAgents System International Foundation for Autonomous Agents and MultiAgent Systems*, 541-549.

Trautman, L. J., & Ormerod, P. C. (2016). Corporate Directors' and Officers' Cybersecurity Standard of Care: The Yahoo Data Breach. *Am. UL Rev.*, *66*(1), 1231.

Yaji, S., Bangera, K., & Neelima, B. (2018). Privacy preserving in blockchain based on partial Homomorphic Encryption system for AI Applications. *25th International conference on High performance computing workshop (HIPCW)*, 81-85.

Yeoh, P. (2017). Regulatory issues in blockchain technology. *Journal of Financial Regulation and Compliance.*, *25*(2), 196–208. doi:10.1108/JFRC-08-2016-0068

Chapter 11
Secure File Storage in Cloud Computing Using a Modified Cryptography Algorithm

Manya Smriti
Vellore Institute of Technology, India

Shruti Varsha Venkatraman
Vellore Institute of Technology, India

Aashish Raj
Vellore Institute of Technology, India

Vaishnavi Raj Shukla
Vellore Institute of Technology, India

Aswani Kumar Aswani Cherukuri
iD https://orcid.org/0000-0001-8455-9108
Vellore Institute of Technology, India

ABSTRACT

This chapter investigates the security issues identified with the file cloud storage to ensure the security of client information in cloud information server. The authors have proposed a modified RSA algorithm with multiple keys and CRT to ensure confidentiality of data coupled with hashing through SHA-512 to maintain integrity. This work has made a secure data exchange app where files are encrypted using the RSA-CRT algorithm and hashed later. On successfully implementing the work, they observed that the proposed technique is more secure than the original RSA algorithm and RSA-CRT. Furthermore, it enhanced the algorithm performance for decryption because it employed the CRT for decryption; thus, the proposed technique proved to be faster than RSA with multi keys.

DOI: 10.4018/978-1-7998-8367-8.ch011

INTRODUCTION

The algorithm of RSA is an asymmetric cryptography technique. This is working on two keys, i.e. public key and private key. The proposed model in our work takes four prime evaluating techniques and discovers extension to build up a far-off information reviewing strategy that can be utilized to check the uprightness of the redistributed information in numbers for modified RSA. Instead of sending one public key directly, send two public keys to the receiver. However, there is the problem of the speed, so that in RSA decryption used the Chinese remainder theorem to enhancement the speed of RSA decryption.

BACKGROUND

Literature Survey

Yang et al. (Yang & Jia, 2012) proposed a proficient and intrinsically secure dynamic reviewing convention. It secures the information protection against the reviewer by consolidating the cryptography strategy with the bi-linearity property of bi-linear paring instead of utilizing the veil method. In this manner, their multi-cloud clump reviewing convention does not require any extra coordinator. Their cluster reviewing convention can likewise bolster the clump examining for numerous proprietors. Moreover, their evaluating conspire brings about less correspondence cost and less calculation cost of the evaluator by moving the registering loads of evaluating from the inspector to the worker, which enormously im- proves the evaluating execution and can be applied to enormous scope distributed storage frameworks.

Li et al. (Li et al., 2017) concentrated on the issue of the cloud information stockpiling and planned to give a methodology that could stay away from the cloud administrators arriving at client' delicate information. Tending to this objective, they proposed a novel methodology entitled as Security-Aware Effective Distributed Storage (SA-EDS) model. In this model, they utilized their proposed calculations, including Alternative Data Distribution (AD2), Secure Efficient Data Distributions (SED2) and Efficient Data Conflation (ED- Con) calculations. Their exploratory assessments had demonstrated that their proposed plan could viably shield significant dangers from the cloud side. The calculation time was shorter than current dynamic methodologies. Future work would address making sure about information duplications so as to increment the degree of information accessibility since any of datacentre's down will cause the disappointment of information recoveries.

Bindu et al. (Shwetha Bindu & Yadaiah, 2011), contemplated the issue of information security in cloud servers. To en- sure the accuracy of clients' information in cloud information server, they proposed a viable and adaptable plan with unequivocal unique information support, including square change, delete, and join. They use erasure-correcting code in the record dissemination planning to give repetition equality vectors and assurance the information reliability. Their plan achieves the joining of capacity rightness protection and information defilement has been recognized during the capacity accuracy check over the circulated workers. Their plan is exceptionally productive and tough to Byzantine disappointment, noxious information alteration assault, and even worker intriguing assaults. They accept that information stockpiling security in Cloud Computing, a zone loaded with difficulties and of prevailing essentials, is still in its early stages to be distinguished. They imagine a few potential bearings for future examination on this territory. It permits Third Parity Auditor to review the cloud information stockpiling without requesting clients' time, likelihood.

Sookhak (Sookhak, 2015) examines the issue of extra handling time in the current distributed computing. It proposed a topical scientific classification based on the best in class information evaluating techniques to meet the necessities to distinguish the holes and remarkable issues in the zone of information stockpiling trustworthiness of distributed computing. The subjective examination is utilized to analyze the current strategies and feature the points of interest and impediments of them and open issues and difficulties of information inspecting plans in cloud and portable distributed computing condition that have not been tended to yet were distinguished and featured. The current information inspecting approaches were actualized in the genuine distributed computing condition, and the benchmark test was utilized to assess such strategies dependent on the calculation and correspondence cost on the customer and worker side. In addition, the effect of dynamic information update tasks was breaking down on the current information approaches in the genuine condition. It examined the impact of dynamic information update procedure for the enormous scope document size. At last, the effect of regular information refreshes was assessed for various size of the documents. Another far off information evaluating strategy was proposed based on mathematical mark procedure to satisfy the target of productive answer for checking the honesty of the redistributed information in distributed computing. The proposed conspire addresses the issue of extra calculation and correspondence cost for cloud information stockpiling framework. The D&CT information structure likewise enables their strategy to be pertinent for huge scope information with least preparing time on the customer. The proposed information examining plan is executed in the genuine condition by utilizing java and C++ language to address the target of assessing DRDA technique. The presentation of the DRDA plot was approved by utilizing the benchmark test in the copying condition and broke down the DRDA conspire by utilizing unmistakable boundaries, for example, length of mark, document size, and the likelihood of identification. The various situations likewise characterized to assess the proposed strategy.

Moreover, it broke down the quality of the security based on mathematic to approve and verify the security of the DRDA technique. The outcomes indicated that the D&CT information structure lessens the handling season of dynamic information update activities by diminishing the quantity of moving. Furthermore, the D&CT information structure significantly declines the preparing season of dynamic information update for enormous scope re-appropriated record in distributed computing.

Chambre et al. (Shimbre & Deshpande, 2015) talks about the record circulation and SHA-1 strategy. At the point when the document is conveyed, then information is likewise isolated into numerous workers. So here the need of information security emerges. Each square of record contains its own hash code, utilizing hash code which will improve client verification process; just approved individual can get to the information. Here, the information is encoded utilizing propelled encryption standard, so information is effectively and safely put away on cloud. Outsider reviewer is utilized for open inspecting. This paper talks about the treatment of some security issues like Fast mistake limitation, information honesty, information security. The proposed plan permits clients to review the information with lightweight correspondence and calculation cost. Examination shows that the proposed framework is profoundly effective against noxious information adjustment assault and worker plotting assault. Execution and broad security examination shows that proposed frameworks are provably secure and exceptionally productive. They show that their plan is profoundly productive for worker conspiring assault and vindictive information adjustment assault with least calculation overhead. Execution investigation and broad security shows that the proposed plot is provably secure and profoundly productive. Behl (Behl, 2011) investigated the security issues identified with the cloud. The paper likewise talks about the current security ways to deal with secure the cloud framework and applications and their disadvantages.

There are various security challenges in the haze of which, this paper has attempted to address the most widely recognized and basic ones. A protected cloud is unthinkable except if the virtual condition viz. foundation, VM, interfaces, organize transmissions are secure. Cloud condition request much over the customary security arrangements, which do not plan well to the virtualized situations, in view of the mind-boggling and dynamic nature of the distributed computing. As a venturing stone, cloud suppliers and clients should cooperate on characterizing the prerequisites and the points of interest. It is 220 2011 World Congress on Information and Communication Technologies certain that new virtualization-mindful security arrangements ought to be actualized to guarantee the pre-emptive security to the general framework. The cloud security arrangements ought to have the knowledge to act naturally safeguarding and be able to give constant checking, discovery and avoidance of known and obscure dangers.

Usman et al. (Usman et al., 2017) scrambled mystery information in compacted video transfers is a moderately new examination region which is drawing in consideration of scientists. This is basically because of protection and security issues worried about the open mists. In this article, a made sure about conspire has been introduced which shrouds the mystery information in HEVC encoded video transfer, i.e., in packed area. The proposed plot comprises three significant stages: video encoding, information encryption, and unscrambling with/without interpreting. The proposed conspire attempts to keep up the first video transfer size after encryption with- out influencing the visual nature of video information. In this way, it creates a perfect stage for constant video applications. The mystery information is appropriated in encoded video transfer, so it is hard for programmers to remove whole mystery information. This is be- cause of the way that programmers do not have the foggiest idea about the specific areas and examples of the concealing plan, regardless of whether they take the mystery key. Another significant bit of leeway is that their proposed conspire completely bolsters the encoding and unraveling structure of the HEVC standard. The video transfer with encoded mystery information can undoubtedly be decoded without undermining or indicating extra concealed data. Test results have demonstrated that the proposed plot keeps up the visual quality with a slight trade-off on expanding the size of the encoded video transfer.

Garg et al. (Garg & Sharma, 2014) discussed that at the point when an asset obliged cell phone stores its information on the cloud, there is consistently a major worry of whether the cloud specialist orga- nization stores the documents accurately or not. Security is the principle worry in portable distributed computing. The proposed instrument gives a security component to making sure about the information in portable distributed computing with RSA calculation and hash work. This exploration paper has pro- posed an instrument to give classification and honesty to the information put away in portable cloud. The proposed plot utilizes RSA calculation with other encryption decoding procedures to make sure about the information in such a way that no spillage of information on cloud could be performed. In this plan, encryption is utilized to give security to the information while in communication. Since the scrambled record is put away on the cloud, so client can accept that his information is secure. In the plan record, just in scrambled structure is moved over the channel, which lessens the issue of data divulgence. No, third individual or gatecrasher can get the document since that individual do not knows the key of information proprietor. There is consistently an extension for development in each field of work, so here too. One of the suspicion made in all the models of security are that the TP An is nonpartisan. All the calculations and confirmations are offloaded to TP A, so there is a need to make TP A safer. Future work could be investigating the utilizations of other systems applied in secure capacity administrations of portable cloud condition. Some work should likewise be possible to diminish the overhead of versatile terminal.

Samir et al. proposed model in the paper takes 4 prime number in RSA and instead of using one public key, 2 public key is sent to the receiver. The problem of speed is sorted out by using RSA with

Chinese Remainder Theorem. Chinese Remainder Theorem, CRT, is a theorem in mathematics that can be used in cryptography .Its application is computing, which is very important in regard to calculations of algorithmic and computations modular. The Chinese remainder theorem (CRT) determines a single integer from its remainders from a set of modulos. It has also got applications in digital signal processing. CRT allows for RSA algorithm implementation very efficiently. If the same message is encrypted using random key more than one time makes the ciphertext look different every time is used here. The comparison in the paper clearly states the all-time encryption and decryption of RSA-CRT is nearly half to that of RSA. For a 640 bit length plaintext, RSA-CRT to RSA time taken is 26:42. The paper shows in-depth research about how it claims RSA-CRT an enhanced algorithm than RSA.

Pant et al. (Pant et al., 2015) discussed information and data security as a most significant issue of cloud processing and IT industry. In this paper they utilize some strategy to make sure about information in cloud or web. This paper examined security issues in distributed computing frameworks and how they can be forestalled, here they use cryptography and steganography strategy together to make sure about information. RSA calculation is safer than other calculation. They incorporate RSA calculation with other calculation to give greater security to information. In steganography, they get scrambled picture, which appears to be identical to a unique picture by the natural eye. In the event that they examination the picture double codes then the distinctions would be seen. Else they are incapable of recognizing the first picture. The methodology they have use in this paper will assist with making a solid structure for the security of information in distributed computing field or web.

Somani et al. (Somani et al., 2010) discussed that among the numerous IT powerhouses driven by pat- terns in distributed computing has not dicey. It gives nearly everybody has brought uplifting news. For ventures, cloud processing is deserving of thought and attempt to fabricate busi- ness frameworks as a path for organizations along these lines can without a doubt realize lower costs, higher benefits and more decision; for huge scope industry, After the monetary unrest will be the expense of framework for huge scope pressure appears to be likely; de- signers, when in the face of distributed computing, through the PaaS model can adequately improve their own limit, Therefore, the effect of cloud processing on the ISV is the biggest of the numerous jobs; for architects and engineers are concerned. There is the approach of cloud registering will undoubtedly birth various new openings. The mists will develop in size as before long as accessible transfer speed and the relating administration model develop enough, distributed computing will bring a progressive change in the Internet. Cloud register- ing reported a minimal effort supercomputing administrations to give the plausibility, while there are an enormous number of producers behind, there is no uncertainty that distributed computing has a splendid future.

Arora et al. (Arora et al., 2013) discussed in this paper, encryption calculations have been proposed to make cloud information secure, helpless and offered worry to security issues, challenges and further- more examinations have been made between AES, DES, Blowfish and RSA calculations to locate the best security calculation, which must be utilized in distributed computing for making cloud information secure and not to be hacked by assailants. Encryption calculations assume a significant job in informa- tion security on cloud, and by examination of various boundaries utilized in calculations, it has been discovered that AES calculation utilizes least an ideal opportunity to execute cloud information. Blowfish calculation has least memory prerequisite. DES calculation expends least encryption time. RSA devours longest memory size and encryption time. By doing execution for all calculations in IDE apparatus and JDK 1.7, the ideal yield for the information on distributed computing has been accomplished. In the present time request of cloud is expanding, so the security of the cloud and client is on top concern.

Henceforth, proposed calculations are useful for the present prerequisite. In future a few correlations with various methodologies and results to show the adequacy of the proposed structure can be given.

Ruj et al. (Ruj et al., 2012) discussed a security safeguarding access control plot that gives fine-grained get to control and confirms clients who store data in the cloud. The cloud anyway does not have the foggiest idea about the personality of the client who stores data, however just confirm the client's accreditations. Key appropriation is done in a decentralized manner. One restriction is that the cloud knows the entrance strategy for each record put away in the cloud. In future, they might want to ensure the security of client traits as well. In this paper, they propose another security saving validated access control conspire to make sure about mists' information. In the proposed plot, the cloud checks the valid-ness of the client without realizing the client's personality before putting away data. Likewise, their plan has the additional element of access control where just legitimate clients can unscramble the put away data. The plot forestalls replay assaults and supports creation, adjustment, also, perusing information put away in the cloud. In addition, their validation also gets to control plot is decentralized and vigorous, in contrast to others getting to control plans intended for mists brought together. The correspondence, calculation, and capacity overheads are tantamount to brought together methodologies.

Subashini et al. (Subashini & Kavitha, 2011) discussed in this paper, they examined the issues in security in in- formation capacity in cloud condition. This makes the information priceless regardless of whether an interloper gains admittance to this information. Even though this model will require some quantifiable exertion to be actualized continuously, it gives the essential answer for a situation like the cloud, indicating an antagonistic potential to turn into the cutting edge undertaking condition. Executing such a model during the prior periods of the development of the framework will be generally simpler as for actualizing it after part of information take exile in the cloud. This model in blend with their multi-level security model for making sure about information over transmission will give legitimate crossbars in the wires of malevolent clients.

Wang et al. (Wang et al., 2010) discussed cloud computing has been imagined as the next-gen of big business IT. As opposed to conventional venture IT arrangements, where the IT administrations are under appropriate physical, coherent, and faculty controls, distributed computing moves the application programming and databases to workers in enormous server farms on the Internet, where the administration of the information and administrations are not completely dependable. In this article they center around cloud information stockpiling security. They first present a organize engineering for viably portraying, creating, also, assessing secure in- formation stockpiling issues. Through inside and out investigation, some current information stockpiling security building squares are inspected. The advantages and disad-vantages of their pragmatic ramifications in the setting of distributed computing are summed up. Further testing issues for open examining administrations that should be engaged on are talked about as well. They accept security in cloud computing, a region brimming with difficulties and of vital significance, is still in its outset presently yet will pull in colossal measures of research exertion for a long time to come.

Zhou et al. (Zhou et al., 2013) discussed in this paper, first it proposes RBE plot that accomplishes proficient client disavowal. At that point, they introduced a RBAC based distributed storage design which permits an association to store information safely in an open cloud, while keeping up the delicate data identified with the association's structure in a private cloud. At that point, they have built up a safe distributed storage framework engineering and have indicated that the framework has a few unrivaled attributes, for example, steady size cipher text and decoding key. Their trials see that both encryption and decoding calculations are effective on the customer side, and decoding time at the cloud can be decreased by having different processors, which is normal in a cloud condition. They accept that the proposed framework can be valuable in business circumstances as it catches handy access arrangements dependent on jobs in an adaptable way. What's more, it gives secure information stockpiling in the cloud authorizing these get to strategies.

Hardik et al. (Gandhi & Gupta, 2015) discussed that in the current scenario, everything is being transferred on the web and other communication medium. We need to make our data secure from all other attacker and unauthorized person. By the use of Magic Rectangle, we can have different ciphertext for the same character. This approach gives enhancement to the public key cryptosystem. This work prohibits any intruders from obtaining the plain text in a readable form. The security aspect is enhanced as there is no repetition of values in Magic rectangle. Even if the intruders found the initial values of MR, it is very difficult to trace the row/column. One of the issues in the proposed work is additional time needed for the construction of Magic rectangle initially.

Shinde et al. (Shinde & Fadewar, 2008) discussed in this paper talks about the RSA cryptography algorithm. After the author gave a brief list and notes on cryptographic goals, they then elaborated on the working of the RSA cryptographic algorithm. How the keys are generated, and how the encryption and decryption is done. CRT is then introduced with an elaborate functioning. The author then shows the steps to using RSA with CRT, how to use them together in the process of encryption and decryption. The proposed approach (RSA-CRT) is then analyzed on the basis of security and performance. An approach of implementing the said proposed approach is done in java, displaying the message, the sender's and receiver's public and private keys and the encryption and decryption. The paper then concludes that the encryption is more effective with CRT.

Lakshmi and Chandravathi (Lakshmi, 2020) discussed in this paper the author discussed that the private data is prone to numerous noxious attacks. Henceforth, the requirement for ensuring secret data has gotten a significant challenge over the Internet. Cryptographic techniques are the most ideal decision for giving protection from pernicious attacks. By applying different strategies, data can be secured. For making sure about data over the cloud is another significant test, which is still must be thought of. The Homomorphic Encryption is a promising technique for making sure about data in the cloud. In this paper the author proposed RSA calculation utilizing numerous public key sets with Homomorphic Encryption. The thought is to produce a critical pair from numerous keys utilizing RSA homomorphic encryption, which is halfway homomorphic in nature, rather than a solitary key pair. This strategy uses one key for encryption and the other for decryption. The excellence of this plan is that a solitary key pair is chosen from numerous key sets which communicate with different users. Different key age strategies use some numerical rationale for acquiring public key straightforwardly, when contrasted with RSA with single key. Thusly, the attacks for finding the private key are halted.

Kim et al. (Kim et al., 2020) discussed that private exponent in RSA is generated from public exponent which are pre-selected by using Euclid's algorithm. It is nearly as same as modulus number in terms of bit size. So, reduction in private and public exponent is not easy in RSA during key generation. CRT method discussed in which exponent is reduced and a fast and more secure method was introduced to reduce exponent. The paper discussed about prime number generation mechanism as well.

Balaji et al. (Balaji et al., 2018) discussed the limitations of Efficiencies in Cloud resource management which are largely determined by pre-set rules and are reactive. To overcome this, the authors adopted a cloud resource management done by a predictive method. AWS t2 micro instance was used to host a read-intensive application for on-off timesheets, and using historical data, simulation based workload patterns were made. Comparisons were made between the existing and proposed methods which showed that the proposed method had reduced the errors, decreased the waiting time for users, increased number of requests and improved utilization of resources.

Balaji et al. (Balaji et al., 2019) discussed in this paper that by assuming enterprise workloads are constant, resource provisioning becomes ineffective. By analyzing synthetic bursty workloads, the current research aims to address this challenge. The researchers used Hurst Exponent and Sample Entropy metrics to build resource provisioning models. NASA datasets were used to compare the performance of the proposed method with the baseline reactive approach and the index of dispersion method.

Narayanan et al. (Narayanan & Cherukuri, 2018) discussed that To acquire current information about a patient, along with tracking purpose, the Data Lake has to be moved to a Cloud for analyzing and analyzing the data would require moving the data to a Cloud. Based on this research, the authors recommend using Data Lake in Cloud as a cloud-based integration framework. The work presented here extends the information integration architecture through the design of using a mathematical model (Petri Net) to verify an architecture for Data Lake in Cloud.

Balaji et al. (Balaji et al., 2014) discussed that using predefined limits, cloud service providers provide or de-provision resources based on average consumption. As a consequence, it does not fully address the diverse range of enterprise use cases. There have been few cases reported of resource management using predictive techniques, even though they could perform more effectively. To manage resources effectively in a cloud environment, it is crucial to establish a model that can predict how the system will perform under load. As the metric for monitoring resource utilization, they used Request rate to compare the performances of two such predictions models, Holt-Winter and ARIMA. Several selected ARIMA models were shown to perform better than the Holt-Winter model, which would subsequently be useful for managing resources on the cloud if data request rates followed a similar trend

PROBLEM DEFINITION

In Cloud Storage, we share data among many clients, server and people. Thus, the security of information present in the cloud is not guaranteed since it is easy for an intruder to access and demolish the first type of information. So, there is a requirement of some plainly key which help us to do cross breed encryption and protect the data. The algorithm of RSA is an asymmetric cryptography technique, this is working on two keys, i.e. public key and private key. The proposed model takes four prime numbers in RSA. Instead of sending one public key directly, send two public keys to the receiver. But there is the problem of the speed, so that in RSA decryption used the Chinese remainder theorem to enhance RSA decryption speed.

Contribution of the Work

Our work contributes the following:

1.   New approach of the RSA algorithm: Modified RSA with CRT and multiple keys:

IN ITSELF, the RSA algorithm is an asymmetric algorithm, which is deemed to be secure, but lacks in the speed component. Especially when the prime numbers used to generate keys are very large, the time it takes to compute all the necessary computations can be long as it has to ensure the security.

Thus with our proposed approach, we are implementing both security and speed. With CRT in the midst of this approach, it breaks down the main parts of the algorithm to increase the throughput rate up to 4 times. This is done by partitioning the following:

DP; DQ; DR; DS < D and CP; CQ; CR; CS < C

By doing this, CRT reduces the size of the numbers to less than half their original sizes, which would automatically speed up the algorithm, making it take lesser time to compute.

RSA with more than 2 prime numbers – RSA with multiple keys helps to ensure more security. In the normal RSA algorithm, there are 2 prime numbers present, which would be undergoing a few computations to generate a public key and a private keys, which in turn are used in the encryption and decryption process.

In RSA with multiple keys, the number of prime numbers are doubled. There are 4 prime numbers, which in turn will be undergoing computations to generate 4 keys. With the doubling of the prime numbers, naturally, all the computation processes will be doubled as well. There will 2 public keys and 2 private keys generated.

Encryption and decryption which had one step each in the normal RSA, now in RSA with multiple keys has two steps each. Both sets of public and private keys are used in the encryption and decryption processes. Double the amount of encryption and decryption are done which increases the security.

2.   Hash to ensure authenticity and integrity of message:

Hash algorithms, particularly the SHA-512, are known for ensuring the authenticity and integrity of the messages sent from person to person. We are using SHA-512 for the same. We hash the message after it is read from the file and store the hash in the database for further use in the receiver's end.

When the receiver is done with the decryption, and the message is uncovered, our pro- posed algorithm then hashes the decrypted message to compare with the other hash. If both the hashes match, then it implies that the message is authentic and has integrity. Otherwise, it shows a breach and that the message has lost its authenticity and integrity.

3.   Generating prime numbers from the user's password:

Normally, a function is used to generate random large prime numbers, which is in turn used for key generation. It does have its advantages. Nevertheless, we are proposing a new way of generating prime numbers: generating them from the user's password. By using the password of the user who is trying to log in to the portal or interface, specific arithmetic operations are done on the user's password.

Taking the asci value of the password, operations such as multiplication, addition, multiplying the squares of the asci values, or adding the squares of the asci values are done. These operations will gener- ate 4 prime numbers, and the same operation will not be done to generate all the numbers.

Thus we generated a method for computing big prime numbers, and it isn't needed to be saved in the database. And this approach is also unique. The password is only known to the user, so we need to keep the password secure, which is necessary for every application or website. We didn't save the private key in the database so even if the database is attacked, the attacker will just get encrypted text in a binary form which is almost impossible to decrypt without knowing the segment size and the private key and both aren't available anywhere, they are generated when only we decipher the text in the application and it makes this process very much efficient and secure.

4.   Another level of security for the ciphertext:

Considering the normal RSA algorithm, the ciphertext is an integer which is sent to the receiver for decryption. In case, an attacker gets or finds the public key, they can crack the ciphertext to access the message being sent by attacks.
Our approach does the following:

a.   Converts the message into its ASCII value.
b.   Each ASCII value, which is a decimal number, is encrypted.
c.   Each ciphertext is converted to its binary equivalent and appended as a long binary string and stored in the database to be used by the receiver for decryption.

With the above steps in our approach, we can ensure that an attacker will find it extremely difficult to find out the number of bits that the binary string should be split into. With a binary string that is very long, figuring out its original form, whether it is an integer, an octal number, or a text would be incredibly hard. It would be a long process of trial error which would mostly end fruitless.

PROPOSED MODEL

Detailed Architecture

Figure 1 shows that for the first time, if a user signup for the portal, a dynamic table is created in the database for the user which stores his/her password for the portal. A separate table each for storing the private key and public key of every user. All the password/keys of the user is stored by applying cryptographic hash function MD5 in database as storing plain text passwords in the database is no less than a sin.

When the user login successfully to the portal, he is redirected to his chatbox.(To do so, the contact's stored in the database is extracted dynamically). All the previous exchanged files appears in the chatbox.

Figure 2 shows that when a file is sent, the file is uploaded in the database which serves as a Cloud to the user. Now, the file stored in the database is actually large binary values(as a result of RSA-CRT encryption). For implementing RSA-CRT, public key and private key is retrieved from the database. SHA-1 is used for ensuring integrity of the data. So the third party has no access to the data sent and received between two users. It acts as cloud since the user need not download the exchanged file, just by clicking on the file, he can view the current and previously exchanged file.

Algorithm Architecture:

Figure 1. Storing the log in information and generation of public and private key in the database

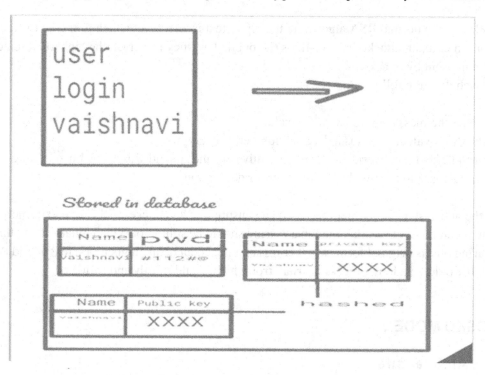

Figure 2. The sender sending a text file to a receiver, which is read, encrypted and decrypted by RSA-CRT with multiple keys and verified for authenticity and integrity using Hash.

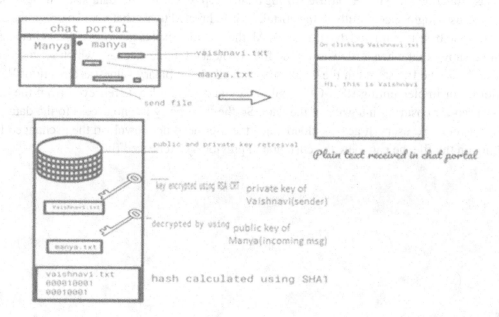

Figure 3 shows algorithm flow in the sender's side. The key generation process is initiated when the user/sender logs in to the interface. As the proposed approach is Modified RSA with CRT, the number of steps in the RSA key generation and encryption decryption is doubled. Four big prime numbers are generated. Let them be 'p','q','r' and 's'. Components of the keys ie., 'n' and 'z' are calculated using the generated primes. Their Euler Totient value of the components are also computed. Another set of components of the keys are enumerated, namely: 'I and 'g'. Following that the main elements of the keys are then determined using the enumerated numbers. The keys are generated and determined in this order. The file uploaded by the sender is read by the algorithm, which then converts each character into its ASCII decimal equivalent. Along with that, the context on the file is hashed using SHA-512 and saved in the database for verifying in the receiver's end. Each ASCII decimal equivalent is encrypted using the Modified RSA steps and stored in an array. Each element of the cipher array is then converted to its binary equivalent with a common block size, and appended. This binary string is then saved in the database for the receivers to use for decryption.

Figure 4 shows algorithm flow in the receiver's side: The algorithm in the receiver's side first accesses the database for the binary string. The block size splits the string, and each block is stored in an array. Each binary element is converted to its decimal equivalent. Decryption is done for each decimal equivalent by the steps of Modified RSA. After each decryption, the computed values are again saved in an array. These values are then converted into their ASCII character equivalent. And they are appended as a string to put together the content. This string is hashed with SHA-512. It is compared with the hash value already stored in the database to verify for authenticity and integrity. If the hashes are the same, the context is written to a file and made viewable to the receiver who can access it.

Functionality

Figure 5 shows a gist of application we have made, a secure data exchange app where files are encrypted using the RSA-CRT algorithm. For the first time, if a user signup for the portal, a dynamic table is created in the database for the user which stores his/her password for the portal. A separate table each for storing the private key and public key of every user. All the password/keys of the user is stored by applying cryptographic hash function MD5 in database as storing plain text passwords in the database is no less than a sin.

When the user login successfully to the portal, he is redirected to his chatbox. (To do so, the contact's stored in the database is extracted dynamically). All the previous exchanged files appear in the chatbox.

Now when the user sends a file? What happens?

When a file is sent, the file is uploaded in the database which serves as a Cloud to the user. Now, the file stored in the database (which will be used further for retrieval purpose by the user) is actually large binary values (as a result of RSA-CRT encryption). For implementing RSA-CRT, public key and private key is retrieved from the database. SHA-1 is used for ensuring the integrity of the data (Fig 2). So the third party has no access to the data sent and received between two users. It acts as cloud since the user need not download the exchanged file, just by clicking on the file, he can view the current and previously exchanged file.

Overview of Algorithm in work:

Figure 3. Flow of the algorithm in the sender's side. This shows the key genera- tion and encryption of the RSA-CRT with multiple keys algorithm.

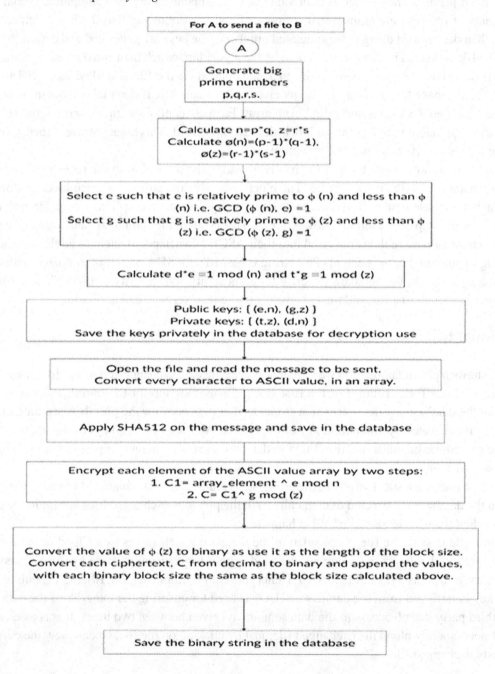

Figure 4. Flow of the algorithm in the receiver's side. This shows the decryption and verification using hash.

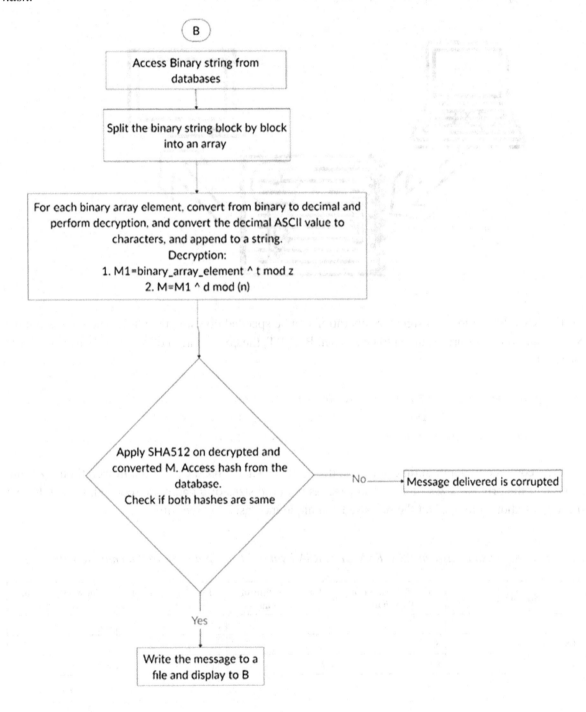

Figure 5. Functions of the algorithm and chat platform. A user can chat privately, and send files which will be encrypted and decrypted using Modified RSA-CRT.

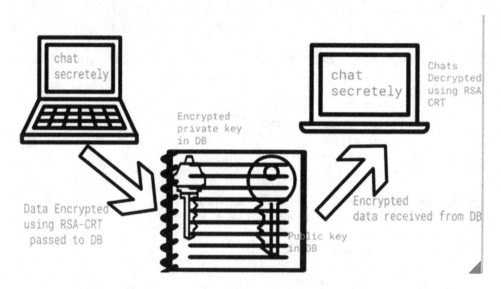

The RSA decryption and signature operation can be speeded up using the CRT, where the modulus N (i.e. and Q) factors are assumed to be known. By CRT, the computation of M can be partitioned into four parts:

```
mp = Cp^dp mod p mq = Cq^dq mod q mr = Cr^dr mod r ms = Cs^ds mod s Where
Cp = C1 mod p Cq = C1 mod q Cr = C1 mod r Cs = C1 mod s And
C1 = Ct mod (z). [using the first private key (t,z)]
```

This reduces computation time since dp, dq, dr, ds< D and Cp,Cq,Cr,Cs< C. In fact, their sizes are about half the original sizes. In the ideal case, as both the sizes of d and n are reduced, we can have a speedup of about 4 times. But the proposed technique increased the security.

Table 1. Comparison between RSA, RSA-CRT, RSA by multi keys and proposed technique with results.

Size in bits	Enc & Dec time of RSA in ms	Enc & Dec time of RSA in ms	Enc & Dec time of RSA in ms	Enc & Dec time of RSA in ms
640	42	26	84	66
1040	48	29	93	71
1136	63	32	113	85

The proposed technique is more secure as compared to the original RSA algorithm and RSA-CRT. And it enhanced the performance of the algorithm in decryption because it used the CRT in decryption, thus the proposed technique faster than RSA by multi keys. It reduces the cost of computation. Although it takes a long time to perform it as compared to the original RSA.

RSA USING MULTI-KEY AND CHINESE REMAINDER THEOREM

Take a document from the cloud, which is to be sent to another person. The document will be chomped by a Hash function into a few lines and will have a referral pair of words such as "message digest". Using our software, we will encrypt the message using our private key which gives the digital signature. RSA with multiple keys and CRT will then be used to encrypt the signature with the receiver's public key. The receiver can decrypt the ciphertext to plain text using their private key and our public key to verify the signature.

The proposed algorithm is trying to modify the RSA cryptosystem by improving its speed by using the Chinese remainder theorem and its security by taking 4 prime numbers instead of 2 and two public key pairs instead of one (Fig 3).

The procedure for generating the key:-

1. We generate four large prime numbers p, q, r and s
2. We calculate the value of (n, z)

    n = pq

    z = rs.
3. We find the value of ϕ(n) and ϕ(z) ϕ(n)= (p − 1)(q − 1)

    ϕ(z) = (r − 1)(s − 1).
4. We choose random integers e, g such that $1 < e < n$ and gcd(e, ϕ(n)) = 1

    $1 < g < z$ and gcd(g, ϕ(z)) = 1.
5. We calculate the value of d and t such that ed = 1 mod (ϕ(n)).

    tg = 1 mod (ϕ(z)).
6. We calculate the value of dp,dq,dr and ds dp = d mod (p − 1)

    dq = d mod (q − 1) dr = d mod (r − 1) ds = d mod (s − 1). NOW,

The Public key KU =< (e, n),(g, z) >

The Private key KV =< t, z, dp, dq, dr, ds>. Encryption for Proposed Technique (Fig 3):

For encryption of the message M, the following steps are as followed:

1. We convert the message M in integer form, in the range [0 to n − 1].
2. We calculate ciphertext C1 using first public key i.e e by

    $C1 = M^e \bmod (n)$
3. We calculate Ciphertext C using second public key g and C1 by $C = C1^g \bmod (z)$.
4. We send the ciphertext C to the receiver. Decryption for Proposed Technique (Fig 4):

For decryption of ciphertext C, we follow these steps:

1. First we find C1 using the first private key (t, z) C1 = Ct mod (z).
2. We do following Calculations Cp = C1 mod p

    Cq = C1 mod q Cr = C1 mod r Cs = C1 mod s
3. Then we calculate:

    $mp = Cp^{dp} \bmod p$ $mq = Cq^{dq} \bmod q$ $mr = Cr^{dr} \bmod r$ $ms = Cs^{ds} \bmod s$
4. Now after combining mp, mq, mr and ms, we get back our original plaintext message M.

Experimental Results

Executing the algorithm to the extent to which it was made, the following results were obtained:

Sample values for variables when p,q,r,s are large values Sample values for variables when p,q,r,s are large values A look and feel of our experimental result:

User logged in:

Fig 6 shows the login user interface of our chat portal where the registered user can login.

Table 2. Unveiling the algorithm behind - sample values for variables when p,q,r,s are small values

5.   The original text file (help_enc txt before getting encrypted

Figure 7 shows the text file the user wants to send using the chat portal.

6.   Now uploading this file to the cloud
7.   The encrypted file which is stored in database

Figure 9 shows the encrypted text stored in our database, ensuring secure data transmission of the text file uploaded by the user.

Table 3. Sample values for variables when p,q,r,s are large values

VARIABLE	VALUES
P	5760005761
Q	57600032951
R	331776232243207
S	331776351372017
N	331776521631549830711
Z	110075507805606161588078138519
Phin	331776521568189792000
Phiz	110075507805605498035494523296
E	331776521568189791999
G	110075507805605498035494523295
D	331776521568189791999
T	110075507805605498035494523295

Table 4. Output of algorithm

5760005761 =p 57600032951 =q 331776232243207 =r 331776351372017 =s
331776521631549830711 =n 1100755078056061615880781385519 =z
331776521568189792000 =phin 1100755078056054980354945223296 =phiz
331776521568189791999 =e 1100755078056054980354945223295 =g
331776521568189791999 =d 1100755078056054980354945223295 =t
001100011011110110011001011101011101110100010111011101000101110111010000100100100100001
Heyyy!!! This work is made by Manya, Aashish, Shruti and Vaishnavi is the messages to be sent. Hashes are the same. Heyyy!!! This work is made by Manya, Aashish, Shruti and Vaishnavi

Figure 6. Login user interface

Login

Please fill in this form to login to FilmFestival!

manyasmriti

••••••••

Forgot Password?

Login

8.   The decrypted text when the user try to open it from the cloud

User can easily retrieve the file:
Figure 10 shows the decrypted text when the user at the other end(receiver) try to open the file from the cloud.
Files stored in the db:
Figure 11 shows files name stored in the database.

Figure 7. Text file the user wants to send (before encryption).

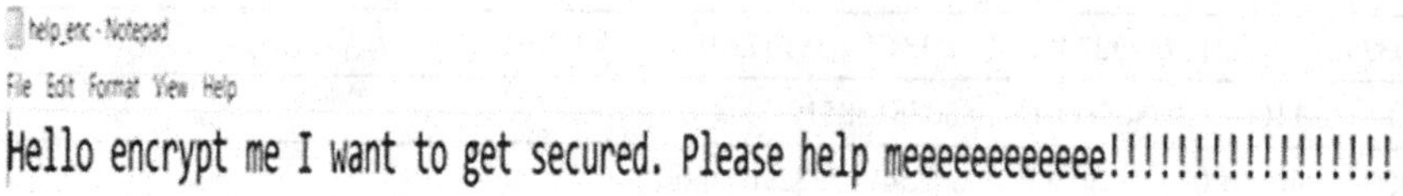

Figure 8. Uploading text file in the interface and cloud.

Figure 9. Encrypted text of the text file uploaded by the user.

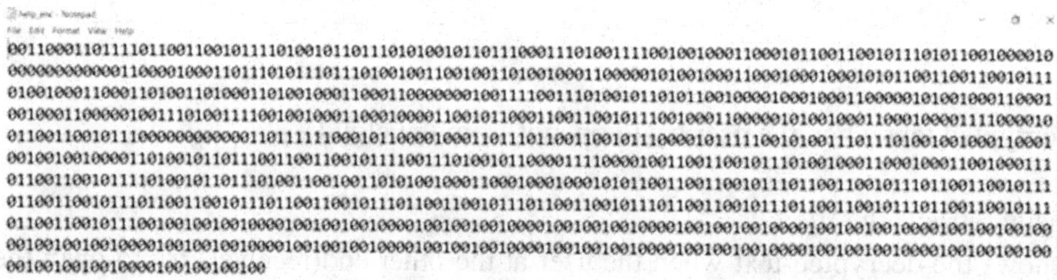

Figure 10. Decrypted text file which the receiver will be able to view.

Figure 11. The file which the sender uploaded is stored in the database.

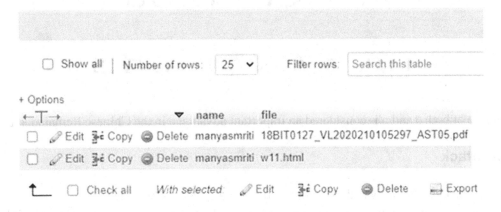

ANALYSIS

Attacks of RSA that can be mitigated using RSA-CRT:

Mitigation of attacks on RSA-CRT: Low exponent attack d is the private exponent in RSA.
Let's see it in detail:

- Given input, m, raise it to the d-th power modulo p and modulo q. The results interme- diate are then combined through addition and multiplication with some constant predefined to compute the final result.
- Since the exponentiation modular is performed on half the bit size of n, the execution time is less than 4 times.
- In RSA,

Decryption M=Cd mod n
Rely directly on size of d and n.
But in RSA-CRT:
After combining mp, mq, mr and ms, we get back our original plaintext message M.

Figure 12. Calculating mp, mq, mr and ms in RSA-CRT

$$mp = Cp^{dp} \bmod p$$

$$mq = Cq^{dq} \bmod q$$

$$mr = Cr^{dr} \bmod r$$

$$ms = Cs^{ds} \bmod s$$

Reduced size of both d and n is considered an important advantage in the Chinese Remainder Theorem.

Timing Attack

The timing attack can be mitigated by incorporating Montgomery Multiplication.

Montgomery multiplication is modular multiplication that allows computing such mul- tiplications faster. Instead of dividing the product and subtracting n multiple times, it adds multiples of n to cancel out the lower bits and then just discards the lower bits.

Benefits of using Multi-Keys RSA-CRT over RSA

1.   Secure option for application needing faster communication:

5 files are encrypted and decrypted using RSA and RSA-CRT. The time taken for encryption and de-cryption is as follows.

Table 5. The results of comparison time RSA encryption and RSA-CRT 1024 bits

File	Enc of RSA in nano-sec	Enc of RSA-CRT in nano-sec
1	330,130	371,148
2	316,803	348,592
3	330,131	358,845
4	344,485	375,250
5	351,661	382,426

Table 6. The results of comparison time decryption RSA and RSA-CRT 1024 bits

File	Dec of RSA in nano-sec	Dec of RSA-CRT in nano-sec
1	103,534,963	29,710,330
2	102,998,756	29,400,697
3	103,437,564	29,477,594
4	103,300,180	29,538,084
5	103,515,483	29,730,836

We can see that on average encryption of RSA-CRT is 367252.2(Table 4) while that of RSA is 334642. Thus the RSA-CRT takes 33610.2 nanoseconds more than RSA while encrypting 1024 bit block. But while decryption, on average, decryption of RSA-CRT is 29,571,508.2 while that of RSA is 103,357,389. Thus the RSA-CRT takes 73,785,800.8 nanoseconds less than RSA while decrypting 1024 bit block (Table 5).

Seeing the overall mechanism of encryption and decryption RSA-CRT is 3 times faster than RSA by 73,752,270.6 nanoseconds while applying the mechanism. This proves that despite of computational overhead, RSA- CRT is faster than RSA.

Though the computational overhead is high, time taken by this mechanism is less. Thus it is a better option to be used in fast communication applications like transaction-oriented or business plans oriented. But more memory would have to be used as the number of variables in more with the modified approach. Therefore, the main limitations in this approach is the overhead time and the memory to be used for the same, which can be overcome with future research and improvements.

1. Key Generation Overhead but is less vulnerable to attacks

Attacks like Fault Injection or Side-Channel Analysis can't be mitigated using RSA but RSA- CRT can protect user's data from these attacks. RSA-CRT prevent the attacker from obtain- ing the signature when a fault has been induced during the computation. Not only this, it makes other attacks(with big prime numbers) like factoring large number or common modu- lus highly infeasible to be done in the exchanging data's lifetime.

Timing attacks on RSA- CRT is highly infeasible since in timing attack precise time of decryption the card takes can help an attacker find or discover the private decryption exponent d. But in RSA-CRT, the decryption time is 3 times lesser than RSA (which is safe since it's still in use).

2. Multi-keys with RSA-CRT makes attacking highly in- feasible in the data's lifetime

Calculating private keys (t,z,dp,dq,dr,ds) where t is obtained by tg = 1 mod (φ(z)). (g is random integers such that gcd(g, φ(z)) = 1). dp = d mod (p − 1) dq = d mod (q − 1) dr = d mod (r − 1) ds = d mod (s − 1). Is highly infeasible in the data's lifetime.

The private key calculation of RSA is just {d,n} which is comparatively more prone to be hacked in data's lifetime.

3. Reduction in the value of d and n can still yield some promising result in RSA-CRT with multi-keys.

In the field of cryptosystem, many algorithms uses functionality of modular computation. The size of the exponent decryption, d and the modulus, n is very important because the complexity of the decryption in RSA depends directly on it. The exponent decryption specifies the numbers of multiplication modular, there are necessary to perform the exponentiation. The modulus, n play an important role in determined the size of the in- intermediate results. A way to reduce the size of both d and n is by using the Chinese Remainder theorem since the exponentiation modular is performed on half the bit size of n.

CONCLUSION

We proposed a technique which is based on traditional RSA, but we improved it by using multiple keys for more security and applied the Chinese remainder theorem for faster computation. We implemented our proposed technique to store a file in the cloud, which is a chatting application focused more on security of text files. This work has made a secure data exchange app where files are encrypted using RSA-CRT algorithm and hashed later. We observed that the proposed technique is more secure as compared to the original RSA algorithm and RSA-CRT.

REFERENCES

Arora, R., Parashar, A., & Transforming, C. C. I. (2013). Secure user data in cloud computing using encryption algorithms. *International Journal of Engineering Research and Applications, 3*(4), 1922–1926.

Balaji, M., Kumar, C. A., & Rao, G. S. V. (2018). Predictive Cloud resource management framework for enterprise workloads. *Journal of King Saud University-Computer and Information Sciences, 30*(3), 404–415. doi:10.1016/j.jksuci.2016.10.005

Balaji, M., Kumar, C. A., & Rao, G. S. V. (2019). Non-linear analysis of bursty workloads using dual metrics for better cloud resource management. *Journal of Ambient Intelligence and Humanized Computing, 10*(12), 4977–4992. doi:10.100712652-019-01183-8

Balaji, M., Rao, G. S. V., & Kumar, C. A. (2014). A comparitive study of predictive models for cloud infrastructure management. In *2014 14th IEEE/ACM International Symposium on Cluster, Cloud and Grid Computing* (pp. 923-926). IEEE. 10.1109/CCGrid.2014.32

Behl, A. (2011). Emerging security challenges in cloud computing: An insight to cloud security challenges and their mitigation. *2011 World Congress on Information and Communication Technologies, 21*, 217–222.

Gandhi, & Gupta. (2015). A Research on Enhancing Public Key Cryptography by the Use of MRGA with RSA and N-Prime RSA. *International Journal for Innovative Research in Science and Technology, 16*, 72–79.

Garg, P., & Sharma, V. (2014). An efficient and secure data storage in Mobile Cloud Com- puting through RSA and Hash function. *2014 International Conference on Issues and Challenges in Intelligent Computing Techniques (ICICT)*, 334–339.

Kim, G.-C., Li, S.-C., & Hwang, H.-C. (2020). Fast rebalanced RSA signature scheme with typical prime generation. *Theoretical Computer Science, 830-831*, 1–19. doi:10.1016/j.tcs.2020.04.024

Lakshmi, B. (2020). *The Dark Phase of Cultural Conflict in The Novel 'Twilight in Delhi'*. Academic Press.

Li, Y., Gai, K., Qiu, L., Qiu, M., & Zhao, H. (2017). Intelligent cryptogra- phy approach for secure distributed big data storage in cloud computing. *Information Sciences, 387*, 103–115. doi:10.1016/j.ins.2016.09.005

Narayanan, M., & Cherukuri, A. K. (2018). Verification of cloud based information integration architecture using colored petri nets. *International Journal of Computer Network and Information Security, 12*(2), 1–11. doi:10.5815/ijcnis.2018.02.01

Pant, V. K., Prakash, J., & Asthana, A. (2015). Three-step data security model for cloud com- puting based on RSA and steganography. *2015 International Conference on Green Computing and Internet of Things (ICGCIoT)*, 490–494. 10.1109/ICGCIoT.2015.7380514

Ruj, S., Stojmenovic, M., & Nayak, A. (2012). Privacy-preserving access control with authen- tication for securing data in clouds. *IEEE/ACM International Symposium on Cluster, Cloud and Grid Computing*, 556–563.

Shimbre, N., & Deshpande, P. (2015). Enhancing distributed data storage security for cloud computing using TPA and AES algorithm. *International Conference on Computing Communication Control and Automation*, 35–39. 10.1109/ICCUBEA.2015.16

Shinde, G. N., & Fadewar, H. S. (2008). Faster RSA algorithm for decryption using Chinese re- mainder theorem. *ICCES: International Conference on Computational & Experimental Engineering and Sciences*, 255–262.

Shwetha Bindu & Yadaiah. (2011). Secure Data Storage In Cloud Computing. *International Journal of Research in Computer Science, 1*(1), 63–73.

Somani, U., Lakhani, K., & Mundra, M. (2010). Implementing digital signature with RSA en- cryption algorithm to enhance the Data Security of cloud in Cloud Computing. *2010 First International Conference On Parallel, Distributed and Grid Computing*, 211– 216.

Sookhak, M. (2015). *Dynamic remote data auditing for securing big data storage in cloud computing* (Doctoral dissertation). University of Malaya.

Subashini, S., & Kavitha, V. (2011). A metadata-based storage model for securing data in a cloud environment. *2011 International Conference on Cyber-Enabled Distributed Computing and Knowledge Discovery*, 429–434.

Usman, M., Jan, M. A., & He, X. (2017). Cryptography-based secure data storage and sharing using HEVC and public clouds. *Information Sciences, 387*, 90–102. doi:10.1016/j.ins.2016.08.059

Wang, C., Ren, K., Lou, W., & Li, J. (2010). Toward publicly auditable secure cloud data storage services. *IEEE Network, 24*(4), 19–24. doi:10.1109/MNET.2010.5510914

Yang, K., & Jia, X. (2012). An efficient and secure dynamic auditing protocol for data storage in cloud computing. *IEEE Transactions on Parallel and Distributed Systems*, *24*(9), 1717–1726. doi:10.1109/TPDS.2012.278

Zhou, L., Varadharajan, V., & Hitchens, M. (2013). Vijay Varadharajan, and Michael Hitchens. Achieving Secure Role-Based Access Control on Encrypted Data in Cloud Storage. *IEEE Transactions on Information Forensics and Security*, *8*(12), 1947–1960. doi:10.1109/TIFS.2013.2286456

Chapter 12
IoT Applications for Coronavirus Industry Protection:
Smart Mask and Smart Badge

Maissa Daoud

University of Sfax, Tunisia

ABSTRACT

In this chapter, an overview of two IoT applications, smart badge and smart mask, are used to protect employees working in a crowded environment. The smart mask protects the wearer from inhaling very small microbes that are transmitted through the airways (such as influenza virus or coronavirus), filters the air, controls the presence of CO2, and measures the body temperature. The smart badge measures the wearer temperature. It is equipped with an SOS panic alarm for indoor and outdoor workers. By pressing the SOS button, the device communicates with pre-recorded IDs so that the victim can talk and alert the emergency services. Thanks to the GPS functionality, it is possible to precisely locate the user via a Google Map link.

INTRODUCTION

SARS-CoV-2, the virus that causes COVID-19, can be spread from person to person by droplets produced when coughing or breathing during close contact with an infected person. Infection can also occur without direct contact, when these droplets land on objects and surfaces around the infected person and the other person touches these objects or surfaces and then touches the eyes, nose or mouth. That's why it's important to stay 1 to 2 metres (3-6 feet) away from the person who is sick. Because some people do not have symptoms when they are infected with the virus, a physical distance of one to two metres should be maintained, whether the other person appears to be sick or not (Chamola, Hassija, Gupta, & Guizani, 2020).

The most common symptoms of COVID-19 are fever, cough and fatigue. Some patients may experience loss of taste or smell, conjunctivitis, headache, muscle aches, congestion, runny nose, sore throat, diarrhea, nausea or vomiting, and various types of rash. Some people become infected but have no symp-

DOI: 10.4018/978-1-7998-8367-8.ch012

toms and do not feel sick. Most people (about 80%) recover from the disease without needing special care. About 1 in 6 people infected with COVID-19 become seriously ill and develop severe symptoms of COVID-19, which include difficulty or shortness of breath, confusion, loss of appetite, persistent pain or pressure in the chest, and require hospitalization. . Older people and those with underlying medical conditions such as high blood pressure, heart problems or diabetes are more susceptible to developing serious illness. People with fever, cough and difficulty breathing should seek medical attention (Henderi, Maulana, Warnars, Setiyadi & Qurrohman, 2020; Haritha, Swaroop & Mounika, 2020).

You can reduce the possibility of contracting or spreading COVID-19 by taking some of the following precautions. Keep at least 1 to 2 metres (3 to 6 feet) of physical distance between you and others, whether or not they have symptoms. Wear a mask as part of the overall public health measures to prevent the spread of COVID-19 even if you are not symptomatic or infected. For this purpose, intelligent masks are designed, whose role is to measure the temperature of the human body, filter the breathing air and control the presence of CO_2 (Li, et al. 2021; Baluprithviraj, Bharathi, Chendhuran & Lokeshwaran, 2021; Rahman, et al. 2020). In the industry, and in order to protect employers from the contamination of the corona virus, badges are designed to measure the temperature of the human body and control the employers around this badge. the intelligent mask and badge communicate remotely with objects located in the same environment through the Internet of Things network (IoT) (Chandra, et al. 2019; Mikroyannidis, Domingue, Bachler & Quick, 2018; Javali & Revadigar, 2012; João, et al. 2021).

The term Internet of Things refers to the network of devices capable of collecting and sharing data with other devices on the same network, as this allows things to be detected and controlled remotely via the existing network infrastructure, which creates many opportunities for seamless integration. of computer systems in the materialist world (Garg & Dave, 2019; Gupta & Johari, 2019; Desai & Toravi, 2017).

In this chapter, an overview of the two IOT applications (smart badge and smart mask) used to protect employees working in a crowded environment. The study covers its components and its operation mode.

THE SMART BADGE

In the face of the ongoing corona virus pandemic, businesses and industries need to ensure social distancing and secure contact tracing to enable their employees to feel more confident about working in a co-located physical workplace. The ability to automate the monitoring of new security policies, while empowering employees as part of the new normality of business operations, is essential for any organization.

Whether in an office, factory or construction site, each employee can be equipped with a compact portable proximity sensor that allows easy monitoring of interactions in common areas, also working with security badges for access control and smart masks. When the sensors register that two or more people have exceeded the security limit, it alerts them with an audible or visual alarm.

System Description

By entering the company as an employee, we wear our badge and register our data with the RFID TAG, which is linked to an employee ID card. At this moment, the operating cycle of this badge begins (Figure 1).

Figure 1. Flowchart of the badge operation

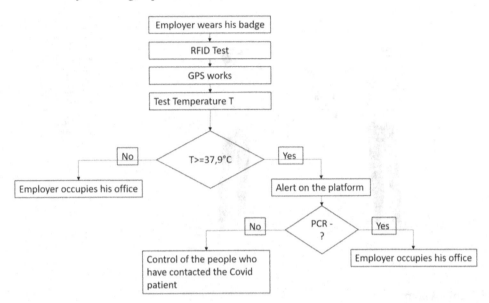

Before entering the company and after the registration of the data. The badge will measure the temperature by means of a small temperature sensor located in the collar of the badge which is in contact with the skin. In this way, the temperature is measured during the entire working time in the company.

- If the measured temperature is higher than 37.9 °C, the badge signals an alert on the platform controlled by an employee and consequently the corona service will be called to perform a PCR test which will take 48 hours. During this time the employee is confined.
- If his PCR is positive, all the employees who contacted him before the 48 hours are called to do this test.
- If the PCR is negative, the employee returns to work
- If the temperature is strictly below 37.9°C, nothing to report

Components and Technologies Involved

1. BLE Proximity

The smart badge detects other smart badges in the vicinity using the BLE beacon and scanning (Figure 2). The devices send an alert when certain risk levels are exceeded.

Figure 2. BLE proximity

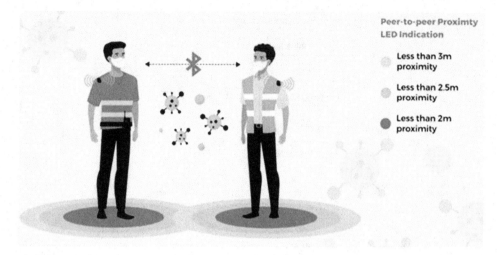

2.   SOS Panic Alarm

The SOS panic alarm is used for indoor and outdoor worker badges. By pressing the SOS button, the device communicates with pre-registered IDs so that the victim can speak and alert the emergency services. Thanks to the GPS functionality, it is possible to locate the user precisely via a Google Map link.

3.   Long Range Wide-Area network (LoRa WAN) Protocol

LoRaWAN is a telecommunication protocol for low-speed communication. Objects with low power consumption communicating using LoRa technology are connected to the Internet via gateways, thus participating in the Internet of Things. This protocol is used in smart cities, industrial monitoring and agriculture. The modulation technology linked to LoRaWAN is LoRa, created in 2009 by the Grenoble start-up Cycleo and acquired by Semtech in 2012. Semtech promotes its LoRa platform through the LoRa Alliance, of which it is a member. The LoRaWAN protocol on the LoRa physical layer allows to connect sensors or objects requiring a long battery life, in a reduced volume and cost (Figure 3).

Figure 3. LoRaWAN network protocols

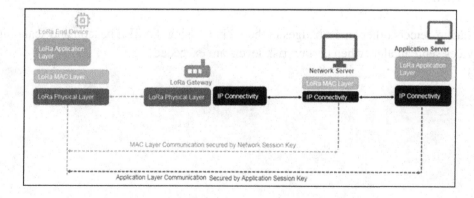

The terminals send data to the gateways and they transmit them to the network server, which in turn transmits them to the application server. The data routing and battery optimization is performed by the cloud. It also provides secure communication.

Since LoRaWAN devices can communicate with the network server whenever there is a change in the sensor or when a timer is activated. They can wake up and talk to the server at any time.

4.   Geolocation System by Satellite (GPS)

The principle of operation of GPS is based on the measurement of the distance from a receiver to several satellites. Each satellite emits a signal, which is received by the receiver, allowing the distance between the transmitter and the receiver to be measured very precisely, thanks to the travel time. The GPS will be used to find the location of the workers inside the company.

In this project we used the NEO-6M GPS module (Figure 4). It is a high performance full-featured GPS receiver with an integrated 25 x 25 x 4 mm ceramic antenna, which offers powerful satellite search capability. With the power and signal indicators, you can monitor the status of the module. With the data backup battery, the module can save data in case of accidental power failure.

Figure 4. NEO-6M GPS module

5. Bluetooth Low Energy (BLE)

The BLE, offering easy and reliable access. It is popular with consumer electronics manufacturers, mobile application developers and engineers. It is increasingly suitable for all things related to the Internet of Things that require less energy.

The major advantage of Bluetooth Low Energy is without doubt its low energy consumption. energy consumption. Used for periodic transfer of small amounts of data at short range, BLE is easy to deploy. In general, BLE consumes half as much power as Bluetooth. Finally, the cost is relatively low and the battery life is not negligible. The BLE has different types of connections. A BLE connected object can have up to 4 different functions:

- The Broadcaster: It can act as a server. The Broadcaster: It can act as a server and regularly transmits data to a device, but it does not accept any incoming connections.
- The "Observer": In the second stage, the object can only listen and interpret the data sent by a broadcaster. In this situation, the object cannot send any connections to the server.
- The "Central": often a smartphone or a tablet. It is an element that interacts in two different ways: either in advertising mode or in connected mode. It is then the leader and it is from it that the data exchange starts.
- The "Peripheral": it accepts connections from the central and sends it data periodically. This system aims to package the data in a universal way via the protocol so that it is understood by the other peripherals.

6. Skin Temperature Sensor

With this sensor (Figure 5), body temperature can be measured more accurately than with conventional thermometers. In addition, the sensor can be integrated into virtually any wearable skin contact device.

Figure 5. Skin temperature sensor

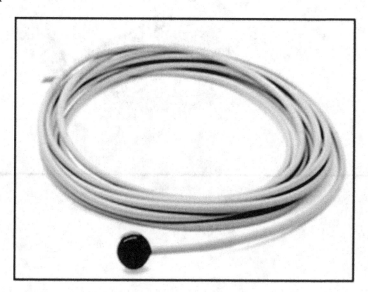

Thanks to its miniaturization, the sensor can be integrated into almost any portable device that comes into contact with the skin. For this reason, it is be used in this study, as we will be testing the temperature of the worker.

7.   Edge Computing

Edge Computing is an open distributed computing architecture (Figure 6). It offers decentralized processing power. (Saini, K., 2018; Saini, K., 2019). Thus, rather than being transmitted to a remote Data Center, data is processed directly by the device that generates it (connected object, smartphone...) or by a local computer or server. Specifically, Edge Computing can be thought of as a mesh network of Micro Data Centers that process or store critical data locally. The data is then transmitted to a central data center or cloud storage with a footprint of less than 10 square meters.

Figure 6. Edge computing flowchart

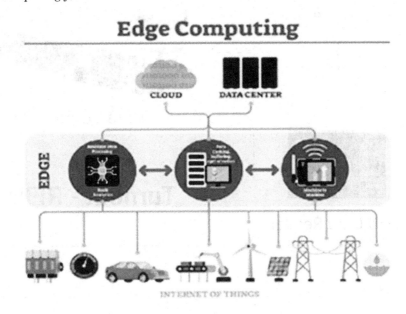

Edge Computing is most often used in the area of the Internet of Things. Some of the extensive data collected by connected devices is processed locally, to reduce traffic to the Cloud or Data Centres and to allow analysis of important data in real time (or near real time). The Edge Computing was used for proximity detection and exposure assessment.

8.   The Radio Frequency IDentification (RFID)

The radio identification is a method of storing and retrieving data remotely using markers called radio tags. The latter are small objects, such as self-adhesive labels, which can be glued or incorporated into objects or products and even implanted into living organisms (animals, human body). The radio tags comprise an antenna associated with a microchip which enables them to receive and respond to radio to receive and respond to radio requests from the transceiver (Figure 7).

These electronic chips contain an identifier and possibly additional data. This identification technology can be used to identify: individuals, by being integrated into passports, transport cards, payment cards or employer cards for check-in purposes.

Figure 7. RFID communication

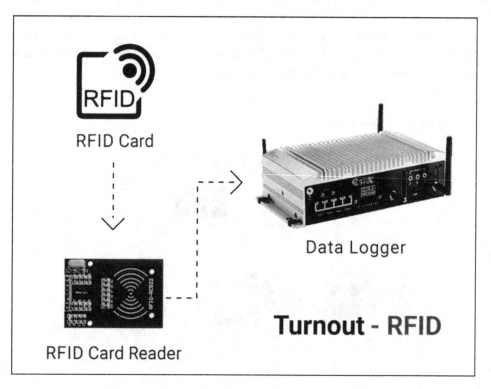

9. WIFI Protocol

WiFi is a set of wireless communication protocols governed by the standards of the IEEE 802.11 group (ISO/IEC 8802-11). A WiFi network allows several computer devices (computer, router, smartphone, modem, internet, etc.) to be linked by radio waves within a computer network in order to transmit data between them at high speed.

The wifi is used to connect all the badges with the platform to identify if there is a case of covid, a person who has confronted a contaminated worker or presses the SOS button and also if there is a location to be disinfected.

THE SMART MASK

Generally, a mask protects the wearer from inhaling very small microbes that are transmitted through the airways (such as influenza, coronavirus or tuberculosis virus). In addition to that, the smart mask measures the temperature of its wearer, measures the temperature of objects around it, measures the level of CO_2 and filters the breathing air (Figure 8).

Figure 8. Smart mask picture

 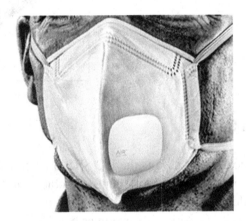

Temperature Measurement

To measure the temperature, we used the MLX90164 temperature sensor (Figure 9). This cyber-tronic-looking sensor hides a secret behind its shimmering eye. Different from most temperature sensors, this sensor measures infrared light bouncing off distant objects so it can detect temperature without physical touching. Simply point the sensor at what you want to measure and it will detect the temperature by absorbing the emitted IR waves.

This sensor is used in many applications such as: Precision temperature measurement (non-contact), temperature measurement in the medical world, body temperature measurement, sensor for mobile air conditioning systems, temperature measurement for air conditioning systems in commercial, industrial and residential areas, windscreen fogging detection, food monitoring, temperature control in printers and copiers, and thermal alarm.

It is a non-contact infrared temperature sensor for measuring ambient and object temperature. The module communicates with a microcontroller via a PWN output or an I2C link. Since it does not touch the object it is measuring, it can detect a temperature range that most digital sensors cannot: from -70 degrees to +380 degrees. It takes the measurement over a 90 degrees angle of view, so it can be useful for determining the temperature of an area.

Figure 9. MLX90164 temperature sensor picture

Motion Sensor

The motion sensor used is the HC-SR505 (Figure 10). This PIR (Pyroelectric InfraRed) sensor measures the infrared (IR) light emitted by objects in the detection area. It is very easy to use because it already delivers a HIGH signal if something moves in the detection area. This HIGH signal lasts for about 8 seconds, which is sometimes considered a disadvantage. Unfortunately, this drawback cannot be solved in software, i.e. adding a workaround to the source code does not work. The module has an operating voltage between 4.5V and 20V. According to the data sheet, the sensor detects movement up to a distance of 3 m.

Figure 10. HC-SR505 motion sensor picture

Gaz Sensor

The gaz sensor used is the MG-811 (Figure 11). It detects the presence of CO_2. A 6V booster allows the sensor to be brought up to temperature for accurate measurement. It is characterized by its high sensitivity and fast response time. The module has an analogue output and a digital ON/OFF output. The module is connected to an analogue input of an Arduino compatible board.

Figure 11. MG-811 gaz sensor picture

Ventilators

Inside the mask there are two ventilators (Figure 12). The air is absorbed, filtered and exhaled. The mask adapts to the wearer's breathing, making it safe and comfortable. To do this, the sensors detect the wearer's breathing cycle and volume and allow the ventilators to be adjusted with three different speeds. In short, the ventilators automatically accelerate to facilitate air entry and slow down to reduce resistance during exhalation to facilitate breathing.

Figure 12. Ventilators picture

CONCLUSION

In this chapter, a detailed study of two IOT applications (smart badge and smart mask) used to protect employees working in a crowded environment. The smart mask measures the wearer temperature and protects him from inhaling very small microbes that are transmitted through the airways (such as influenza virus or corona virus). The smart badge measures the wearer temperature. It is equipped with an SOS panic alarm for indoor and outdoor workers. By pressing the SOS button, the device communicates with pre-recorded IDs so that the victim can talk and alert the emergency services.

REFERENCES

Baluprithviraj, K. N., Bharathi, K. R., Chendhuran, S., & Lokeshwaran, P. (2021). Artificial Intelligence based Smart Door with Face Mask Detection. *IEEE International Conference on Artificial Intelligence and Smart Systems (ICAIS)*, 543-548. 10.1109/ICAIS50930.2021.9395807

Chamola, V., Hassija, V., Gupta, V., & Guizani, M. (2020). A Comprehensive Review of the COVID-19 Pandemic and the Role of IoT, Drones, AI, Blockchain, and 5G in Managing its Impact. *IEEE Access: Practical Innovations, Open Solutions, 8*, 90225–90265. doi:10.1109/ACCESS.2020.2992341

Chandra, Y. U. (2019). Smart E-badge for Student Activities in Smart Campus. *IEEE International Conference on ICT for Smart Society (ICISS)*, 1-6. 10.1109/ICISS48059.2019.8969806

Desai, M. R., & Toravi, S. (2017). A Smart Sensor Interface for Smart Homes and Heart Beat Monitoring using WSN in IoT Environment. *IEEE International Conference on Current Trends in Computer, Electrical, Electronics and Communication (CTCEEC)*, 74-77. 10.1109/CTCEEC.2017.8455124

Garg, H., & Dave, M. (2019). Securing IoT Devices and Securely Connecting the Dots Using REST API and Middleware. *IEEE International Conference on Internet of Things: Smart Innovation and Usages (IoT-SIU)*, 1-6. 10.1109/IoT-SIU.2019.8777334

Gupta, A. K., & Johari, R. (2019). IOT based Electrical Device Surveillance and Control System. *IEEE International Conference on Internet of Things: Smart Innovation and Usages (IoT-SIU)*, 1-5. 10.1109/IoT-SIU.2019.8777342

Haritha, D., Swaroop, N., & Mounika, M. (2020). Prediction of COVID-19 Cases Using CNN with X-rays. *IEEE International Conference on Computing, Communication and Security (ICCCS)*, 1-6. 10.1109/ICCCS49678.2020.9276753

Henderi. (2020). Model Decision Support System for Diagnosis COVID-19 Using Forward Chaining: A Case in Indonesia. *8th International Conference on Cyber and IT Service Management (CITSM)*, 1-4. 10.1109/CITSM50537.2020.9268853

Javali, C., & Revadigar, G. (2012). Wireless Smart Badge based on IEEE 802.15.4 LRWPAN. *IEEE World Congress on Information and Communication Technologies*, 367-372. 10.1109/WICT.2012.6409104

João, D. V., Lodetti, P. Z., dos Santos, A. B., Izumida Martins, M. A., De Francisci, S., & Brandao Almeida, J. F. (2021). A Smart Badge Implementation on Electrical Power Sector for Safety Improvement for Workforce - A Study Case. *IEEE Power & Energy Society Innovative Smart Grid Technologies Conference*, 1–5. Advance online publication. doi:10.1109/ISGT49243.2021.9372220

Li, C. H. (2021). Development of IoT-based Smart Recycling Machine to collect the wasted Non-woven Fabric Face Mask (NFM). *IEEE International Symposium on Product Compliance Engineering-Asia (ISPCE-CN)*, 1-5. 10.1109/ISPCE-CN51288.2020.9321851

Mikroyannidis, A., Domingue, J., Bachler, M., & Quick, K. (2018). Smart Blockchain Badges for Data Science Education. *IEEE Frontiers in Education Conference (FIE)*, 1-5. 10.1109/FIE.2018.8659012

Rahman, M. M. (2020). An Automated System to Limit COVID-19 Using Facial Mask Detection in Smart City Network. *IEEE International IOT, Electronics and Mechatronics Conference (IEMTRONICS)*, 1-5. 10.1109/IEMTRONICS51293.2020.9216386

Saini, K. (2018). A Future's Dominant Technology Blockchain: Digital Transformation. *IEEE International Conference on Computing, Power and Communication Technologies*, 937-940. 10.1109/GUCON.2018.8675075

Saini, K. (2019). Recent Advances and Future Research Directions in Edge Cloud Framework. *International Journal of Engineering and Advanced Technology*, 9(2), 1–6. doi:10.35940/ijeat.B3090.129219

Chapter 13
Reliable Blockchain–Aided Searchable Attribute–Based Encryption for Cloud–IoT

Ambika N.

https://orcid.org/0000-0003-4452-5514

St. Francis College, India

ABSTRACT

The work utilizes an alliance blockchain, where a lot of foreordained hubs control the agreement convention. Different devices can produce information and send the information to the information pool. All agreement hubs cooperate to update the client repudiation list that improves the unwavering quality of the frame. Clients submit search demands through the blockchain. A client sends a fractional token to the blockchain, and agreement hubs produce the total with the client's trait keys. At that point, the cloud can play out a quest with the total token for the client. The cloud asks the related time-coordinated pre-unscrambling key of the client from the blockchain to pre-decode. The framework is proportionate to a release board where we record all client open personality keys, client unscrambling keys, key update messages, and pre-decoding keys. The cloud can utilize those keys to pre-decrypt for clients, and accord hubs are liable for refreshing keys for non-renounced clients. The proposal increases security by 3.82% and improves trust by 5.09%.

INTRODUCTION

The Internet-of-things (Ambika, 2019) (Alaba, 2017) (Nagaraj, 2021) makes it easy for humans by decreasing their effort. These devices communicate with each other with varying capabilities using a common platform. The cloud supports enormous data storage. The transmission between the IoT devices and the cloud needs some amount of security. Some of the applications making use of these devices include smart homes (Verma & Sood, 2018), hospitals (Ambika N., 2020)(Abdelgawad, Yelamarthi, & Khattab, 2016), industry (A & K, 2016), smart building (Akkaya, Guvenc, Aygun, Pala, & Kadri, 2015) and cities(Alrashdi, Alqazzaz, Aloufi, Alharthi, Zohdy, & Ming, 2019). The devices do not have enough

DOI: 10.4018/978-1-7998-8367-8.ch013

space to store large amounts of data. Hence cloud is used for storage. Using The devices can upload data from anywhere, anytime using Internet services.

A blockchain (Atlam & Wills, 2019) is a dispersed record that comprises a consistently developing arrangement of evidence. The appropriated idea of blockchains suggests no single substance controls the information, but it takes interest peers together to approve the credibility of records. These records are in blocks that are connected utilizing cryptographic hashes, thus the name blockchain. Blockchain-based innovations boost an organization of companions to make calculations towards an agreement in the organization. The blockchain arrangement (Chen, Xu, Lu, & Chen, 2018)(Dorri, Kanhere, Jurdak, & Gauravaram, 2017) is the Bitcoin cryptographic money. The Bitcoin blockchain keeps up all switches from the underlying square, alluded to as the beginning square. The exchange has sender, recipient, the measure of the moved Bitcoin money, and the mark (sender). For the trading to remember, the blockchain transmits to the blockchain network. The purported diggers assume the liability to check new exchanges and propose the following square that incorporates the confirmed trade. Excavators compensate with Bitcoins and exchange expenses for their computational work.

The work (Liu S., Yu, Xiao, Wan, Wang, & Yan, 2020) utilizes an alliance blockchain, where foreordained (believed) hubs control agreement convention. Different devices can produce information and send the information to the information pool. At that point, the agreement hubs run the accord convention to update the chain and keep all devices in this framework conceding to a steady state. All agreement hubs cooperate to update the client repudiation list that improves the unwavering quality of the frame. Clients submit search demands through the blockchain. A client sends a fractional token to the blockchain, and agreement hubs produce the total with the client's trait keys. It can play out a quest with the total pledge for the client. It asks related time-coordinated pre-unscrambling key of the client from the blockchain to pre-decode. The framework is proportionate to a release board where we record all client open personality keys, client unscrambling keys, key update messages, and pre-decoding keys. It can utilize those keys to pre-decrypt the clients, and accord hubs are liable for a refreshing credential for non-renounced clients. The contribution is an improvement compared to the previous work. The proposal uses the Merkle root method to generate a hash value. It increases security by 3.82%. The previously generated value prefixes to the data. The new hash value suffixes to the data before transmission. It improves reliability by 5.09% compared to (Liu S., Yu, Xiao, Wan, Wang, & Yan, 2020).

The chapter has seven subdivisions. The literature survey follows the introduction in section two. Segment three briefs background of the work. Paragraph four details the previous contribution. Subdivision five explains the proposed work. Segment six provides an analysis of the work. The chapter concludes in section seven.

LITERATURE SURVEY

The section contains similar contributions to discussions. The work (Liu S., Yu, Xiao, Wan, Wang, & Yan, 2020) utilizes an alliance blockchain, where foreordained (believed) hubs control agreement convention. Different devices can produce information and send the information to the information pool. At that point, the agreement hubs run the accord convention to update the chain and keep all devices in this framework conceding to a steady state. All agreement hubs cooperate to update the client repudiation list that improves the unwavering quality of the frame. Clients submit search demands through the blockchain. A client sends a fractional token to the blockchain, and agreement hubs produce the total with the client's trait keys. It can play out a quest with the total pledge for the client. It asks related time-coordinated pre-unscrambling key of the client from the blockchain to pre-decode. The framework is proportionate to a release board where we record all client open personality keys, client unscrambling keys, key update messages, and pre-decoding keys. It can utilize those keys to pre-decrypt the clients, and accord hubs are liable for a refreshing credential for non-renounced clients.

The work (Shafagh, Burkhalter, Hithnawi, & Duquennoy, 2017) decouples the control and information plane of our IoT disseminated capacity framework. In the framework, the control plane isolates the rationalist of the information plane. They utilize an openly evident blockchain to make a responsible appropriated framework and bootstrap trust in an untrusted network without a focal trust element. The exchanges comprise responsibility for streams and relating access permissions. They utilize the blockchain to store access authorizations safely. Access rights concede per information stream. The information proprietor can deny the sharing of an information stream. For any solicitation to recover information, the capacity hub first checks the blockchain for access rights. To disavow admittance to an information stream, the information proprietor refreshes the encryption key. They store information pieces forming sequences. The information lump scrambles at the source with symmetric code AES-GCM. In the capacity layer, they stockpile key-esteem sets. The IoT doors fill in as an intermediary stockpiling hub at the front of the capacity layer. The entryway pushes the lumps utilizing the FIFO standard into the capacity layer.

The new engineering (Manzoor, Liyanage, Braeke, Kanhere, & Ylianttila, 2019) is dependent on the components of a blockchain. It is re-encryption for secure putting away and sharing of the sensor information. They think about four substances in the framework: IoT sensors, information requester, cloud supplier, and the blockchain. The sensors' proprietor actuates the sensors and registers them on the blockchain using contract work. After enrollment, the sensor's proprietor gives the sensor the necessary key material with the end goal. The deliberate information transmits to the distributed storage worker. A client demands admittance to one (or a gathering of) sensor(s) of the proprietor using a keen agreement work. After getting the solicitation, an agreement is created and mined on the blockchain. The requester connects with the blockchain to share the public cryptographic key and deals with all the budgetary-related exchanges. On accepting the client demand, distributed storage communicates by the blockchain. The product channels the information as indicated by the solicitation. The re-encryption cryptographic key from the sensor proprietor is refreshed on the smart contract when the client demand is gotten. He unscrambles and re-scrambles data and puts it in an impermanent area. The encoded information is transiently put away on the worker, and an exchange containing the location of the put-away information undergoes mining on the blockchain. When the data undergoes preparation, the requester is told of the impermanent area by the blockchain. The requester can unscramble the information utilizing its private cryptographic key. They propose to apply a Certificate-Based Proxy ReEncryption (CB-PRE) plot, which comprises seven polynomial-time calculations.

The framework (Dwivedi, Srivastava, Dhar, & Singh, 2019) comprises five sections containing the Overlay organization, cloud stockpiling, Healthcare suppliers, Smart agreements, and Patient outfitting with medical services wearable IoT gadgets. The distributed storage bunches client's information in indistinguishable squares related to an extraordinary square number. These mists are associated with overlay organizations. The data is put away into the precinct, and the cloud worker sends the hash of the information squares to the overlay organization. The hash of the information is determined utilizing Merkle Tree. The system acknowledges the root hash. It includes the past esteem producing a chain. It comprises explicit hubs to demonstrate confirmation with a legitimate endorsement. It can be transferred or confirmed before making a record on the organization. When approved, he will have the option to sign information/exchanges over the organization carefully. To expand network adaptability and keep away from network delay, they bunch the hubs as numerous groups. Each bunch has one Cluster Head that deals with the public keys of the devices. Any device joined with any bunch can change the group whenever in the event of deferral. The instrument appends to a bunch and can change the group head. The group head keeps the public keys of requesters that can get to the information of a specific patient. The insurance agencies or patients delegate the medical services suppliers to perform clinical tests. Medical care specialist organizations manage the treatment of patients once they get a caution from the organization. They likewise treat them as a hub in the organization and are approved to get specific patient information from the cloud. Intelligent contracts permit the making of arrangements in any IoT gadgets and execute when given conditions meet. When readings obtain from the wearable instrument that doesn't follow the showed run, the intelligent agreement will send an alarm message to the approved individual or medical care supplier. It stores the irregular information so medical care suppliers can get the patient circulatory strain readings. The IoT gadget will gather all wellbeing information from the patient. Such information could be pulsed, resting conditions, or strolling separation to give some examples. Patients themselves are the proprietors of their data. They are liable for allowing, denying, or repudiating information access from some other gatherings. On the off chance, the tolerant requirements of clinical treatment will impart individual wellbeing information to the ideal specialist. After treatment, the patient can deny further admittance to the specialist, medical care supplier, or medical coverage organization.

Patients' information gathered undergo grouping by wellbeing sensors (Obour Agyekum, Xia, Sifah, Gao, Xia, & Guizani, 2019) that are generally bound and transferred onto a cloud worker in the wake of recording. Before a patient's clinical information moves to a cloud worker, the patient encodes their data characteristics. It shows the entrance benefit on the data. The patient gives the subtleties of all approved clients to the blockchain's preparing hub. Accordingly, admittance to a patient's information can be conceivable if the client fulfills the trait set and utilizes the private key identified with that property set. The information Owner is the element obtained. Access conceives if the private key of the information client compares to the quality set determined by the information proprietor. Information User is the element that needs to utilize the information from the proprietor. Both the information proprietor and user ought to enroll in the blockchain. Cloud Server is the archive of the data from the proprietor. The cloud worker using the correspondence channel sends all the encoded records. Blockchain networks comprise the accompanying substances. Guarantor substance enrolls the members (information proprietor and clients) on the blockchain network. It gives out enrollment keys to them and fills in as their character (ID). The verifier can fill in as a validation unit, checks whether a client makes an entrance demand or an information proprietor transfers its information onto the storage. The handling hub is the heartbeat of the blockchain network. The element performs all cycles.

The work (Liu B., Yu, Chen, Xu, & Zhu, 2017) has four sections- Data Owners Application (DOA), Data Shopper Application, Cloud Storage Service, and Blockchain. The CSS divides into private CSS and public CSS. The information trustworthiness confirmation will include different DOAs and DCAs. Information Integrity Service (DIS) has its basis in the Blockchain framework. The individuals who need DIS should begin blockchain customers on their hubs first. Every device is allowed to join or leave the blockchain network. To disentangle the proposed administration, it uses Cloud Storage Service. Information Integrity Service (DIS) actualizes by a brilliant agreement living on the blockchain. The usage is completely decentralized, which empowers higher effectiveness and better dependability of DIS. Information Integrity Service actualizes by an intelligent contract. The data to be recorded in blockchain through shrewd agreements ought to be encoded locally. The record of each gathering associates with the accord. After the blockchain administration begins, the blockchain information on a hub synchronizes with the entire blockchain network. DOA should compose data into blockchain through a brilliant agreement to get substantial and open to different devices after the accord of the blockchain.

DroneChain (Liang, Zhao, Shetty, & Li, 2017) comprises four principal segments- drones, control frameworks, cloud workers, and blockchain networks. At least one automaton can shape an automaton group to perform complex commissions. The Control framework can be appointed and communicate with an automaton bunch for information assortment and commission appropriation. The cloud worker gives the limit of capacity to information gathered by drones and provides ongoing information preparation and information investigation to encourage future dynamics. The blockchain, a decentralized organization, is utilized for information approval and resilience. It needs to speak with a control framework through a delegate to convey the gathered information or the flight status information and get the commands. The control framework assembles information from automatons or automatons bunches and transmits orders to alter the flight development. The control framework serves as uncertain to total the data from drones. It hashes the first information for uprightness assurance, and afterward, sends both unique information and hashed information to both the blockchain network and the cloud. The blockchain organization undergoes usage for three purposes. Every hashed information passages are transferred to the blockchain network for trustworthiness security and could be put away in an appropriate way that guarantees steadiness. The cloud information base stores the first information gathered from drones, orders sent by the control framework, and information access from cloud workers and reviewers. Information access is made responsible by a unique mark for each entrance, which is likewise put away in the data set. A daemon cycle will look into every information section in both the information base and the block. To approve the information record, the cloud worker is liable for mentioning to the blockchain network for a blockchain receipt as a lasting verification of information integrity. The chain network works for consistency check intermittently.

The authors (Samaniego & Deters, 2016) actualize virtual assets as simultaneous go-schedules in a Golang program. The virtual strength is a capacity characterized in the language Golang. The source code of all virtual benefits is put away in a code archive for the example information base. At runtime, the executive chooses the virtual assets and assembles them into at least one Golang application. The Golang capacities add to the source code. It has a program that aggregates for the objective stage. The director puts the code onto a consent-based blockchain and educates the edge segment to download the code from the blockchain. Virtual benefit deactivates either by advising the host program to obstruct its go-work or by recompiling another host program. Changing virtual assets requires the making of another host program. The Edison module is a Framework on a Chip (SoC) containing a 500 MHz double center, double-strung Intel Atom, and a 100 MHz 32-bit Intel Quark microcontroller. The two sheets utilized in the examinations are both associated with a similar shared Wi-Fi organization. In the principal analysis, each board runs one virtual asset. One virtual benefit sends 1000 successive solicitations to the virtual strength on the other board. After sending the solicitation, the virtual one sits tight for the affirmation and proceeds with the following solicitation.

BaDS design (Zhang, He, & Choo, 2018.) comprises the accompanying members: IoT gadgets, Data Owner, Blockchain Network, and Cloud. IoT gadgets gather information and send information to the organization layer. Such instruments are additionally answerable for information obtaining, fundamental preparation, encryption, and transmission. The devices can ordinarily distantly demand access and handle the orders. When the gadgets need to ask for information from different gadgets, they ought to distribute a comparing solicitation to the cloud or the information owner. There is an exceptionally enormous number of information proprietors that partitions into heads. The executives are mindful of confirming the participants. The agreement calculation in the framework is the Byzantine adaptation to internal failure component PBFT instead of Proof of Work (POW) utilized in Bitcoin. The texture contains verification hubs and requesting hubs. When the devices get an exchange, they will check and pack them into the blockchain. Cloud is utilized to store the encoded gadgets' information and sends a relating demand exchange to the blockchain organization to inquiry permission of the instrument when the cloud gets a solicitation from IoT gadgets.

Every hub (Kim & Lee, 2018) imparts its data to devices in various areas employing correspondence with the worker, which goes about as a door. It plays out encryption by making n re-encryption keys and sends these to the intermediary worker. The worker at that point creates ciphertexts that permit different hubs to decode the writings, diminishing the encryption of figuring trouble for every device. In the plan, a client may acquire the last information by unscrambling the privileges of data(indicated by their rank). If the two clients have similar credits, they will have indistinguishable decoding right. If their properties contrast, other clients undergo disavowing. In the proposed information-sharing plan, there is no requirement for the denial of the client ascribes. Client A exchanges the encryption key to client B, that wishes to get to the familiar data by re-encoding the encryption key. It can decode the scrambled information, utilizing its credits dependent on the quality public key of client B. The proposed strategy takes out pointless cycles along these lines giving expanded effectiveness and more secure information sharing.

LES (Al Salami, Baek, Salah, & Damiani, 2016) utilizes brilliant home applications. It very well may be applied in the accompanying situation: Suppose that a client is attempting to open the front entryway of his home distantly. In the house, a keen lock framework usage brings security. The client will make an impression on open the entrance through his cell phone. Notwithstanding, the message that orders the brilliant lock framework to open the portal contains delicate data of entryway bolting or not. This data can be helpful for a robber who is attempting to break into the house. The plan has two-sub calculations - KEYEncrypt and DATAEncrypt. The first one encodes a meeting key, and the last is to scramble messages under the picked key. This plan is character-based, which means the public keys utilized for this plan are only personality strings, which needn't bother with authentication. The character-based property ends up helping oversee encryption keys for intelligent home gadgets.

A lightweight is no pairing ECC-Based ABE (Yao, Chen, & Tian, 2015). It conspires to address the information security and protection issues in the IoT. The proposed ABE plan's security relies upon the ECDDH issue rather than bilinear Diffie–Hellman suspicion, which can diminish the calculation overhead and correspondence overhead. The security verification acts in a property-based specific set model. The elliptic Curve is an integrated Encryption Scheme. It has information privacy and information uprightness for clients, which embraces ECDH to create a sharing mystery, from which the encryption key and the MAC key determines individually. A KP-ABE conspires with four calculations. The Setup calculation randomizes computation and is controlled by the position. It yields the public credential boundaries and the ace key. The distributed border has the key mystery of location. The Encrypt calculation is a randomized calculation, controlled by the sender. It yields figure text by taking the message to be encoded. The traits set that the information client ought to fulfill, and the public credential boundaries as info. The Key-Generation calculation is randomized. It is controlled by the power and takes an entrance structure and the ace key as info. It yields the unscrambling credential relating to the entrance structure. The Decrypt calculation is controlled by the collector, which takes the code text encoded under the ascribes set, the unscrambling key D for access control structure, alongside the public credential boundaries as info. If control structure esteem compares to 1, it unscrambles the code text and yields a message.

BACKGROUND

Merkle Root: A Merkle root is a mathematical way to deal with check the data on a Merkle tree. They are used in computerized cash to guarantee data squares went between peers on a mutual framework. They are vital to the estimation needed to keep up cryptographic types of monetary transactions like bitcoin and ether. A hash tree encodes the blockchain data gainfully and securely. It engages by lively checking of the blockchain data on the dispersed compose. Each trade occurring on the blockchain orchestrate has a hash related to it. These hashes embedding as a treelike structure has the ultimate objective that each hash is associated with its parent following a parent-kid treelike association.

Assume that two instant messages hashing is at level 1. Leave the content alone T_1 and T_2. Let the resultant hash esteem Hm_1 got from hashing of T_1. Notation (1) is the representation of the same. Let the derived hash esteem Hm_2 be inferred by hashing the content T_2. Notation (2) denotes the same. The parent of these two hash esteems is spoken to by Hm_{12}. The equivalent got by hashing both the writings T_1 and T_2. Notation (3) represents the same.

$$Hm_1 \rightarrow hash\left(T_1\right). \tag{1}$$

$$Hm_2 \rightarrow hash\left(T_2\right). \tag{2}$$

$$Hm_{12} \rightarrow hash\left(T_1 + T_2\right). \tag{3}$$

PREVIOUS CONTRIBUTION

The previous contribution (Liu S., Yu, Xiao, Wan, Wang, & Yan, 2020) has four participants. Any IoT gadget can produce information. Information proprietors are liable for scrambling the data and creating lists. It receives ciphertexts. Information users (DU) utilizes their private character keys to produce the token and send it to the blockchain. After accepting the half-decoded ciphertext from the sender, DUs can use their private character keys to unscramble the information. The alliance blockchain utilized in the framework is a shared organization made by a set out of pre-selected confided in understanding hubs, an information pool, and an appropriated edge. BC introduces the framework public key (Ambika & Raju, 2010), store client shared character keys, instate client unscrambling keys, produce key update messages, and create pre-decoding keys. The agreements of the hubs cooperate to restore the client repudiation list. The cloud worker is the capacity place where we store the monstrous encoded IoT information. The storage is liable for looking and pre-unscrambling for clients. The calculation produces and distributes the worldwide public key. The accord hubs utilize the Pedersen mystery Sharing convention and the Reciprocal Protocol to choose the ace key together. When an information client needs to join this framework, it runs the calculation to create its personality key pair. At that point, it sends the ID to BC to store. In the following stage, agreement hubs will utilize ID to produce the shared decoding key for this client. This public unscrambling key creates this current client's pre-decoding key. At long last, Cloud (Aazam, Khan, Alsaffar, & Huh, 2014)(Aceto, Botta, Donato, & W., 2013) can utilize the pre-decoding credential to pre-unscramble for this client. Each time a client disavows, agreement hubs run the Revoke calculation to refresh the denial list. In the credential production step, three sorts of keys are created by agreement hubs. The client public unscrambling key depends on the client information. The subsequent are key update messages. It connects with the client denial list, time checks, and state marks. The last one is client pre-decoding key is utilized by Cloud to pre-decode for clients.

PROPOSED WORK

Table 1. Notations used in the work

Notations used	Description
N	Network under study
S_i	Server under consideration
ID_s	Identity of the server
U_i	user in the network
ID_u	Identity of the user
$Data_i$	Transmitted data
$Hash_{pre}$	Previous hash value
$Hash_{post}$	New hash value

1. 1. **Public Key Generation by Server** - The proposal increases reliability by using the Merkle root concept. The base station or the server uses this concept to generate a public hash value. It broadcast it to its users. Notation (4) denotes the same. S_i is the server used and ID_s is the identity of the server S_i at time $Time_i$.

$$S_i \rightarrow hash\left(ID_S\right).$$

(4)

2. 2. **Registration of the User** - The user device also generates a hash value using the Merkle root concept. The user device concatenates the obtained and generated hash value during the registration procedure. Notation (5) denotes the same. Let U_i be the user and let ID_u be the identity of the user.

$$U_i \rightarrow hash\left(ID_u\right).$$

(5)

This hash value is attached to every message dispatching to the server. Every session has a different hash value. It prefixes previous hash value $hash_{pre}$, followed by data $Data_i$ and postfixes the new hash value hash$_{post}$. Notation (6) denotes the same. Hence the reliability and security of the network increases compared to previous contribution (Liu S., Yu, Xiao, Wan, Wang, & Yan, 2020).

$$U_i \rightarrow S_i : hash_{pre} \| Data_i \| hash_{post} . \tag{6}$$

ANALYSIS OF THE WORK

The accord hubs (Liu S., Yu, Xiao, Wan, Wang, & Yan, 2020) utilize the Pedersen mystery Sharing convention and the Reciprocal Protocol to choose the ace key together. When an information client needs to join this framework, it runs the calculation to create its personality key pair. At that point, it sends the ID to BC to store. In the following stage, agreement hubs will utilize ID to produce the shared decoding key for this client. This public unscrambling key creates this current client's pre-decoding key. At long last, Cloud (Aazam, Khan, Alsaffar, & Huh, 2014)(Aceto, Botta, Donato, & W., 2013) can utilize the pre-decoding credential to pre-unscramble for this client. Each time a client disavows, agreement hubs run the Revoke calculation to refresh the denial list. In the credential production step, three sorts of keys are created by agreement hubs. The first is the clients' public unscrambling key. It depends on the clients' information. The subsequent key update messages connect with the client denial list, time checks, and state marks. The last one is client's pre-decoding key is utilized by Cloud to pre-decode for clients. The simulation is performed in NS2. Table 2 contains the parameters used in the simulation.

Table 2. Parameters used in the study

Parameters used	Description
Area of surveillance	200m *200 m
Number of devices considered	5
Length of identification	24 bits
Length of hash value generated	12 bits
Simulation time	60 ms

Table 3. Algorithm used to generate hash value

Input: Identification of the device (24 bits) *Step 1*: Interchange bits in odd and even positions *Step 2:* For i= 1 to 24 Resultant [i] = Xor operation extreme bits *Step 3:* For i= 1 to 12 Divide into 2 groups Apply round right shift on both the groups Step 4: Merge both the groups

The proposal uses the Merkle root to produce a hash value. The server uses the same concept to generate the hash value using its identity. This value is transmitted to the users. Similarly, user devices calculate the hash value using their identity. It prefixes the previous hash value to the data and suffixes the new hash value. It transmits it to the server. The hash value changes for every session. It increases security (Abd El-Latif, et al., 2020) by 3.82%. As the previous hash value is prefixed to the data, reliability (Ahmad, 2014) is increased by 5.09% of the network. The same is represented in figure 1 and figure 2.

Figure 1. Comparison of security in the network

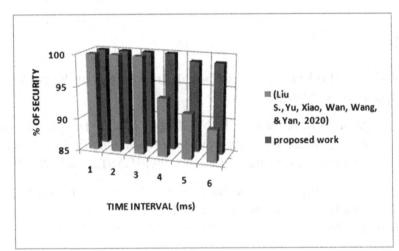

Figure 2. Comparison of reliability in the network

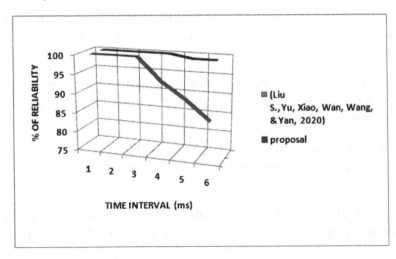

CONCLUSION

The IoT devices are of a different caliber. These instruments use a shared platform to communicate with each other. They do not have enough space to store, hence use a cloud facility. The storage facility provides ample warehousing. Using blockchain enhances the reliability of the transmitted data. The proposal uses the Merkle root to generate the hash value. This method is used by the user and the server to change its credential for every session. The methodology increases security by 3.82%. The data is prefixed by the previously generated hash value and postfixed by the new value. Hence the technique improves trust by 5.09%.

REFERENCES

A, B., & K, M. V. (2016). Blockchain platform for industrial internet of things. *Journal of software Engineering and Applications, 9*(10), 533.

Aazam, M., Khan, I., Alsaffar, A. A., & Huh, E. N. (2014). Cloud of Things: Integrating Internet of Things with Cloud Computing and the Issues Involved. In *International Bhurban Conference on Applied Sciences & Technology*. Islamabad, Pakistan: IEEE. 10.1109/IBCAST.2014.6778179

Abd El-Latif, A., Abd-El-Atty, B., Venegas-Andraca, S., Elwahsh, H., Piran, M., & Bashir, A. (2020). Providing End-to-End Security Using Quantum Walks in IoT Networks. *IEEE Access: Practical Innovations, Open Solutions, 8*, 92687–92696. doi:10.1109/ACCESS.2020.2992820

Abdelgawad, A., Yelamarthi, K., & Khattab, A. (2016). IoT-based health monitoring system for active and assisted living. In *International Conference on Smart Objects and Technologies for Social Good* (pp. 11-20). Venice, Italy: Springer.

Aceto, G., Botta, A., de Donato, W., & Pescapè, A. (2013). Cloud monitoring: A Survey. *Computer Networks, 57*(9), 2093–2115. doi:10.1016/j.comnet.2013.04.001

Ahmad, M. (2014). Reliability Models for the Internet of Things: A Paradigm Shift. In *IEEE International Symposium on Software Reliability Engineering Workshops*. Naples, Italy: IEEE. 10.1109/ISSREW.2014.107

Akkaya, K., Guvenc, I., Aygun, R., Pala, N., & Kadri, A. (2015). *IoT-based occupancy monitoring techniques for energy-efficient smart buildings. In IEEE Wireless Communications and Networking Conference Workshops (WCNCW)*. IEEE.

Al Salami, S., Baek, J., Salah, K., & Damiani, E. (2016). Lightweight encryption for smart home. In *11th International Conference on Availability, Reliability and Security (ARES)* (pp. 382-388). Salzburg, Austria: IEEE.

Alaba, F. A., Othman, M., Hashem, I. A. T., & Alotaibi, F. (2017). Internet of Things security: A survey. *Journal of Network and Computer Applications, 88*, 10–28. doi:10.1016/j.jnca.2017.04.002

Alrashdi, I., Alqazzaz, A., Aloufi, E., Alharthi, R., Zohdy, M., & Ming, H. (2019). Ad-iot: Anomaly detection of iot cyberattacks in smart city using machine learning. In *9th Annual Computing and Communication Workshop and Conference (CCWC)* (pp. 305-310). 10.1109/CCWC.2019.8666450

Ambika, N. (2019). Energy-Perceptive Authentication in Virtual Private Networks Using GPS Data. In Security, Privacy and Trust in the IoT Environment (pp. 25-38). Springer.

Ambika, N. (2020). Encryption of Data in Cloud-Based Industrial IoT Devices. In S. Pal & V. G. Díaz (Eds.), *IoT: Security and Privacy Paradigm* (pp. 111–129). CRC press, Taylor & Francis Group.

Ambika, N. (2020). Methodical IoT-Based Information System in Healthcare. In C. Chakraborthy (Ed.), Smart Medical Data Sensing and IoT Systems Design in Healthcare (pp. 155-177). Bangalore, India: IGI Global.

Ambika, N., & Raju, G. T. (2010). *Figment Authentication Scheme in Wireless Sensor Network. In Security Technology, Disaster Recovery and Business Continuity.* Springer, Berlin, Heidelberg.

Atlam, H. F., & Wills, G. B. (2019). Technical aspects of blockchain and IoT. In Role of Blockchain Technology in IoT Applications (Vol. 115). doi:10.1016/bs.adcom.2018.10.006

Chen, G., Xu, B., Lu, M., & Chen, N. S. (2018). Exploring blockchain technology and its potential applications for education. *Smart Learning Environments, 5*(1), 1. doi:10.118640561-017-0050-x

Dorri, A., Kanhere, S. S., Jurdak, R., & Gauravaram, P. (2017). *Blockchain for IoT security and privacy: The case study of a smart home. In IEEE international conference on pervasive computing and communications workshops.* IEEE.

Dwivedi, A. D., Srivastava, G., Dhar, S., & Singh, R. (2019). A decentralized privacy-preserving healthcare blockchain for IoT. *Sensors (Basel), 19*(2), 1–17. doi:10.339019020326 PMID:30650612

Kim, S., & Lee, I. (2018). IoT device security based on proxy re-encryption. *Journal of Ambient Intelligence and Humanized Computing, 9*(4), 1267–1273. doi:10.100712652-017-0602-5

Liang, X., Zhao, J., Shetty, S., & Li, D. (2017). Towards data assurance and resilience in IoT using blockchain. In *IEEE Military Communications Conference (MILCOM* (pp. 261-266). Baltimore, MD: IEEE. 10.1109/MILCOM.2017.8170858

Liu, B., Yu, X. L., Chen, S., Xu, X., & Zhu, L. (2017). Blockchain based data integrity service framework for IoT data. In *IEEE International Conference on Web Services (ICWS)* (pp. 468-475). Honolulu, HI: IEEE. 10.1109/ICWS.2017.54

Liu, S., Yu, J., Xiao, Y., Wan, Z., Wang, S., & Yan, B. (2020, May). BC-SABE: Blockchain-aided Searchable Attribute-based Encryption for Cloud-IoT. *IEEE Internet of Things Journal, 7*(9), 1–17. doi:10.1109/JIOT.2020.2993231

Manzoor, A., Liyanage, M., Braeke, A., Kanhere, S. S., & Ylianttila, M. (2019). Blockchain based proxy re-encryption scheme for secure IoT data sharing. In *International Conference on Blockchain and Cryptocurrency (ICBC)* (pp. 99-103). IEEE. 10.1109/BLOC.2019.8751336

Nagaraj, A. (2021). Introduction to Sensors in IoT and Cloud Computing Applications. Bentham Science Publishers. doi:10.2174/97898114793591210101

Obour Agyekum, K. O., Xia, Q., Sifah, E. B., Gao, J., Xia, H. D., & Guizani, M. (2019). A Secured Proxy-Based Data Sharing Module in IoT Environments Using Blockchain. *Sensors (Basel)*, *19*(5), 1–20. doi:10.339019051235 PMID:30862110

Samaniego, M., & Deters, R. (2016). Hosting virtual iot resources on edge-hosts with blockchain. In *IEEE International Conference on Computer and Information Technology (CIT)* (pp. 116-119). Nadi, Fiji: IEEE. 10.1109/CIT.2016.71

Shafagh, H., Burkhalter, L., Hithnawi, A., & Duquennoy, S. (2017). Towards blockchain-based auditable storage and sharing of iot data. In *Proceedings of the 2017 on Cloud Computing Security Workshop* (pp. 45-50). ACM. 10.1145/3140649.3140656

Verma, P., & Sood, S. K. (2018). Fog assisted-IoT enabled patient health monitoring in smart homes. *IEEE Internet of Things Journal*, *5*(3), 1789–1796. doi:10.1109/JIOT.2018.2803201

Yao, X., Chen, Z., & Tian, Y. (2015). A lightweight attribute-based encryption scheme for the Internet of Things. *Future Generation Computer Systems*, *49*, 104–112. doi:10.1016/j.future.2014.10.010

Zhang, Y., He, D., & Choo, K. K. (2018). BaDS: Blockchain-based architecture for data sharing with ABS and CP-ABE in IoT. *Wireless Communications and Mobile Computing*, *2018*, 1–10. doi:10.1155/2018/2783658

Chapter 14
Retail and Internet of Things:
A Digital Transformation

Reena Malik

Chitkara Business School, Chitkara University, Punjab, India

ABSTRACT

The Indian retail sector is transforming rapidly propelled by rising household income, technology advancements, e-commerce, and increased expectations. Radical changes are evident in the retail landscape with the advent of the internet. New innovative technologies are being used by the retailers in order to provide seamless and unique shopping experience to the customer. Internet of things is one of the technologies creating competitive advantage in the world of retailing, and now smart retailing is in trend to cater to enhanced customer expectations. This study aims to understand concept and explain applications of internet of things in retailing and also discusses IoT as an opportunity for retailers, companies using IoT technology, and obstacles in adopting IoT especially in the retail sector.

INTRODUCTION

The advent of internet give rise to technological advance world and Internet of things is the new buzz terminology which is used for machine to machine connectivity. The internet of things is shaping almost all business sectors and retailing is one of them making retailing smarter beyond our imagination. Internet of things is a combination of artificial intelligence and machine learning making the collected data useful for the marketers. One best example of IoT is at your home fridge reminding you about milk requirement and controlling your air conditioner while sitting at office. Internet of things will prove disruptive to the retail industry (Gregory, 2015). Internet of things has a strong impact on retailing and retailers are now focusing on providing better in store shopping experience for the customers making it much more unique, efficient and of course profitable as IoT offers the ability to interact with both devices and people which further provides information on brand performance, present and potential customers, customer engagement, introducing new product, store layout optimization. Companies like American Apparel, Kroger, Tesco, Wal-Mart has been using robotics, RFID tags for enhanced customer service and brand experience. Digital technologies have opened the doors of availability of diverse and

DOI: 10.4018/978-1-7998-8367-8.ch014

rich information for the customers and the way it can be accessed on multiple devices. The prevailing competition has given customers a lot of choice to choose from. Digital transformation provides various tools to analyze these vast choices like business analytics and other predictive tools which helps retailers to understand customers and framing marketing strategies accordingly. Every customer is different and wants to access the information in their own way as consumers are more aware about all the possibilities, thus digital retailing provides different channels to choose from like physical store, online store, social media platform and mobile communications as well. IoT assists customers and salesperson to locate goods where stores are equipped with sensors which lowers down the requirement of sales staff as the details can be provided on digital display. IoT proved very helpful in delivering the right product at right time ensuring maintained condition from shipment to arrival. It also aids in saving energy and costs, helps businesses to save money as the technology enabled devices can automatically keeps check on wastage. IoT in retail has witnessed strong shift in consumption, shopping behavior. According to Capgemini, 2020 report, 69% percent of consumers overall – and more than 80% of consumers in China and India – prefer to shop with retailers who are using automation and believe that automation can be the solution for the problems experienced while shopping in store.

REVIEW OF LITERATURE

Retail sector is changing drastically with the advent of internet and technological advancements. As it is not about only selling products, but providing exclusive purchase journey by providing interactive and engaging customer experience (G.J. ten Bok, 2016). Internet of things is one of the innovate things been adopted by retail sector also considered a way of achieving competitive advantage (G.J. ten Bok, 2016). Auto-ID Labs originated the tem internet of things while working on networked RFID infrastructure at the Massachusetts Institute of Technology (Wortmann and Flüchter, 2015). Omnichannel experience in retail is being provided by various ways like RFID tags, sensors, virtual reality, Wi-Fi (Iotuk.org.uk, 2017). IoT has been used for linking actual and virtual world together providing 24x7connectivity. It has also used by the retailers for identifying right customer at right time (Vermesan et al., 2009). Retailers are identifying needs of customers thus improving sales (Maltseva, 2018). Enhance customer loyalty can be achieved by introducing new and innovative techniques that provide better shopping experience (Mckinsey.com, 2016). The importance of providing customer a unique experience by using AI and IoT techniques is of utmost value as it drives the sales (Mohapatra and V. Krishnan, 2018). E-shopping carts or smart carts which leads to enhance user experience and drive numbers (Pavaluru, 2017). The study by Atos, investigated about the future of retailing and the impact of technology on current retail outlets. IoT in order to penetrate technology will provide unique opportunities for developing innovative business models to increase the market share and capturing more market (Narasimha, Vijaya. 2015). According to McKinsey report on IoT, retail environments are being considered as physical spaces to purchase different offerings (product or service) by the marketers including traditional retail outlets and showrooms like bank branches, sports complexes etc. Customers are now expecting a better shopping experience with application of advance technology due to advent of internet and technological advancements in the sector. Internet of things has been considered as new wave of e-commerce in the world of retailing for providing unique shopping journey every time.

TECHNOLOGIES USED IN RETAILING

Facing competition from e-commerce businesses retailers trying to implement technology of Internet of things in order to optimize store layout, inventories and staff deployment. There are different technologies used in retailing for providing seamless shopping experience to customers.

1. **Radio Frequency Identification-** RFID tags are used for quick identification and tracking of products which can be done by attaching these tags or in build at time of manufacturing consisting of a chip, identifiable by reader device which finally makes the inventory checking process way easier than earlier. RFID tags can also be used for better customer experience in store by using reader devices mounted on walls. This saves customer time and also replaces cashier staff thus, saving labor costs as well. (Manyika et al., 2015).

2. **Sensors-** such sensors helps in collecting data for existing staff and customers which further can provide relevant inputs. These sensors and cameras also help in regulating temperature, path taken by customers, unusual activity, facial recognition, maintenance etc.

3. **Wi-Fi-** this is the most used technology in retail outlets and stores, according to Global data survey, by using organization wi-fi customers are signing in and giving access to use their information for marketing purposes as their full profile can be tracked. Retailers can avail the information regarding number of customers in an area.

4. **Beacons-** Bluetooth based technology beacons has the ability to identify and send personal, customized messages to customers if they are in nearby the product provided enabled Bluetooth or app installed. Most of companies tested this technology for marketing purposes example Tesco and Unilever in promotion of their magnum ice cream.

5. **Digital Signage-** with this technology marketer can provide better customer experience by tailoring billboards in real time to customer segments for promoting products and interacting with customers. By tailoring messages retailers can improve their marketing efforts towards a target group.

6. **Augmented Reality-** Using IoT based augmented reality unique experience of virtual fitting or trial rooms can be extended to customers. Providing customers certain wearables like smart watches, glasses (3D) attached with sensors and cameras in order to interact better as customer expect to have certain facilities like AR in retail stores now-a days for better purchase experience and increased sales. Retailers can avail information about types of products are in store, products mostly tried by customers but never bought and products oftenly bought together (Lawrence, 2016).

7. **IoT Payments-** providing customers with varied options like payment through mobile phones or QR codes which provides customers convenience of making payment anytime, anywhere.

AUTOMATED CUSTOMER SHOPPING JOURNEY

- Self identification- identifies that customer has entered the store premises; automated shelves keeps track on customer moves in aisle and accordingly suggests required products.

- Product Information- Information about the product is being provided where technology integrates shelves with online platforms, where screen will provide user comments about the product. Augmented reality images of models wearing require dress can be shown assisting customer.
- In store navigation- this assists customer about store layout and availability of products, automated robots explaining product features and also act as shopping trolley.
- Selecting product- such technologies are used which assists customer in selecting required products like in store mirrors which are connected with store app allowing customer to try on virtually.
- Automated Checkout- self checkout can be provided when using technologies like facial recognition, bar codes, mobile phones and sensors etc.
- Final payment- sensors based technology or RFID codes help customers making payment in fraction of seconds.

GROWING ACCEPTANCE OF INTERNET OF THINGS IN INDIA

IoT earlier was used by the marketers for location based marketing those who are using internet, but now retailers are collecting valuable information that helps in better targeting which provides premium shopping experience. Recent studies claim that the number of IoT connected devices to reach 20.4 billion in 2020 as compared to 6.4 billion in 2016 globally. In India, growth is slow as the technology came very late in India as compared to developed countries but the adoption rate is increasing. Retailers are using IoT to enhance customer experience.

Listed below are some of the applications widely used in retailing

Managing supply chain: Retailers by applying innovative elements of IoT like RFID tags can easily have a check on the movement of inventory right from the manufacturer to the store and finally till the customer buy it. Real time track of transportation duration and temperature requirements for product especially in case of perishable goods can be done by using IoT techniques.

Smart CRM: Providing enhanced purchase experience to customers is very crucial now a-days and with the help of IoT technology the data can be leveraged from installed cameras, mobile devices, videos and social media platforms. The data on consumer purchase behavior collected from these sources can easily be converted into valuable information about present and future plans of purchasing. Making cordial relation with the customers is essence of retailing and adding component 'smart' makes it even more crucial (Manyika et al., 2015). Salesperson can adjust their shopping experience accordingly on the basis of past purchase information of customers by using face recognition software. Smart CRM also allows salesperson to understand customers' nature and personality by going through his personal profile. Smart CRM is emerging more as a strategy than technology.

Smart Inventory Management: By applying smart inventory management systems like digital price tags, digital information about products, digital display, RFID will help in maintaining inventory level smartly and recognizing low levels then placing order automatically, otherwise managing inventory levels is very hectic for retailers and also costs much.

Automated Checkouts: The process of checkout is generally not liked by customers because of long queues at the counter even some customers may leave without purchasing anything due to this botheration. Automated point of sale or accepting payment through mobile phones can be the solution and with this conversion rate can also be increased. It automatically scans items present in the shopping cart being linked with customer bank, charges total amount to customer paying account through their mobile phones. System read all RFID tags and transfers this information to wireless paying system at the time customer existing store. Automated checkouts makes customer more satisfied as it saves a lot of time and costs too for enterprises. Using automated checkouts companies can save staff costs as it reduces cashier requirement by 75% (Manyika et al., 2015). MagicBand, by Disney is an example of such technology in use which allows customer to have automated access of their rooms, card free payments and it is also provides useful information by tracking customer activities for providing better services (ComQi, 2015).

Monitoring Foot Traffic: IoT can be useful for monitoring time spend and tracking movements by customer for searching one or other product. In order to track customer movement heat sensors are being used by Hugo Boss which allows placing high price products areas (Gregory, 2015). Such optimization in store layout can contribute an increase of 5% in productivity (Manyika, et al., 2015). By using IoT one can also measure consumers' interest regarding certain products present on the shelves (Parada et al., 2015). RFID is capable of providing a digital identity to all products across categories measuring reading time. With the help of LDR sensors placed behind the products allows managers to know about pick up status of product by flashing light on sensor. Managers can process this information in form of inventory management. For efficient customer visit store layouts can be tweaked. Moreover existing in store experience can be customized by observing real time store traffic. It would be helpful for framing marketing strategies and tactics to target customers

Smart Maintenance: Mostly stores are installed with different complex equipments like refrigerators, air conditioners etc. with the help of IoT (fitted sensors) the maintenance issues or temperature issues can be forecasted beforehand providing food safety, saving cost and energy.

Automated Warehouse: By applying IoT one can monitor sales in real time and missed in store sales and helps in inventory management as well. As these technologies help in maintain optimum stock level and reordering whenever shortfall occurs for the same.

Smart Transportation: IoT assists in tracking transportation in real time using GPS and provides fair, shortest and safer route for the same. Any kind of frill and wastage on the way can be monitored by this technology. This would help in reducing costs.

RETAILING AND BIG DATA

Big data enables making decisions on the basis of data, which is being prevalent from past decades. By using IoT retailers can extract detailed data which can be used in reliable ways for large businesses. When it comes to IoT environment it is the sensors and devices which provide information about previously unconnected processes (Howe, 2014). Abundant information is available in retail about transactions, pricing, browsing history, time spend and sales behavior. Moreover, one can predict market trends by looking at social media (ComQi, 2015). Generally people follow other people reference to follow trend (Manyika et al., 2011). Retailers can combine relevant information with the help of Internet of Things in order to predict demand, they can also adjust current inventory and prices on basis of hourly demand with real-time analytics, (Pittman, 2013). Tracking customer activity via IoT generates massive data which can be utilized for specific segmentation (personalization) allowing retailers to move from traditional to modern outlook. Tracking individual customer behavior allows retailers to go for micro-segmentation where retailers easily identify customer's need and do customization for which customers are ready to pay a little extra for the same (Wolfgang et al., 2016).

Table 1. Glimpse of future stores

Journey of retail	Traditional outlook	Modern outlook
Creating awareness	Use of print ad, television and leaflets etc.	Notification on customers' mobile, predictive analysis of data compiled from social media platforms.
Research and information	Personal interview with staff, use of in store sign for directions.	Virtual shelves, digital display, kiosks, automated sales assistant, aisles, use of tablets, digital description of products
Trial and selection	In store trial rooms	Virtual fitting and trial rooms, augmented reality, customization
Purchasing	In store physical checkout counter	Digital wallets, click and collect, mobile payments etc.
Customer loyalty	Traditional programmes generally card based.	Service bundling, automatic discounts, subscription based programmes, database information
Supply chain	Tradional inventory/warehouse management	Delivery via drones, automated delivery, digital monitoring, use of sensors and cameras etc.
People	Traditional training of human resource	Use of KPI's, digital training, use of smart systems.

Source: author compilation

COMPANIES APPLYING IoT TECHNOLOGY

Growing demand for innovating from customers' compelling companies to adopt newer smart technologies as customer wants more interactive tools in order to make the shopping experience more interesting (Pantano, 2014).

Global Companies

- At Lowe's, "Lowebots" shelves are been scanned many a times in a day for product replenishment.
- Walmart, is using different cameras at in-store for detecting empty shelves, spoiled food, ripe items, and floor spills.
- Consumer habits are being tested and tracked with sensors used in cooler doors at Walgreens.
- Metro AG contract with Sensei, which offers various technical solutions for measuring customer traffic in the store, out of stock items by using video-recognition.
- Ahold Delhaize invested in more than five hundred robots for identifying any liquid spills in the warehouse or outlet.
- Kroger's 'EDGE' are using digital shelves offering lightings which are enabled with sensors in order to reduce the consumption of electricity.
- Falabella, a department store at South American department using robots to click and collect orders whenever customers come to receive their orders.
- Albertsons and Ahold renowned retailers automated their retail store for fulfilling orders and other operations.
- Suning.com, an electronic store at China, integrated their shelves with online platform offered by organization, with screens which provides product information along with user comments.

- Zara's, fashion retailer at their stores offering augmented reality images of models to the customers on display.
- Kroger's using digital shelves which helps in identifying shoppers next move and suggests products.
- JD.com's self-service shops using facial recognition for granting access to customers.
- A.S Watson,beauty retailer invested in-store mirrors which are connected to with the store app where customers can try varied makeup colors virtually.

Indian Companies

- Traditional retail, renowned clothing brand launched a store at Bengaluru, offering ready to wear experience just with a click on I-pad.
- Capillary technologies, a commerce platform company developed automated visitor counter powered by machine learning for retail outlets for analyzing consumer behavior.
- Myntra, renowned online commerce platform launched its first offline store equipped with VR gadgets.

OPPORTUNITY FOR RETAILERS

Technology of Internet of things offers various opportunities to retailers broadly in the areas of supply chain, better customer experience and value streams. Though, IoT seems friction but it is becoming reality and provides platform to retailers in order to build an improved ecosystem that connects physical and digital world. Tracking customers' movements through IoT (smart mirror, digital signage, smart shelves, contactless checkouts, robots for browsing desired product, IoT enabled in store promotions etc.) leverage retailers to utilize the copious amount of data to provide seamless experience to customers and improve store layout and framing strategies for merchandise placement. Companies are utilizing newer technologies like big data, cloud computing often called as 'Industrial internet' to achieve operational efficiency and fostering innovation. It is estimated that Internet of things and industrial internet together add more than $14 trillion to the global economy by 2030 (ComQi., 2015).To optimize complex supply chain technologies like data visualization help employees to track inventories across supply chain. Automated smart tags allow managers to adjust prices in real time to suit the requirements of demand and supply or any effect of promotional schemes. Retailers are creating new channels. Almost all homely products are becoming part of IoT ecosystem from household products to fitness products for e.g. Iris platform by Lowe's designated as 'smart home hub' capable of communicating with any device utilizing networking technologies like Wi-Fi or Z-Wave allows replenishment of medicines, glossaries and toiletries. No doubt, that retailer has realized the importance of technological advancements in retailing world and they are also applying these technologies while offering any product or service. Internet of things is newer technology which is getting huge popularity now-a-days which provides customer a blended channel and unique experience of shopping. The things are being connected with the online platforms in order to provide seamless and unique shopping journey. The technological advancement not only making customers delightful but also providing ample opportunities to the retailers in terms of increased market share, revenue, brand image and customer retention and loyalty.

HINDRANCES IN ADOPTING IoT

(Pantano, 2014) identified uncertainty towards acceptance of new technology in retail. Attitude of customers, retailer and employee is crucial for accepting any new technology especially in retail. Customers' usage has been widely predicted by companies by applying Technology Acceptance Models but when it comes to employee's acceptance it is still a matter of concern and needs attention. Security and privacy needs to be created for widespread adoption of IoT technology along with marketing and ethical perspectives (Tan, et al., 2010). There exists huge risk of tampering data being unattended most of the times. Password protection is required which is hard to realize owing to limited computing capabilities (Atzori, et al., 2010). A survey conducted by TRUSTe revealed that (78%) of Internet users disagreed that the benefits of smart devices outweighed the privacy concerns. This makes it evident that IoT acceptance depends on user's privacy (Lee, et al., 2015). Another significant factor is trust that makes the environment of IoT more challenging. Being smart objects when they take decisions it becomes hindrance for trust between human and objects (Miorandi, et al., 2012). Growth of IoT technology impacts daily activities of retailers and become challenging for them to collaborate with such technology. The present situation requires not only to understand the technology but to accept the same for making value additions to their businesses. With the incredibly huge data generated by IoT, data management has become even more challenging task (Manyika et al., 2015). Knowing customers and selling products is not enough, working and collaborating with data is required. Undoubtedly need for different types of sales support is reduced owing to smart retailing but at the same time requirement for data analysts and designers for smart CRM system has been increased. Mckinsey estimated 1.5 million managers requirement that possess analytical skills for making effective business decisions.

CONCLUSION

Products and machines are being fitted with sensors enabling communication among devices. Use of technology like artificial intelligence, internet of things, augmented reality is the need of the hour especially in the world of retailing where every customer is different and satisfying their enhanced expectations due to technological advancements has become even challenging for marketers. Internet of things has the ability to offer a large number of applications, of which a very little is available to our society (Atzori, Iera, Morabito, 2010). The power of data analytics and artificial intelligence can be utilized by the marketers for maintaining databases, analyzing information and targeting customers for better marketing efforts. Internet of things can be considered as ideal technological platform for making collaborations among organizations, suppliers, manufacturers and retailers. Leveraging IoT surely help companies in adapting and thriving especially in the period of uncertainty. It enables costs to drive down, adapting and responding to change, loyal customers. Retailers should choose such a platform that fosters them to grow and expand their IoT infrastructure in the market like Samsung ARTIK. Moreover, IoT technology help retailers in predicting the market return (ComQi, 2015). They need to embrace this new technology in order to have exciting and fruitful opportunities and beating the competition. This paper explores the importance of internet of things in retailing and organizations using this technology for smart retailing. Further research can be done to access the impact of IoT in area like infrastructure management, IT and financial management etc. this study used secondary data further research can be done analyzing customer experience and satisfaction in IoT enabled stores by collecting primary data.

REFERENCES

Atos. (2013). *The Future of In-store shopping*. https://atos.net/wpcontent/uploads/2017/10/01122013AscentWhitePaperFutureInStoreShopping.pdf

Atzori, L., Iera, A., & Morabito, G. (2010). The Internet of Things: A survey. *Computer Networks*, *54*(15), 2787–2805. doi:10.1016/j.comnet.2010.05.010

Bok, B. T. (2016). *Innovating the retail industry: an IoT approach*. University of Twente Student Theses. https://essay.utwente.nl/69982/

ComQi. (2015, July). *How Iot is Reinventing Retail*. http://www.comqi.com/wpcontent/uploads/2015/08/How-IoT-is-ReinventingRetail.pdf

Delloite. (2018). *Media & Entertainment Industry Outlook*. Available: https://www2.deloitte.com/us/en/pages/technology-mediaandtelecommunications/articles/media-and-entertainmentindustry-outlook-trends.html

D.S. & S. K. (2021). Statistical Assessment of Hybrid Blockchain for SME Sector. *WSEAS Transactions on Systems And Control, 16*. doi:10.37394/23203.2021.16.6

Global Retail Trends. (2018). Available https://assets.kpmg/content/dam/kpmg/xx/pdf/2018/03/global-retail-trends-2018.pdf

Gregory, J. (2015). *The Internet of Things: Revolutionizing the Retail Industry*. Accenture.

Howe, K. (2014). *Beyond Big Data: How Next-Generation Shopper Analytics and the Internet of Everything Transform the Retail Business*. Cisco.

K. (2018). A Future's Dominant Technology Blockchain: Digital Transformation. *IEEE International Conference on Computing, Power and Communication Technologies 2018 (GUCON 2018)*.

Lawrence, C. (2016, May). *How IoT is changing the fashion retail experience*. https://readwrite.com/2016/05/17/how-iot-is-changingthe-fashion-retail-experience-vr4/

Lee, I., & Lee, K. (2015). The Internet of Things (IoT): Applications, investments, and challenges for enterprises. *Business Horizons*, *58*(4), 431–440. doi:10.1016/j.bushor.2015.03.008

Manyika, J., Chui, M., Bisson, P., Woetzel, J., Dobbs, R., Bughin, J., & Aharon, D. (2015). *The Internet of Things: Mapping the Value Beyond the Hype*. McKinsey Global Institute.

Manyika, J., Chui, M., Brad, B., Bughin, J., Dobbs, R., Roxburgh, C., & Hung Byers, A. (2011). *Big data: The next frontier for innovation, competition, and productivity*. McKinsey Global Institute.

McKinsey Global Institute (MGI). (2016). *Digital Europe: Pushing the Frontier, Capturin the Benefits*. McKinsey Global Institute.

Miorandi, D., Sicari, S., Pellegrini De, F., & Chlamtac, I. (2012). *Internet of Things; Vision, applications and research challenges*. Academic Press.

Mohapatra, B., & Krishnan, V. (2018). *Customer experience for retail Industry.* https://www.infosys.com/Oracle/whitepapers/Documents/customer-experience-retail-industry.pdf

Narasimha Murthy, D., & Vijaya Kumar, B. (2015). Internet Of Things (Iot): Is Iot A Disruptive Technology Or A Disruptive Business Model? *Indian Journal of Marketing, 45*(8), 18–27. doi:10.17010/ijom/2015/v45/i8/79915

Nayyar, S. (2019). *The Impact Of Internet Of Things On The Fashion Retail Sector Bringing Experience To Retail.* . doi:10.13140/RG.2.2.32135.04008

Pantona, E. (2014, March). Innovation Drivers in the Retail Industry. *International Journal of Information Management, 34*(3), 344–350. doi:10.1016/j.ijinfomgt.2014.03.002

Pavaluru. (2017). *From Shopping Cart to SMART Kart.* Available: https://www.evry.com/globalassets/india/what-we-do/retail-- logistics/smart-kart---white-paper/smart-kart---whitepaper.pdf

Pittman, D. (2013, January). *Big Data in Retail - Examples in Action.* Academic Press.

Tan, L., & Wang, N. (2010). Future Internet: The Internet of Things. *3rd International Conference on Advanced Computer Theory and Engineering.*

Vermesan, O., Friess, P., Guillemin, P., Sundmaeker, H., Eisenhauer, M., Moessner, K., Le Gall, F., & Cousin, P. (2013). *Internet of Things Strategic Research and Innovation Agenda.* Academic Press.

Wortmann, F., & Flüchter, K. (2015). Internet of Things. *Business & Information Systems Engineering, 57*(3), 221–224. doi:10.100712599-015-0383-3

Chapter 15
IoT–Based Smart Gardening System Using the Cloud

Sudha Senthilkumar

School of Computer Science and Engineering, Vellore Institute of Technology, Vellore, India

Meghena Danasekar

School of Information Technology and Engineering, Vellore Institute of Technology, Vellore, India

Brindha K.

School of Information Technology and Engineering, Vellore Institute of Technology, Vellore, India

ABSTRACT

Gardening is a nice activity. It is not possible to monitor and tend to a garden 24 hours a day, so we need a smart gardening system that can monitor and tend to the garden as we want it. In today's busy world, we forget to nourish and water plants that make our home clean and soothing. It would be really helpful if we get a notification on our phones about our plant health and needs. Taking account of this, the authors came up with the idea of building a smart garden with an IoT plant monitoring system. After the data is processed and verified, a notification is sent about the plant's health. An automated gardening system is designed to enable us to manage gardening, including monitoring moisture, temperature, and humidity. This chapter is on an IoT-based smart garden monitoring system which senses the requirement of the plant and provides it with water as the soil loses its moisture. Thing-speak and Blynk application are used to view sensor data from remote locations.

INTRODUCTION

Automation rules the world nowadays. It is a technique of using computers or mobile phones in monitoring and controlling the simple parameters of day to day life. The standard of our life will be nourished by the practice of using automation for simple things. Using the concept of IOT we make sensors to communicate with each other which are powerful in automation. The important aspect of this prototype is that it saves cost and ensures safety. When people try to make plantings and set up their own

DOI: 10.4018/978-1-7998-8367-8.ch015

garden, they were cautious in maintenance at only in their beginning stages. As days go on due to lack of maintenance the plants get destroyed. This prototype will help people to automatically monitor the parameters and ensures maintenance of the garden. It plays a vital role and serves as a good companion for plants. IOT provides solutions for various problems and it allows things to be sensed or controlled remotely in network infrastructure.

In all of human history the most powerful and important creation is the Internet. The integrated part of future internet is IoT. In the field of business, social process, information and communication, the things are expected to become active participants by using IoT. They need to be enabled in order to interact with the environment and communicate among themselves by transforming and exchanging the data and information sensed about the environment. It reacts automatically to the real world events and is influenced by the processes that create services and trigger actions with or without human intervention.

The number of companies to help enable their IoT (Internet of Things) ideas. And as a result, we hear about new ideas and solutions that are already solving business challenges with M2M (Machine to Machine) communication. And today, we want to highlight some of the most compelling IoT applications in another industry—agriculture. Agriculture IoT is becoming one of the fastest growing fields (pun intended) within the IoT. Today, more than ever, farmers have to more effectively utilize and conserve their resources. That's where the need for data comes in, and M2M communication has made the ongoing collection of that info easy.(Tzounis et al., 2017) (Khan et al., 2017)

There is increased pressure on existing water allocations and has increased the importance of water management for the sustainability of irrigated agriculture. The objectives idea is: To optimize the water supply to crops, to reduce manual intervention, to make the irrigation system smart, autonomous and efficient. According to the mental health problem in elderly, gardening and IoT technology, they propose the IoT Planting for the elderly that is controlled by Android application which help mental health and memory's problem in elderly. We use the application to reduce spaces between elderly and technology by use planting tree's activity as an intermediate and avoid accident from planting trees activity. Smart Terrace Garden In the paper problem is systems are too expensive and not compatible with the app or both. A solution of this problem is it will help to save time, money and help the environment through reducing water loss. The proposed system is composed of three main components: monitoring node, central node, and the cloud.

This is an IOT based system to check the plant soil, temperature, water and cold level of plant using sensors, all these descriptions will be notified, and all this information should be saved on cloud through IOT.

LITERATURE SURVEY

The author Byoungwook Min et al (Min & Park, 2017) explored the potentials of a smart indoor gardening system that links gardening activities and the IoT technology. The benefits of gardening have been emphasized to improve the quality of life. However, a number of reasons due to a lack of gardening culture and apartment housing systems limit personal gardening in Korea. Thus, indoor gardening has been paid attention as an alternative, but it is still a challenge. Previous studies and practices have shown that the IoT technology can be applied to numerous occasions, and can feasibly provide a solution to these gardening issues. This paper proposes a possible smart indoor gardening system to cope with the issues.

Thamaraimanalan et al (Thamaraimanalan et al., 2018) proposed a system which consists of a central microcontroller to which other objects are connected. The smart garden consists of NodeMCU as a hub to which different types of sensors such as moisture sensor, humidity sensor, temperature sensor and ultrasonic sensor are connected. The ultrasonic sensor is connected to a water tank which indicated the level of water in the tank. Other sensors are connected to their respective positions and these sensors send the data to NodeMCU which consists of an inbuilt Wi-Fi technology. Firebase is a database available on the internet in which real-time values of the sensor are updated every second. Android application is developed using android studio software. Within the software, the connectivity between the application and firebase will be made. So, the user can monitor the parameters from anywhere. Watering of garden varies with the type of soil. Hence the values of the sensors are predetermined for automation purposes inside the software. Whenever the user 27 finds need of watering the garden, a switch in the application will automate the process. This helps in complete maintenance of the garden.

Phytotron (Ait Abdelouahid et al., 2020) also called growth chambers are research installations where environmental parameters such as temperature, humidity, irrigation, conductivity, lighting, and CO2 are finely controlled. This kind of installation allows us on one hand to measure the impact of environment change and on the other hand to optimize the natural grow of plants. With the democratization of the materials, cloud computing and new possibilities offered by Internet of Things (IoT). Therefore, it is possible to develop a low-cost personal phytotron. In this paper, we propose to use connected things to develop a personal growth chamber with the aim to produce fresh vegetable in urban context.

Mitul et al (Sheth & Rupani, 2019) proposed the Global Sensing enabled by Wireless Sensor Network (WSN) cut crosswise over numerous zones of current living. This provides the potentiality to compute, and understand the environmental indicators. In today's digital world, a person expects Automatization which makes the task easy, comfortable, fast and efficient. The idea is to advance our traditional system to a Smart Automated System for supplying water in home gardening, farms fields, etc. In this system, we use soil wetness detector, temperature detector and humidity detector that are mounted at the root space of the plants. The values recognize by the system are conveyed to the base station. The target is to fetch data and sync those values with internet using Wifi. It notifies the user as the water level goes down below the set point. This paper shows that making use of NodeMCU we can do observing of circuit diagrams using wireless technology and shows the result using Blynk App. As it detects low wetness and warm temperature, a message is passed between NodeMCU and Blynk App and it automatically starts the motor in home gardening, farm, etc.

Sachin et al (Samonte et al., 2019) The Cloud-based techniques emerging Internet of Things (IoT) with Wireless Sensor Networks (WSNs) are enabling many new applications and new opportunities to people in VANET scenario. This paper presents a smart home gardening system; which is able to gather real-time data with various parameters used in gardening system. The technology used in this paper is going to help the society in terms of economic impact. Home gardening is considered an essential new trend for the awareness of the society towards environment. The efficient wireless communication using smart sensors facilitates cost effective solutions to real-time home gardening management system. Precision home gardening management system may optimize resources utilizations, smart sensors deployment and improves society awareness towards pollution free environment. This paper presents the design, implementation and validation process of new innovative technologies which can gather data related to home gardening like humidity, temperature, fertilizers compositions, and many more, push gathered data into VANET cloud for analysis, generate alerts and notify it to user for appropriate actions. In this paper, we present Cloud-based IoT technologies in VANET implementation for smart home gardening management system, which primarily focuses on real-world challenge of developing pollution free smart home in cities. We demonstrate the implementation of proposed system and discuss the results.(Sharma et al., 2020)

Burton et al (Burton et al., 2018) explored the usage of WI-FI potentiometry in discipline settings for in situ N monitoring. We report a disposable IoT gardening soil sheet, able to studying real–time soil nitrate awareness at some stage in leaching and irrigation events. The nitrate doped polypyrrole ion selective electrode (N-doped PPy ISE) sensor array sheet functions a fault tolerant circuit layout multiplexed to an oxidation and discount potentiometer which could unexpectedly discover nitrate degrees in soil leachates. Measurement statistics are transmitted thru Waspmote ZB Pro SMA 5dBi radio, 6600mAh rechargeable battery, 7.4-volt solar panel, and a Meshlium ZigBee PRO get right of entry to factor to cloud server and mobile tool. This paper investigates the gardening IoT sheets as a feasible tool for in situ nitrate mapping, and to probably help ordinary domestic and commercial gardeners reduce excessive fertilizer utility.

Omary et al (Al-Omary et al., 2018) proposed a cloud based Internet of Things (IoT) smart garden monitoring and irrigation machine the usage of Arduino Uno. The watering requirement for a plant may be adjusted via tracking the soil moisture. Measuring the soil moisture of the plant offers statistics if the plant is ideally watered, over watered or underneath watered. The proposed gadget video display units and keeps two quantities of the garden, the lawn soil moisture content and light intensity. This is accomplished the usage of soil moisture sensors and mild intensity sensor. The monitored records is sent constantly to ThinkSpeak IoT cloud. In the cloud the statistics amassed from the device is analyzed and while a goal threshold of soil moister is reached, an movement is sent as a result from the cloud to the lawn automated watering system to irrigate the lawn. Arduino Uno microcontroller is used to put in force the gadget control unit. IoT is used to maintain the lawn proprietor updated approximately the fame of the sprinklers. Information from the sensors is often up to date on a ThinSpeack IoT cloud and the person can check the water sprinklers reputation at any time. In addition, the sensor readings are transmitted to a ThingSpeak channel to generate graphs for evaluation.

Homera et al (Durani et al., 2018) proposed a method which encompass functionality of node esp8266 are related with both of above given house application like fan, light, water pump, gardening with help of coding and website hosting on line with net server. All the functionality is treated by using Mobile App created in android utility, from which residence software are managed with assist of internet. This paper is clarifying that tracking of circuit gadgets via wi-fi using Node MCU and controlling the usage of App Blynk. According to requirement of need one could connect multiple tool like sensors, appliance and plenty of more till eight.

After studying the existing system (Domb, 2019) (Jabbar et al., 2018) we have proposed the system which consists several advantages. It usually consists of a central microcontroller to which other objects are connected. The smart garden consists of NodeMCU as a hub to which different types of sensors such as moisture sensor, humidity sensor, temperature sensor and ultrasonic sensor are connected. The ultrasonic sensor is connected to a water tank which indicated the level of water in the tank. Other sensors are connected to their respective positions and these sensors send the data to NodeMCU which consists of an inbuilt Wi-Fi technology. Firebase is a database available on the internet in which real-time values of the sensor are updated every second. Android application is developed using android studio software. Within the software, the connectivity between the application and firebase will be made. So, the user can monitor the parameters 25 from anywhere. Watering of garden varies with the type of soil. Hence the values of the sensors are predetermined for automation purposes inside the software. Whenever the user finds need of watering the garden, a switch in the application will automate the process. This helps in complete maintenance of the garden.

Advantages

- The system can be operated from anywhere in the world, with help of the blynk app which acts as a virtual switch. (Darby, 2018) (Singh et al., 2018)
- The RFID sensor, provides security and helps us against burglars and unauthorized access.
- It is available at low cost.
- Managing all of your devices from one place. The convenience factor is enormous.
- Flexibility for new devices and appliances.
- Control functions using Blynk app which acts as a virtual switch for the smart gardening system.
- Increased energy efficiency.
- Improved appliance functionality.
- Smart gardening management insight.
- Reduce human efforts: As this system works automatically humans do not require
- To apply more efforts.
- Multitasking: Multiple functions are done at the same time without the efforts of the human.
- Reduce time: As this system is multitasking so the time required will be less.

PROPOSED SYSTEM ARCHITECTURE

Arduino IDE

- The ARDUINO integrated development environment (IDE) is a cross stage application (for Windows, macOS, Linux) that is written in the programming language Java.
- It is utilized write and upload programs to Arduino compatible boards, but also, with the help of 3rd party cores, other vendor development boards. (Singh et al., 2018) (Govindraj et al., 2017)
- The Arduino IDE additionally supports the languages C and C++ utilizing exceptional guidelines of code organizing.
- The Arduino IDE supplies a software library from the wiring venture, which gives numerous basic info and yield methodology.
- It empowers us to program the ESP8266WiFi module with the direct and earth shattering LUA programming language or Arduino IDE.

Blynk Application

- Blynk is a hardware-agnostic IoT platform with white-label mobile apps, private clouds, device management, data analytics, and machine learning. (Zaidan & Zaidan, 2020) (Alaa et al., 2017)
- Join the most popular IoT platform to connect your devices to the cloud, design apps to control them, analyze telemetry data, and manage your deployed products at scale.

- It is a new platform that allows you to quickly build interfaces for controlling and monitoring your hardware projects from your iOS and Android device.
- After downloading the Blynk app, you can create a project dashboard and arrange buttons, sliders, graphs, and other widgets onto the screen.

Figure 1. System architecture

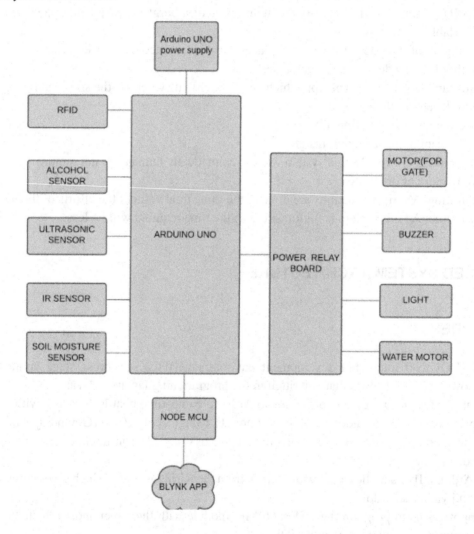

Figure 1 represents the overall system architecture of our proposed system which integrates all the sensors and blank application. (Chen et al., 2017)

NodeMCU

NodeMCU shown in Figure 2 is an open source IoT platform. It includes firmware which runs on the ESP8266 Wi-Fi SoC from Espressif Systems, and hardware which is based on the ESP-12 module. The

13 term "NodeMCU" by default refers to the firmware rather than the development kits. The firmware uses the Lua scripting language. It is based on the eLua project, and built on the Espressif Non-OS SDK for ESP8266. It uses many open source projects, such as lua-cjson, and spiffs. The NodeMCU ESP8266 development board comes with the ESP-12E module containing ESP8266 chip having Tensilica Xtensa 32-bit LX106 RISC microprocessor. This microprocessor supports RTOS and operates at 80MHz to 160 MHz adjustable clock frequency. NodeMCU has 128 KB RAM and 4MB of Flash memory to store data and programs. Its high processing power with in-built Wi-Fi / Bluetooth and Deep Sleep Operating features make it ideal for IoT projects.

Figure 2. NodeMCU

Arduino Uno

Arduino Uno shown in figure 3 is a microcontroller board based on the ATmega328P (data sheet). It has 14 digital input/output pins (of which 6 can be used as PWM outputs), 6 analog inputs, a 16 MHz ceramic resonator (CSTCE16M0V53-R0), a USB connection, a power jack, an ICSP header and a reset button. It contains everything needed to support the microcontroller; simply connect it to a computer with a USB cable or power it with a AC-to-DC adapter or battery to get started. You can tinker with your Uno without worrying too much about doing something wrong, worst case scenario you can replace the chip for a few dollars and start over again.

Figure 3. Arduino Uno

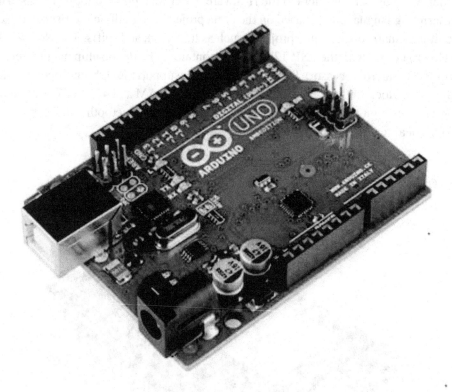

Soil Moisture Sensor

The Soil Moisture Sensor shown in figure 4 uses capacitance to measure the water content of soil (by measuring the dielectric permittivity of the soil, which is a function of the water content). Simply insert this rugged sensor into the soil to be tested, and the volumetric water content of the soil is reported in percent. The working of the soil moisture sensor is pretty straightforward. The fork-shaped probe with two exposed conductors, acts as a variable resistor (just like a potentiometer) whose resistance varies according to the water content in the soil. This resistance is inversely proportional to the soil moisture:

- The more water in the soil means better conductivity and will result in a lower resistance.
- The less water in the soil means poor conductivity and will result in a higher resistance.

The sensor produces an output voltage according to the resistance, which by measuring we can determine the moisture level. The sensor also contains an electronic module that connects the probe to the Arduino. The module produces an output voltage according to the resistance of the probe and is made available at an Analog Output (AO) pin. The module has a built-in potentiometer for sensitivity adjustment of the digital output (DO). You can set a threshold by using a potentiometer; So that when the moisture level exceeds the threshold value, the module will output LOW otherwise HIGH. This setup is very useful when you want to trigger an action when certain threshold is reached.

Figure 4. Soil moisture sensor

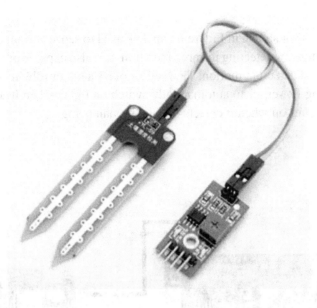

Automated Water Sprinkler Sensor: (Submersible Mini Water Pump)

Micro DC 3-6V Micro Submersible Pump Mini water pump shown in Figure 5 For Fountain Garden Mini water circulation System DIY project. This is a low cost, small size Submersible Pump Motor which can be operated from a 3 ~ 6V power supply. It can take up to 120 liters per hour with very low current consumption of 220mA. Just connect tube pipe to the motor outlet, submerge it in water and power it. Make sure that the water level is always higher than the motor. Dry run may damage the motor due to heating and it will also produce.

Figure 5. Automated water sprinkler sensor

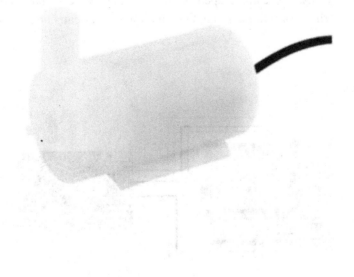

IR Sensor

An infrared sensor is a sensor shown in Figure 6 which is used to sense certain characteristics of its surroundings by either emitting or detecting infrared radiation. It is also capable of measuring the heat being emitted by the objects and detecting motion. This sensor plays a major role in smart city monitoring. In this system, we are using IR sensor to automatically switch on lights when it detects any humans. The light automatically switches on when it detects the any human being.

Figure 6. IR sensor

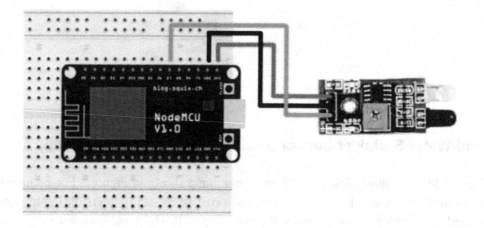

RFID Sensor

RFID stands for Radio Frequency Identification shown in Figure 7 and it's a non-contact technology that's broadly used in many industries for tasks such as personnel tracking, access control, supply chain management, books tracking in libraries, tollgate systems and so on. In our system, we use RFID for tollgate systems. We have used id card to open the door. When any car enters the toll door, it shows unauthorized access and the door will not open. Only authorized car can enter the tollgate without paying money.

Figure 7. RFID sensor

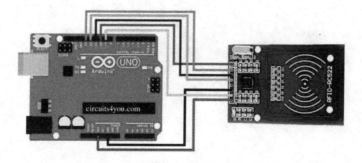

IOT Module- Blynk App

BLYNK shown in figure 8 is the most popular IoT platform to connect your devices to the cloud. BLYNK is a digital dashboard where you can build a graphic interface for your project by simply dragging and dropping widgets .It supports a wide range of Hardware including Arduino, Nodemcu, Raspberry PI & others. Blynk was designed for the Internet of Things. It can control hardware remotely, it can display sensor data, it can store data and visualize it.

Figure 8. Blynk app

Complete Design:

Figure 9.

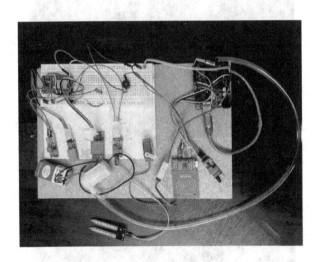

RESULTS

Blynk App

The below diagram shows the Blank application output.

Figure 10.

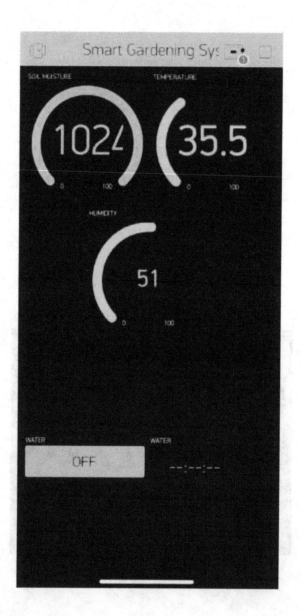

Figure 11.

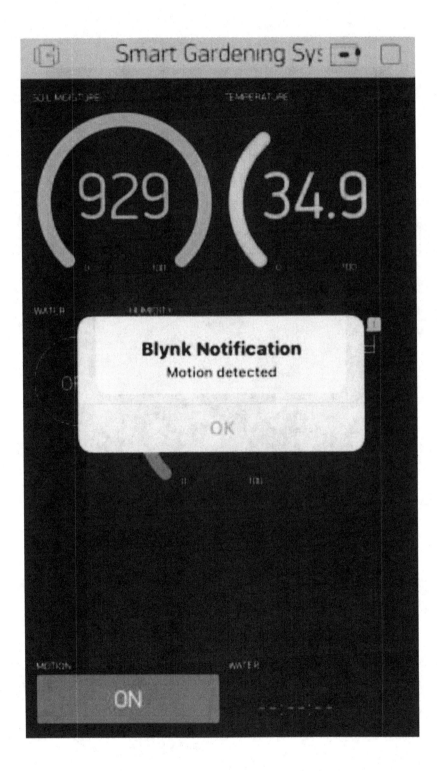

Figure 12.

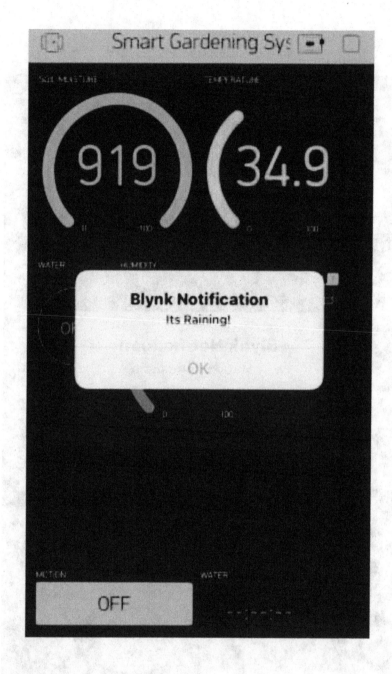

Figure 13.

CONCLUSION AND FUTURE SCOPE

We have successfully made a food quality monitoring system using NodeMCU and Blynk cloud platform. This system blinks an LED if the readings of temperature and humidity go beyond the set threshold. Several such sensors can be placed in go-downs and storage containers to be of practical application. This system will help keep food at optimal levels of temperature and humidity and increase the shelf life of the plants. The implementation of Smart Garden system using the Internet of Things has been verified to satisfactorily work by connecting different parameters of the soil to the cloud and was successfully controlled remotely through a mobile application. The system designed not only monitors the sensor data, like moisture, humidity, temperature and ultrasonic but also actuates other parameters according to the requirement, for example, if the water level in tank is reduced to a minimum value then the motor switch is turned on automatically to the water level of the tank reaches the maximum value. The initial cost and the installation of this system are cheap and hence it can be implemented anywhere. With the development of sensor technology, the system can be elevated to the next level which helps the users to utilize their investment in an economic manner. If soil nutrient sensors can be installed, then the system can be modified to supply fertilizers to the garden precisely. This system saves manpower and efficiently utilizes the water resources available ultimately leading to more profit. The feedback provided by the system will improve the implementation of the gardening process.

We can successfully implement our project as a cheap alternative to the exiting smart gardening monitoring techniques. We could also create an app interfacing with our project to provide a more immersive and better experience.

REFERENCES

Ait Abdelouahid, R., Debauche, O., Mahmoudi, S., Marzak, A., Manneback, P., & Lebeau, F. (2020). *Open phytotron: A new iot device for home gardening.* Academic Press.

Al-Omary, A., AlSabbagh, H. M., & Al-Rizzo, H. (2018). *Cloud based IoT for smart garden watering system using Arduino Uno.* Academic Press.

Alaa, M., Zaidan, A. A., Zaidan, B. B., Talal, M., & Kiah, M. L. M. (2017). A review of smart home applications based on Internet of Things. *Journal of Network and Computer Applications*, *97*, 48–65. doi:10.1016/j.jnca.2017.08.017

Burton, L., Dave, N., Fernandez, R. E., Jayachandran, K., & Bhansali, S. (2018). Smart gardening IoT soil sheets for real-time nutrient analysis. *Journal of the Electrochemical Society*, *165*(8), B3157–B3162. doi:10.1149/2.0201808jes

Chen, M., Yang, J., Zhu, X., Wang, X., Liu, M., & Song, J. (2017). Smart home 2.0: Innovative smart home system powered by botanical IoT and emotion detection. *Mobile Networks and Applications*, *22*(6), 1159–1169. doi:10.100711036-017-0866-1

Darby, S. J. (2018). Smart technology in the home: Time for more clarity. *Building Research and Information*, *46*(1), 140–147. doi:10.1080/09613218.2017.1301707

Domb, M. (2019). Smart home systems based on internet of things. In *Internet of Things (IoT) for Automated and Smart Applications*. IntechOpen. doi:10.5772/intechopen.84894

Durani, H., Sheth, M., Vaghasia, M., & Kotech, S. (2018, April). Smart automated home application using IoT with Blynk app. In *2018 Second International Conference on Inventive Communication and Computational Technologies (ICICCT)* (pp. 393-397). IEEE. 10.1109/ICICCT.2018.8473224

Govindraj, V., Sathiyanarayanan, M., & Abubakar, B. (2017, August). Customary homes to smart homes using Internet of Things (IoT) and mobile application. In *2017 International Conference On Smart Technologies For Smart Nation (SmartTechCon)* (pp. 1059-1063). IEEE. 10.1109/SmartTechCon.2017.8358532

Jabbar, W. A., Alsibai, M. H., Amran, N. S. S., & Mahayadin, S. K. (2018, June). Design and implementation of IoT-based automation system for smart home. In *2018 International Symposium on Networks, Computers and Communications (ISNCC)* (pp. 1-6). IEEE. 10.1109/ISNCC.2018.8531006

Khan, W. Z., Aalsalem, M. Y., Khan, M. K., & Arshad, Q. (2017). When social objects collaborate: Concepts, processing elements, attacks and challenges. *Computers & Electrical Engineering*, *58*, 397–411. doi:10.1016/j.compeleceng.2016.11.014

Min, B., & Park, S. J. (2017). A smart indoor gardening system using IoT technology. In *Advances in Computer Science and Ubiquitous Computing* (pp. 683–687). Springer.

Samonte, M. J. C., Signo, E. P. E., Gayomali, R. J. M., Rey, W. P., & Serrano, E. A. (2019, March). PHYTO: An IoT urban gardening mobile app. In *Proceedings of the 2019 2nd International Conference on Information Science and Systems* (pp. 135-139). 10.1145/3322645.3322659

Sharma, S., Sharma, A., Goel, T., Deoli, R., & Mohan, S. (2020, July). Smart Home Gardening Management System: A Cloud-Based Internet-of-Things (IoT) Application in VANET. In *2020 11th International Conference on Computing, Communication and Networking Technologies (ICCCNT)* (pp. 1-5). IEEE.

Sheth, M., & Rupani, P. (2019, April). Smart Gardening Automation using IoT With BLYNK App. In *2019 3rd International Conference on Trends in Electronics and Informatics (ICOEI)* (pp. 266-270). IEEE. 10.1109/ICOEI.2019.8862591

Singh, H., Pallagani, V., Khandelwal, V., & Venkanna, U. (2018, March). IoT based smart home automation system using sensor node. In *2018 4th International Conference on Recent Advances in Information Technology (RAIT)* (pp. 1-5). IEEE. 10.1109/RAIT.2018.8389037

Thamaraimanalan, T., Vivekk, S. P., Satheeshkumar, G., & Saravanan, P. (2018). Smart garden monitoring system using IoT. *Asian Journal of Applied Science and Technology*, *2*(2), 186–192.

Tzounis, A., Katsoulas, N., Bartzanas, T., & Kittas, C. (2017). Internet of Things in agriculture, recent advances and future challenges. *Biosystems Engineering*, *164*, 31–48. doi:10.1016/j.biosystemseng.2017.09.007

Zaidan, A. A., & Zaidan, B. B. (2020). A review on intelligent process for smart home applications based on IoT: Coherent taxonomy, motivation, open challenges, and recommendations. *Artificial Intelligence Review*, *53*(1), 141–165. doi:10.100710462-018-9648-9

Compilation of References

Al-Omary, A., AlSabbagh, H. M., & Al-Rizzo, H. (2018). *Cloud based IoT for smart garden watering system using Arduino Uno*. Academic Press.

Dubovitskaya, A., Xu, Z., Ryu, S., Schumacher, M., & Wang, F. (2017). *Secure and Trustable Electronic Medical Records Sharing using Blockchain*. arXiv preprint arXiv:1709.06528.

Pant, V. K., Prakash, J., & Asthana, A. (2015). Three-step data security model for cloud com- puting based on RSA and steganography. *2015 International Conference on Green Computing and Internet of Things (ICGCIoT)*, 490–494. 10.1109/ICGCIoT.2015.7380514

Shafee, A. (2020). Botnets and their detection techniques. *Networks Computers and Communications (ISNCC) International Symposium on*, 1-6.

Zwolenski, M., & Weatherill, L. (2014). The digital universe: Rich data and the increasing value of the Internet of Things. *Austral. J. Telecommunication. Digit. Econ.*, 2(3), 47. doi:10.7790/ajtde.v2n3.47

Al-Qamash & Soliman. (2018). Cloud, Fog, and Edge Computing: A Software Engineering Perspective. *2018 International Conference on Computer and Applications (ICCA)*. 10.1109/COMAPP.2018.8460443

Durani, H., Sheth, M., Vaghasia, M., & Kotech, S. (2018, April). Smart automated home application using IoT with Blynk app. In *2018 Second International Conference on Inventive Communication and Computational Technologies (ICICCT)* (pp. 393-397). IEEE. 10.1109/ICICCT.2018.8473224

How Blockchain Can Fight Fraud Based on Know-Your-Customer Data. (2019). Available: https://www.nasdaq.com/articles/how-blockchain-can-fight-fraud-based-know-your-customer-data-2019-02-11.

Peters, G., Panayi, E., & Chapelle, A. (2015, November). Trends in cryptocurrencies and blockchain technologies: A monetary theory and regulation perspective. *J. Financial Perspect.*, 3(3), 1–25.

Somani, U., Lakhani, K., & Mundra, M. (2010). Implementing digital signature with RSA en- cryption algorithm to enhance the Data Security of cloud in Cloud Computing. *2010 First International Conference On Parallel, Distributed and Grid Computing*, 211– 216.

Al-Jaroodi, J., & Mohamed, N. (2019). Blockchain in industries: A survey. *IEEE Access: Practical Innovations, Open Solutions*, 7, 36500–36515. doi:10.1109/ACCESS.2019.2903554

Arora, R., Parashar, A., & Transforming, C. C. I. (2013). Secure user data in cloud computing using encryption algorithms. *International Journal of Engineering Research and Applications*, 3(4), 1922–1926.

Dolui & Datta. (2017). Comparison of edge computing implementations: Fog computing, cloudlet and mobile edge computing. *Global Internet of Things Summit (GIoTS)*. doi:10.1109/GIOTS.2017.8016213

Domb, M. (2019). Smart home systems based on internet of things. In *Internet of Things (IoT) for Automated and Smart Applications*. IntechOpen. doi:10.5772/intechopen.84894

Kolias, C., Kambourakis, G., Stavrou, A., & Voas, J. (2017). DDoS in the IoT: Mirai and other botnets. *Computer*, *50*(7), 80–84. doi:10.1109/MC.2017.201

Francis, T., & Madhiajagan, M. (2017). A Comparison of Cloud Execution Mechanisms: Fog, Edge and Clone Cloud Computing. *Proc. EECSI*, 446-450. 10.11591/eecsi.v4.1032

Jabbar, W. A., Alsibai, M. H., Amran, N. S. S., & Mahayadin, S. K. (2018, June). Design and implementation of IoT-based automation system for smart home. In *2018 International Symposium on Networks, Computers and Communications (ISNCC)* (pp. 1-6). IEEE. 10.1109/ISNCC.2018.8531006

Klessig, H., Ohmann, D., Reppas, A. I., Hatzikirou, H., Abedi, M., Simsek, M., & Fettweis, G. P. (2016). From immune cells to self-organizing ultra-dense small cell networks. *IEEE Journal on Selected Areas in Communications*, *34*(4), 800–811. doi:10.1109/JSAC.2016.2544638

Ruj, S., Stojmenovic, M., & Nayak, A. (2012). Privacy-preserving access control with authen- tication for securing data in clouds. *IEEE/ACM International Symposium on Cluster, Cloud and Grid Computing*, 556–563.

Trautman, L. J., & Ormerod, P. C. (2016). Corporate Directors' and Officers' Cybersecurity Standard of Care: The Yahoo Data Breach. *Am. UL Rev.*, *66*(1), 1231.

Aazam, M., Zeadally, S., & Harras, K. A. (2018). Fog computing architecture, evaluation, and future research directions. *IEEE Communications Magazine*, *56*(5), 46–52. doi:10.1109/MCOM.2018.1700707

Darby, S. J. (2018). Smart technology in the home: Time for more clarity. *Building Research and Information*, *46*(1), 140–147. doi:10.1080/09613218.2017.1301707

Kshetri, N. (2017). Can blockchain strengthen the internet of things? *IT Professional*, *19*(4), 68–72. doi:10.1109/MITP.2017.3051335

Mafakheri, B., Subramanya, T., Goratti, L., & Riggio, R. (2018). Blockchainbased Infrastructure Sharing in 5G Small Cell Networks. *14th International Conference on Network and Service Management (CNSM)*.

Subashini, S., & Kavitha, V. (2011). A metadata-based storage model for securing data in a cloud environment. *2011 International Conference on Cyber-Enabled Distributed Computing and Knowledge Discovery*, 429–434.

Alrawais, A., Alhothaily, A., Hu, C., & Cheng, X. (2017). Fog computing for the internet of things: Security and privacy issues. *IEEE Internet Computing*, *21*(2), 34–42. doi:10.1109/MIC.2017.37

Mistry, I., Tanwar, S., Tyagi, S., & Kumar, N. (2020). Blockchain for 5Genabled IoT for Industrial Automation: A Systematic Review, Solutions, and Challenges. *Mechanical Systems and Signal Processing*, *135*, 106382. doi:10.1016/j.ymssp.2019.106382

Singh, H., Pallagani, V., Khandelwal, V., & Venkanna, U. (2018, March). IoT based smart home automation system using sensor node. In *2018 4th International Conference on Recent Advances in Information Technology (RAIT)* (pp. 1-5). IEEE. 10.1109/RAIT.2018.8389037

Wang, C., Ren, K., Lou, W., & Li, J. (2010). Toward publicly auditable secure cloud data storage services. *IEEE Network*, *24*(4), 19–24. doi:10.1109/MNET.2010.5510914

Yeoh, P. (2017). Regulatory issues in blockchain technology. *Journal of Financial Regulation and Compliance.*, *25*(2), 196–208. doi:10.1108/JFRC-08-2016-0068

Global Mobile Suppliers Association. (2015). *The Road to 5G: Drivers, applications, requirements and technical development*. Global Mobile Suppliers Association.

Zhou, L., Varadharajan, V., & Hitchens, M. (2013). Vijay Varadharajan, and Michael Hitchens. Achieving Secure Role-Based Access Control on Encrypted Data in Cloud Storage. *IEEE Transactions on Information Forensics and Security*, *8*(12), 1947–1960. doi:10.1109/TIFS.2013.2286456

Gandhi, & Gupta. (2015). A Research on Enhancing Public Key Cryptography by the Use of MRGA with RSA and N-Prime RSA. *International Journal for Innovative Research in Science and Technology*, *16*, 72–79.

Govindraj, V., Sathiyanarayanan, M., & Abubakar, B. (2017, August). Customary homes to smart homes using Internet of Things (IoT) and mobile application. In *2017 International Conference On Smart Technologies For Smart Nation (SmartTechCon)* (pp. 1059-1063). IEEE. 10.1109/SmartTechCon.2017.8358532

Liyanage, M., Ahmad, I., Abro, A. B., Gurtov, A., & Ylianttila, M. (2018). *A Comprehensive Guide to 5G Security*. John Wiley & Sons. doi:10.1002/9781119293071

Satyanarayanan, M. (2017). The Emergence of Edge Computing. *IEEE Computer Society*, *50*(1), 30–39. doi:10.1109/MC.2017.9

Bangui, H., Rakrak, S., Raghay, S., & Buhnova, B. (2018). Moving to the Edge-Cloud-of-Things: Recent Advances and Future Research Directions. *Electronics (Basel)*, *7*(309), 309. Advance online publication. doi:10.3390/electronics7110309

Shinde, G. N., & Fadewar, H. S. (2008). Faster RSA algorithm for decryption using Chinese re- mainder theorem. *ICCES: International Conference on Computational & Experimental Engineering and Sciences*, 255–262.

Zaidan, A. A., & Zaidan, B. B. (2020). A review on intelligent process for smart home applications based on IoT: Coherent taxonomy, motivation, open challenges, and recommendations. *Artificial Intelligence Review*, *53*(1), 141–165. doi:10.100710462-018-9648-9

Alaa, M., Zaidan, A. A., Zaidan, B. B., Talal, M., & Kiah, M. L. M. (2017). A review of smart home applications based on Internet of Things. *Journal of Network and Computer Applications*, *97*, 48–65. doi:10.1016/j.jnca.2017.08.017

Lakshmi, B. (2020). *The Dark Phase of Cultural Conflict in The Novel 'Twilight in Delhi'*. Academic Press.

Popovski, Trillingsgaard, Simeone, & Durisi. (2018). 5G Wireless Network Slicing for eMBB, URLLC, and mMTC: A communication-theoretic view. *IEEE Access*, *6*(55), 765–779.

Abbott, F. (2000). Distributed Governance at the WTO-WIPO: An Evolving Model For Open-Architecture Integrated Governance. *Journal of International Economic Law*, *3*(1), 63–81. doi:10.1093/jiel/3.1.63

Kaushik, A., Choudhary, A., Ektare, C., Thomas, D., & Akram, S. (2017). Blockchain – Literature Survey. *2nd IEEE International Conference On Recent Trends in Electronics Information & Communication Technology (RTEICT)*. 10.1109/RTEICT.2017.8256979

Min, B., & Park, S. J. (2017). A smart indoor gardening system using IoT technology. In *Advances in Computer Science and Ubiquitous Computing* (pp. 683–687). Springer.

Shi, W., Pallis, G., & Xu, Z. (2019, August). Edge Computing. *Proceedings of the IEEE*, *107*(8), 1474–1481. doi:10.1109/JPROC.2019.2928287

Yang, K., & Jia, X. (2012). An efficient and secure dynamic auditing protocol for data storage in cloud computing. *IEEE Transactions on Parallel and Distributed Systems*, *24*(9), 1717–1726. doi:10.1109/TPDS.2012.278

Chen, M., Yang, J., Zhu, X., Wang, X., Liu, M., & Song, J. (2017). Smart home 2.0: Innovative smart home system powered by botanical IoT and emotion detection. *Mobile Networks and Applications*, 22(6), 1159–1169. doi:10.100711036-017-0866-1

Jain, A., & Singhal, P. (2016). Fog computing: Driving force behind the emergence of edge computing. *2016 International Conference System Modeling & Advancement in Research Trends (SMART)*, 294-297. 10.1109/SYSMART.2016.7894538

Kim, G.-C., Li, S.-C., & Hwang, H.-C. (2020). Fast rebalanced RSA signature scheme with typical prime generation. *Theoretical Computer Science*, 830-831, 1–19. doi:10.1016/j.tcs.2020.04.024

Yang, R., Yu, F. R., Si, P., Yang, Z., & Zhang, Y. (2019). Integrated blockchain and edge computing systems: A survey, some research issues and challenges. *IEEE Communications Surveys and Tutorials*, 21(2), 1508–1532. doi:10.1109/COMST.2019.2894727

Balaji, M., Kumar, C. A., & Rao, G. S. V. (2018). Predictive Cloud resource management framework for enterprise workloads. *Journal of King Saud University-Computer and Information Sciences*, 30(3), 404–415. doi:10.1016/j.jksuci.2016.10.005

Stanciu, A. (2017). Blockchain based distributed control system for edge computing. In *2017 21st International Conference, on Control Systems and Computer Science (CSCS)*, (pp. 667–671). IEEE. 10.1109/CSCS.2017.102

Taleb, T., Dutta, S., Ksentini, A., Iqbal, M., & Flinck, H. (2017). Mobile edge computing potential in making cities smarter. *IEEE Communications Magazine*, 55(3), 38–43. doi:10.1109/MCOM.2017.1600249CM

Balaji, M., Kumar, C. A., & Rao, G. S. V. (2019). Non-linear analysis of bursty workloads using dual metrics for better cloud resource management. *Journal of Ambient Intelligence and Humanized Computing*, 10(12), 4977–4992. doi:10.100712652-019-01183-8

Rehman, M. H., Jayaraman, P. P., Malik, S. R., Khan, A. R., & Gaber, M. M. (2017). RedEdge: A Novel Architecture for Big Data Processing in Mobile Edge Computing Environments. *J. Sens. Actuator Network.*, 6(3), 17. doi:10.3390/jsan6030017

Zheng, Z., Xie, S., Dai, H.-N., Chen, X., & Wang, H. (2018). Blockchain challenges and opportunities: A survey. *International Journal of Web and Grid Services*, 14(4), 352–375. doi:10.1504/IJWGS.2018.095647

Kim, Kim, & Park. (2017). *A combined network control approach for the edge cloud and LPWAN-based IoT services.* doi:10.1002/cpe.4406

Narayanan, M., & Cherukuri, A. K. (2018). Verification of cloud based information integration architecture using colored petri nets. *International Journal of Computer Network and Information Security*, 12(2), 1–11. doi:10.5815/ijcnis.2018.02.01

Balaji, M., Rao, G. S. V., & Kumar, C. A. (2014). A comparitive study of predictive models for cloud infrastructure management. In *2014 14th IEEE/ACM International Symposium on Cluster, Cloud and Grid Computing* (pp. 923-926). IEEE. 10.1109/CCGrid.2014.32

Jain, K., & Mohapatra, S. (2019). Taxonomy of Edge Computing: Challenges, Opportunities, and Data Reduction Methods. In *Al-Turjman Fields, Edge Computing. EAI/Springer Innovations in Communication and Computing*. Springer. doi:10.1007/978-3-319-99061-3_4

Abbas, N. (2018). Mobile edge computing: A survey. *IEEE IOT J.*, 5(1), 450–465.

Ai, Y., Peng, M., & Zhang, K. (2018). Edge cloud computing technologies for internet of things: A primer. *Digital Communication Network.*, 4(2), 77–86. doi:10.1016/j.dcan.2017.07.001

Lopez, P. G. (2015). Edge-centric computing: Vision and challenges. *ACM SIGCOMM Computational Communication Rev., 45*(5), 37–42.

Roman, R., Lopez, J., & Mambo, M. (2016). A survey and analysis of security threats and challenges. *Future Generation Computer Systems, 78*, 680–698. doi:10.1016/j.future.2016.11.009

Shi, W., & Dustdar, S. (2016, May). The promise of edge computing. *Comput, 49*(5), 78–81. doi:10.1109/MC.2016.145

Allenby, B. R. (2012). *The Theory and Practice of Sustainable Engineering* (1st ed.). Pearson Prentice Hall.

Aste, T. D. M. T., Tasca, P., & Di Matteo, T. (2017). Blockchain Technologies: The Foreseeable Impact on Society and Industry. *Computer, 50*(9), 18–28. doi:10.1109/MC.2017.3571064

Bonomi, F., Milito, R., Zhu, J., & Addepalli, S. (2012). Fog computing and its role in the Internet of Things. *Proc. 1st Ed. MCC Workshop Mobile Cloud Comput.*, 13–16. 10.1145/2342509.2342513

Jena, S. R., Shanmugam, R., Saini, K., & Kumar, S. (2020). Cloud Computing Tools: Inside Views and Analysis. *International Conference on Smart Sustainable Intelligent Computing and Applications under ICITETM2020*, 382-391.

Li, Y., Gai, K., Qiu, L., Qiu, M., & Zhao, H. (2017). Intelligent cryptogra- phy approach for secure distributed big data storage in cloud computing. *Information Sciences, 387*, 103–115. doi:10.1016/j.ins.2016.09.005

Thamaraimanalan, T., Vivekk, S. P., Satheeshkumar, G., & Saravanan, P. (2018). Smart garden monitoring system using IoT. *Asian Journal of Applied Science and Technology, 2*(2), 186–192.

Salman, O., Elhajj, I., Kayssi, A., & Chehab, A. (2015). Edge computing enabling the Internet of Things. *Proc. IEEE World Forum Internet of Things (WFIOT)*, 603–608. 10.1109/WF-IoT.2015.7389122

Tong, L., Li, Y., & Gao, W. (2016). A hierarchical edge cloud architecture for mobile computing. *Proc. IEEE Int. Conf. Computational Communication (INFOCOM)*, 1–9. 10.1109/INFOCOM.2016.7524340

Bastug, E., Bennis, M., & Debbah, M. (2014, August). Living on the edge: The role of proactive caching in 5G wireless networks. *IEEE Communications Magazine, 52*(8), 82–89. doi:10.1109/MCOM.2014.6871674

Ait Abdelouahid, R., Debauche, O., Mahmoudi, S., Marzak, A., Manneback, P., & Lebeau, F. (2020). *Open phytotron: A new iot device for home gardening*. Academic Press.

Almeida, V., Getschko, D., & Afonso, C. (2015). The Origin and Evolution of Multistakeholder Models. *IEEE Internet Computing, 19*(1), 74–79. doi:10.1109/MIC.2015.15

Gupta, Y., Shorey, R., Kulkarni, D., & Tew, J. (2018). The Applicability of Blockchain in the Internet of Things. *10th International Conference on Communication Systems & Networks (COMSNETS)*. 10.1109/COMSNETS.2018.8328273

Hu, Y. C., Patel, M., Sabella, D., Sprecher, N., & Young, V. (2015). *Mobile edge computing—A key technology towards 5G*. ETSI, Sophia Antipolis, France.

Kumari, K., & Saini, K. (2019). CFDD (CounterFeit Drug Detection) using Blockchain in the Pharmaceutical Industry. *International Journal of Engineering Research & Technology, 8*(12), 591-594.

Shwetha Bindu & Yadaiah. (2011). Secure Data Storage In Cloud Computing. *International Journal of Research in Computer Science, 1*(1), 63–73.

Antonopoulos, A. (2014). *Bitcoin Security Model: Trust by Computation*. O'Reilly-Radar. Retrieved from http://radar.oreilly.com/2014/02/bitcoin-security-model-trust-by-computation.html

Dinh, T. N., & Thai, M. T. (2018). AI and Blockchain: A Disruptive Integration. *Computer, 51*(September), 48–53. doi:10.1109/MC.2018.3620971

Kavita. (2018). A Future's Dominant Technology Blockchain: Digital Transformation. *IEEE International Conference on Computing, Power and Communication Technologies 2018 (GUCON 2018).* doi:10.1109/GUCON.2018.8675075

Ravi, J., Shi, W., & Xu, C.-Z. (2005, March). Personalized email management at network edges. *IEEE Internet Computing, 9*(2), 54–60. doi:10.1109/MIC.2005.44

Sheth, M., & Rupani, P. (2019, April). Smart Gardening Automation using IoT With BLYNK App. In *2019 3rd International Conference on Trends in Electronics and Informatics (ICOEI)* (pp. 266-270). IEEE. 10.1109/ICOEI.2019.8862591

Sookhak, M. (2015). *Dynamic remote data auditing for securing big data storage in cloud computing* (Doctoral dissertation). University of Malaya.

Ansell, C., & Gash, A. (2007). Collaborative Governance in Theory and Practice. *Journal of Public Administration: Research and Theory, 18*(4), 543–571. doi:10.1093/jopart/mum032

Litke, A., Anagnostopoulos, D., & Varvarigou, T. (2019, January). Blockchains for supply chain management: Architectural elements and challenges towards a global scale deployment. *Logistics, 3*(1), 5. doi:10.3390/logistics3010005

Samonte, M. J. C., Signo, E. P. E., Gayomali, R. J. M., Rey, W. P., & Serrano, E. A. (2019, March). PHYTO: An IoT urban gardening mobile app. In *Proceedings of the 2019 2nd International Conference on Information Science and Systems* (pp. 135-139). 10.1145/3322645.3322659

Satyanarayanan, M., Bahl, P., Caceres, R., & Davies, N. (2009, October/December). The case for VM-based cloudlets in mobile computing. *IEEE Pervasive Computing, 8*(4), 14–23. doi:10.1109/MPRV.2009.82

Shimbre, N., & Deshpande, P. (2015). Enhancing distributed data storage security for cloud computing using TPA and AES algorithm. *International Conference on Computing Communication Control and Automation,* 35–39. 10.1109/ICCUBEA.2015.16

Alkadi, O., Moustafa, N., & Turnbull, B. (2020). A Review of Intrusion Detection and Blockchain Applications in the Cloud: Approaches Challenges and Solutions. *Access IEEE, 8,* 104893–104917. doi:10.1109/ACCESS.2020.2999715

Behl, A. (2011). Emerging security challenges in cloud computing: An insight to cloud security challenges and their mitigation. *2011 World Congress on Information and Communication Technologies, 21,* 217–222.

Dutta & Saini. (2019). Evolution of Blockchain Technology in Business Applications. *Journal of Emerging Technologies and Innovative Research, 6*(9), 240-244.

Sharma, S., Sharma, A., Goel, T., Deoli, R., & Mohan, S. (2020, July). Smart Home Gardening Management System: A Cloud-Based Internet-of-Things (IoT) Application in VANET. In *2020 11th International Conference on Computing, Communication and Networking Technologies (ICCCNT)* (pp. 1-5). IEEE.

Shi, W., Cao, J., Zhang, Q., Li, Y., & Xu, L. (2016, October). Edge computing: Vision and challenges. *IEEE Internet of Things Journal, 3*(5), 637–646. doi:10.1109/JIOT.2016.2579198

Yaji, S., Bangera, K., & Neelima, B. (2018). Privacy preserving in blockchain based on partial Homomorphic Encryption system for AI Applications. *25th International conference on High performance computing workshop (HIPCW),* 81-85.

Dutta, S., & Saini, K. (2021a). Securing Data: A Study on Different Transform Domain Techniques. *WSEAS Transactions on Systems And Control, 16.* doi:10.37394/23203.2021.16.8

Gochhayat, S. P., Shetty, S., Mukkamala, R., Foytik, P., Kamhoua, G. A., & Njilla, L. (2020). Measuring Decentrality in Blockchain Based Systems. *Access IEEE*, 8, 178372–178390. doi:10.1109/ACCESS.2020.3026577

Mylrea, M., & Gourisetti, S. N. G. (2017). Blockchain for small grid resilience:Exchanging distributed energy at speed, scale and security. *Resilience Week*, (Sep), 18–23.

Symeonides, M., Trihinas, D., Georgiou, Z., Pallis, G., & Dikaiakos, M. (2019). Query-driven descriptive analytics for IoT and edge computing. *Proc. IEEE Int. Conf. Cloud Eng. (IC2E)*, 1–11. 10.1109/IC2E.2019.00-12

Tzounis, A., Katsoulas, N., Bartzanas, T., & Kittas, C. (2017). Internet of Things in agriculture, recent advances and future challenges. *Biosystems Engineering*, 164, 31–48. doi:10.1016/j.biosystemseng.2017.09.007

Usman, M., Jan, M. A., & He, X. (2017). Cryptography-based secure data storage and sharing using HEVC and public clouds. *Information Sciences*, 387, 90–102. doi:10.1016/j.ins.2016.08.059

Dutta, S., & Saini, K. (2021b). Statistical Assessment of Hybrid Blockchain for SME Sector. *WSEAS Transactions on Systems And Control, 16*. doi:10.37394/23203.2021.16.6

Garg, P., & Sharma, V. (2014). An efficient and secure data storage in Mobile Cloud Com- puting through RSA and Hash function. *2014 International Conference on Issues and Challenges in Intelligent Computing Techniques (ICICT)*, 334–339.

Khan, W. Z., Aalsalem, M. Y., Khan, M. K., & Arshad, Q. (2017). When social objects collaborate: Concepts, processing elements, attacks and challenges. *Computers & Electrical Engineering*, 58, 397–411. doi:10.1016/j.compeleceng.2016.11.014

Strobel, V., Ferrer, E. C., & Dorigo, M. (2018). Managing byzantine robots via blockchain technology in a swarm robotics collective decision making scenario. *Proc.17th Int. Conf. Auto. Agents MultiAgents System International Foundation for Autonomous Agents and MultiAgent Systems*, 541-549.

Vakali, A., & Pallis, G. (2003, November). Content delivery networks: Status and trends. *IEEE Internet Computing*, 7(6), 68–74. doi:10.1109/MIC.2003.1250586

Zou, Y., Meng, T., Zhang, P., Zhang, W., & Li, H. (2020). Focus on Blockchain: A Comprehensive Survey on Academic and Application. *Access IEEE*, 8, 187182–187201. doi:10.1109/ACCESS.2020.3030491

Burton, L., Dave, N., Fernandez, R. E., Jayachandran, K., & Bhansali, S. (2018). Smart gardening IoT soil sheets for real-time nutrient analysis. *Journal of the Electrochemical Society*, 165(8), B3157–B3162. doi:10.1149/2.0201808jes

Kblaw, Azaria, Halamka, & Lippman. (2016). A Case Study for Blockchain in Healthcare. "MedRec" prototype for electronic health records and Medical research data. Proceedings of IEEE Open & Big Data Conference, 13.

Naz, S., & Lee, S. U.-J. (2020). Why the new consensus mechanism is needed in blockchain technology? *Blockchain Computing and Applications (BCCA) Second International Conference on*, 92-99.

Xu, Z.-W. (2014, January). Cloud-sea computing systems: Towards thousand-fold improvement in performance per watt for the coming zetta-byte era. *J. Computational Science Technol.*, 29(2), 177–181. doi:10.100711390-014-1420-2

A, B., & K, M. V. (2016). Blockchain platform for industrial internet of things. *Journal of software Engineering and Applications, 9*(10), 533.

Aazam, M., Khan, I., Alsaffar, A. A., & Huh, E. N. (2014). Cloud of Things: Integrating Internet of Things with Cloud Computing and the Issues Involved. In *International Bhurban Conference on Applied Sciences & Technology*. Islamabad, Pakistan: IEEE. 10.1109/IBCAST.2014.6778179

Abbas, K., Afaq, M., Khan, T. A., & Song, W.-C. (2020). A blockchain and machine learning-based drug supply chain management and recommendation system for smart pharmaceutical industry. *Electronics (Switzerland), 9*(5), 852.

Abd El-Latif, A., Abd-El-Atty, B., Venegas-Andraca, S., Elwahsh, H., Piran, M., & Bashir, A. (2020). Providing End-to-End Security Using Quantum Walks in IoT Networks. *IEEE Access: Practical Innovations, Open Solutions*, *8*, 92687–92696. doi:10.1109/ACCESS.2020.2992820

Abdelgawad, A., Yelamarthi, K., & Khattab, A. (2016). IoT-based health monitoring system for active and assisted living. In *International Conference on Smart Objects and Technologies for Social Good* (pp. 11-20). Venice, Italy: Springer.

Aceto, G., Botta, A., de Donato, W., & Pescapè, A. (2013). Cloud monitoring: A Survey. *Computer Networks*, *57*(9), 2093–2115. doi:10.1016/j.comnet.2013.04.001

Adiguna, T. (2016). Secure H. 264 Video Coding using AES/CFB/PKCS5 padding encryption on various video frames (I, P, B). In *2016 10th International Conference on Telecommunication Systems Services and Applications (TSSA)* (pp. 1-5). IEEE.

Ahlborn, Bachmann, Biegel, Bienert, & Falk. (n.d.). *Technology Scenario 'Artificial Intelligence in Industrie 4.0.'* Academic Press.

Ahmadi, V., Benjelloun, S., El Kik, M., Sharma, T., Chi, H., & Zhou, W. (2020). Drug Governance: IoT-based Blockchain Implementation in the Pharmaceutical Supply Chain. *6th International Conference on Mobile and Secure Services, MOBISECSERV 2020*, 1–8. 10.1109/MobiSecServ48690.2020.9042950

Ahmad, M. (2014). Reliability Models for the Internet of Things: A Paradigm Shift. In *IEEE International Symposium on Software Reliability Engineering Workshops*. Naples, Italy: IEEE. 10.1109/ISSREW.2014.107

Akkaya, K., Guvenc, I., Aygun, R., Pala, N., & Kadri, A. (2015). *IoT-based occupancy monitoring techniques for energy-efficient smart buildings. In IEEE Wireless Communications and Networking Conference Workshops (WCNCW)*. IEEE.

Al Salami, S., Baek, J., Salah, K., & Damiani, E. (2016). Lightweight encryption for smart home. In *11th International Conference on Availability, Reliability and Security (ARES)* (pp. 382-388). Salzburg, Austria: IEEE.

Alaba, F. A., Othman, M., Hashem, I. A. T., & Alotaibi, F. (2017). Internet of Things security: A survey. *Journal of Network and Computer Applications*, *88*, 10–28. doi:10.1016/j.jnca.2017.04.002

Alangot, B., & Achuthan, K. (2017, August). Trace and track: Enhanced pharma supply chain infrastructure to prevent fraud. In *International Conference on Ubiquitous Communications and Network Computing* (pp. 189-195). Springer.

Al-Fuqaha, A., Guizani, M., Mohammadi, M., Aledhari, M., & Ayyash, M. (2015). Internet of things: A survey on enabling technologies, protocols, and applications. *IEEE Communications Surveys and Tutorials*, *17*(4), 2347–2376.

Al-Garadi, M. A., Mohamed, A., Al-Ali, A. K., Du, X., Ali, I., & Guizani, M. (2020). A survey of machine and deep learning methods for internet of things (IoT) security. *IEEE Communications Surveys and Tutorials*, *22*(3), 1646–1685.

Alhussein, M., Muhammad, G., Hossain, M. S., & Amin, S. U. (2018). Cognitive IoT-cloud integration for smart healthcare: Case study for epileptic seizure detection and monitoring. *Mobile Networks and Applications*, *23*(6), 1624–1635. doi:10.100711036-018-1113-0

Alkadi, O., Moustafa, N., Turnbull, B., & Choo, K. K. (2020). A deep blockchain framework-enabled collaborative intrusion detection for protecting iot and cloud networks. *IEEE Internet of Things Journal*, 1–12.

Almuhammadi, A. (2021, March). Review of the Role of IoT in Managing COVID-19 in Saudi Arabia. In *2021 8th International Conference on Computing for Sustainable Global Development (INDIACom)* (pp. 439-444). IEEE.

Alrashdi, I., Alqazzaz, A., Aloufi, E., Alharthi, R., Zohdy, M., & Ming, H. (2019). Ad-iot: Anomaly detection of iot cyberattacks in smart city using machine learning. In *9th Annual Computing and Communication Workshop and Conference (CCWC)* (pp. 305-310). 10.1109/CCWC.2019.8666450

Alsaffar, D. M., Almutiri, A. S., Alqahtani, B., Alamri, R. M., Alqahtani, H. F., Alqahtani, N. N., & Ali, A. A. (2020). Image Encryption Based on AES and RSA Algorithms. In *2020 3rd International Conference on Computer Applications & Information Security (ICCAIS)* (pp. 1-5). IEEE.

Al-Turjman, F., & Malekloo, A. (2019). Smart parking in IoT-enabled cities: A survey. *Sustainable Cities and Society*, *49*, 101608.

Amanullah, M. A., Habeeb, R. A. A., Nasaruddin, F. H., Gani, A., Ahmed, E., Nainar, A. S. M., ... Imran, M. (2020). Deep learning and big data technologies for IoT security. *Computer Communications*, *151*, 495–517.

Ambika, N. (2019). Energy-Perceptive Authentication in Virtual Private Networks Using GPS Data. In Security, Privacy and Trust in the IoT Environment (pp. 25-38). Springer.

Ambika, N. (2020). Methodical IoT-Based Information System in Healthcare. In C. Chakraborthy (Ed.), Smart Medical Data Sensing and IoT Systems Design in Healthcare (pp. 155-177). Bangalore, India: IGI Global.

Ambika, N. (2020). Encryption of Data in Cloud-Based Industrial IoT Devices. In S. Pal & V. G. Díaz (Eds.), *IoT: Security and Privacy Paradigm* (pp. 111–129). CRC Press, Taylor & Francis Group.

Ambika, N., & Raju, G. T. (2010). *Figment Authentication Scheme in Wireless Sensor Network. In Security Technology, Disaster Recovery and Business Continuity*. Springer, Berlin, Heidelberg.

Anand, R., Niyas, K., Gupta, S., & Revathy, S. (2020). Anti-counterfeit on medicine detection using blockchain technology. *Lecture Notes in Networks and Systems*, *89*, 1223–1232. doi:10.1007/978-981-15-0146-3_119

An, J., Li, W., Le Gall, F., Kovac, E., Kim, J., Taleb, T., & Song, J. (2019). EiF: Toward an elastic IoT fog framework for AI services. *IEEE Communications Magazine*, *57*(5), 28–33.

Anon. (2018). 2018 Major Pharma Packaging Trends. In *Pharmaceutical Processing*. Advantage Business Media.

Arksey, H., & O'Malley, L. (2005). Scoping studies: Towards a methodological framework. *International Journal of Social Research Methodology: Theory and Practice*, *8*(1), 19–32. doi:10.1080/1364557032000119616

Armitage, A., & Keeble-allen, D. (2008). Undertaking a Structured Literature Review or Structuring a Literature Review: Tales from the... by Academic Conferences and publishing International – Issuu. *7th European Conference on ...*, *6(2)*, 103–114.

Arom-oon, U. (2017). An AES cryptosystem for small scale network. In *2017 Third Asian Conference on Defence Technology (ACDT)* (pp. 49-53). IEEE. 10.1109/ACDT.2017.7886156

Atlam, H. F., & Wills, G. B. (2019). Technical aspects of blockchain and IoT. In Role of Blockchain Technology in IoT Applications (Vol. 115). doi:10.1016/bs.adcom.2018.10.006

Atlam, H. F., Walters, R. J., & Wills, G. B. (2018). Fog computing and the internet of things: A review. *Big Data and Cognitive Computing*, *2*(2), 10.

Atos. (2013). *The Future of In-store shopping*. https://atos.net/wpcontent/uploads/2017/10/01122013AscentWhitePaperFutureInStoreShopping.pdf

Atzori, L., Iera, A., & Morabito, G. (2010). The internet of things: A Survey. *Computer Networks*, *54*(15), 2787–2805. doi:10.1016/j.comnet.2010.05.010

Azimi, I., Anzanpour, A., Rahmani, A. M., Pahikkala, T., Levorato, M., Liljeberg, P., & Dutt, N. (2017). HiCH: Hierarchical fog-assisted computing architecture for healthcare IoT. *ACM Transactions on Embedded Computing Systems*, *16*(5s), 1–20.

Baluprithviraj, K. N., Bharathi, K. R., Chendhuran, S., & Lokeshwaran, P. (2021). Artificial Intelligence based Smart Door with Face Mask Detection. *IEEE International Conference on Artificial Intelligence and Smart Systems (ICAIS)*, 543-548. 10.1109/ICAIS50930.2021.9395807

Barchetti, U., Bucciero, A., De Blasi, M., Guido, A. L., Mainetti, L., & Patrono, L. (2010). Impact of RFID, EPC and B2B on traceability management of the pharmaceutical supply chain. *Proceeding - 5th International Conference on Computer Sciences and Convergence Information Technology, ICCIT 2010*, 58–63. 10.1109/ICCIT.2010.5711029

Belda, R., De Fez, I., Arce, P., & Guerri, J. C. (2018). Look ahead: a DASH adaptation algorithm. In *2018 IEEE International Symposium on Broadband Multimedia Systems and Broadcasting (BMSB)* (pp. 1-5). IEEE.

Benatia, M. A., De Sa, V. E., Baudry, D., Delalin, H., & Halftermeyer, P. (2018, March). A framework for big data driven product traceability system. In *2018 4th international conference on advanced technologies for signal and image processing (ATSIP)* (pp. 1-7). IEEE. 10.1109/ATSIP.2018.8364340

Ben-Daya, M., Hassini, E., & Bahroun, Z. (2019). Internet of things and supply chain management: A literature review. *International Journal of Production Research*, *57*(15–16), 4719–4742. doi:10.1080/00207543.2017.1402140

Bento documentation for conversion from mp4 to HLS. (n.d.). https://www.bento4.com/documentation/mp42hls/

Bhat, B., Ali, A. W., & Gupta, A. (2015). DES and AES performance evaluation. In *International Conference on Computing, Communication & Automation* (pp. 887-890). IEEE. 10.1109/CCAA.2015.7148500

Bhattacharya, S., Maddikunta, P. K. R., Pham, Q. V., Gadekallu, T. R., Chowdhary, C. L., Alazab, M., & Piran, M. J. (2021). Deep learning and medical image processing for coronavirus (COVID-19) pandemic: A survey. *Sustainable Cities and Society*, *65*, 102589.

Bocek, T., Rodrigues, B. B., Strasser, T., & Stiller, B. (2017). Blockchains everywhere - A use-case of blockchains in the pharma supply-chain. *Proceedings of the IM 2017 - 2017 IFIP/IEEE International Symposium on Integrated Network and Service Management*, 772–777. 10.23919/INM.2017.7987376

Bok, B. T. (2016). *Innovating the retail industry: an IoT approach*. University of Twente Student Theses. https://essay.utwente.nl/69982/

Botcha, K. M., & Chakravarthy, V. V. (2019, June). Enhancing traceability in pharmaceutical supply chain using Internet of Things (IoT) and blockchain. In *2019 IEEE International Conference on Intelligent Systems and Green Technology (ICISGT)* (pp. 45-453). IEEE. 10.1109/ICISGT44072.2019.00025

Bryatov, S. R., & Borodinov, A. (2019, May). Blockchain technology in the pharmaceutical supply chain: Researching a business model based on Hyperledger Fabric. In *Proceedings of the International Conference on Information Technology and Nanotechnology (ITNT)* (pp. 21-24). 10.18287/1613-0073-2019-2416-134-140

BudimanBadarsyah, I., & Rosmansyah, Y. (2014). Digital rights management with ABAC implementation to improve enterprise document protection. In *2014 8th International Conference on Telecommunication Systems Services and Applications (TSSA)* (pp. 1-6). IEEE.

Chakkarwar, V., & Tamane, S. (2020). Social Media Analytics during Pandemic for Covid19 using Topic Modeling. *IEEE International Conference on Smart Innovations in Design, Environment, Management, Planning and Computing (ICSIDEMPC)*, 279-282. 10.1109/ICSIDEMPC49020.2020.9299617

Chakraborty, P., Dev, S., & Naganur, R. H. (2015). Dynamic http live streaming method for live feeds. In *2015 International Conference on Computational Intelligence and Communication Networks (CICN)* (pp. 1394-1398). IEEE. 10.1109/CICN.2015.333

Chamola, V., Hassija, V., Gupta, V., & Guizani, M. (2020). A Comprehensive Review of the COVID-19 Pandemic and the Role of IoT, Drones, AI, Blockchain, and 5G in Managing its Impact. *IEEE Access: Practical Innovations, Open Solutions*, 8, 90225–90265. doi:10.1109/ACCESS.2020.2992341

Chandra, Y. U. (2019). Smart E-badge for Student Activities in Smart Campus. *IEEE International Conference on ICT for Smart Society (ICISS)*, 1-6. 10.1109/ICISS48059.2019.8969806

Chanson, M., Bogner, A., Bilgeri, D., Fleisch, E., & Wortmann, F. (2019). Blockchain for the IoT: Privacy-preserving protection of sensor data. *Journal of the Association for Information Systems*, 20(9), 1271–1307. doi:10.17705/1jais.00567

Chen, C.-C., Su, W.-T., Hung, M.-H., & Lin, Z.-H. (2018). Map–Reduce–Style Job Offloading Using Historical Manufacturing Behavior for Edge Devices in Smart Factory. *IEEE Robotics and Automation Letters*, 3(4), 2918–2925. doi:10.1109/LRA.2018.2847746

Chen, D. (2021). All-round and Accurate Online Education Model amid COVID19. *IEEE/WIC/ACM International Joint Conference on Web Intelligence and Intelligent Agent Technology (WI-IAT)*, 713-717. 10.1109/WIIAT50758.2020.00109

Chen, G., Xu, B., Lu, M., & Chen, N. S. (2018). Exploring blockchain technology and its potential applications for education. *Smart Learning Environments*, 5(1), 1. doi:10.118640561-017-0050-x

Chiacchio, F., Compagno, L., D'Urso, D., Velardita, L., & Sandner, P. (2020). A decentralized application for the traceability process in the pharma industry. *Procedia Manufacturing, 42*, 362–369.

Chiang, M., & Zhang, T. (2016). Fog and IoT: An overview of research opportunities. *IEEE Internet of Things Journal*, 3(6), 854-864.

Chien, C.-F., & Chen, C.-C. (2020). Data-Driven Framework for Tool Health Monitoring and Maintenance Strategy for Smart Manufacturing. *IEEE Transactions on Semiconductor Manufacturing*, 33(4), 644–652. doi:10.1109/TSM.2020.3024284

Chifor, B. C., Bica, I., Patriciu, V. V., & Pop, F. (2018). A security authorization scheme for smart home Internet of Things devices. *Future Generation Computer Systems*, 86, 740–749.

Chitre, M., Sapkal, S., Adhikari, A., & Mulla, S. (2019). Monitoring counterfeit drugs using counterchain. *2019 6th IEEE International Conference on Advances in Computing, Communication and Control, ICAC3 2019.* 10.1109/ICAC347590.2019.9036794

Choi, C., & Choi, J. (2019). Ontology-based security context reasoning for power IoT-cloud security service. *IEEE Access: Practical Innovations, Open Solutions*, 7, 110510–110517. doi:10.1109/ACCESS.2019.2933859

Chui, M., Manyika, J., Miremadi, M., Henke, N., Chung, R., Nel, P., & Malhotra, S. (2018). *Notes from the AI frontier. Insights from hundreds of use cases.* McKinsey & Company.

Clauson, K. A., Breeden, E. A., Davidson, C., & Mackey, T. K. (2018). Leveraging Blockchain Technology to Enhance Supply Chain Management in Healthcare: An Exploration of Challenges and Opportunities in the Health Supply Chain. *Blockchain in Healthcare Today*, 1(0), 1–12.

ComQi. (2015, July). *How Iot is Reinventing Retail.* http://www.comqi.com/wpcontent/uploads/2015/08/How-IoT-is-ReinventingRetail.pdf

Crisostomo, A. S. I., Balida, D. A. R., & Gustilo, R. C. (2020). K- means Clustering of Online Learning Profiles of Higher Education Teachers and Students Amid Covid19 Pandemic. *IEEE International Conference on Humanoid, Nanotechnology, Information Technology, Communication and Control, Environment, and Management (HNICEM),* 1-5. 10.1109/HNICEM51456.2020.9400036

Da Xu, L., He, W., & Li, S. (2014). Internet of things in industries: A survey. *IEEE Transactions on Industrial Informatics, 10*(4), 2233–2243. doi:10.1109/TII.2014.2300753

Dastjerdi, A. V., Gupta, H., Calheiros, R. N., Ghosh, S. K., & Buyya, R. (2016). Fog computing: Principles, architectures, and applications. In *Internet of things* (pp. 61–75). Morgan Kaufmann.

De Aguiar, E. J., Faiçal, B. S., Krishnamachari, B., & Ueyama, J. (2020). A Survey of Blockchain-Based Strategies for Healthcare. *ACM Computing Surveys, 53*(2), 1–27. doi:10.1145/3376915

Delloite. (2018). *Media & Entertainment Industry Outlook.* Available: https://www2.deloitte.com/us/en/pages/technology-mediaandtelecommunications/articles/media-and-entertainmentindustry-outlook-trends.html

Desai, M. R., & Toravi, S. (2017). A Smart Sensor Interface for Smart Homes and Heart Beat Monitoring using WSN in IoT Environment. *IEEE International Conference on Current Trends in Computer, Electrical, Electronics and Communication (CTCEEC),* 74-77. 10.1109/CTCEEC.2017.8455124

Diro, A. A., & Chilamkurti, N. (2018). Distributed attack detection scheme using deep learning approach for Internet of Things. *Future Generation Computer Systems, 82,* 761–768. doi:10.1016/j.future.2017.08.043

Diro, A., & Chilamkurti, N. (2018). Leveraging LSTM networks for attack detection in fog-to-things communications. *IEEE Communications Magazine, 56*(9), 124–130. doi:10.1109/MCOM.2018.1701270

Dong, B., Chen, Z., Tang, L.-A., Chen, H., Wang, H., Zhang, K., Lin, Y., & Li, Z. (2021). Anomalous Event Sequence Detection. *IEEE Intelligent Systems, 36*(3), 5–13. doi:10.1109/MIS.2020.3041174

Dorri, A., Kanhere, S. S., Jurdak, R., & Gauravaram, P. (2017). *Blockchain for IoT security and privacy: The case study of a smart home. In IEEE international conference on pervasive computing and communications workshops.* IEEE.

Doukas, C., & Maglogiannis, I. (2012). Bringing IoT and Cloud Computing towards Pervasive Healthcare. 6 international conference on innovative mobile and internet services in ubiquitous computing.

Dwivedi, S.K., Amin, R., & Vollala, S. (2020b). Blockchain based secured information sharing protocol in supply chain management system with key distribution mechanism. *Journal of Information Security and Applications, 54.*

Dwivedi, A. D., Srivastava, G., Dhar, S., & Singh, R. (2019). A decentralized privacy-preserving healthcare blockchain for IoT. *Sensors (Basel), 19*(2), 1–17. doi:10.339019020326 PMID:30650612

Elhoseny, M., Shankar, K., Lakshmanaprabu, S. K., Maseleno, A., & Arunkumar, N. (2018). Hybrid optimization with cryptography encryption for medical image security in Internet of Things. *Neural Computing & Applications,* 1–15. doi:10.100700521-018-3801-x

Elshamy, A. M., Abdelghany, M. A., Alhamad, A. Q., Hamed, H. F., Kelash, H. M., & Hussein, A. I. (2017). Secure implementation for video streams based on fully and permutation encryption techniques. In *2017 International Conference on Computer and Applications (ICCA)* (pp. 50-55). IEEE. 10.1109/COMAPP.2017.8079738

Elsisi, M., Tran, M.-Q., Mahmoud, K., Mansour, D.-E. A., Lehtonen, M., & Darwish, M. M. F. (2021). Towards Secured Online Monitoring for Digitalized GIS Against Cyber-Attacks Based on IoT and Machine Learning. *IEEE Access: Practical Innovations, Open Solutions, 9,* 78415–78427. doi:10.1109/ACCESS.2021.3083499

Essien, A., & Giannetti, C. (2020). A Deep Learning Model for Smart Manufacturing Using Convolutional LSTM Neural Network Autoencoders. *IEEE Transactions on Industrial Informatics*, *16*(9), 6069–6078. doi:10.1109/TII.2020.2967556

Exoplayer documentation. (n.d.). https://exoplayer.dev/hls.html

Farahani, B., Firouzi, F., Chang, V., Badaroglu, M., Constant, N., & Mankodiya, K. (2018). Towards fog-driven IoT eHealth: Promises and challenges of IoT in medicine and healthcare. *Future Generation Computer Systems*, *78*, 659–676.

Fernández-Caramés, T. M., & Fraga-Lamas, P. (2019). A Review on the Application of Blockchain to the Next Generation of Cybersecure Industry 4.0 Smart Factories. *IEEE Access: Practical Innovations, Open Solutions*, *7*, 45201–45218. doi:10.1109/ACCESS.2019.2908780

FFMPEG documentation. (n.d.). https://ffmpeg.org/ffmpeg-formats.html

Floissac, N., & L'Hyver, Y. (2011). From AES-128 to AES-192 and AES-256, how to adapt differential fault analysis attacks on key expansion. In *2011 Workshop on Fault Diagnosis and Tolerance in Cryptography* (pp. 43-53). IEEE. 10.1109/FDTC.2011.15

Gams, M., Gu, I. Y. H., Härmä, A., Muñoz, A., & Tam, V. (2019). Artificial intelligence and ambient intelligence. *Journal of Ambient Intelligence and Smart Environments*, *11*(1), 71–86.

Garcia, D., Astorga, J., & Jacob, E. (2018). Innovating at the Connected Industry: SDN and NFV Experiences and Lessons Learned. *2018 IEEE 26th International Conference on Network Protocols (ICNP)*, 245–246. 10.1109/ICNP.2018.00035

Garg, H., & Dave, M. (2019). Securing IoT Devices and SecurelyConnecting the Dots Using REST API and Middleware. *International Conference on Internet of Things: Smart Innovation and Usages (IoT-SIU)*, 1-6. 10.1109/IoT-SIU.2019.8777334

Gawade, P., & Joshi, P. S. (2020). Personification and Safety during pandemic of COVID19 using Machine Learning. *IEEE International Conference on Electronics, Communication and Aerospace Technology (ICECA)*, 1582-1587. 10.1109/ICECA49313.2020.9297555

Gill, H. (n.d.). *From Vision to Reality: Cyber-Physical Systems*. Academic Press.

Global Retail Trends. (2018). Available https://assets.kpmg/content/dam/kpmg/xx/pdf/2018/03/globalretail-trends-2018.pdf

Gluhak, A., Krco, S., Nati, M., Pfisterer, D., Mitton, N., & Razafindralambo, T. (2011). A survey on facilities for experimental internet of things research. *IEEE Communications Magazine*, *49*(11), 58–67.

Goudarzi, M., Wu, H., Palaniswami, M., & Buyya, R. (2020). An application placement technique for concurrent IoT applications in edge and fog computing environments. *IEEE Transactions on Mobile Computing*, *20*(4), 1298–1311.

Greer, C., Burns, M., Wollman, D., & Griffor, E. (2019). Cyber-physical systems and internet of things (NIST SP 1900-202; p. NIST SP 1900-202). National Institute of Standards and Technology. doi:10.6028/NIST.SP.1900-202

Gregory, J. (2015). *The Internet of Things: Revolutionizing the Retail Industry*. Accenture.

Gupta, A. K., & Johari, R. (2019). IOT based Electrical Device Surveillance and Control System. *IEEE International Conference on Internet of Things: Smart Innovation and Usages (IoT-SIU)*, 1-5. 10.1109/IoT-SIU.2019.8777342

Hameed, K. (2021). An Approach to design Human Assisting Prototype Robot for providing Fast and hygienically secure environment to Clinical professionals in order to fight against COVID19 in Hospitals, *IEEE International IOT, Electronics and Mechatronics Conference (IEMTRONICS)*, 1-7. 10.1109/IEMTRONICS52119.2021.9422658

Han, S., Go, Y., Noh, H., & Song, H. (2019). Cooperative server-client http adaptive streaming system for live video streaming. In *2019 International Conference on Information Networking (ICOIN)* (pp. 176-180). IEEE. 10.1109/ICOIN.2019.8718151

Haritha, D., Swaroop, N., & Mounika, M. (2020). Prediction of COVID-19 Cases Using CNN with X-rays. *IEEE International Conference on Computing, Communication and Security (ICCCS)*, 1-6. 10.1109/ICCCS49678.2020.9276753

Harris, R. M. (2020). Data Warehousing and Decision Support System Effectiveness Demonstrated in Service Recovery During COVID19 Health Pandemic. *IEEE International Conference on Open Source Systems and Technologies (ICOSST)*, 1-5. 10.1109/ICOSST51357.2020.9333019

Hasan, H., AlHadhrami, E., AlDhaheri, A., Salah, K., & Jayaraman, R. (2019). Smart contract-based approach for efficient shipment management. *Computers and Industrial Engineering*, *136*(July), 149–159.

Hassan, H. E. R., Tahoun, M., & ElTaweel, G. S. (2020). A robust computational DRM framework for protecting multimedia contents using AES and ECC. *Alexandria Engineering Journal*, *59*(3), 1275–1286. doi:10.1016/j.aej.2020.02.020

Hastig, G. M., & Sodhi, M. S. (2020). Blockchain for Supply Chain Traceability: Business Requirements and Critical Success Factors. *Production and Operations Management*, *29*(4), 935–954. doi:10.1111/poms.13147

Haughwout, J. (2018). Tracking medicine by transparent blockchain. *Pharmaceutical Processing*, *33*(1), 24–26.

Hemalatha, K., Yadav, P. K., & Ramasubramanian, N. (2015). Adaptive bitrate transcoding for power efficient video streaming in mobile devices. In *2015 3rd International Conference on Signal Processing, Communication and Networking (ICSCN)* (pp. 1-5). IEEE. 10.1109/ICSCN.2015.7219825

Henderi. (2020). Model Decision Support System for Diagnosis COVID-19 Using Forward Chaining: A Case in Indonesia. *8th International Conference on Cyber and IT Service Management (CITSM)*, 1-4. 10.1109/CITSM50537.2020.9268853

Henning Kagermann. (2011, April 1). *Industrie 4.0: Mit dem Internet der Dinge auf dem Weg zur 4. industriellen Revolution - ingenieur.de*. Ingenieur.de - Jobbörse Und Nachrichtenportal Für Ingenieure. https://www.ingenieur.de/technik/fachbereiche/produktion/industrie-40-mit-internet-dinge-weg-4-industriellen-revolution/

Hindrayani, K. M., Fahrudin, T. M., Prismahardi Aji, R., & Safitri, E. M. (2020). Indonesian Stock Price Prediction including Covid19 Era Using Decision Tree Regression. *IEEE International Seminar on Research of Information Technology and Intelligent Systems (ISRITI)*, 344-347. 10.1109/ISRITI51436.2020.9315484

HLS Article by Apple Inc. (n.d.). https://developer.apple.com/streaming/

Hongsongkiat, T., & Chongstitvatana, P. (2014). AES implementation for RFID Tags: The hardware and software approaches. In *2014 International Computer Science and Engineering Conference (ICSEC)* (pp. 118-123). IEEE. 10.1109/ICSEC.2014.6978180

Howe, K. (2014). *Beyond Big Data: How Next-Generation Shopper Analytics and the Internet of Everything Transform the Retail Business*. Cisco.

Huang, Y., Wu, J., & Long, C. (2018). Drugledger: A practical blockchain system for drug traceability and regulation. *Proceedings - IEEE 2018 International Congress on Cybermatics: 2018 IEEE Conferences on Internet of Things, Green Computing and Communications, Cyber, Physical and Social Computing, Smart Data, Blockchain, Computer and Information Technology, iThings/Gree.*, 1137–1144. 10.1109/Cybermatics_2018.2018.00206

Hu, P., Dhelim, S., Ning, H., & Qiu, T. (2017). Survey on fog computing: Architecture, key technologies, applications and open issues. *Journal of Network and Computer Applications*, *98*, 27–42.

Hyperledger. (2019). *Case Study: How Walmart brought unprecedented transparency to the food supply chain with Hyperledger Fabric Challenge.* Author.

Intizar Ali, M., Patel, P., & Breslin, J., Harik, R., & Sheth, A. (2021). Cognitive Digital Twins for Smart Manufacturing. *IEEE Intelligent Systems*, *36*(2), 96–100. doi:10.1109/MIS.2021.3062437

Jain, N., Shrivastava, H., & Moghe, A. A. (2020). Production-ready environment for HLS Player using FFmpeg with automation on S3 Bucket using Ansible. In *2nd International Conference on Data, Engineering and Applications (IDEA)* (pp. 1-4). IEEE.

Jamil, F., Hang, L., Kim, K., & Kim, D. (2019). A novel medical blockchain model for drug supply chain integrity management in a smart hospital. Electronics, 8(5). doi:10.3390/electronics8050505

Jangir, S., Muzumdar, A., Jaiswal, A., Modi, C. N., Chandel, S., & Vyjayanthi, C. (2019). A Novel Framework for Pharmaceutical Supply Chain Management using Distributed Ledger and Smart Contracts. *2019 10th International Conference on Computing, Communication and Networking Technologies, ICCCNT 2019.* 10.1109/ICCCNT45670.2019.8944829

Jansen, C., & Jeschke, S. (2018). Mitigating risks of digitalization through managed industrial security services. *AI & Society*, *33*(2), 163–173. doi:10.100700146-018-0812-1

Javali, C., & Revadigar, G. (2012). Wireless Smart Badge based on IEEE 802.15.4 LRWPAN. *IEEE World Congress on Information and Communication Technologies*, 367-372. 10.1109/WICT.2012.6409104

Jha, S., Kumar, R., Chatterjee, J. M., & Khari, M. (2019). Collaborative handshaking approaches between internet of computing and internet of things towards a smart world: A review from 2009–2017. *Telecommunication Systems*, *70*(4), 617–634. doi:10.100711235-018-0481-x

João, D. V., Lodetti, P. Z., dos Santos, A. B., Izumida Martins, M. A., De Francisci, S., & Brandao Almeida, J. F. (2021). A Smart Badge Implementation on Electrical Power Sector for Safety Improvement for Workforce - A Study Case. *IEEE Power & Energy Society Innovative Smart Grid Technologies Conference*, 1–5. Advance online publication. doi:10.1109/ISGT49243.2021.9372220

Jugović, D., & Banduka, M. L. (2017). Extending and integration of HLS software support in Android based systems. In *2017 25th Telecommunication Forum (TELFOR)* (pp. 1-4). IEEE.

K. (2018). A Future's Dominant Technology Blockchain: Digital Transformation. *IEEE International Conference on Computing, Power and Communication Technologies 2018 (GUCON 2018).*

Kabir, S. (2021). Internet of Things and Safety Assurance of Cooperative Cyber-Physical Systems: Opportunities and Challenges. *IEEE Internet of Things Magazine*, *4*(2), 74–78. doi:10.1109/IOTM.0001.2000062

Kamble, S.S., Gunasekaran, A., & Sharma, R. (2020). Modeling the blockchain enabled traceability in agriculture supply chain. *International Journal of Information Management*, *52*(June).

Khant, S., & Patel, A. (2021). COVID19 Remote Engineering Education: Learning of an Embedded System with Practical Perspective. *IEEE International Conference on Innovative Practices in Technology and Management (ICIPTM)*, 15-19. 10.1109/ICIPTM52218.2021.9388360

Khari, M., Garg, A. K., Gandomi, A. H., Gupta, R., Patan, R., & Balusamy, B. (2019). Securing data in Internet of Things (IoT) using cryptography and steganography techniques. *IEEE Transactions on Systems, Man, and Cybernetics. Systems*, *50*(1), 73–80. doi:10.1109/TSMC.2019.2903785

Kharrufa, H., Al-Kashoash, H. A., & Kemp, A. H. (2019). RPL-based routing protocols in IoT applications: A Review. *IEEE Sensors Journal*, *19*(15), 5952–5967.

Kim, H. M., & Laskowski, M. (2018b). Toward an ontology-driven blockchain design for supply-chain provenance. *Intelligent Systems in Accounting, Finance & Management, 25*(1), 18–27. doi:10.1002/isaf.1424

Kim, S., & Lee, I. (2018). IoT device security based on proxy re-encryption. *Journal of Ambient Intelligence and Humanized Computing, 9*(4), 1267–1273. doi:10.100712652-017-0602-5

Kiss, M., Breda, G., & Muha, L. (2019). Information security aspects of Industry 4.0. *Procedia Manufacturing, 32*, 848–855. doi:10.1016/j.promfg.2019.02.293

Kovacevic, M., Kovacevic, B., Stefanovic, D., & Novak, S. (2015). Automated monitoring of HTTP live streaming QoE factors on Android STB. In *2015 IEEE 1st International Workshop on Consumer Electronics (CE WS)* (pp. 72-75). IEEE. 10.1109/CEWS.2015.7867159

Krishnamoorthy, S., Dua, A., & Gupta, S. (2021). Role of emerging technologies in future IoT-driven Healthcare 4.0 technologies: A survey, current challenges and future directions. *Journal of Ambient Intelligence and Humanized Computing*, 1–47.

Kshetri, N. (2018). 1 Blockchain's roles in meeting key supply chain management objectives. *International Journal of Information Management, 39*(June), 80–89. . doi:10.1016/j.ijinfomgt.2017.12.005

Kuchta, M., & Miklošík, A. (2017). Evolution of digital video consumption patterns. *Communication Today, 8*(2), 58–69.

Kumar, R., & Tripathi, R. (2019). Traceability of counterfeit medicine supply chain through Blockchain. *2019 11th International Conference on Communication Systems and Networks, COMSNETS 2019*, 568–570. 10.1109/COMSNETS.2019.8711418

Kumar, A., Choudhary, D., Raju, M. S., Chaudhary, D. K., & Sagar, R. K. (2019). Combating counterfeit drugs: A quantitative analysis on cracking down the fake drug industry by using blockchain technology. *Proceedings of the 9th International Conference On Cloud Computing, Data Science and Engineering, Confluence 2019.*, 174–178. 10.1109/CONFLUENCE.2019.8776891

Kumar, A., Sharma, K., Singh, H., Naugriya, S. G., Gill, S. S., & Buyya, R. (2021). A drone-based networked system and methods for combating coronavirus disease (COVID-19) pandemic. *Future Generation Computer Systems, 115*, 1–19.

Kumari, R., & Saini, K. (2021). Advanced Automobile Manufacturing: An Industry 4.0. *15th INDIACom*, 899-904. Doi:10.1109/INDIACom51348.2021.00161

Kumari, K., & Saini, K. (2020). Data handling & drug traceability: Blockchain meets healthcare to combat counterfeit drugs. *International Journal of Scientific and Technology Research, 9*(3), 728–731.

Kumar, Y., Munjal, R., & Sharma, H. (2011). Comparison of symmetric and asymmetric cryptography with existing vulnerabilities and countermeasures. *International Journal of Computer Science and Management Studies, 11*(03), 60–63.

Lalmuanawma, S., Hussain, J., & Chhakchhuak, L. (2020). Applications of machine learning and artificial intelligence for Covid-19 (SARS-CoV-2) pandemic: A review. *Chaos, Solitons, and Fractals*, 110059.

Lawrence, C. (2016, May). *How IoT is changing the fashion retail experience.* https://readwrite.com/2016/05/17/how-iot-is-changingthe-fashion-retail-experience-vr4/

Lee, C. K. M., Huo, Y. Z., Zhang, S. Z., & Ng, K. K. H. (2020). Design of a Smart Manufacturing System With the Application of Multi-Access Edge Computing and Blockchain Technology. *IEEE Access: Practical Innovations, Open Solutions, 8*, 28659–28667. doi:10.1109/ACCESS.2020.2972284

Lee, I., & Lee, K. (2015). The Internet of Things (IoT): Applications, investments, and challenges for enterprises. *Business Horizons*, *58*(4), 431–440. doi:10.1016/j.bushor.2015.03.008

Lee, N. Y., & Lee, T. Y. (2009). User friendly digital rights management system based on smart cards. In *2009 Fifth International Conference on Intelligent Information Hiding and Multimedia Signal Processing* (pp. 869-872). IEEE. 10.1109/IIH-MSP.2009.130

Lemley, J., Bazrafkan, S., & Corcoran, P. (2017). Deep Learning for Consumer Devices and Services: Pushing the limits for machine learning, artificial intelligence, and computer vision. *IEEE Consumer Electronics Magazine*, *6*(2), 48–56. doi:10.1109/MCE.2016.2640698

Letaief, K. B., Chen, W., Shi, Y., Zhang, J., & Zhang, Y. J. A. (2019). The roadmap to 6G: AI empowered wireless networks. *IEEE Communications Magazine*, *57*(8), 84–90.

Liang, X., Zhao, J., Shetty, S., & Li, D. (2017). Towards data assurance and resilience in IoT using blockchain. In *IEEE Military Communications Conference (MILCOM* (pp. 261-266). Baltimore, MD: IEEE. 10.1109/MILCOM.2017.8170858

Li, C. H. (2021). Development of IoT-based Smart Recycling Machine to collect the wasted Non-woven Fabric Face Mask (NFM). *IEEE International Symposium on Product Compliance Engineering-Asia (ISPCE-CN)*, 1-5. 10.1109/ISPCE-CN51288.2020.9321851

Lin, J., Yu, W., Zhang, N., Yang, X., Zhang, H., & Zhao, W. (2017). A survey on internet of things: Architecture, enabling technologies, security and privacy, and applications. *IEEE Internet of Things Journal*, *4*(5), 1125–1142.

Liu, C., Ren, W., Zhang, B., & Lv, C. (2011). The application of soil temperature measurement by LM35 temperature sensors. *IEEE Proceedings of International Conference on Electronic & Mechanical Engineering and Information Technology*, 1825-1828. 10.1109/EMEIT.2011.6023459

Liu, B., Yu, X. L., Chen, S., Xu, X., & Zhu, L. (2017). Blockchain based data integrity service framework for IoT data. In *IEEE International Conference on Web Services (ICWS)* (pp. 468-475). Honolulu, HI: IEEE. 10.1109/ICWS.2017.54

Liu, S., Yu, J., Xiao, Y., Wan, Z., Wang, S., & Yan, B. (2020, May). BC-SABE: Blockchain-aided Searchable Attribute-based Encryption for Cloud-IoT. *IEEE Internet of Things Journal*, *7*(9), 1–17. doi:10.1109/JIOT.2020.2993231

López, T. S., Ranasinghe, D. C., Harrison, M., & McFarlane, D. (2012). Adding sense to the Internet of Things. *Personal and Ubiquitous Computing*, *16*(3), 291–308.

Mahmud, R., Kotagiri, R., & Buyya, R. (2018). Fog computing: A taxonomy, survey and future directions. In *Internet of everything* (pp. 103–130). Springer.

Mantravadi, S., Schnyder, R., Møller, C., & Brunoe, T. D. (2020). Securing IT/OT Links for Low Power IIoT Devices: Design Considerations for Industry 4.0. *IEEE Access: Practical Innovations, Open Solutions*, *8*, 200305–200321. doi:10.1109/ACCESS.2020.3035963

Manyika, J., Chui, M., Bisson, P., Woetzel, J., Dobbs, R., Bughin, J., & Aharon, D. (2015). *The Internet of Things: Mapping the Value Beyond the Hype*. McKinsey Global Institute.

Manyika, J., Chui, M., Brad, B., Bughin, J., Dobbs, R., Roxburgh, C., & Hung Byers, A. (2011). *Big data: The next frontier for innovation, competition, and productivity*. McKinsey Global Institute.

Manzoor, A., Liyanage, M., Braeke, A., Kanhere, S. S., & Ylianttila, M. (2019). Blockchain based proxy re-encryption scheme for secure IoT data sharing. In *International Conference on Blockchain and Cryptocurrency (ICBC)* (pp. 99-103). IEEE. 10.1109/BLOC.2019.8751336

Maqsood, F., Ahmed, M., Ali, M. M., & Shah, M. A. (2017). Cryptography: A comparative analysis for modern techniques. *International Journal of Advanced Computer Science and Applications, 8*(6), 442–448. doi:10.14569/IJACSA.2017.080659

Marbury, D. (2019). How Blockchain Can Reduce Waste, Fraud in Pharmacy. *Drug Topics, 163*(1), 30–31.

Markarian, J. (2018). Modernizing Pharma Manufacturing. *Pharmaceutical Technology, 42*(4), 20–25.

Masek, P., Masek, J., Frantik, P., Fujdiak, R., Ometov, A., Hosek, J., Andreev, S., Mlynek, P., & Misurec, J. (2016). A Harmonized Perspective on Transportation Management in Smart Cities: The Novel IoT-Driven Environment for Road Traffic Modeling. *Sensors (Basel), 16*(11), 1872. doi:10.339016111872 PMID:27834796

McKinsey Global Institute (MGI). (2016). *Digital Europe: Pushing the Frontier, Capturin the Benefits*. McKinsey Global Institute.

Meurer, R. S., Mück, T. R., & Fröhlich, A. A. (2013). An Implementation of the AES cipher using HLS. In *2013 III Brazilian Symposium on Computing Systems Engineering* (pp. 113-118). IEEE. 10.1109/SBESC.2013.36

Meyliana & Surjandy. (2019). Success factor of implementation blockchain technology in pharmaceutical industry: A literature review. *2019 6th International Conference on Information Technology, Computer and Electrical Engineering, ICITACEE 2019.*

Mikroyannidis, A., Domingue, J., Bachler, M., & Quick, K. (2018). Smart Blockchain Badges for Data Science Education. *IEEE Frontiers in Education Conference (FIE)*, 1-5. 10.1109/FIE.2018.8659012

Miladinovic, I., & Schefer-Wenzl, S. (2018). NFV enabled IoT architecture for an operating room environment. *IEEE World Forum on Internet of Things (WF-IoT)*, 98-102. 10.1109/WF-IoT.2018.8355128

Miorandi, D., Sicari, S., Pellegrini De, F., & Chlamtac, I. (2012). *Internet of Things; Vision, applications and research challenges*. Academic Press.

Mnaoui, Y., Najoua, A., & Ouajji, H. (2020). Analyzing COVID19 Crisis in North Africa: Using Health Indicators. *IEEE International Conference on Electronics, Control, Optimization and Computer Science (ICECOCS)*, 1-5. 10.1109/ICECOCS50124.2020.9314612

Mohapatra, B., & Krishnan, V. (2018). *Customer experience for retail Industry*. https://www.infosys.com/Oracle/white-papers/Documents/customer-experience-retail-industry.pdf

Molina, J. C., Delgado, D. T., & Tarazona, G. (2019). Using blockchain for traceability in the drug supply chain. *Communications in Computer and Information Science, 1027*, 536–548. doi:10.1007/978-3-030-21451-7_46

Mukesh, P. S., Pandya, M. S., & Pathak, S. (2013). Enhancing AES algorithm with arithmetic coding. In *2013 International Conference on Green Computing, Communication and Conservation of Energy (ICGCE)* (pp. 83-86). IEEE. 10.1109/ICGCE.2013.6823404

Mukherjee, M., Shu, L., & Wang, D. (2018). Survey of fog computing: Fundamental, network applications, and research challenges. *IEEE Communications Surveys and Tutorials, 20*(3), 1826–1857.

Muladi. (2020). Development of The Personnel Monitoring System Using Mobile Application and Real-Time Database During the COVID19 Pandemic. *IEEE International Seminar on Research of Information Technology and Intelligent Systems (ISRITI)*, 371-376. 10.1109/ISRITI51436.2020.9315377

Musamih, A., Salah, K., Jayaraman, R., Arshad, J., Debe, M., Al-Hammadi, Y., & Ellahham, S. (2021). A Blockchain-Based Approach for Drug Traceability in Healthcare Supply Chain. *IEEE Access: Practical Innovations, Open Solutions, 9*, 9728–9743. doi:10.1109/ACCESS.2021.3049920

Mushtaq, M. F., Jamel, S., Disina, A. H., Pindar, Z. A., Shakir, N. S. A., & Deris, M. M. (2017). A survey on the cryptographic encryption algorithms. *International Journal of Advanced Computer Science and Applications, 8*(11), 333–344.

Nagaraj, A. (2021). Introduction to Sensors in IoT and Cloud Computing Applications. Bentham Science Publishers. do i:10.2174/97898114793591210101

Naha, R. K., Garg, S., Georgakopoulos, D., Jayaraman, P. P., Gao, L., Xiang, Y., & Ranjan, R. (2018). Fog computing: Survey of trends, architectures, requirements, and research directions. *IEEE Access: Practical Innovations, Open Solutions, 6*, 47980–48009.

Narasimha Murthy, D., & Vijaya Kumar, B. (2015). Internet Of Things (Iot): Is Iot A Disruptive Technology Or A Disruptive Business Model? *Indian Journal of Marketing, 45*(8), 18–27. doi:10.17010/ijom/2015/v45/i8/79915

Nasution, T. H., & Harahap, L. A. (2020). Predict the Percentage Error of LM35 Temperature Sensor Readings using Simple Linear Regression Analysis. *IEEE International Conference on Electrical, Telecommunication and Computer Engineering (ELTICOM)*, 242-245. 10.1109/ELTICOM50775.2020.9230472

Nayyar, S. (2019). *The Impact Of Internet Of Things On The Fashion Retail Sector Bringing Experience To Retail.* . doi:10.13140/RG.2.2.32135.04008

News from the Lab Archive: January 2004 to September 2015. (n.d.). Retrieved June 23, 2021, from https://archive.f-secure.com/weblog/archives/00002718.html

Ni, J., Zhang, K., Lin, X., & Shen, X. (2017). Securing fog computing for internet of things applications: Challenges and solutions. *IEEE Communications Surveys and Tutorials, 20*(1), 601–628.

Obour Agyekum, K. O., Xia, Q., Sifah, E. B., Gao, J., Xia, H. D., & Guizani, M. (2019). A Secured Proxy-Based Data Sharing Module in IoT Environments Using Blockchain. *Sensors (Basel), 19*(5), 1–20. doi:10.339019051235 PMID:30862110

Okoli, C. (2015). A Guide to Conducting a Standalone Systematic Literature Review. *Communications of the Association for Information Systems, 37*(1), 879–910. doi:10.17705/1CAIS.03743

Olson-Hazboun, S. K., Howe, P. D., & Leiserowitz, A. (2018). 'The influence of extractive activities on public support for renewable energy policy'. *Energy Policy, 123*, 117–126. doi:10.1016/j.enpol.2018.08.044

Oyman, O., & Singh, S. (2012). Quality of experience for HTTP adaptive streaming services. *IEEE Communications Magazine, 50*(4), 20–27. doi:10.1109/MCOM.2012.6178830

Panda, M. (2019). Text And Image Encryption Decryption Using Symmetric Key Algorithms On Different Platforms. *Int. J. Sci. Technol. Res, 8*(09).

Pandey, P., & Litoriya, R. (2020). Securing E-health Networks from Counterfeit Medicine Penetration Using Blockchain. *Wireless Personal Communications*. Advance online publication. doi:10.100711277-020-07041-7

Pantona, E. (2014, March). Innovation Drivers in the Retail Industry. *International Journal of Information Management, 34*(3), 344–350. doi:10.1016/j.ijinfomgt.2014.03.002

Papert, M., Rimpler, P., & Pflaum, A. (2016a). Enhancing supply chain visibility in a pharmaceutical supply chain: Solutions based on automatic identification technology. *International Journal of Physical Distribution & Logistics Management, 46*(9), 859–884. doi:10.1108/IJPDLM-06-2016-0151

Parthornratt, T., Burapanonte, N., & Gunjarueg, W. (2016). People identification and counting system using raspberry Pi (AU-PiCC: Raspberry Pi customer counter). *IEEE International Conference on Electronics, Information, and Communications (ICEIC)*, 1-5. 10.1109/ELINFOCOM.2016.7563020

Patel, K. K., Patel, S. M., & Scholar, P. G. (2016). Internet of Things-IOT: Definition, Characteristics, Architecture, Enabling Technologies, Application & Future Challenges. *International Journal of Engineering Science and Computing, 6*(5), 1–10.

Pavaluru. (2017). *From Shopping Cart to SMART Kart.* Available: https://www.evry.com/globalassets/india/what-we-do/retail-- logistics/smart-kart---white-paper/smart-kart---whitepaper.pdf

Pech, M., Vrchota, J., & Bednář, J. (2021). Predictive Maintenance and Intelligent Sensors in Smart Factory [Review]. *Sensors (Basel), 21*(4), 1470. doi:10.339021041470 PMID:33672479

Pereira, T., Barreto, L., & Amaral, A. (2017). Network and information security challenges within Industry 4.0 paradigm. *Procedia Manufacturing, 13*, 1253–1260. doi:10.1016/j.promfg.2017.09.047

Perera, C., Qin, Y., Estrella, J. C., Reiff-Marganiec, S., & Vasilakos, A. V. (2017). Fog computing for sustainable smart cities: A survey. *ACM Computing Surveys, 50*(3), 1–43.

Pham, Q. V., Nguyen, D. C., Huynh-The, T., Hwang, W. J., & Pathirana, P. N. (2020). *Artificial intelligence (AI) and big data for coronavirus (COVID-19) pandemic: A survey on the state-of-the-arts.* Academic Press.

Pittman, D. (2013, January). *Big Data in Retail - Examples in Action.* Academic Press.

Plakhotnikov, D. P., & Kotova, E. E. (2020). The Use of Artificial Intelligence in Cyber-Physical Systems. *2020 XXIII International Conference on Soft Computing and Measurements (SCM)*, 238–241. 10.1109/SCM50615.2020.9198749

Popay, J., Roberts, H., Sowden, A., Petticrew, M., Arai, L., Rodgers, M., ... Duffy, S. (2006). *Guidance on the conduct of narrative synthesis in systematic reviews. A product from the ESRC methods programme version.* Academic Press.

Premkumar, A., & C, S. (2020). Application of Blockchain and IoT towards. *Die Pharmazeutische Industrie*, 729–733.

Princy, P. (2015). A comparison of symmetric key algorithms DES, AES, Blowfish, RC4, RC6: A survey. *International Journal of Computer Science and Engineering Technology, 6*(5), 328–331.

Qjidaa, M. (2020). Early detection of COVID19 by deep learning transfer Model for populations in isolated rural areas. *International Conference on Intelligent Systems and Computer Vision (ISCV)*, 1-5. 10.1109/ISCV49265.2020.9204099

Rabah, K. (2018). Convergence of AI, IoT, big data and blockchain: A review. *The Lake Institute Journal, 1*(1), 1-18.

Radanović, I., & Likić, R. (2018). Opportunities for Use of Blockchain Technology in Medicine. *Applied Health Economics and Health Policy, 16*(5), 583–590.

Rahim, R., Pranolo, A., Hadi, R., Nurdiyanto, H., Napitupulu, D., Ahmar, A. S., . . . Abdullah, D. (2018). Digital Signature Security in Data Communication. doi:10.2991/icedutech-17.2018.34

Rahim, Z. A., & Iqbal, M. S. (2020). Malaysia Chapter on University Roles to Support the Frontliners during COVID19 Pandemic. *International Conference on Assistive and Rehabilitation Technologies (iCareTech)*, 5-9. 10.1109/iCareTech49914.2020.00013

Rahman, M. M. (2020). An Automated System to Limit COVID-19 Using Facial Mask Detection in Smart City Network. *IEEE International IOT, Electronics and Mechatronics Conference (IEMTRONICS)*, 1-5. 10.1109/IEMTRONICS51293.2020.9216386

Raj, R., Rai, N., & Agarwal, S. (2019). Anticounterfeiting in Pharmaceutical Supply Chain by establishing Proof of Ownership. *IEEE Region 10 Annual International Conference, Proceedings/TENCON*, 1572–1577. 10.1109/TENCON.2019.8929271

Raj, M., Gupta, S., Chamola, V., Elhence, A., Garg, T., Atiquzzaman, M., & Niyato, D. (2021). A survey on the role of Internet of Things for adopting and promoting Agriculture 4.0. *Journal of Network and Computer Applications*, 103107.

Raj, P., Saini, K., & Surianarayanan, C. (2020). *Identification of Blockchain-Enabled Opportunities and Their Business Values: Interoperability of Blockchain. In Blockchain Technology and Applications*. Auerbach Publications. doi:10.1201/9781003081487

Rasheed, J., Jamil, A., Hameed, A. A., Aftab, U., Aftab, J., Shah, S. A., & Draheim, D. (2020). A survey on artificial intelligence approaches in supporting frontline workers and decision makers for COVID-19 pandemic. *Chaos, Solitons, and Fractals*, 110337.

Rathore, S., & Park, J. H. (2018). Semi-supervised learning based distributed attack detection framework for IoT. *Applied Soft Computing*, *72*, 79–89. doi:10.1016/j.asoc.2018.05.049

Recommendations for implementing the strategic initiative INDUSTRIE 4.0. Final report of the Industrie 4.0 Working Group. (n.d.). *Acatech - National Academy of Science and Engineering*. Retrieved June 6, 2021, from https://en.acatech. de/publication/recommendations-for-implementing-the-strategic-initiative-industrie-4-0-final-report-of-the-industrie-4-0-working-group/

Redman, R. (2019). Walmart joins FDA blockchain pilot for prescription drugs. *Supermarket News*, 1–3.

Rejeb, A., Keogh, J. G., & Treiblmaier, H. (2019). Leveraging the Internet of Things and blockchain technology in Supply Chain Management. *Future Internet*, *11*(7), 10–11. doi:10.3390/fi11070161

Rotunno, G., Mannarelli, C., Guglielmelli, P., Pacilli, A., Pancrazzi, A., Pieri, L., Fanelli, T., Bosi, A., & Vannucchi, A. M. (2014). Impact of calreticulin mutations on clinical and hematological phenotype and outcome in essential thrombocythemia. *Blood*, *123*(10), 1552–1555. doi:10.1182/blood-2013-11-538983 PMID:24371211

Sahoo, M., Singhar, S. S., Nayak, B., & Mohanta, B. K. (2019). A Blockchain Based Framework Secured by ECDSA to Curb Drug Counterfeiting. *2019 10th International Conference on Computing, Communication and Networking Technologies, ICCCNT 2019*. 10.1109/ICCCNT45670.2019.8944772

Saini, K. (2019). Recent Advances and Future Research Directions in Edge Cloud Framework. *International Journal of Engineering and Advanced Technology*, *9*(2), 439–444. Advance online publication. doi:10.35940/ijeat.B3090.129219

Saini, K., Agarwal, V., Varshney, A., & Gupta, A. (2018). E2EE For Data Security For Hybrid Cloud Services: A Novel Approach. *IEEE International Conference on Advances in Computing, Communication Control and Networking*, 340-347. 10.1109/ICACCCN.2018.8748782

Saleem, T. J., & Chishti, M. A. (2019). Deep learning for Internet of Things data analytics. *Procedia Computer Science*, *163*, 381–390.

Samaniego, M., & Deters, R. (2016). Hosting virtual iot resources on edge-hosts with blockchain. In *IEEE International Conference on Computer and Information Technology (CIT)* (pp. 116-119). Nadi, Fiji: IEEE. 10.1109/CIT.2016.71

Sanida, T., Sideris, A., & Dasygenis, M. (2020). Accelerating the AES Algorithm using OpenCL. In *2020 9th International Conference on Modern Circuits and Systems Technologies (MOCAST)* (pp. 1-4). IEEE.

Sarkar, S., Chatterjee, S., & Misra, S. (2015). Assessment of the Suitability of Fog Computing in the Context of Internet of Things. *IEEE Transactions on Cloud Computing*, *6*(1), 46–59.

Sasiain, J., Sanz, A., Astorga, J., & Jacob, E. (2020). Towards Flexible Integration of 5G and IIoT Technologies in Industry 4.0: A Practical Use Case. *Applied Sciences (Basel, Switzerland)*, *10*(21), 7670. doi:10.3390/app10217670

Saunders, M. N., Altinay, L., & Riordan, K. (2009). The management of post-merger cultural integration: Implications from the hotel industry. *Service Industries Journal*, *29*(10), 1359–1375. doi:10.1080/02642060903026213

Settanni, E., Harrington, T.S., & Srai, J.S. (2017). Pharmaceutical supply chain models: A synthesis from a systems view of operations research. *Operations Research Perspectives*, *4*, 74–95.

Shafagh, H., Burkhalter, L., Hithnawi, A., & Duquennoy, S. (2017). Towards blockchain-based auditable storage and sharing of iot data. In *Proceedings of the 2017 on Cloud Computing Security Workshop* (pp. 45-50). ACM. 10.1145/3140649.3140656

Shang, C., & You, F. (2019). Data Analytics and Machine Learning for Smart Process Manufacturing: Recent Advances and Perspectives in the Big Data Era. *Engineering*, *5*(6), 1010–1016. doi:10.1016/j.eng.2019.01.019

Shanley, A. (2018). FDA Provides More Clarity on DSCSA. *Pharmaceutical Technology Europe*, *30*(11), 36–37.

Shanley, A. (2017). Real-Time Logistics: Internet of things, advanced analytics, and blockchain solutions such as smart contracts promise to give manufacturers more control over products and supply chains. *Pharmaceutical Technology Europe*, *29*(10), 46–48.

Sharma, M. (2021). Drone Technology for Assisting COVID-19 Victims in Remote Areas: Opportunity and Challenges. *Journal of Medical Systems*, *45*(9), 1–2. doi:10.100710916-021-01759-y PMID:34322759

Sheppard, N. P., Safavi-Naini, R., & Jafari, M. (2009). A digital rights management model for healthcare. In *2009 IEEE International Symposium on Policies for Distributed Systems and Networks* (pp. 106-109). IEEE. 10.1109/POLICY.2009.8

Sheth, K., Patel, K., Shah, H., Tanwar, S., Gupta, R., & Kumar, N. (2020). A taxonomy of AI techniques for 6G communication networks. *Computer Communications*, *161*, 279–303.

Shi, J., Yi, D., & Kuang, J. (2019). Pharmaceutical Supply Chain Management System with Integration of IoT and Blockchain Technology. Lecture Notes in Computer Science (including subseries Lecture Notes in Artificial Intelligence and Lecture Notes in Bioinformatics), 11911 LNCS, 97–108. doi:10.1007/978-3-030-34083-4_10

Sinclair, D., Shahriar, H., & Zhang, C. (2019, January). Security requirement prototyping with hyperledger composer for drug supply chain: a blockchain application. In *Proceedings of the 3rd International Conference on Cryptography, Security and Privacy* (pp. 158-163). 10.1145/3309074.3309104

Singh, P., & Kaur, R. (2020). An integrated fog and Artificial Intelligence smart health framework to predict and prevent COVID-19. *Global Transitions*, *2*, 283-292.

Singh, G. (2013). A study of encryption algorithms (RSA, DES, 3DES and AES) for information security. *International Journal of Computers and Applications*, *67*(19).

Singh, S. K., Rathore, S., & Park, J. H. (2020). Blockiotintelligence: A blockchain-enabled intelligent IoT architecture with artificial intelligence. *Future Generation Computer Systems*, *110*, 721–743.

Sodagar, I. (2011). The mpeg-dash standard for multimedia streaming over the internet. *IEEE MultiMedia*, *18*(4), 62–67. doi:10.1109/MMUL.2011.71

Song, Y., Liu, T., Wei, T., Wang, X., Tao, Z., & Chen, M. (2020). Fda3: Federated defense against adversarial attacks for cloud-based iiot applications. *IEEE Transactions on Industrial Informatics*, 1–8. doi:10.1109/TII.2020.3005969

Soumya, R. J., Shanmugam, R., Saini, K., & Kumar, S. (2020). Cloud Computing Tools: Inside Views and Analysis. *International Conference on Smart Sustainable Intelligent Computing and Applications*, 382-391.

Srivastava, S., Bhadauria, A., Dhaneshwar, S., & Gupta, S. (2019). Traceability and transparency in supply chain management system of pharmaceutical goods through block chain. *International Journal of Scientific and Technology Research*, *8*(12), 3201–3206.

Sunny, J., Undralla, N., & Pillai, V. M. (2020). Supply chain transparency through blockchain-based traceability: An overview with demonstration. *Computers & Industrial Engineering*, *150*, 106895. doi:10.1016/j.cie.2020.106895

Swapnarekha, H., Behera, H. S., Nayak, J., & Naik, B. (2020). Role of intelligent computing in COVID-19 prognosis: A state-of-the-art review. *Chaos, Solitons, and Fractals*, *138*, 109947.

Sylim, P., Liu, F., Marcelo, A., & Fontelo, P. (2018a). Blockchain technology for detecting falsified and substandard drugs in distribution: Pharmaceutical supply chain intervention. *Journal of Medical Internet Research*, *20*(9), 1–12. PMID:30213780

Tan, L., & Wang, N. (2010). Future Internet: The Internet of Things. *3rd International Conference on Advanced Computer Theory and Engineering*.

Thaul, S. (2015). Pharmaceutical supply chain security. *Securing the Pharmaceutical Supply Chain: Issues and Perspectives*, 1–26.

Thepade, S. D., Chaudhari, P. R., Dindorkar, M. R., & Bang, S. V. (2020). Covid19 Identification using Machine Learning Classifiers with Histogram of Luminance Chroma Features of Chest X-ray images. *IEEE Bombay Section Signature Conference (IBSSC)*, 36-41. 10.1109/IBSSC51096.2020.9332160

Thepade, S. D., & Jadhav, K. (2020). Covid19 Identification from Chest X-Ray Images using Local Binary Patterns with assorted Machine Learning Classifiers. *IEEE Bombay Section Signature Conference (IBSSC)*, 46-51. 10.1109/IBSSC51096.2020.9332158

Tian, Z., Luo, C., Qiu, J., Du, X., & Guizani, M. (2019). A distributed deep learning system for web attack detection on edge devices. *IEEE Transactions on Industrial Informatics*, *16*(3), 1963–1971. doi:10.1109/TII.2019.2938778

Ting, S. L., Kwok, S. K., Tsang, A. H. C., & Lee, W. B. (2010). Enhancing the information transmission for pharmaceutical supply chain based on Radio Frequency Identification (RFID) and internet of things. *SCMIS 2010 - Proceedings of 2010 8th International Conference on Supply Chain Management and Information Systems: Logistics Systems and Engineering*.

Tranfield, D., Denyer, D., & Smart, P. (2003). Towards a Methodology for Developing Evidence-Informed Management Knowledge by Means of Systematic Review. *British Journal of Management*, *14*(3), 207–222. doi:10.1111/1467-8551.00375

Treiblmaier, H. (2019). Toward More Rigorous Blockchain Research: Recommendations for Writing Blockchain Case Studies. *Frontiers in Blockchain*, *2*(May), 1–15. doi:10.3389/fbloc.2019.00003

Tsaur, W. J. (2012). Strengthening digital rights management using a new driver-hidden rootkit. *IEEE Transactions on Consumer Electronics*, *58*(2), 479–483. doi:10.1109/TCE.2012.6227450

Tseng, J.-H., Liao, Y.-C., Chong, B., & Liao, S.-W. (2018). Governance on the drug supply chain via gcoin blockchain. *International Journal of Environmental Research and Public Health*, *15*(6), 1055. doi:10.3390/ijerph15061055 PMID:29882861

Tuli, S., Tuli, S., Tuli, R., & Gill, S. S. (2020). Predicting the growth and trend of COVID-19 pandemic using machine learning and cloud computing. *Internet of Things*, *11*, 100222.

Tuptuk, N., & Hailes, S. (n.d.). *The cyberattack on Ukraine's power grid is a warning of what's to come*. The Conversation. Retrieved June 21, 2021, from https://theconversation.com/the-cyberattack-on-ukraines-power-grid-is-a-warning-of-whats-to-come-52832

Uddin, M., Salah, K., Jayaraman, R., Pesic, S., & Ellahham, S. (2021). Blockchain for drug traceability: Architectures and open challenges. *Health Informatics Journal, 27*(2). doi:10.1177/14604582211011228 PMID:33899576

Varun, S. S., & Nagaraj, R. (2021). Covid19 tracking algorithm and conceptualization of an associated patient monitoring system. *International Conference on Trends in Electronics and Informatics (ICOEI)*, 1549-1553. 10.1109/ICOEI51242.2021.9452910

Vecchione, A. (2017). Blockchain tech could track pharmacy supply chain. *Drug Topics, 161*(11).

Verma, P., & Sood, S. K. (2018). Fog assisted-IoT enabled patient health monitoring in smart homes. *IEEE Internet of Things Journal, 5*(3), 1789–1796. doi:10.1109/JIOT.2018.2803201

Vermesan, O., Friess, P., Guillemin, P., Sundmaeker, H., Eisenhauer, M., Moessner, K., Le Gall, F., & Cousin, P. (2013). *Internet of Things Strategic Research and Innovation Agenda*. Academic Press.

Vishwakarma, S. K., Upadhyaya, P., Kumari, B., & Mishra, A. K. (2019). Smart Energy Efficient Home Automation System Using IoT. *IEEE International Conference on Internet of Things: Smart Innovation and Usages (IoT-SIU)*, 1-4. 10.1109/IoT-SIU.2019.8777607

Welbourne, E., Battle, L., Cole, G., Gould, K., Rector, K., Raymer, S., ... Borriello, G. (2009). Building the internet of things using RFID: The RFID ecosystem experience. *IEEE Internet Computing, 13*(3), 48–55.

What's New in the 2019 Cost of a Data Breach Report. (2019, July 23). *Security Intelligence*. https://securityintelligence.com/posts/whats-new-in-the-2019-cost-of-a-data-breach-report/

WHO. (2010). *Monitoring the Building Blocks of Health Systems : a Handbook of Indicators and.* WHO.

Wortmann, F., & Flüchter, K. (2015). Internet of Things. *Business & Information Systems Engineering, 57*(3), 221–224. doi:10.100712599-015-0383-3

Wu, H., Li, Z., King, B., Miled, Z. B., Wassick, J., & Tazelaar, J. (2017). A distributed ledger for supply chain physical distribution visibility. Information, 8(4). doi:10.3390/info8040137

Xie, W., Wang, B., Ye, Z., Wu, W., You, J., & Zhou, Q. (2019). Simulation-based Blockchain Design to Secure Biopharmaceutical Supply Chain. *Proceedings - Winter Simulation Conference*, 797–808. 10.1109/WSC40007.2019.9004696

Yadav, A.S., Selva, N.S., & Tandon, A. (2020). Medicine manufacturing industries supply chain management for blockchain application using artificial neural networks. *International Journal of Advanced Science and Technology, 29*(8), 1294–1301.

Yadav, P., & Vishwakarma, S. (2019). Application of Internet of Things and Big Data towards a Smart City. *IEEE International Conference On Internet of Things: Smart Innovation and Usages (IoT-SIU)*, 1-5. 10.1109/IoT-SIU.2018.8519920

Yamanoor, N. S., & Yamanoor, S. (2017). High quality, low cost education with the Raspberry Pi. *IEEE Global Humanitarian Technology Conference (GHTC)*, 1-5. 10.1109/GHTC.2017.8239274

Yao, X., Chen, Z., & Tian, Y. (2015). A lightweight attribute-based encryption scheme for the Internet of Things. *Future Generation Computer Systems, 49*, 104–112. doi:10.1016/j.future.2014.10.010

Yong, B., Shen, J., Liu, X., Li, F., Chen, H., & Zhou, Q. (2020). An intelligent blockchain-based system for safe vaccine supply and supervision. *International Journal of Information Management, 52*, 52. doi:10.1016/j.ijinfomgt.2019.10.009

Yousef pour, A., Fung, C., Nguyen, T., Kadiyala, K., Jalali, F., Niakanlahiji, A., ... Jue, J. P. (2019). All one needs to know about fog computing and related edge computing paradigms: A complete survey. *Journal of Systems Architecture, 98*, 289–330.

Zhang, P., Zhou, M., & Fortino, G. (2018). Security and trust issues in fog computing: A survey. *Future Generation Computer Systems*, *88*, 16–27.

Zhang, Y., He, D., & Choo, K. K. (2018). BaDS: Blockchain-based architecture for data sharing with ABS and CP-ABE in IoT. *Wireless Communications and Mobile Computing*, *2018*, 1–10. doi:10.1155/2018/2783658

Zhou, W., Jia, Y., Peng, A., Zhang, Y., & Liu, P. (2018). The effect of iot new features on security and privacy: New threats, existing solutions, and challenges yet to be solved. *IEEE Internet of Things Journal*, *6*(2), 1606–1616.

Zhou, W., & Piramuthu, S. (2014, June). Security/privacy of wearable fitness tracking IoT devices. In *2014 9th Iberian Conference on Information Systems and Technologies (CISTI)* (pp. 1-5). IEEE. 10.1109/CISTI.2014.6877073

Zhou, Y., Cahya, S., Combs, S. A., Nicolaou, C. A., Wang, J., Desai, P. V., & Shen, J. (2019). Exploring Tunable Hyper-parameters for Deep Neural Networks with Industrial ADME Data Sets. *Journal of Chemical Information and Modeling*, *59*(3), 1005–1016. doi:10.1021/acs.jcim.8b00671 PMID:30586300

Zikria, Y. B., Afzal, M. K., Ishmanov, F., Kim, S. W., & Yu, H. (2018). A survey on routing protocols supported by the Contiki Internet of things operating system. *Future Generation Computer Systems*, *82*, 200–219.

About the Contributors

Pethuru Raj has been working in the Site Reliability Engineering (SRE) Center of Excellence, Reliance Jio Infocomm Ltd. (RJIL), Bangalore. My previous stints are in IBM Cloud center of Excellence (CoE), Wipro consulting services (WCS), and Robert Bosch Corporate Research (CR). In total, I have gained more than 17 years of IT industry experience and 8 years of research experience. Finished the CSIR-sponsored PhD degree at Anna University, Chennai and continued with the UGC-sponsored postdoctoral research in the Department of Computer Science and Automation, Indian Institute of Science, Bangalore. Thereafter, I was granted a couple of international research fellowships (JSPS and JST) to work as a research scientist for 3.5 years in two leading Japanese universities. Published more than 40 research papers in peer-reviewed journals such as IEEE, ACM, Springer-Verlag, Inderscience, etc. Have authored and edited 16 books thus far and focus on some of the emerging technologies such as IoT, Cognitive Analytics, Blockchain, Digital Twin, Docker Containerization, Data Science, Microservices Architecture, fog / edge computing, Artificial intelligence (AI), etc.

* * *

Syed Imran Ali is a Senior Lecturer of Logistics and Supply Chain Management at Huddersfield Business School, University of Huddersfield. Imran engages widely with the industry and has research interests in digitalisation of supply chains, supply chain data analytics, industry 4.0 applications (AI, IoT, Blockchain, Digital Twin) and innovation. He is currently conducting research in the usage of technologies broadly in the logistics and supply chain to make the data-driven decisions with more accuracy and efficiency. He has published in academic and managerial journals including International Journal of Production Economics, International Journal of Production Research, Computers and Operations Research and International Business Review. ORCiDs: 0000-0002-6553-8210.

Aswani Kumar Cherukuri, Professor of School of Information Technology & Engineering, Vellore Institute of Technology, Vellore, India. He has 20+ years of teaching and research experience. His research interests include Machine Learning, Information Security and Quantum Computing. He has more than 150 publications in book chapters, international journals and conferences. He is a member of IEEE and a senior member of ACM. Further, he is a distinguished speaker of ACM & Vice-chair of IEEE Taskforce on educational data mining.

Maissa Daoud was born in Sfax, Tunisia, in 1987. She received the applied license in Science and Information of Communication and Technology Diploma, and the Applied Master degree in Industrial media and portable systems from the higher institute of electronics and communication of Sfax "ISECS", respectively, in 2009 and 2012. In 2014, she obtained the research Master degree in telecommunication, network and electronic systems from the National School of Electronic and telecommunication "ENET'COM". She received her Ph.D. degree in 2019 in electronics at the National School of Engineers in Sfax "ENIS". Her research interest is the design of low voltage low power analog integrated circuit design in CMOS technology for biomedical implant.

Bhavisha Dholakia is an undergraduate student of Information technology at Vellore Institute of Technology. She will be receiving her bachelor's degree (B.Tech) in 2021. Her research interests includes Network Security, Artificial Intelligence and web languages.

Saugata Dutta received his bachelor of computer science from Alagappa University, Tamil Nadu, India and received his Master of Computer Science from Punjab Technical University, Punjab, India. He has 6 publications in the field of Network security and Blockchain technology. He is presently doing research in Blockchain technology from Galgotias University, Greater Noida, India and associated with an IT company as Head of Department in Information Technology.

N. S. Gowri Ganesh received the B.E. degree in Electronics and Communication Engineering and the M.E. in Computer Science and Engineering from Bharathiar University, Coimbatore, India, in 1993, and 2000 respectively and Ph.D. degree in Computer Science and Engineering from Anna University, Chennai in 2015. In 1993, he joined the Numeric Power Systems Ltd., an Uninterrupted power Supply manufacturing Industry and worked in the Research and Development, Production and Quality Department. He worked as Senior Technical support Engineer for technical support(off-shore) cases for Sybase Inc. He worked as a Lecturer in Sathyabama Institute of Science and Technology, Chennai and R.R. Engineering College, Tiruchengode between 2001 and 2004. In 2004, he worked as Senior Lecturer in Siva Subramania Nadar College, Chennai. He joined the Centre for Development of Advanced Computing (C-DAC), is the premier R&D organization of the Ministry of Electronics and Information Technology (MeitY) for carrying out R&D in IT, Electronics and associated areas, as Senior Engineer in 2006. He worked in various opensource projects and was involved with the first seed version of Indian version of Linux – BOSS (www.bosslinux.in). He was the SEPG Head for acquiring CMMI Level 3 for C-DAC,Chennai. He is presently working as Professor in the Department of Information Technology, at MallaReddy college of Engineering and Technology, Hyderabad from 2016. He is a Life Member of the Indian Society for Technical Education (ISTE).He is also the member of International Association of Engineers(IAENG), and Computer Science Teachers association(CSTeachers.org). He was one of the coordinator, Organizing secretary for the First, Third International Conference on SoftComputing and Signal Processing (ICSCSP) - Springer held in MallaReddy College of Engineering and Technology, Hyderabad. He had published in various Scopus, sci journals and conferences. His recent contribution is In blockchain, published as a chapter titled "Identification of Blockchain-Enabled Opportunities and Their Business Values: Interoperability of Blockchain" in a Taylor & Francis book "Blockchain Technology and Applications" edited by Pethuru Raj, Kavita Saini, Chellammal Surianarayanan https://doi.org/10.1201/9781003081487 His research interests are Cloud computing, AI, Machine learning, Provenance, Blockchain, IOT, and webservices.

Shashank Gupta is an Assistant Professor in the Department of Computer Science & Information Systems, Birla Institute of Technology & Science, Pilani, Pilani Campus since 2017. He is an active member of Disruptive Technologies (DT) Lab. He has received his PhD from National Institute of Technology Kurukshetra, Haryana in Web Security in 2017, M.Tech. (CSE) from Central University of Rajasthan in 2012 and B.E (IT) from University of Pune in 2009. His research interest specializes in the areas of Privacy and Security, Internet of Things (IoT), Fog Computing, Internet of Vehicles (IoVs) and some related areas of high performance computing. He has recently contributed his research work in the related areas of HTML5 injection attacks, IoT healthcare systems, IoT-driven precision agriculture, cryptocurrencies related to blockchain, etc. He has published numerous research articles in various top tier conferences and journals such as Future Generation Computer Systems (FGCS), Elsevier, Journal of Network and Computer Applications (JNCA), Journal of Ambient Intelligence and Humanized Computing (AIHC), Springer, NSS, Globecom, ICC, FIPS, etc. He is also a Senior member of IEEE and professional member of ACM. In addition, he is a part of program/review committee of various top-tier conferences, transactions and journals, and also served as PI/Co-PI for numerous sponsored research grants. He has also filed a few patents related to web security.

Brindha K. received her Ph.D. degree in Cloud Security from VIT University, Vellore, Tamilnadu, India. She is an Associate Professor in VIT, Vellore for the School of Information Science and Engineering. She has authored and co-authored over 35 research publications in peer-reviewed reputed journals and 15 conference proceedings. She has authored over 6 books. She has served as the reviewer for various international journals. She has been honoured by VIT as an active researcher for the last seven years. Her current areas of interest include IoT, Cloud, and Big data, Blockchain, Data Security, Machine learning and Deep learning.

Aditya Kaushik is a student at Vellore Institute of Technology, Vellore pursuing his B.Tech in the field of Information Technology. Aditya has a keen interest in Network Security Fundamentals, Cyber Security, data science, and software development. Aditya has also worked with the Entrepreneurship Cell as a board member during his time in college.

R. Nagarajan received his B.E. in Electrical and Electronics Engineering from Madurai Kamarajar University, Madurai, India, in 1997. He received his M.E. in Power Electronics and Drives from Anna University, Chennai, India, in 2008. He received his Ph.D in Electrical Engineering from Anna University, Chennai, India, in 2014. He has worked in the industry as an Electrical Engineer. He is currently working as Professor of Electrical and Electronics Engineering at Gnanamani College of Technology, Namakkal, Tamilnadu, India. He has published more than 70 papers in International Journals and Conferences. His research interest includes Power Electronics, Power System, Communication Engineering, Network Security, Soft Computing Techniques, Cloud Computing, Big Data Analysis and Renewable Energy Sources.

Dhaya R. has 16 years experience in teaching and research in the field of Computer Science and Engineering. She published more than 80 research papers in peer reviewed international Journals. She was the recipient of IEI Young women Engineer award. Her areas of interests are wireless sensor networks, embedded systems, Machine Learning, Communication Systems.

Kanthavel R. has 22 years experience in teaching and research in the field of information and Communication Engineering. He has the credit of more than 100 research articles in peer reviewed international Journals. His areas of interests are computer networking, Machine Learning and AI, Cooperative communication, computing and mobile networks.

Aashish Raj is an undergraduate student of the information technology program of Vellore institute of technology, Vellore.

Oshin Rawlley is pursuing Ph.D. under the supervision of Dr. Shashank Gupta, Assistant Professor, Department of Computer Science and Information Systems, BITS Pilani. Her research interests are IoT, Fog computing. She has conferred her MTech degree in Computer Science & engineering from Amity University, Noida (UP), in 2018. She has received her B.Tech. degree in Computer Science & Engineering from Rajiv Gandhi Proudyogiki Vishwavidyalaya, Bhopal (MP), India, in 2015. Oshin Rawlley did her schooling from St. Joseph's Convent School Bhopal, MP.

Kazim Rizvi is a student of Information Technology at Vellore Institute of Technology and will be receiving the Bachelor's degree (B.Tech) in 2021. He is interested in finding/building solutions with the help of technology and making a difference through it. His research interests include Security, Algorithms and Machine Learning.

Kannadhasan S. is working as an Assistant Professor in the department of Electronics and Communication Engineering in Cheran College of Engineering, karur, Tamilnadu, India. He is currently doing research in the field of Smart Antenna for Anna University. He is ten years of teaching and research experience. He obtained his B.E in ECE from Sethu Institute of Technology, Kariapatti in 2009 and M.E in Communication Systems from Velammal College of Engineering and Technology, Madurai in 2013. He obtained his M.B.A in Human Resources Management from Tamilnadu Open University, Chennai. He obtained his PGVLSI in Post Graduate diploma in VLSI design from Annamalai University, Chidambaram in 2011 and PGDCA in Post Graduate diploma in Computer Applications from Tamil University in 2014. He obtained his PGDRD in Post Graduate diploma in Rural Development from Indira Gandhi National Open University in 2016. He has published around 10 papers in the reputed indexed international journals and more than 85 papers presented/published in national, international journal and conferences. Besides he has contributed a book chapter also. He also serves as a board member, reviewer, speaker, advisory and technical committee of various colleges and conferences. He is also to attend the various workshop, seminar, conferences, faculty development programme, STTP and Online courses. His areas of interest are Smart Antennas, Digital Signal Processing, Wireless Communication, Wireless Networks, Embedded System, Network Security, Optical Communication, Microwave Antennas, Electromagnetic Compatibility and Interference, Antenna Wave Propagation and Soft Computing techniques. He is Member of IEEE, ISTE, IEI, IETE, CSI and EAI Community.

Varsha Shruti is an undergraduate student of information technology program of Vellore Institute of Technology, Vellore.

Vaishnavi Raj Shukla is undergraduate student of information technology program of Vellore Institute of Technology, Vellore.

Manya Smriti (18BIT0127) is an undergraduate student of information technology program of Vellore Institute of Technology, Vellore.

Chandra Mouliswaran Subramanian is working as the Faculty in School of Information Technology and Engineering, VIT University, Vellore, India. He holds Ph.D. Degree in Information Technology from Vellore Institute of Technology, Vellore. He also possesses M.E. degree in Computer Science and Engineering from Anna University, Chennai and B.E. Degree in Computer Science and Engineering from University of Madras. He has more than 17 years of experience in teaching Engineering education and two years of experience in industry. His current research interests are knowledge representation, formal concept analysis, semantic web and ontology and information security. Dr. Chandra Mouliswaran S. has published many research articles in various national, international journals and conferences. He is the member of CSI. He is the reviewer of many international journals and conferences.

Yuan Sun engages widely with the industry and has research interests in supply chain management, procurement management and manufacturing operations. She is also interested in the usage of technology for solving supply chain problems.

N. G. Mukunth Venkatesh is a student current pursuing his B.E. Computer Science and Engineering in Panimalar Engineering College, Chennai, India. His interest is in Cyber Security and particularly in offensive programming and had participated in various Capture The Flag (CTF) competitions and have decent ranking in India level. He has also completed (CEH) Certified Ethical Hacker.

Index

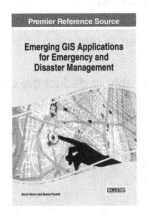
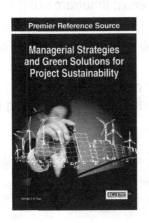

www.igi-global.com

Publisher of Peer-Reviewed, Timely, and
Innovative Academic Research Since 1988

IGI Global's Transformative Open Access (OA) Model:
How to Turn Your University Library's Database Acquisitions Into a Source of OA Funding

Well in advance of Plan S, IGI Global unveiled their OA Fee Waiver (Read & Publish) Initiative. Under this initiative, librarians who invest in IGI Global's InfoSci-Books and/or InfoSci-Journals databases will be able to subsidize their patrons' OA article processing charges (APCs) when their work is submitted and accepted (after the peer review process) into an IGI Global journal.

How Does it Work?

Step 1: **Library Invests in the InfoSci-Databases:** A library perpetually purchases or subscribes to the InfoSci-Books, InfoSci-Journals, or discipline/subject databases.

Step 2: **IGI Global Matches the Library Investment with OA Subsidies Fund:** IGI Global provides a fund to go towards subsidizing the OA APCs for the library's patrons.

Step 3: **Patron of the Library is Accepted into IGI Global Journal (After Peer Review):** When a patron's paper is accepted into an IGI Global journal, they option to have their paper published under a traditional publishing model or as OA.

Step 4: **IGI Global Will Deduct APC Cost from OA Subsidies Fund:** If the author decides to publish under OA, the OA APC fee will be deducted from the OA subsidies fund.

Step 5: **Author's Work Becomes Freely Available:** The patron's work will be freely available under CC BY copyright license, enabling them to share it freely with the academic community.

Note: This fund will be offered on an annual basis and will renew as the subscription is renewed for each year thereafter. IGI Global will manage the fund and award the APC waivers unless the librarian has a preference as to how the funds should be managed.

Hear From the Experts on This Initiative:

"I'm very happy to have been able to make one of my recent research contributions *freely available* along with having access to the *valuable resources* found within IGI Global's InfoSci-Journals database."

– Prof. Stuart Palmer,
Deakin University, Australia

"Receiving the support from IGI Global's OA Fee Waiver Initiative *encourages me to continue my research work without any hesitation.*"

– Prof. Wenlong Liu, College of Economics and Management at Nanjing University of Aeronautics & Astronautics, China

For More Information, Scan the QR Code or Contact:
IGI Global's Digital Resources Team at eresources@igi-global.com.

Printed in the United States
by Baker & Taylor Publisher Services